A POCKET GUIDE TO

Wines,

Wineries,

Vineyards,

& Vines

KONRAD EJBICH

For Talin

Library and Archives Canada Cataloguing in Publication

Ejbich, Konrad
    A pocket guide to Ontario wines, wineries, vineyards, & vines / Konrad Ejbich.

Includes index.
ISBN 13: 978-0-7710-3055-0
ISBN 10: 0-7710-3055-X

    1. Wineries – Ontario – Guidebooks.   2. Wines and wine making – Ontario – Guidebooks.   3. Ontario – Guidebooks.
I. Title.

TP559.C3E53 2005   663.2'009713   C2005-902308-2

We acknowledge the financial support of the Government of Canada through the Book Publishing Industry Development Program and that of the Government of Ontario through the Ontario Media Development Corporation's Ontario Book Initiative. We further acknowledge the support of the Canada Council for the Arts and the Ontario Arts Council for our publishing program.

Typeset in Gill Sans by M&S, Toronto
Printed and bound in Canada

McClelland & Stewart Ltd.
75 Sherbourne Street
Toronto, Ontario
M5A 2P9
www.mcclelland.com

2 3 4 5   09 08 07 06 05

Contents

Contents

Introduction

As a neophyte wine lover in the late 1970s, I often became frustrated when visiting the Canadian wine section of the local liquor store. Buying from those shelves was a toss of the dice. So much had been written about wines from the rest of the world, and so little about what was made here. Like most aficionados at the time, I tasted and read voraciously about the classic wines of the world; but unlike many who narrowed their drinking to their favourite regions, I wanted to explore all the tastes of the world, and began to develop an eclectic cellar with a special corner set aside for good Canadian wines.

Later, when I switched career paths from professional photographer to wine merchant, I wanted to have in my collection exceptional domestic wines with which to surprise foreign wine producers. To this day, it gives me great pleasure to shock a disbelieving guest by serving a "mystery bottle," then unveiling it as Canadian. (Many people who travel to Europe, and especially to France, tend to bring home a bottle or several. To this day, I carry Canadian wines there!)

So I started to compile my own notes, including the names and vintages of reliable Ontario wines as well as other useful tidbits of trivia I'd pick up here and there. At first, I kept all of this information on a little card I carried in my wallet. That expanded into a carefully folded sheet of paper, then a piece of foolscap. Ultimately, my "cribsheet" grew into a stack of cards too thick and bulky to carry around.

As my cellar grew, so did my wine library. The first book I purchased was Hugh Johnson's 1977 *Pocket Encyclopedia of Wine* – the first edition. I carried it everywhere and read it over and over again. It was very helpful to me when I was starting out. Other wine books were published and I'd read them all, but I repurchased the Hugh Johnson with each annual edition. Later, in the 1980s and early 1990s, when Ontario wines began to improve dramatically, winning many international awards and accolades, I was repeatedly disappointed with Hugh Johnson's pitiful section about Canadian regions and producers. Many new wine books were launched in those years as consumer awareness exploded worldwide, but there was no buyer's guide to Ontario wines. For two reasons, one selfish and one altruistic, I decided to take up the challenge myself. That's what this book is all about.

When I became old enough to drink legally, there were 6 wineries in Ontario, but there was a striking similarity to what they produced. It was all dreck. By 1988, after much cajoling by the wine-drinking public and by the wine press, and under threat of becoming insignificant under new rules of the Free Trade Agreement, Ontario wineries relented by establishing a set of rules and standards to guide the industry. This was the Vintners Quality Alliance (VQA). Only wines that adhered to certain minimum guidelines would have the VQA stamp of approval. These standards were and remain low, but in the industry's defence, they succeeded in eliminating that one wine we all hated to drink . . . the dreck.

By 1990, there were 21 wineries and within 3 years that had grown to 33. Today the number has surpassed 110. More licences are currently under review by Ontario's Alcohol and Gaming Commission, and as many as 125 wineries could be in full production by the end of next year.

Naturally, this underlines one of the hazards of producing this book. From the very start, I wanted this to be the most comprehensive reference on Ontario wines ever written. It may well be, but some players inevitably will be missing from this first edition. I could write forever and not be finished as there is so much change occurring every day. My apologies to the newbies who are excluded. I simply had to draw the line somewhere. You may also find limited information on some not-so-new wineries. Some owners chose not to co-operate while others said they were too busy to respond to my questionnaires, requests for samples, and persistent warnings that time was running out. I hope they'll reconsider in time for the next edition.

Yes, I did say "requests for samples." This book contains reviews of thousands of wines. Almost all of the most recent vintages were acquired by contacting the wineries, explaining the project, and asking them to ship me one bottle of each product they sell. Almost every winery provided me at least a partial selection of their products and many sent their entire portfolio. Diligently, I tasted every one. I could not have written this book without their co-operation.

I also dug into my own cellar for almost all the older vintages reviewed in this guide, opening one bottle of every Ontario wine I owned. In some cases, where there was a corked or tired bottle, I opened a second sample if I had one, to ensure my notes would be as fair and accurate as possible. Even though most of the older wines are no longer available for sale, many certainly do exist in the cellars of casual collectors and serious connoisseurs. The purpose of opening these older wines was twofold: to find out if they are still alive and if they can be kept longer and, if so, just how good they are; and, by opening a series of, say, Pinot Noirs from Inniskillin and Château des Charmes side by side, to establish an approximate average potential longevity for the varietal, for the producer, or for the region. This was particularly instructive as I was able to establish boundaries for specific grape varieties, wine styles, and wine brands.

The tasting notes of older vintages will benefit you, even if you don't have any in your own cellar. This is explained in the section about how to use this guide.

All the notes are mine and mine alone. I tasted these wines without the assistance of a panel or committee. These are my opinions. At the risk of sounding immodest, I have a fairly high opinion of my own tasting abilities and an even higher opinion of my standard for honesty in my comments. More than 28 years of tasting thoughtfully, curiously, critically, interrogatively, and meticulously, I have discovered that no one knows more about my likes and dislikes than I do. That said, my purpose as a professional wine taster and critic is to set aside my personal biases and judge every wine on its own merits. Whether I would choose to drink any particular wine for personal enjoyment is irrelevant when deciding whether that specimen is well made. I assess wines objectively on their correctness according to set standards for purity, intensity, harmony, texture, varietal typicity, technical competence, and condition, and subjectively on their style and expression of terroir.

To achieve this I tasted almost every bottle under what one might call clinical conditions, with an eye to being scrupulously fair to every winery and every wine. That means:

I tasted alone.

I tasted in a standard white-walled tasting room where every glass was identical in size and shape and every glass was meticulously cleaned. The room was ventilated with fresh air and the lighting was bright and even.

I tasted only fresh bottles, not previously opened samples from a tasting bar or someone's refrigerator.

I took all the time required with every sample. Sometimes, that meant retasting the same bottle of wine over several days to observe its evolution.

I did not taste side by side with winemakers to avoid being influenced in any way. Nor did I taste in darkened underground cellars with various winemaking smells, odour of cleansers, or damp musty walls.

I did not taste in retail shops where there is uneven lighting, wildly different colours, and, often, the distraction of people milling about.

I did not taste over dinner or snacks to avoid the influence that spices and cooking smells may have.

There were exceptions to these rules: wines were tasted as part of judging sessions such as the Ontario Wine Awards, when a panel of 4 or 5 judges assesses large numbers of wines at a single sitting. Nevertheless, the conditions are always excellent and judges cannot influence one another. We are too individualistic and most definitely too opinionated to listen to others. In addition, there were a few wines of exceptional age or rarity that were opened by friends and colleagues – bottles of historical significance that, had I insisted on taking them home to my own tasting room, I would never have tasted. Finally, in a very few cases, where wineries simply would not provide samples for tasting, their wines may have been assessed at a trade function, consumer wine show, or elsewhere under "less than ideal conditions." This is noted in the appropriate sections.

There are no photographs, no labels, and no logos in this book. There is no advertising, no patronage, no sponsorship program, and, consequently, no advantage to larger, richer, or more imposing wineries. The content within these pages is straightforward reportage. My prime concern is the person who puts his or her money on the counter in a wine or liquor store, i.e., you, the consumer.

The ratings are clear, concise, and honest. I tell you not only which wines to buy, but which ones to avoid. This has its hazards too, because telling a winemaker you don't like his wine is akin to telling a dad his baby is ugly. But my goal, as I've stated before, is to help you to buy the right Ontario wine, not to win friends in the wine industry.

How to Use This Guide

To get the most use from the least space, I've used a number of short forms, abbreviations, symbols, and codes throughout the book.

Officially Designated Viticultural Areas (VA)

[NP]   wine from the Niagara Peninsula viticultural area
[LENS]   from the Lake Erie North Shore viticultural area
[PI]   from the Pelee Island viticultural area
[Ont]   from hybrid grapes, blended VAs, or a declassified VA

Other Designations and Abbreviations

[PEC]   from Prince Edward County, a de facto wine region but not yet officially designated as such. The Vintners Quality Alliance (VQA) requires there be a minimum of 5 wine-grape wineries with a minimum of 5 ha each and an average harvest for all of them of 500 t. per year. Alternatively, a region can demonstrate that wines critically acknowledged as being "of distinguishable character" are consistently produced.

[nonVQA] a wine that, for any number of reasons, is not qualified to carry a VQA designation. It may be produced or blended using grapes grown outside of an officially designated viticultural area. It may be produced in one of the officially designated viticultural areas by a winery that is not a member of the Wine Council of Ontario or which has chosen not to submit its wine for approval by the VQA tasting panel. Most likely, it was produced from the legal minimum of Canadian wine blended with imported juice. In the latter case, it would be labelled "Product of Canada" and may have a line at the bottom of the label reading, "Cellared and bottled in Canada."

[preVQA] any wine produced before 1988, the year the VQA established viticultural boundaries, guarantees of origin, and standards of production.

[QC]	quality certified – a designation that applies to fruit wines only.

NV	a non-vintage wine

Quality Ratings

☒	(00-49)	**flawed:** undrinkable
☐	(50-69)	**poor:** safe, but best to look for alternatives
☆	(70-73)	**unremarkable:** drinkable, if nothing else is available
★	(74-76)	**passable:** should be consumed without fanfare
★☆	(77-79)	**average:** often served at banquets and charity functions
★★	(80-82)	**good:** decent everyday wine
★★☆	(83-84)	**above average:** good value if the price is right
★★★	(85-86)	**admirable:** well made, noticeable aroma and taste
★★★☆	(87-89)	**fine:** worth seeking out
★★★★	(90-93)	**terrific:** expect an exceptional experience
★★★★☆	(94-97)	**outstanding:** highly desirable at any price
★★★★★	(97-100)	**great:** one for the record books

Drinkability Assessments

↑	Much too young. Needs significantly more aging.
↗	Can be drunk now, but will improve with further aging.
→	At its peak now, but may still hold for some time.
↘	In decline and should be drunk soon.
↓	Kaput.
↻	For quick turnover. At its best when released. Cannot improve.

For many of the wines recorded here, I provide a "window of drinkability" (e.g., Drink 2006-2012). This is the range of years during which the wine will remain at its peak. If you like to drink your wines "fresh," i.e., with lots of vigorous, juicy, youthful flavours and assertive tannins, consume them closer to the earlier date mentioned; however, if you prefer your wines to taste softer, more mature, and fully developed, store them away until closer to the later date recommended.

Here's how the tasting notes of older vintages will benefit you, even if you don't have any yourself: You're standing in front of a selection of Ontario wines with this book in hand. The specific vintage you are looking at is not listed in the book because it was released after publication, but two or more previous vintages are listed with detailed notes. You can compare the quality of those wines and deduce the relative quality of the bottle in front of you. You can also surmise something about its style and predict the ideal time to drink it.

Blending Information

Many wines are blends of two or more grape varieties. Where information is available and useful I have included the breakdown by percentage using the following format:

For example:	*Stands for:*
(CS30/M70)	30% Cabernet Sauvignon, 70% Merlot
(M50/Mal20/S15/V15)	50% Merlot, 20% Malbec, 15% Syrah, 15% Viognier

Abbreviations used:

BN	Baco Noir
C	Chardonnay
CB	Chenin Blanc
CF	Cabernet Franc
CM	Chardonnay Musqué
CS	Cabernet Sauvignon
Gam	Gamay
Gew	Gewürztraminer
M	Merlot
Mal	Malbec
MF	Marechal Foch
PB	Pinot Blanc
PG	Pinot Gris
PM	Pinot Meunier
PN	Pinot Noir
PV	Petit Verdot
R	Riesling
S	Syrah
SB	Sauvignon Blanc
Sem	Semillon
SvB	Seyval Blanc
V	Viognier
VB	Vidal Blanc

Sample listings:

Chardonnay [nonVQA] **2001** ☒ This wine is flawed. Avoid like the plague.

Gamay Rosé [Ont] **NV** ★ ★ ↻ Pale pink shade with strawberry aroma. Taste seems sweet but finishes dry. No need to age, it's not capable of improvement.

Meritage, Sunnyside Farm [NP] **2002** ★ ★ ☆ ↗ Not bad but will improve with ideal storage. Drink now-2010. **1998** ★ ★ ★ ★ → Ready to drink, can be kept but unlikely to improve further. **1996** ↓ Over the hill.

Grape Varieties Authorized for Planting in Ontario (and a Word on the Significance of Soil and Vine Density)

There are thousands of grape varieties grown around the world. Some taste delicious when squeezed to make fresh juice or are best eaten fresh as table grapes. Others are better dried in the sun as raisins. Some are fine for jams, jellies, condiments, or, simply, as an ingredient in cooking. Still others excel at nothing more than climbing the brick walls of your house and making it look like an old country château. Very cool.

Over the centuries, very few grape varieties have proven themselves to be ideal for being turned into wine. *Vitis vinifera* – when translated from Latin: the vine that makes wine – is believed to have originated in the Middle East or Europe. There are hundreds of varieties of vinifera, each of which develops different olfactory (smell) and gustatory (taste) characteristics – some strong, pungent, and unpleasant and some intensely seductive with ethereal nuances that appeal to our inner core.

There are other species of the genus *Vitis*, of which some are more and some are less suitable for winemaking. These include, but are not limited to: *Vitis amurensis*, native to the Orient, as well as *Vitis rupestris*, *Vitis riparia*, and the unfortunate *Vitis labrusca*, which grow wild in the fields and forests of North America.

Over the past 2 centuries, plant breeders have spent an immeasurable amount of time crossbreeding grape varieties to create new varieties, some better resistant to certain vine diseases, some more tolerant to cold temperatures, and others simply more productive. Hybrid varieties created from exclusively *Vitis vinifera* parentage are called vinifera crossings, whereas varieties created by crossing the European vine with North American or other varieties are called interspecific crossings or interspecies. Any variety created by crossing grape types, whether all vinifera or interspecies, may colloquially be referred to as a hybrid variety.

Grapes that have been manipulated genetically, by adding the gene of a non-*Vitis* plant variety are called transgenic. In Ontario, experiments were done more than a decade ago to insert the genes of a wild northern broccoli plant into a Cabernet Franc (vinifera) grape to increase its resistance to cold. Officially, it was referred to as transgenic; unofficially, it was called Cabernet Frankenstein.

The following list includes only those varieties that have been approved for winemaking by the Vintners Quality Alliance Ontario (VQAO). Not every grape is cultivated in the province (and planting some of them wouldn't exactly be the wisest choice), but growers certainly would be permitted to plant them.

White Grapes

Aligoté (Vinifera) – Though it does achieve good body and balance in exceptionally hot vintages in Burgundy, these are only occasional successes. Aligoté generally produces highly acidic wines with little flavour in average years and should therefore be drunk quite young (within 3 years of harvest) or blended with a more flavourful, low-acid variety. Its higher yields do not compensate for its bland taste. The French have solved the acid problem by creating the cocktail called Kir. It's made by adding 1 oz. of super-sweet crème de cassis to 5 oz. of Aligoté. The best straight Aligoté I have ever tasted was produced by Aubert de Villaine (owner of Romanée Conti) at Bouzeron in the Côte Chalonnaise of Burgundy. (A tray of warm gougères improved the tasting.) But the variety's general lack of distinctive flavours makes it quite a suitable match for food, especially hors d'oeuvres, fish, seafood, and light pasta dishes.

Aurore (Interspecific crossing) – An early ripening, frost-resistant, French-American hybrid variety grown in Canada and the northeastern United States. According to VQAO rules, it is allowed only for blending purposes and is prohibited from carrying its own VQA designation. There is a distinct freshness to the taste and a strong aroma moderately reminiscent of Tokay-Pinot Gris vinified in the Alsace style. Andrés Wines bottled some tasty Aurore in the late 1970s and early 1980s; however, these days it disappears into generic blends only. (a.k.a. Aurora, Seibel 5279)

Auxerrois (Vinifera) – A variety that's widely grown in Alsace, predominantly for blending in Edelzwicker, a local specialty. It provides high yields of low-acid wine that, if severely thinned at veraison, is capable of yielding a decent wine with the bouquet of honeyed nuts. Regrettably, most producers overcrop, resulting in wines of low flavour concentration. After successfully surviving severe winter frosts in Ontario in 1992, Auxerrois has become one of the favoured grapes for new plantings. Jordan Wines of British Columbia (now part of the Vincor group of wineries) was the first to produce a commercial Auxerrois from grapes grown by George Heiss, founder of Gray Monk Cellars. At that time, Jordan's then winemaker, Josef Zimmermann, called it "the future Chardonnay of the Okanagan." It is still referred to as "Pinot Auxerrois" by some producers, erroneously, as it is not a true member of the Pinot family.

Bacchus (Vinifera crossing) – One of numerous German crossings of Riesling-x-Silvaner with Müller-Thurgau. It can produce aromatic wines when fully ripened but merely insipid ones in less than stellar years. Its main advantage over Riesling is that it ripens early and yields relatively full-bodied wines. Disadvantages are low yields and propensity to attract vine diseases.

Chardonnay (Vinifera) – The "Gucci" grape, according to Allan Schmidt, president of Vineland Estates. It is one of the most prized, most planted white wine grapes in the world. Consumers like the taste (and the fact that it's easy to pronounce), while grape growers and wine-makers like the profits. It's easy to grow, easy to work with in the cellar, and versatile at the table as a food wine. Careful vineyard management is required as it is sensitive to spring frosts, oidium (mildew), *coulure* (sparse bunches), and *Botrytis cinerea* (gray rot). Chardonnay is delicious when fermented in stainless steel and bottled early; its taste will be crisp and fruity in a light, lemon-lime style, except when given a secondary malolactic fermentation or *sur lie* treatment, whence it softens, yielding fuller and creamier pear, melon, and, occasionally, peach flavours. When barrel-fermented, barrel-aged, and bottle-aged under appropriate conditions, it can develop superb, rich, full-bodied, buttery, nutty, toasty flavours of great depth, complexity, and elegance. Among the aroma descriptors, one finds dried flowers as well as fresh flower pollens, peach, fig, orange, lemon, and other white-fleshed fruits (pineapple, mango, guava, etc.), brown sugar, butterscotch, toffee, caramel, and other interpretations of cooked or burnt sugar, butter, cocoa butter, vanilla, coconut (especially when aged in American oak), hazelnut, mocha, roasted coffee, smoke, spice, herbs, dill, pickle, celery, and asparagus. Chardonnay harvested late in the season can also develop nuances of honey, sage, apricot, papaya, and molasses.

Chardonnay Musqué (Vinifera) – Ampelographers refer to this variety as "Clone 77." Paul Bosc, the founder of Château des Charmes winery, calls his "Clone 809." It isn't certain if it is a spontaneous clonal mutation or a natural crossing of Chardonnay with Muscat. Characteristics are identical in every way to common Chardonnay, except that it has an exceptionally strong aroma and taste, with distinct hints of Muscat on the nose and Viognier nuances on the palate. In general, it is preferred with minimal barrel influence or bottle-aging, although I have tasted some lively older samples. It's grown by several Ontario wineries, although only in the past few years have more wineries begun to bottle it as a single varietal.

Chasselas (Vinifera) – Once widely planted, especially throughout Switzerland and in France's Alsace and Savoie regions, this classic variety now seems to be falling out of favour. In Canada, there are a few hectares planted in the Okanagan Valley. It yields crisp wines of nondescript character. *(a.k.a. Chasselas Doré, Dorin, Fendant)*

Chenin Blanc (Vinifera) – Originally from the Loire region of France, where it is used to produce sweet (Vouvray), dry (Savennière), and occasionally sparkling wines. This white variety is gaining supporters in Canada, with Henry of Pelham the first winery to plant it in the Niagara Peninsula. There's growing acreage in Ontario and, increasingly, it is left for later harvesting through December or January to make icewine. It is notable for its racy acidity, delicate, floral aroma, and distinct, ripe honeydew melon flavours. Additional descriptors frequently include herbs, fresh-cut grass, pear, pumpkin, and applesauce. *(a.k.a. Pineau de la Loire)*

Colombard (Vinifera) – In France, it is used in the production of cheap table wine or distilled for the making of brandy. California's colombards are far more interesting because of the standard practice of cool fermenting, which brings out more floral fruitiness in the wine. It is generally a straightforward wine with balanced acidity. Ontario's biggest grower is Murray Puddicombe. He matures his in oak for a short period, giving it fuller body, some butteriness, and a degree of complexity. It should be drunk young as it does not improve with aging. *(a.k.a. Columbard, French Colombard)*

Couderc (Interspecific crossing) – Several versions, grown primarily as a rootstock variety. The most common is Couderc-3309.

Ehrenfelser (Vinifera crossing) – One of the more successful German Riesling-x-Silvaner crossings of the previous century, Ehrenfelser was widely grown in the Rhine Valley. It offers much of the aromatic character of Riesling but has similar acidity, giving it some ability to age. In British Columbia, some wineries produce an attractive late-harvest version. Its biggest liability has to be its name. Canadians tend to avoid wines with Germanic names. It's hard enough to convince them to buy Riesling.

Faberrebe (Vinifera crossing) – A German crossing of Pinot Blanc and Müller-Thurgau, it yields wines with a moderate degree of elegance and relatively undistinguished Muscat-like flavours. It is used primarily for blending.

Furmint (Vinifera) – The famous white grape of Hungary's marvellous late-harvest Tokaji wines is notable for its high acidity, spicy flavour, and for the ease with which it acquires *Botrytis cinerea*, i.e., the highly desirable noble rot. Crown Bench Estate Winery is the only grower currently cultivating it in Ontario.

Gewürztraminer (Vinifera) – Widely grown throughout the world, it is gaining popularity with Ontario grape growers. "Gewürz," as it is casually referred to, can produce harmonious wines of intense perfume and great complexity. Alas, most Canadian producers select the wrong clone (opting for volume rather than taste), overcrop (more volume), pick too early (no character) or too late (too little acidity), and/or vinify, leaving too much residual sugar (yech!), thereby delivering less than exciting results. The best examples, like those from France's Alsace region, will have relatively high alcohol (12.5%), pungent flavours that stay long on the palate, a thick, almost oily texture (umami), and natural, palate-cleansing acidity. Great Gewürztraminer can be long-lived, say, 15 to 20 years. Typical aroma descriptors include allspice, cloves, nutmeg, lanolin, honey, rose, honeysuckle, jasmine, bergamot, apricot, pineapple, lychee, tropical fruits, ginger, and wildflowers. *(a.k.a. Traminer)*

Goldburger (Vinifera crossing) – A crossing of Welschriesling and Orangetraube used primarily to add colour to other, paler wines. Ontario's Colio Estate was the only winery I recall ever to have bottled it as a single varietal. These days, it is used primarily as a blending grape.

Grüner Veltliner (Vinifera) – The main grape of Austria has been grown in Canada for some time by Inniskillin's founding winemaker, Karl Kaiser, not surprisingly an Austrian by birth. It produces medium-bodied wines that are relatively high in acid, with a slight prickle on the tongue. It often has an assertive aroma that includes nuances of white pepper, celery, musk, and spice. Although Austrian winemakers will age it for 20 or 30 years, it is most enjoyable while it is still young and sprightly. These days, Kaiser blends his harvest with other varieties, but in the heady days when French Beaujolais Nouveau was at its height of marketing madness, Kaiser turned his Grüner Veltliner into the traditional Austrian-style *heuriger*, which is a crisp, tart, refreshing wine that's still working and fermenting in the glass. Regrettably, consumers didn't get it and the liquor board didn't like the idea of an "unfinished" wine on the market. It was too much trouble, so the winery gave up. It was so-o-o yummy. *(a.k.a. Veltliner)*

Hibernal (Interspecific crossing) – This white grape was developed at the Geisenheim Institute in Germany as a crossing of Riesling and Chancellor, which itself is a Seibel crossing. It is cold-tolerant, has aromatic and stylistic characteristics mildly similar to Riesling or Gewürztraminer, and can be harvested late to produce sweet wines. Its popularity is highest in that winter wonderland, Prince Edward County, and in the heat-challenged vineyards of Muskoka and the Ottawa Valley. *(a.k.a. GM-322-58)*

Kerner (Vinifera crossing) – A reliable German crossing bred from Trollinger and Riesling parentage. As it's an exceptionally high-yielding grape, aggressive pruning is usually required to control it. Its wine has a coarse, spicy taste that combines the aromatics of Muscat and the acidic, green-fruit characteristics of Riesling. It yields a wine with fullish body and lively acidity. The best examples age surprisingly well, some lasting as long as 10 years. *(a.k.a. Trollinger-x-Riesling)*

Madeleine Angevine (Vinifera crossing) – A very early ripening crossing of Précoce de Malingre and Madeleine Royale developed in the Loire region of France. It is grown predominantly as a table grape, but when fermented into wine, it can develop a strong, floral aroma. For early consumption.

Madeleine Silvaner (Vinifera crossing) – A low-cropping, early maturing variety that prefers much cooler sites. It emits a strong, floral aroma when it begins to ripen, attracting hungry wasps. Taste is reminiscent of Muscat.

Malvasia (Vinifera) – Thought to be of Greek origin, it is one of the oldest varieties known. Consequently, it is grown in most wine regions of the world, producing wines of substance and savour. It is most often turned into a sweet wine with high alcohol, either natural or fortified. *(a.k.a. Malmsey, Malvasia Bianca)*

Matsvani (Vinifera) – This white variety originates in Georgia. That's Georgia next door to Armenia, not the southern U.S. state on the eastern seaboard. It is highly resistant to cold temperatures, but there's not much else to recommend it to growers.

Mélon de Bourgogne (Vinifera) – This grape's other name is Muscadet, which gives you an idea in what part of the world it originates. Mélon handles cold winters quite well and provides relatively high yields of light-bodied, high-acid, flavour-free wine to complement shellfish. Unfortunately, it is also highly prone to crown gall, a vine disease that chokes off the plant when tumourlike growths appear at the graft point. Mélon matures quickly, but does not keep well. It is at its best when it has spent a few months in the barrel on the lees, highlighting its freshness and sprightliness on the palate. Malivoire makes a very good one. *(a.k.a. Melon)*

Morio Muscat (Vinifera crossing) – A crossing of Silvaner with Pinot Blanc, it yields highly perfumed wines that some tasters believe are aromatically over the top. Morio Muscat is a late ripener and prone to rot in anything less than ideal conditions, so it is the rare winemaker who is willing to give it a chance. Look for fine, dry, spicy, floral examples made by Hillebrand and Peller Estates. *(a.k.a. Muscat)*

Müller-Thurgau (Vinifera crossing) – One of the oldest vinifera crossings of Riesling-x-Silvaner was bred by famous plant physiologist Dr. Müller of the town of Thurgau in Switzerland. Its wine is usually low in acidity with a lightish, floral aroma and relatively nondescript taste. (Jancis Robinson calls it "mousy.") It is used mainly as a blending base with more aromatic grapes and is the base wine for most cheap German Liebfraumilch. If produced as a single varietal, it's best drunk young. Not many Canadian growers are willing to plant Müller-Thurgau for it is quite susceptible to frost damage. *(a.k.a. Rivaner)*

Muscadelle (Vinifera) – A filler grape in white Bordeaux blends. Not much character on its own.

Muscat (Vinifera) – The grapiest of grapes, Muscat has a profound floral-perfumy aroma that delights about as many tasters as it offends. There are 4 clonal variations of the grape: the best is Muscat á Petits Grains, followed by Muscat of Alexandria, Muscat Hamburg, and the relatively ordinary Muscat Ottonel, which is the variety authorized for cultivating in Ontario. The wine can be produced in the sweet, sparkling Asti style, the rich, still Beaumes-de-Venise style, or in the bone-dry style of high-alcohol, Alsatian versions. Eminently enjoyable but, sadly, it is underappreciated by most Canadian consumers. Lime, orange blossom, honey, bergamot, perfume, wildflowers, and spice are typical flavour characteristics of its wine.

Optima (Vinifera crossing): An early ripening crossing of Riesling-x-Silvaner and Müller-Thurgau, it makes very ordinary dry wines; but when affected by *Botrytis cinerea*, it produces superlative late-harvest, sweet wines.

Oraniensteiner (Vinifera crossing) – A German crossing developed at the Geisenheim Institute of Riesling and Silvaner parentage. It yields a high-acid wine with a strong spiced-orange bouquet and taste.

Ortega (Vinifera crossing) – A German crossing of Müller-Thurgau and Siegerrebe, it is suited to cool climate regions but must be harvested at just the right moment. Too early and it yields a bitter-green, tart wine and too late and it becomes dull, alcoholic, and characterless. Useful primarily for blending purposes.

Perle of C'saba (Vinifera crossing) – An early ripening crossing of Gewürztraminer with Müller-Thurgau with good frost resistance. Wine made from Perle tends to be light and soft, with a floral nuance, but certainly not to the same degree as its parent, Gewürztraminer. *(a.k.a. Pearl of Csaba)*

Pinot Blanc (Vinifera) – This variety is the white sister to Pinot Gris, Pinot Meunier, Pinot Noir, and the rare Pinot Verte and looks identical to them until the grape bunches actually begin to ripen and change colour. It's a marvellous food wine with its subtle (read, nondescript) bouquet and harmonious dry finish. An unblended Pinot Blanc will have muted acidity, nuances of apple, pear, peach, or vanilla, an occasional hint of almonds or spice in the bouquet, and a rather full-bodied palate. It does well in damp, gravelly soils. *(a.k.a. Clevner in Hungary; Pinot Bianco in Italy; Weissburgunder in Austria and Germany)*

Pinot Gris (Vinifera) – This natural mutation of Pinot Noir produces full-bodied wines with a rich, golden colour and a noble scent that can be as simple as honeyed pears or as fragrant and complex as ripe and spicy Gewürztraminer. In general, it prefers a warm climate, and is notorious for rapidly losing acidity as sugars rise at harvest time. Nevertheless, in cool climates with cold fall nights, it can produce deliciously spicy late-harvest wines that become more complex with age. In the past, it was overlooked by Canadian growers; however, today more of this fine variety is finding its way into Ontario vineyards. The worst thing that can happen to this variety is to have it pushed into producing high volumes of tart, flavourless wine, often called Pinot Grigio. The wine should be thick and oily in texture with concentrated flavours and potential to improve in flavour, with up to 20 years aging. *(a.k.a. Grauburgunder, Rulander in Austria; Pinot Grigio in Italy; Szürkebarát in Hungary; Tokay d'Alsace, Tokay Pinot Gris in France)*

Pollux (Interspecific crossing) – Vineland Estates may still grow this white variety as a blending grape. Its true value lies in its winter hardiness, its high productivity, and its nondescript taste profile that rarely interferes with the better grapes with which it is blended.

Riesling (Vinifera) – The classic grape of Germany and France's Alsace region is grown throughout Canada and is deeply appreciated by connoisseurs. Regrettably, the general public isn't as taken with it as the wine-loving community is. Riesling is usually vinified without much intervention, so it is one of the best varieties to express the soil on which it is grown. A perfect Riesling has ferocious acidity, a high degree of refinement in the bouquet, which can display nuances of apricot, peach, pear, apple, citrus, mango, papaya, pineapple, or various and sundry wildflowers, but is almost always somewhat spicy and honeyed. After 3 or 4 years, it can develop an enticing, sweet "petrol" nose, reminiscent of wildflowers, rose, wintergreen, benzene, diesel, or furnace oil. These last few may sound off-putting but are actually highly desirable. Some wineries blend back a small amount of unfermented grape juice (sussreserve) to the finished wine in order to achieve higher natural fruitiness without affecting the balance of sweetness and acidity. Riesling's racy acidity makes it quite age-worthy

– 20 to 50 years – especially when late harvested or produced as icewine. Riesling can be vinified still or sparkling, bone dry or intensely sweet, and may have a low alcohol level ranging from 7.5% to 10.5%. *(a.k.a. Johannisberg Riesling, White Riesling in United States; Johannisberger in Switzerland; Rhine Riesling in Australia; Riesling Renano in Italy)*

Rkatsiteli (Vinifera) – The most planted variety of the former Soviet wine industry, its greatest asset is its winter hardiness, not its taste. Mineral flavours combine with herbal aromas and fairly high acidity. *(a.k.a. Rkatziteli)*

Sauvignon Blanc (Vinifera) – Not really suited to Ontario's climate, it nevertheless is one of the most widely planted white vinifera varieties after Chardonnay. It prefers hot days and cool nights but does not take well to high humidity or rich soils. Some characteristic olfactory descriptors include fresh-cut grass, day-old hay, green bell pepper, dill weed, green beans, asparagus, green olives, pea shoots, celery, radish, Granny Smith apple, evergreen sap (pine, cedar), spearmint, peppermint, citrus fruits (especially grapefruit, lime, and mandarin), gooseberry, flowers, and honey. Its strong, aromatic character makes it one of the few varieties able to mask (to a limited degree) the unpleasant taint of Asian lady beetle (see main entry in "A to Z"). *(a.k.a. Fume Blanc)*

Savagnin (Vinifera) – Common only in the Jura region of France where it is used to make the fine, sherrylike *vin jaune* wines of which the greatest is Château Chalon, but rare everywhere else. Château des Charmes introduced it to Niagara more than a decade ago but may tear it out as it does not sell well in Ontario. This late-ripening variety expresses the terroir well, offering some spicy, nutty, musky aromas, and has an uncanny ability to age. *(a.k.a. Salvagnin, Savagnin Blanc in France; Edeltraube in Germany)*

Scheurebe (Vinifera crossing) – A Riesling-x-Silvaner crossing that gives forth high yields but prefers to be planted in a region with a long growing season, as it is a late ripener. It has fine acidity, approaching that of Riesling, a floral, spicy, berry bouquet that often resembles black currant (it's highly unusual for a white variety to show characteristics of red fruits or berries), along with full body and a pronounced taste. It is grown predominantly in the warmer regions of Germany and Austria. A well-made Scheurebe can age for several years. Pelee Island is the only Ontario winery I know to cultivate this grape.

Schönberger (Vinifera crossing) – This aromatic pink-skinned variety is most often used as a table grape in northern Italy. A crossing of Pinot Noir, Chasselas, and Muscat Hamburg, it is a good performer in the vineyard and delivers low acidity, fullish body, and an unexciting aroma not unlike bad Gewürztraminer.

Sémillon (Vinifera) – A genuine character actor, Sémillon is capable of playing many roles. It is a fine team player (together with Sauvignon Blanc) in France, producing some of the great, long-lived dry wines of Graves and sweet unfortified wines of Sauternes and Barsac. It also does an amazing monologue, yielding rich, buttery wines in Australia and crisp, green, flinty wines in New Zealand. Sémillon performs best in cooler climates, as lack of acidity is always an issue.

Seyval Blanc (Interspecific crossing) – One of the few Euro-American crossings that, thankfully, does not have that foxy taste characteristic of many other native hybrids. Seyval Blanc is a high-yielding (up to 10 t. per acre), extremely hardy variety, suited to cooler regions such as those in Canada, the northeastern United States, and Great Britain. The wine has little personality, though a whiff of grapefruit or honey can occasionally be detected. Nevertheless, it perplexes me that so many Ontario growers devote so much valuable vineyard space to this otherwise useless variety. *(a.k.a. Seyve-Villard 5-276)*

Siegerrebe (Vinifera crossing) – The main claim to fame of this pink-skinned, early ripening crossing of Madeleine Angevine with Gewürztraminer is its ability to produce high sugar levels. Unfortunately, its aroma is so strong it overpowers any wine with which it is blended. I know of no Ontario grower who has planted it here; however, Domaine de Chaberton grows a few hectares of it in the Fraser River Valley.

Siegfriedrebe (Interspecific Crossing) – A convoluted crossing of Oberlin 595-SP, a seedling of the Oberlin Noir vine that itself is a crossing of *Vitis riparia*-x-Gamay Noir with Riesling. Ultimately, it was deemed to be unsuitable for winemaking, so why did the VQA approve its use? *(a.k.a. Siegfried, Sigfried Rebe)*

Silvaner (Vinifera) – It's uncertain to me if the German wine industry values this variety more for its high productivity in the vineyard or for its prolific nature in the lab. After all, it is the parent plant of countless grape crossings. There's not much more to praise. It makes flavourless, acidic wine with poor structure and is best blended. *(a.k.a. Sylvaner in France; Johannisberg, Gros Rhin, or Gruner in Switzerland)*

Traminer (Vinifera) – A less spicy ancestor of Gewürztraminer. (*Gewürz* is the German word for "spicy.")

Trebbiano (Vinifera) – Widely planted in France, this acidic, high-yielding variety's main purpose in life is to be distilled for the production of brandy. In Italy, it accounts for more wine than any other grape. *(a.k.a. Muscadet Aigre in Bordeaux; St. Émilion in Cognac; Procanico in Umbria; Ugni Blanc in South Africa and elsewhere)*

Verdelet (Interspecific crossing) – I remember drinking some decent Verdelet produced at Mission Hill Vineyards in the Okanagan Valley of British Columbia in the early 1980s. I was under the impression that it had been banned after B.C. accepted VQA standards. Watery in colour, it was strong and flavourful with lemon grass, lime, and herb flavours. Too much for some tastes. *(a.k.a. Seibel 9110)*

Vidal Blanc (Interspecific crossing) – The European grape, Ugni Blanc, crossed with Seibel 4986, results in a thick-skinned, thick-stemmed variety that resists frost well, ripens in cool climates, and manages to achieve high sugar and acid levels. Regrettably, there is little flavour in the dry wines made from it; however, late-harvested versions and especially icewines offer some unique and delicious flavours. Typical descriptors for late harvest and icewines include apricot, guava, lemon, lychee, mango, papaya, peach, pear, and pineapple. *(a.k.a. Vidal 256)*

Vignoles (Interspecific crossing) – Planted in numerous locations in the Finger Lakes district of New York State and in a few vineyards of other eastern states, primarily for the production of sweet, late-harvest wines. Dry versions tend to have a strong aroma (verging on foxy), whereas sweet wines are simply aromatic and quite palatable. *(a.k.a. Ravat, Ravat Blanc)*

Viognier (Vinifera) – The distinctive grape of the northern Rhône that is the basis for Condrieu. It is highly appreciated among connoisseurs for its beguiling scent of peach blossoms, honeysuckle, Turkish delight, lychee, frankincense, and fine perfume. Not many growers choose to cultivate it, though, because it gives notoriously small yields and is finicky about precisely when it wants to be picked. The grape's taste is feeble and bland if not fully ripened and rapidly turns blowsy and dull if overripened.

Welschriesling (Vinifera crossing) – Unrelated to the classic grape of Germany. With the exception of Austria, where it produces opulent, late-harvest, dessert wines, this variety tends to yield overly acidic wines with a green, leafy, or stemmy undertone. *(a.k.a. Laski Riesling in Slovenia; Olaszriesling in Hungary; Riesling Italico in Italy)*

Red Grapes

Baco Noir (Interspecific crossing) – A teinturier (red-fleshed) variety developed late in the 19th century by crossing Folle Blanche with a North American *Vitis riparia*. Produces wines high in extract and acidity with moderate ability to age. Ontario growers like it for its large yields, its ability to ripen early (avoiding unexpected fall frosts), and its general winter-hardiness. The wine usually has a deep purple colour while taste characteristics include acidic blackberry, cranberry, and red-currant flavours and a rustic, smoky, herbaceous, woodsy leafiness. A well-made Baco Noir can age reasonably well. The best ones I've tasted were sweet and fortified in the style of port. *(a.k.a. Baco No. 1)*

Blauburger (Vinifera crossing) – Originating in Austria, this uncommon grape (a crossing of Portugieser and Blaufränkisch) yields wines light in colour and of unremarkable taste.

Cabernet Franc (Vinifera) – This could well be the best red variety for Ontario's Niagara Peninsula and Lake Erie North Shore growing zones, as it ripens at least a week earlier than its "big brother," Cabernet Sauvignon, and has more resistance to our severe winter conditions. The wine it produces is generally lighter in colour, sharper in acidity, and softer in tannic structure than Cabernet Sauvignon. In cool vintages, it can display similar herbaceousness but, with its greater likelihood of ripening, is a surer bet for our short growing season. It displays tremendous elegance, an enticing fruity scent, and a wonderful delicacy. Common descriptors include violets, red currant, black currant, black cherry, olives in brine, green pepper (underripe), red pepper (overripe), cedar, and various herbal notes.

Cabernet Sauvignon (Vinifera) – The main grape of Bordeaux' famous châteaux is planted wherever winemakers believe they can make a red wine with the elegance, finesse, and depth of genuine Bordeaux. Dream on, fellas. In Ontario, Cabernet Sauvignon rarely ripens fully, often resulting in wines that display too much herbaceousness and bitter, vegetal characteristics or, in the worst vintages, downright weediness. Warmer, longer vintages yield riper, fruitier, and better balanced wines. Cabernet Sauvignon can age exceptionally well. Typical descriptors in a young Cabernet Sauvignon include red and black fruits, cassis (black currant), eucalyptus, cranberry, oak, bell pepper, black tea, cherry, blackberry, rhubarb, asparagus, green olive, raspberry, peppermint, cinnamon, dark chocolate, raw potato, soy, molasses, fig, and plum. Older Cabs will also have flavours of prune, leather, humus, mushrooms, and dried fruits.

Castel (Interspecific crossing) – A relatively disease-resistant hybrid whose popularity is growing even though its usefulness is dubious at best. Its value is in its large yields and high sugar levels.

Chambourcin (Interspecific crossing) – A disease-free, heavy-cropping hybrid of French origin. Wines are deeply coloured, quite aromatic, spicy, herbaceous, and often relatively high in alcohol. It contributes body and structure when blended with more flavourful grapes, but offers little character or elegance on its own. It is a late ripener and vulnerable to crown gall disease. *(a.k.a. Johannes-Seyve 26-205)*

Chancellor (Interspecific crossing) – A widely planted teinturier variety that yields a richly coloured, mildly fruity, balanced but flavour-challenged juice. Most Canadian winemakers blend it with other, more assertive varieties. Both Stoney Ridge and B.C.'s Sumac Ridge have used it to produce a port-style wine. This grape was once the most widely used hybrid in France but now is banned. It is highly susceptible to fungal vine diseases, particularly downy mildew and powdery mildew. *(a.k.a. Chancellor Noir, Seibel 7053)*

Chelois (Interspecific crossing) – A teinturier grape grown widely in cool Ontario vineyards since it undergoes a late bud-break, ripens relatively early, and produces a deeply coloured, moderately tannic juice. Flavours tend toward stewed or candied fruit. Unfortunately it is highly susceptible to certain fungal vine diseases and to late-season bunch rot. *(a.k.a. Seibel 10-878)*

De Chaunac (Interspecific crossing) – A widely planted, vigorous, early ripening red grape used primarily for blending purposes in Ontario. Wines are fruity but relatively low in tannins. The variety is quite susceptible to certain soilborne viruses. *(a.k.a. Seibel 9549)*

Dornfelder (Vinifera crossing) – A crossing of Helfensteiner (Frühburgunder-x-Trollinger) and Heroldrebe (Portugieser-x-Limberger), which seems to excite growers more than it does consumers. It grows well, produces high yields, good sugar levels, nice colour, and, according to the bumph, great taste. My experience with the variety is that it has a narrow range of simple flavours.

Gamay Noir (Vinifera) – Officially, it is called Gamay Noir à Jus Blanc to differentiate it from its numerous teinturier clones. This is the cheerful, early ripening grape of Beaujolais, the southernmost district of Burgundy. Typical descriptors include strawberry, raspberry, cranberry, blackberry, cherry, rhubarb, and, occasionally, peppermint. It is the favoured grape for making a "Nouveau" wine for drinking fresh in the late fall and through the winter. By spring it loses its charm. Château des Charmes developed its own unique clone that it has named Gamay "Droit," as the shoots grow upright. It ripens about 16 days later, yielding richer fruit and higher sugar levels.

Lemberger (Vinifera) – A dark-skinned grape that yields a richly coloured red wine that can be compared to a combination of soft, fruity Gamay and well-structured Syrah. The wine is fruity, hearty, and spirited, with racy acidity. It has characteristics similar to Merlot with good colour, fresh raspberry, and black pepper aromatics. It is best drunk young. Walter Strehn was the first to plant it on Pelee Island, although his grapes were usually sold to Colio winery rather than to the Pelee Island winery. Has some potential in Ontario. *(a.k.a. Blaufränkisch in*

Austria; Limberger in Germany; Kékfrankos in Hungary; Franconia in Italy;
Nagyburgundi in Slovakia)

Léon Millot (Interspecific crossing) – A vigorous, early ripening variety now used mostly for blending with paler wines to deepen their colour. Grown extensively in the United Kingdom and in parts of Ontario where growing conditions are wetter and cooler than those in the Niagara Peninsula and Lake Erie North Shore. The wine tends to mature and fade quickly. *(a.k.a. Kuhlmann 194-2)*

Malbec (Vinifera) – A thick-skinned grape that yields a tough, tannic, deeply coloured wine, it was once the star of Cahors while playing a bit part in many Bordeaux wines. Today the best Malbecs are produced in Argentina, where the resulting wine rivals Cabernet Sauvignon in body and structure and Merlot in softness and grace. *(a.k.a. Cot)*

Marechal Foch (Interspecific crossing) – Another deeply coloured, early ripening, frost-resistant, high-yielding teinturier variety widely planted in Ontario's cool-climate vineyards. Descriptors for juvenile Foch include blackberry jam, black raspberries, smoke, and citrus peel, while older ones develop semi-interesting Burgundian nuances of latex rubber, cedar, plum and cherry pie, stewed prunes, spice, saddle leather, decaying autumn leaves, and black forest earth. High acidity, deep colour, and strong, rustic, black-fruit flavours are its signature. Alas, elegance and finesse are not. *(a.k.a. Kuhlmann 188-2)*

Merlot (Vinifera) – Although this variety usually plays second fiddle to Cabernet Sauvignon, it deserves sole credit for one of the world's greatest wines, Château Petrus of Pomerol. Whereas Cabernet Sauvignon gives wine its structure and longevity, Cabernet Franc, its delicacy, fruit, and perfume, Merlot's contribution is fleshiness – soft, luxurious, velvety texture that brings completeness to the blend. Merlot is happiest growing in clay, where it can develop its heady aromas of blueberry, blackberry, black currant, plum, mocha chocolate, thyme, pine sap, and, occasionally, a whiff of soft leather. The biggest drawback to Merlot in Ontario is its sensitivity to cold weather, of which we get more than our share. Crops were almost entirely destroyed during the winters of 1992-1993 and again in 2002-2003.

Michurinetz (Vinifera) – Popular in the vineyards of the former Soviet Republics, primarily for its durability under severe winter conditions. Dr. Roger Dial grew some at his Grand Pré Vineyards in Nova Scotia's Annapolis Valley in the mid-1980s. The wine combined toughness with rustic, leathery, blackberry flavours.

Nebbiolo (Vinifera) – The grape of Italy's famous Barolo and Barbaresco wines. Its wine can be long-lived, ultimately developing luxuriant flavours and captivating aromatics. In Ontario, it is grown by Ridgepoint Vineyard. (a.k.a. *Chiavanesca, Spanna*)

Petit Verdot (Vinifera) – A thick-skinned grape that yields a very tannic, deeply coloured, and highly aromatic wine. For these reasons, it is a useful addition (some would say a key player) in Bordeaux and Meritage wines. It is generally used in tiny proportions so as to not overwhelm the more subtle characteristics of the principle components, Cabernet Sauvignon, Cabernet Franc, and Merlot.

Petite Sirah (Vinifera) – Do not confuse this variety with Petite Syrah, a small-berried version of genuine Syrah grown only in the southern Rhône region of France. It has also been confused with Durif, a grape of little quality once widely grown in the Ardèche region of France. Petite Sirah is grown currently by Marynissen. Grape grower Dieter Guttler also has grown the variety in his Kew Vineyard but uprooted all the vines after 1993 because the specific clone he had planted succumbed to crown gall, a vine disease whose symptoms include tumourlike growths at the graft point. When grown in hot regions such as California, Mexico, Brazil, or Argentina, Petite Sirah develops an intense, attractive purple colour. The wine also exhibits chewy blackberry and black pepper flavours, with hints of prune, chocolate, tobacco, black tea, herbs, earth, and spice, but it tends to be mouth-dryingly tannic. In cooler climates, like that of Ontario, it tends to produce the dark colour and the strong tannins but lacks the sweetness and ripe fruit flavours of physiologic and phenolic maturity.

Pinot Meunier (Vinifera) – Wine aficionados will recognize it as 1 of the 3 grapes used in the production of champagne. It is valued mainly because it breaks bud a week later and ripens a week earlier than its cousin, Pinot Noir. Hillebrand produces one. It has a smidgen more acidity and a soupçon less flavour intensity than Pinot Noir, but, in my opinion, it deserves more play in Ontario vineyards. Should be considered for white and sparkling wine production in cool years, red wine in very hot years. (a.k.a. *Meunier, Müllerrebe, Schwarzriesling*)

Pinot Noir (Vinifera) – Young Pinot Noir can have nuances of violets, peppermint, raspberry, strawberry, cherry, orange peel, tangerine, grapefruit, oak, coffee, chocolate, gingerbread, acacia, cedar, cinnamon, terpine (pine pitch), and quinine. In general, as Pinot ages the flavours slowly shift from fruity to vegetal, earthy, mushroomy (in a perfect world, like truffles), leathery, and gamy. British Master of Wine Michael Broadbent says Pinot's fingerprint is "boiled beetroot." When combined with Chardonnay, as is done in the production of sparkling wine, Pinot Noir's contribution to the blend is fullness, roundness, and fruitiness. (a.k.a. *Blauburgunder, Spätburgunder in Germany; Pinot Nero in Italy; Nagyburgundi in Hungary*)

Pinotage (Vinifera crossing) – This crossing of Pinot Noir and Cinsault is the signature grape of South Africa. It grows well under a variety of conditions and ripens early but requires aggressive pruning in order to accentuate its flavour. The taste is strong and rustic with earth, coffee, leather, smoke, and, often, sausage or bacon fat nuances dominating the stewed cherry and red currant flavours.

Rosette (Interspecific crossing) – Grown widely in upper New York State, this hardy variety is best noted for its ability to ripen in a cool climate. (a.k.a. Seibel 1000)

Rotberger (Vinifera crossing) – Another German crossing (will they ever find their golden fleece?) of Trollinger and Riesling. This red variety makes especially nice rosés and the country's best is the one produced by Gray Monk Cellars in the Okanagan. Don't know of anyone in Ontario growing it.

Samtrot (Vinifera) – A low-yielding clone of Pinot Meunier.

Sangiovese (Vinifera) – The classic Tuscan grape of Brunello di Montalcino, Chianti, Chianti Classico, Carmignano, Vino Nobile di Montepulciano, and spilling over into the regions of Umbria, Marches, and Abruzzo. Characteristic flavours include cranberry, cherry, plum, prune, barnyard, leather, smoke, and, occasionally, licorice and tar. Why any Ontario grower would want to plant it is beyond me. It ripens late into the season, dislikes cool, damp climates, and has thin skins, a combination that easily leads to grape rot in a cool climate. It's also a fickle grape that mutates at the drop of a secateur and, even in good vintages, its juice tends to be hard, tannic, and somewhat acidic. (a.k.a. Brunello, Morellino, Prugnolo, Sangioveto)

St. Laurent (Vinifera) – This ancient variety has been falling out of favour for generations, mainly because it buds early and is therefore susceptible to late-spring frosts. It is grown in parts of Lower Austria and has had some success in South Africa. It yields a velvety, deeply coloured wine similar to, but more rustic in taste than, Pinot Noir.

Sereksia Chornaya (Vinifera) – Originating in Romania, where it has been cultivated since the 14th century, it yields medium-sized bunches of blue-black fruit that produce light-bodied, full-flavoured, fruity red or rosé wines. (a.k.a. Babeasca Neagra)

Shiraz/Syrah (Vinifera) – Wine historians believe this is the oldest of grapes, hailing from the town of Shiraz in ancient Mesopotamia. It's grown in many of the world's warmer wine regions but is best known for its contributions in the Rhône (especially Côte Rôtie and Hermitage) and Australia (where until a few decades ago it was known as the

Hermitage grape). A fair amount is brought in to Canada for blending with domestic wine. Alex Nichol was the first to plant an acre of it in the Okanagan Valley. Currently it is one of the highly desirable varieties, so numerous Ontario growers have started to plant it in recent years. Characteristic flavours include blackberry, crushed black pepper, tar, licorice, and cigar smoke.

Villard Noir (Interspecific crossing) – A double crossing, i.e., a crossing of two previous interspecific crossings, Seibel 6905 and Seibel 7053 (Chancellor). In France, it was widely cultivated, though new plantings are now banned and old ones in rapid decline. Yields enormous amounts of dark-coloured grapes with a vegetal, perhaps even somewhat foxy taste. Used only in low-end blends. *(a.k.a. Villard, Seyve-Villard 18-315)*

Vincent (Interspecific crossing) – A cold-hardy Canadian crossing developed at the Horticultural Research Institute in Vineland. It is a teinturier grape (dark fleshed) used mostly in the production of dessert wines.

Zinfandel (Vinifera) – The only grape with its own cult following. There are "zinfanatics" all over North America, but, not surprisingly, the majority are in California, home of this grape. It can be turned into a cheerful, semi-sweet quaffer or an alcoholic, massive monster. One of the best I have tasted was a port-style wine with a natural alcohol of 18% and enough residual sugar to require a dentist on standby. Typical descriptors include red and black raspberry, raisin, prune, black pepper, mint, and eucalyptus. I know of only one winery growing Zinfandel grapes in Ontario: Reif Estate. *(a.k.a. Plavac Mali in Croatia; Primitivo in Italy)*

Zweigelt (Vinifera crossing) – Some Ontario winemakers have a deep conviction that this recent German crossing of Blaufränkisch and St. Laurent holds great promise in our terroirs. It resists our winters fairly well and yields early and abundantly. The wines are generally deeply coloured with lively acidity and honest berry flavours. Some Zweigelts do age well, but most are drunk young and fruity. I believe it is best suited to making off-dry rosés. *(a.k.a. Zweigeltrebe)*

A Word on the Significance of Soil . . .

That's gneiss, but who gives a schist?
When the discussion begins to focus on specific taste differences based solely on the influence of soil, I go cross-eyed. The relationship is subtle,

and so many other factors can muddle the results. But it goes without saying that the type of soil in which grapes grow has an influence on the taste of the wine, and in this book I make frequent reference to soil types. The influences are twofold.

First, the percentages of silt, sand, loam, clay, alluvium, till, rubble, stones, and other material change soil moisture absorption and the rate of drainage. This affects how much water can be taken up by the vines' root systems and at what rate, as well as how quickly the water will drain away after a heavy rainfall. Grapes generally hate having their roots sit in muck.

The second influence is the chemical composition of the soil and specific proportion of minerals in the soil. Is the soil acidic or alkaline? Does it have more potassium, calcium, magnesium, or iron? What other minerals exist in trace amounts?

The soils of Chablis, in France, are called Kimmeridgian clay because, during the Kimmeridgian period, the area was under water and vast populations of sea life existed in the shallow water. After it dried up, the seabed was left rife with shells. Over the ages, these have desiccated and become part of the soil makeup. This is a lacustrine soil, where material deposited in the lake is later exposed once the lakebed dries up. The high calcium content gives the wine a particular flavour of wet stones and a structure that is lean and firm. White wines grown on this type of soil pair especially well with oysters, mussels, scallops, and other seafood and fish.

In Beaujolais, the single cru with the fruitiest taste grows in the soil with the highest proportion of granite. Gamay is partial to granite. Cabernet Franc and Cabernet Sauvignon prefer to stick their roots in gravel, whereas their buddy Merlot is happiest in clay – red clay, to be precise. Pinot Noir and Chardonnay like calciferous soils: limestone, dolomite, chalk. Gewürztraminer sings in slate, while Riesling does well in a wide variety of sites and reflects their individual terroirs with crystal clarity. Everywhere you go, grapes grown on opposite sides of a road in slightly different soils have subtle differences in taste.

It's not always easy to isolate those parts of the aroma and taste that are most affected by soil. Compare the basic Chardonnays of several Niagara wineries and you may find them very similar. It's likely these companies sourced their grapes from growers scattered throughout the entire region and blended away the individuality of each site. But *single-vineyard* bottlings provide a window into the soil structure of the individual site. Compare and taste individual sites. Single vineyard wines, when collected over several years, provide insight into effects of the site itself as well as a look into how the vineyard responded to the various vintages – how the weather is expressed by the site.

You see now why I go cross-eyed?

. . . and Vine Density

Denser Vines, Denser Flavours?

I also refer frequently in this book to the density at which vines are grown. The theory is that the closer you force vines to grow, the deeper they will send their roots into the ground, struggling to compete for moisture and minerals. The deeper the roots go, the more trace minerals available to be taken up, and the more flavourful the wines will be. And the more plants one grows per acre, the less fruit weight can be taken off each individual vine. If the plant provides all its nutrients to fewer grapes, those grapes will have a greater concentration of flavours.

So, if 2 vineyards each yield 1 t. of grapes and Vineyard A has 1,000 vines per acre while Vineyard B has 2,500, you can bet that Vineyard B grapes will have deeper concentration of flavours and more complexity.

Farmers may space their plants at 10 x 5 ft., or 9 x 4 ft., or 1 m x 80 cm, and so on, depending on soil structure, aspect, grape variety, and even what kind of farm tractor they have . . . one that straddles the vines or one that rolls between the rows. There may be differing results if the rows are laid out on an east-west bias instead of north-south. Every decision made at the time of planting will have an effect on the ultimate quality and style of the wine.

A to Z
of Ontario Wines,
Wineries, Vineyards,
& Vines

- **ABERDEEN VINEYARD (Beamsville, NP)** – The 2.5-acre property itself is owned by David Little, but its use is leased to Aberdeen Vineyards Inc., a partnership between Little and Deborah Paskus. Located 4.8 km from the lake, southeast of the town of Beamsville and just north of Crown Bench Estates, the vineyard has a gentle north-facing grade composed of Chinguacousy clay loam soil over a lime-stone bedrock. There are 2 acres of Chardonnay, underdrained between every row, which Paskus personally thins down to less than 1 t. per acre. Grapes are shared by Closson Chase of Prince Edward County, Tawes Winery of Vineland, and Temkin-Paskus, another joint venture of Paskus with Stephen Temkin.

- **ALEKSANDER ESTATE WINERY** (1542 County Road 34, Ruthven, ON, N0P 2G0 / Phone: 519-326-2024 / Fax: 519-326-1371 / Email: izabela@aleksanderestate.com / Website: www.aleksander estate.com [in development])

(Est. 2005) Although the Bemben family has only recently opened the doors to its wine operation, the dream and the plan are right on track. Polish immigrants Aleksander, his wife, Genowefa, daughter Izabela, and son Lukasz are all very much involved in the business. They have 5 sandy acres planted with Cabernet Franc, Cabernet Sauvignon, Chambourcin, and Riesling. They also buy some Baco Noir from a neighbouring vine-yard. This past summer, Izabela graduated from the Cool Climate Oenology and Viticulture Institute at Brock University. The Bembens also plan to produce fruit wines. Their short-term goal is 2,000 cases. Long-term will depend on the market.

Winemaker: Aleksander Bemben / Vineyard Manager: Aleksander Bemben

Wines not available for appraisal before press time.

- **ALVENTO WINERY** (3048 Second Avenue, R.R.#1, Vineland, ON, L0R 2E0 / Phone: 905-562-1212 / Fax: 905-562-1212 / Email: bmoos@total.net)

(Est. 2001) Alvento means "to the wind" in Italian. For Bruno and Elyane Moos, owners of this new estate winery backing on to Jordan Harbour due east of Vineland Station, it connotes the gentle wind that constantly blows over their young vineyard. Originally from Switzerland, where Bruno was an architect, the couple moved first to Tuscany, where they built a successful winery. They moved again in 2001 to find a new life in the New World, landing here on the advice of friends. Fourteen of their 16 acres are planted; the remaining 2 acres surround their century-old home and the barn Bruno converted into a modern and efficient winery building. In their first year on the property, they planted 1.5 acres of Cabernet Franc, 5 acres of Cabernet Sauvignon, and 2.5 acres each of Merlot and Viognier. The following year they added 2.5 acres of Nebbiolo, completing the vineyard. Vine density throughout is 2,430 plants per acre (6,000 per ha) with vine spacing of 2.6 ft. on 6.5-ft. rows (80 cm on 2 m rows), which is common in Europe but substantially denser than the average Ontario vineyard. The property is generally flat with a few dips and bumps and consists entirely of Vineland reddish-hued lacustrine fine sandy loam. Their first vintage in 2003 yielded only 800 cases of wines. The couple have applied for a retail licence and plan to boost production to 2,500 cases by 2006. In addition to estate-bottled wine, they are developing a small production of traditional balsamic vinegar.

Winemaker: Bruno Moos / Vineyard Manager: Elyane Moos

Cabernet Sauvignon [NP] **2003** ★ ★ ★ ↗ Bright ruby-garnet with a light, fresh berry-fruit aroma. Light-bodied, clean, and harmonious. Drink 2006-2010.

Merlot [NP] **2001** ★ ★ → From purchased grapes. Soft, hint of blueberry, blackberry, and an unfortunate whiff of Asian lady beetle. Mildly tannic. Drink now-2008.

- **Ancient Coast** – National brand owned by Vincor International Inc., Canada's largest wine producer and the thirteenth largest wine company in the world. VQA varietals for immediate consumption produced from purchased hybrid and vinifera grapes.

Tasting notes listed under **Vincor International Inc.**

- **ANDRÉS WINES LTD.** (697 South Service Road, Grimsby, ON, L3M 4E8 / Phone: 905-643-4131 / Toll-Free: 1-800-263-2170, 1-800-610-6610 / Fax: 905-643-4944 / Email: info@andreswines.com / Website: www.andreswines.com)

(Est. 1969) Canada's 2nd largest winery was founded in 1961 in Port Moody, British Columbia, by Hungarian-born Andrew Peller, who already owned a brewery, a newspaper, and a car dealership. Within a year, he opened 2 additional wineries, in Calgary, Alberta, and Truro, Nova Scotia, but it took another 7 years before Andrew's son, Joseph, would be able to enter the Ontario market, and then only by purchasing the money-losing Beau Chatel winery in Winona from Imperial Tobacco. Soon after, Andrés continued its expansion into Saint-Hyacinthe, Quebec, and Morris, Manitoba. The company's single, largest-scale success was the introduction in 1971 of Baby Duck, a sweet-tasting, low-alcohol, sparkling wine marketed to an unsophisticated, young, impressionable audience. Its enormous success drove Andrés share price from $5 in 1972 when the company went public to almost $50 2 years later. Andrés became Canada's biggest winery and Baby Duck accounted for 1 in every 24 bottles sold in the country. Sales of the bubbly peaked at 8 million bottles in 1980. But Baby Duck was as much a success as it was an obstacle to greater success. In later years, few inroads were possible in the premium-priced category as consumers connected the Andrés banner with inexpensive pop wine. Growth continued to come with frequent launches of low-end products such as the widely advertised brands Hochtaler, Domaine D'Or, and Cellar Cask. In 1991, under the direction of grandson John Peller, the company introduced a new label, Peller Estates, for premium imported blends and domestic varietal wines. Then, in 1994, Andrés purchased the Hillebrand winery in Virgil from its German owners. These 2 divisions provided a vehicle for Andrés to penetrate a more sophisticated market and to reach a younger, more modern consumer. In June 2001, Andrés opened the doors to a new showpiece winery for Peller Estates on a 25-acre property within walking distance of Niagara-on-the-Lake, featuring a gorgeous underground barrel cellar and vintage wine library, tasting room, retail shop, and gourmet restaurant. Andrés also produces winemaking kits in Ontario through its subsidiary, Vineco International Products Ltd., located in St. Catharines.

Winemakers: Sean Hails (2002-present); Rob Summers (1997-2001); David Hojnoski (1978-1996); Barry Poag (1970s-1998)

Abbey Label
Franciscan Burgundy [nonVQA] **NV**□↻ Basic dry red plonk.

Andrés Label
Baby Duck [nonVQA] **NV**★↻ Once the top-selling wine in the country. Sweet, grapey, sparkling, and somewhat reminiscent of the purple gum called Thrills.

Boisseau Blanc de Blancs [nonVQA] **NV**☆↻ Generic dry white.

Botticelli Red [nonVQA] **NV**□↻ Sweetish red.

Botticelli White [nonVQA] **NV**□↻ Sweetish white.

Canadian Blush [nonVQA] **NV**□↻ Semi-dry, carbonated, pink plonk.

Canadian Champagne [nonVQA] **NV**☆↻ Dryish, citrusy, carbonated white.

Canadian Dry [nonVQA] **NV**☆↻ Basic dry white plonk.

Cellar Cask [nonVQA] **NV**★☆↻ Generic off-dry and sweet white. Once a heavily advertised big seller, now available only in bag-in-the-box format.

Cellar Reserve Dinner Red [nonVQA] **NV**★↻ Generic, off-dry red.

Hochtaler [nonVQA] **NV**☆↻ Generic, off-dry, balanced, fruity white.

Hochtaler Dry [nonVQA] **NV**☆↻ Generic, dry, fruity white.

Hochtaler Gold Riesling [nonVQA] **NV**☆↻ Generic, off-dry, fruity white.

Kurhauser Trocken Sekt [nonVQA] **NV**☆↻ Generic, off-dry, fruity white.

Madrigal [nonVQA] **NV**★☆↻ A sweet, red, muscat-based aperitif. Spicy, nutty, and a bit cloying.

Spumante Bianco [nonVQA] **NV**☆↻ Generic bubbly. Best with orange juice.

Wintergarten [nonVQA] **NV**☆↻ Generic, semi-dry, aromatic white.

Domaine D'Or Label

Cabernet [nonVQA] **NV**★☆↻ Dry red international blend. Clean, simple, and uncomplicated.

Chardonnay [nonVQA] **NV**★☆↻ Dry white international blend.

Red [nonVQA] **NV**★↻ Generic, off-dry red, offered in multiple sizes.

Superieur Red [nonVQA] **NV**★↻ Generic, off-dry red, sold in multiple sizes.

Superieur White [nonVQA] **NV**★↻ Generic, off-dry white, available in multiple sizes.

White [nonVQA] **NV**★↻ Generic, off-dry white, offered in multiple sizes.

Vineyard Mist Label

Strawberry-Zinfandel [nonVQA] **NV**★★↻ Pretty, pale pink, lightly sparkling, with a smell and taste of, what else, strawberries. Only 6.9% alc./vol.

Hillebrand wines, including Collectors' Choice, Harvest, Stone Road, Trius, and Vineyard Select series, listed separately under Hillebrand Estates.

Peller Estates wines, including Andrew Peller Signature, French Cross, Heritage, Oakridge, Private Reserve, and Vineyard series, listed separately under Peller Estates.

• **ANGELS GATE WINERY** (4260 Mountainview Road, R.R.#2, Beamsville, ON, L0R 1B2 / Phone: 905-563-3942 / Toll-Free: 1-877-264-4283 / Fax: 905-563-4127 / Email: mail@angelsgatewinery.com / Website: www.angelsgatewinery.com)

(Est. 2002) In 1996, a group of 13 investors purchased a 35-acre property lodged more or less across the road from Thirty Bench Winery. It's a gorgeous location with a photogenic pond and gardens and a fabulous vista across the lake to the Toronto skyline. For many years it was an abandoned mink farm. On a moderate, northeast-facing slope composed of Chinguacousy clay loam till with scattered alluvial deposits, the group planted 2 acres each of Cabernet Franc, Cabernet Sauvignon, and Chardonnay plus 1 acre of Gewürztraminer. In 2001, they purchased a second property, an existing 24-acre vineyard on the east side of Beamsville with 22 acres planted to Cabernet Franc, Cabernet Sauvignon, Chardonnay, Merlot, Pinot Noir, Riesling, and Syrah. Here, the terrain is relatively flat (it was an airfield during the 1930s and 1940s) and the soil has a higher proportion of clay in the mix. Last year, the winery jumped at the opportunity to buy a third property, the former Helen Straub Vineyard just up the road from the estate. That parcel had been a supplier of old vines Chardonnay since the winery's inception. It is a 20-acre parcel with Chinguacousy clay loam similar to the soil on the estate. In addition to the 3 acres of Chardonnay planted in 1978, this past summer the winery added 7 acres each of Merlot and Pinot Noir plus 1 acre of Sauvignon Blanc. Currently, Angels Gate harvests 23 t. of fruit from its own holdings. All of it is hand-picked and later hand-sorted at the winery. In addition, another 150 t. of fruit is purchased from Emerald Shore Vineyard, Niagara Bench Farms, and Polana Vineyard. Total production in 2004 was 13,000 cases. The winery's goal is to reach 20,000 cases by 2007.

Winemaker: Natalie Spytkowsky (2000-present) / Vineyard Manager: Claus Wolf, Custom Farm Services

Angels III [NP] **2002**★★★★↑ (CF25/CS25/M50) Solid garnet to the rim. Restrained nose but complexity comes through with aromas of singed oak, green veggies, and black fruits. Mouth-filling and supple with high alcohol, acidity, and tannin. Balanced flavours. Drink 2006-2012.

Cabernet [NP] **2002**★★★☆↑ (CF68/CS32) Garnet with a pink rim and a big, complex raspberry, currant, and cherry bouquet with powerful aromas of oak and smoke. Young, tough, and packed with vibrant fruit and oak flavours. Drink 2006-2010.

Cabernet Franc [NP] **2002**★★★☆↑ Lively garnet colour. Elegant Bordeaux-like nose with nuances of boysenberry, raspberry, and hazelnut. Lean mid-palate with green apple acidity; dry and balanced. Peak drinking: 2006-2012.

Cabernet Franc Icewine [NP]   2001 ★ ★ ★ ★ ★ ↗ Pale salmon shade with a clean, intense, and rich bouquet of strawberry syrup and orange pekoe tea. Thick as runny jam and just as sweet. A lovely, concentrated nectar. Drink now-2014.

Cabernet Sauvignon [NP]   2002 ★ ★ ★ ★ ↗ Deep garnet colour with a ripe cassis, black raspberries, and cherry-flavoured cough-syrup nose. Tart but balanced with good intensity and ample complexity. Already drinking well but can age to 2013.

Chardonnay [NP]   2002 ★ ★ ★ ↻ Light, clean, crisp aroma and supple palate with a mineral backdrop.

Chardonnay, Old Vines, Barrel-Aged [NP]   From the winery-owned Helen Straub Vineyard. 2002 ★ ★ ★ ★ ↗ Pale gold, oaky, herbal, toasty, medicinal aroma with clean, bright vanilla flavours. Big, dry, layered, and complex. Drink now-2009.

Gamay Noir [NP]   2003 ★ ★ ★ ★ → Brilliant ruby with cherry aroma and undertones of thyme and oregano. Big, ripe, clean, and juicy with flavours of apples and strawberry cream. Drink now-2007. **2002** ★ ★ ★ → Ruby-garnet colour with an oaky/vanilla overtone. Fresh and lively taste with hints of strawberry and raspberry and a zippy finish. Drink now-2007.

Gewürztraminer [NP]   2004 ★ ★ ★ ☆ ↗ Very pale gold with an aroma that's just beginning to open up. Hints of bergamot, grapefruit, and violets. Slightly spritzy and crisp with ripe, balanced short flavours. Drink now-2009. **2003** ★ ★ ★ ☆ → Pale straw-gold with lemon, orange, and grapefruit flavours. Superficial but proper. May yet develop depth. Drink now-2007. **2002** ★ ★ ★ ☆ ↗ Straw-gold with a clean nose of honey, oil, and spice. Big, thick palate – a real mouthful – suitable to pair with a stinky Münster cheese. Drink now-2012.

Pinot Noir [NP]   2002 ★ ★ ☆ → Pale garnet hue with a cherry, sandalwood bouquet. A bit hard now with a dusty tannic texture, but I expect it to soften up soon and exhibit intriguing earthy, cherry compote flavours. Drink now-2008. **2000** ★ ★ ★ → Quite pale in colour but has an elegant varietal nose of some depth. Clean flavours of raspberry and cherry with nuances of mocha-chocolate. Drink now.

Riesling [NP]   2004 ★ ★ ★ ↗ Pale gold with a subdued nose of lime and apples. Despite a kiss of sweetness on the palate, it finishes dry. Drink now-2009. **2003** ★ ★ ★ → Lovely honeyed bouquet with mineral notes. Fresh, clean apple flavours with good weight, tight structure, and a yummy finish. Drink now-2010. **2002** ★ ★ ☆ ↗ Straw-green hue. Hint of sulphur off the top, blows off to reveal lemon-lime notes. Crisp acidity, fullish body with a hint of bitterness in the finish. Still unknit. Try after 2005.

Riesling Süssreserve [NP]   2004 ★ ★ ★ ↗ Pale gold with a sweet lemon-pie nose. Soft, sweetish, and balanced. Drink now-2009. **2003** ★ ★ ★ ↗ Pale gold with a floral, lemon aroma and a crisp, tart taste. Ripe fruit with a sweet finish. Drink now-2009.

Rosé [Ont]　A blend of Gamay and Vidal. **2002**★★↻ Nose has some gamy, animal nuances that put me off a bit. Good base for a rose-coloured spritzer.

Rosé Pinot Noir [NP]　**2002**★★★➔ More like a *vin gris*. Good body, lovely flavour, and solid texture. Offers the duo of demure flavours together with buxom mouthfeel.

Sauvignon Blanc [NP]　**2004**★★★☆↻ Silvery gold with a lovely grassy, passionfruit nose. Ripe, sweet, fruity, and balanced.

Vidal Blanc [Ont]　Lightly sweetened with sussreserve. **2003**★★↻ Pale straw-gold colour with apple/pear nose. Clean, pithy grapefruit taste. Seems dull but I blame variety, not winemaking, for that. **2002**★★↻ Fullish grapey nose with nuances of pineapple and grapefruit. Clean and quaffable.

• **Asian Lady Beetle (ALB)** – The multicoloured Asian lady beetle (*Harmonia axyridis*) is an aggressive, non-native species related to the more common North American ladybug (*Hippodamia convergens*). Female Asian lady beetles secrete a pheromone containing methoxypyrazines, primarily to attract male beetles but also to make themselves distasteful to predators. If the bugs are on the vines during harvesting and are frightened or crushed, these chemical secretions end up on the grapes and, ultimately, in the wine. Methoxypyrazines are stable enough to survive heat treatment, fermentation, filtering, and fining, and are noticeable at very low levels. The taint affects a wine's aromas and taste but poses no known health threat to humans. Odours have been described as rancid peanuts, rotting spinach, blue cheese, and vase rot. The Asian lady beetle made its way to North America through a series of accidental and planned releases, which date as far back as 1916. Initially, the bug failed to establish itself on the continent, but the U.S. Department of Agriculture's Agricultural Research Service continued to introduce it into many southern and eastern states throughout the 1970s and 1980s as a biological control against aphids and other soft-bodied insects that harm agricultural crops. As early as 1993, growing populations of the beetle were noticed in American states surrounding Lake Erie and Lake Michigan and particularly in Ohio. The voracious aphid-eating insect spread widely in search of food, finding its way into vineyards at harvest time. The beetle began to cause havoc in the Ontario wine industry as far back as 1999, particularly in the extreme southwestern corner of the province. But in 2001, ideal weather conditions resulted in an explosion in the number of aphids, so Asian lady beetle numbers escalated proportionately and spread into New York State and Niagara Peninsula vineyards. In Ontario, worst hit were vineyards at the foot of the Niagara Escarpment, especially those that lie near soybean farms on the high land above the faultline. That year was especially tragic for growers and winemakers, partly because of the high concentration of beetles but also because the industry had not yet recognized its threat and did nothing to prevent it. Not until spring 2002 did wineries detect a serious problem in tank and barrel samples. Their initial assessment was that drought-stressed vines had produced higher levels of vegetal aromas. The confusion arose because methoxypyrazines exist in many green vegetables, such as asparagus, green beans, and bell peppers, and give Sauvignon Blanc its characteristic herbaceous bouquet. (It is also found in Sémillon and Cabernet Sauvignon, to which it also contributes vegetal notes.) The odour can be particularly difficult to distinguish, even for experienced tasters, in wines made from Sauvignon Blanc or highly aromatic Muscat and Gewürztraminer grapes. At the beginning of 2002, winemakers began to compare notes and whisper among themselves about the unusual, offensive odours, but did not inform the media or the public. As much as 50% of the 2001 vintage was tainted by the bug's smelly secretions, and since grapes are freely bought, sold, and blended throughout the province, the bug's effects are not limited to wines from any producer or region. More than a million litres were held back from the market; some was distilled into vinegar, some blended into nonVQA wines, and the worst of it simply dumped. But many wines did slip through cracks in the system. The LCBO's tasting panel was inexperienced and unaware of the problem at first, but to this day it continues to miss tainted wines, releasing them for sale throughout the province. Some wineries callously pushed affected wines through their own retail stores and, if you attended a charity function any time in 2003 or early 2004 where wine had been donated, the likelihood was high that you would be drinking smelly wine. When the bug reappeared in large numbers in 2003, however, winemakers were ready to try out several new pest-control methods. One of the most successful preventative weapons today is the shaker table, a long stainless-steel table perforated with holes large enough to allow the bugs to drop through but too small to permit grapes to escape. As a further precaution, sorters are instructed to lift away any visible bug using a plastic spoon. And if someone accidentally does touch one of the insects, they are ordered to leave the sorting area immediately to wash their hands. Nevertheless, there were some wines made in 2003 with a whiff of the taint. Curiously, some people claim they like the smell. If you do come across one, do not hesitate to return it with a complaint to the LCBO or winery outlet.

• **ATALICK VINEYARD (St. Catharines, NP)** – Luba and Ernie Atalick farm 24 acres planted with Baco Noir, Cabernet Franc, Chardonnay, Riesling, Syrah, and Vidal Blanc. Their Syrah was lost in the freeze of 2003 and their Cabernet Franc provided only minute crops during the past 2 vintages, but the 2002 CF was exceptional enough to deserve label recognition by Thirty Bench.

B

- **B & V VINEYARD (Vineland, NP)** – Formerly owned by Roger Vail, who currently manages it for new owners. Zweigelt is sold to Lakeview Cellars.

- **BARNES WINES** – Established in St. Catharines in 1873 as The Ontario Grape Growing and Wine Manufacturing Company by George Barnes. It changed hands several times until it was swallowed up by Vincor International Inc.

- **BEAMER FARM (St. Catharines, NP)** – An 80-acre farm on 8th Avenue between 19th Street Louth and 21st Street Louth owned by Howard and Wendy Staff, who own several other sizeable vineyards in the region. According to their daughter, Sue Ann, this flat site situated 5 km from the lake is not suitable for vinifera grapes. Currently 40 acres are dedicated to Concord and 10 acres to Niagara, all of which is sold to the Welch's juice company. The sandy and sandy-clay soil will be replanted to Baco Noir and Vidal grapes in the near future.

- **BEBENEK VINEYARDS (Grimsby, NP)** – George and Elsie Bebenek grow Chardonnay for Kacaba's "old vines" bottling.

- **BELLA VINEYARDS (Cape Vesey, PEC)** – Pat and Heidi del Gatto still work full-time, but weekends and summers are fully committed to establishing their young vineyard and, eventually, building the dream winery. Pat's Italian heritage is rife with winemaking traditions and Heidi's organizational and accounting skills are perfectly matched. Their 74-acre vineyard is a few kilometres east of Waupoos and features 3 types of soils. Generally speaking, it consists of lacustrine materials over limestone till with sections of neutral Waupoos clay, slightly alkaline Somesville clay, and alkaline Ameliasburg clay loam over a fractured limestone base. To date, the couple have planted 1 acre of Chardonnay, .25 acre of Gamay, .5 acre of the white German hybrid, Geisenheim 322, .25 acre of Léon Millot, 2 acres of St. Laurent, and 2 acres of Zweigelt. This past summer they also planted some Pinotage as an experiment. They hope to increase the vineyard up to 40 acres within a few years. For now, their grapes are bottled at Black Prince Winery and are sold under that winery's label.

• **BETHUNE VINEYARD (Niagara Falls, NP)** – On a 4-acre plot located on Warner Road just inside the city boundary of Niagara Falls, George Bethune grows 2 acres of Cabernet Franc at a density of 1,640 plants per acre and 1 acre of Merlot planted at 1,920 vines per acre. The vineyard is virtually flat and fully underdrained, with clay loam soil over a limestone bedrock. All grapes are sold to Inniskillin Wines.

• **BIRCHWOOD ESTATE WINERY LTD.** (4679 Cherry Avenue, Beamsville, ON, L0R 1B1 / Phone: 905-562-8463 / Fax: 905-562-6344 / Email: chevonn@diamondwines.com / Website: www.birchwood wines.ca)

(Est. 2000) In March 2000, Andrew Green, a lawyer and founder of Boka Imports wine agency, purchased the assets of Vine Court Estates from Josef Zimmermann (who also owns King's Court Estate Winery in St. Catharines) and renamed the winery Birchwood. Green hired Murray Marshall as president and assembled additional investors to form Diamond Estates, the nominal owner of Birchwood as well as of Lakeview Cellars Estate Winery. The Birchwood property is located at the top of Cherry Avenue and is visible from the QEW on the opposite side of the South Service Road. It is 10 acres of completely flat Jeddo clay loam till. Six acres of old Seyval Blanc have been torn out and replaced with Cabernet Sauvignon, Chardonnay, and, most recently, Gewürztraminer. There are also 3 acres of Riesling planted by Ron Speranzini in the mid-1990s. The property has a smallish house, winery, retail space, and a massive parking lot to accommodate tour buses. Birchwood's highly visible location has been one of its greatest assets. No fewer than 3 big buses stop here every day, packed with tourists itching to take home some wines not available at local liquor stores. Birchwood's current production is about 7,000 cases and is expected to increase steadily to meet growing demand.
    Winemaker: Tom Green (2000-present)

Baco Noir [Ont] **2003** ★ ☆ ➔ Opaque garnet colour with a creamy, herbal, and smoky blackberry nose. Palate disappoints with overly tart acidity and a hot, volatile finish. **2002** ★ ★ ★ ➔ *Gold, Ontario Wine Awards 2004.* Garnet black hue with an intense bouquet of creamy hot chocolate, allspice, sage, wild game, leather, and sweat. Tart and tannic with strong flavours of black fruits. Drink now-2008.

Cabernet Franc [NP] **2002** ★ ★ ★ ↗ Garnet colour, green, vegetal, closed, and undeveloped nose with nuances of mandarin and oriental spices. Tannic taste with a dusty finish. Needs another year to open up.

Cabernet Franc Icewine [NP] **2003** ★ ★ ★ ➔ *Gold, All Canadian Wine Championships 2004.* Pale tawny-orange with a thick, viscous texture. Strawberry, Rainier cherry, and nut aromas and an intensely sweet finish. Drink now-2008.

Cabernet-Merlot [NP] **2001** ★ ↻ Garnet with a subdued herbal nose. Hints of Asian lady beetle. Light red for quick turnover.

Chardonnay [NP] **2003** ★ ★ ★ ↻ Gold with light aromas of apple, lemon, and a hint of cream. Clean, refreshing, and balanced.

Crescendo [NP] Cabernet Sauvignon fortified to 20% alc./vol. in the style of ruby port. **2001** ★ ★ ★ ☆ ↗ Deep garnet with a bouquet of plums and toasted walnut skins. Thick, creamy, sweet, tasty, fruitcake flavours. This could be brilliant but for the tough tannins in the finish. Drink now-2010.

Gamay Noir [NP] **2003** ★ ★ ★ ↻ Deep cherry hue. Light, soft, fruity, and vinous with clean, fresh, straightforward flavours.

Gewürztraminer-Riesling [NP] **2002** ★ ★ ★ ☆ ↻ Double Gold, American Wine Society 2004. Pale gold with a fruity, mango aroma with undertones of spice. Pleasant spiced honey flavours. Best to drink it now, while it's still young and fresh.

Pinot Noir [NP] **2002** ★ ★ ★ → Gold, American Wine Society 2004. Pale cherry reflections. Restrained nose with more wood than fruit to start. Sweet, ripe fruit, tending to flavours of warmed strawberry, red-cherry, and black-cherry compote. Great balance. Lovely supple texture and clean, lingering pleasant finish. Drink now-2008.

Riesling [NP] **2002** ★ ★ → Straw-green colour with a dull, doughy nose. Soft flat taste. Unexceptional.

Riesling Icewine [NP] **2003** ★ ★ ★ ★ ↗ Straw-gold colour. Wild fruit nose with nuances of apple, lemon, pineapple, pear, and wildflower honey. Tart and lively. Drink now-2013.

Vidal Icewine [NP] **2002** ★ ★ ★ ★ → Gold, Selection Mondiale 2004. Big and fat with flavours of pear syrup and herb-infused roast game. Balanced acidity with a relatively dry finish. Drink now-2010.

Salmon River Label

Cabernet-Merlot [NP, nonVQA] **2003** ★ ★ ☆ → Ruby-garnet hue with a light berry-fruit aroma. Fresh, juicy, and light but well balanced. **2001** ☒ Spoiled by Asian lady beetle.

First Blush [Ont] **2000** ☒ Deeply unpleasant nose of boiled asparagus and wilted celery. Taste is no better.

Pinot Gris-Chardonnay [NP, nonVQA] **2003** ★ ☆ ↻ (C40/PG60) Light gold colour with a vinous, nondescript nose. Good body, pleasant flavour, fine with light foods. **2001** ☒ Severely tainted by Asian lady beetle.

Vidal Icewine [NP] **2001** ★ ★ ★ ☆ → Pale amber-gold with a bouquet of caramelized pear and sautéed pineapple. Rich, sweet, and well balanced. Drink now-2009.

• **BLACK PAW VINEYARD (St. Davids, NP)** – Steve and Vivian Murdza have been growing grapes for other wineries for more than 20 years. In 2004, they joined with Jeff Aubry and David Sheppard to create Coyote's Run Winery. This 34-acre property, just a stone's throw from the winery, is not a part of the operation but sells its fruit exclusively to them. The couple grows Cabernet Franc, Cabernet Sauvignon, Merlot, and Pinot Noir all planted in 1997 and Vidal Blanc planted in 1988. The vines are spaced at 1,600 plants per acre in the iron-rich, dark, clay-dominated soil. There are a few very large rocks scattered throughout the otherwise flat vineyard. Summers here are very hot.

• **BLACK PRINCE WINERY** (13370 Loyalist Parkway [Highway 33], R.R.#1, Picton, ON, K0K 2T0 / Phone: 613-476-4888 / Toll-Free: 1-866-470-9463 / Fax: 613-476-0075 / Email: gwebb@blackprince winery.com / Website: www.blackprincewinery.com)

(Est. 2001) A 50-acre property on the north side of Loyalist Parkway in Picton owned by a group of investors that includes Val O'Donovan, retired chairman and founder of ComDev International, the Opimian Vineyard Trust, and Kylix International Inc., the parent company of Kylix Media, which owns *Wine Tidings* magazine. In 2002, the group planted 8.5 acres of Auxerrois, Cabernet Franc, Chambourcin, Chardonnay, Marechal Foch, Pinot Noir, and Riesling at a vine density of 1,200 per acre. After the winter of 2003, 6 acres remained unscathed. The soil in this south-facing hillside vineyard is Pontypool sandy loam over a limestone base. Black Prince produces a multiplicity of wines, mostly small lots, supporting local growers. Currently, they buy grapes from Sandbanks Estate, Domaine Calcaire, Little Creek Vineyards, Loyalist, Shingle Ridge Vineyard, and Bella Vineyards. Current production is 5,000 cases, half of which is sold outside Ontario and predominantly in the Florida "snowbirds" market. Aim is to grow to 25,000 cases by 2010.

Winemaker: Michael Fallow (2001-present) / Vineyard Manager: Bob Adair

Baco Noir, First Crush [nonVQA] **2003 ★ ★ →** Garnet with a smoky, soft fruity nose. Light, but clean and balanced. Drink now-2006.

Baco Noir Rosé, Nouveau Crush [nonVQA] **2004 ★ ★ ☆ ↻** Bright ruby colour with a tart, fresh, candied aroma. Clean, fresh, pleasant, and uncomplicated.

Cabernet [nonVQA] **2003 ★ ★ ★ →** Deep garnet hue with a bracing raspberry and orange juice nose. Clean red-fruit flavours, silky texture, and light, quick finish. Drink now-2007.

Cabernet Franc [nonVQA] **NV ★ ★ →** Garnet with a shy nose, hinting at raspberry. Lean and clean with a hint of fruitiness. Drink now-2006.

Chardonnay, First Crush [nonVQA] **2004**★ ★ ↻ Pale gold with tiny bubbles forming on the surface and on the inside of the glass. Crisp, tart nose with a spritzy taste of green apple and lemon.

Chardonnay [Ont] **2002**★ ↘ Deep gold with a lemony nose and a flabby, dull, sweetish taste. Over the hill.

Vidal Icewine [LENS] **1999**★ ★ ★ ☆ → Deep golden hue with a honeyed pear aroma. Teeth-rattling sweetness and good acidity. Best now but can age to 2008.

• **BLACK RIVER VINEYARDS (Milford, PEC)** – In addition to growing 5 acres of grapes on the 60-acre property they purchased in 2000, Elia and Gudrun Gallo produce local food and wine publications, including *The Harvest Table* in Prince Edward County and *What's Happening* in Belleville. To date, they have planted Baco Noir, Pinot Gris, Pinot Noir, Sauvignon Blanc, and St. Laurent. Although grapes are not cultivated organically, the Gallos say they do not use any pesticides. Their first small harvest was in 2004. Sometime in the future, the couple intends to start construction on a winery.

• **BOLDT & GUNTER VINEYARDS (Niagara-on-the-Lake, NP)** – When Herbert and Gudrun Konzelmann purchased and combined these 2 contiguous vineyards totalling 30 acres in 1997, they already had 3.25 acres of Riesling and 1.5 acres of Vidal Blanc planted upon them. Since 1999, the Konzelmanns have added 2.25 acres of Cabernet Sauvignon, 6.6 acres of Chardonnay, 12.25 acres of Merlot, 1 acre of Pinot Blanc, 1.3 acres of Shiraz, and .25 acre of Zweigelt. The site is relatively flat with sandy loam soil.

• *Botrytis cinerea* – A mould that grows on the surface of vines. If the weather is poor, the mould will grow rampantly and unevenly, breaking the skins of the grapes and causing unpleasant mouldy smells. If the weather is good, with dewy mornings and warm dry days, the mould will grow only on the surface of the grapes, sending thin root follicles through pores in the skin into the depths of the grape's pulp, where it will use up moisture, slowly shrivelling the grape, concentrating the sugar/water ratio but maintaining the sugar/acid balance. Under the latter conditions, the common English term is "noble rot" (Fr., *pourriture noble*; Ger., *edelfaule*; It., *muffa nobile*), under the former, it is called "gray rot." A wine affected by botrytis is said to be botrytised (not, as I often hear, botrysized.)

• **BOWEN VINEYARD (Jordan, NP)** – The new Le Clos Jordanne winery has negotiated a long-term lease with the Bowen family to cultivate a 25-acre portion of this farm. The site is partially flat, partially sloped, and north-facing, and partially irregular and uneven but all of it is composed of a deep, silty, clay loam with limestone particles sitting on glacial till.

There are almost 16 acres of 4-year-old Pinot Noir, 8.5 acres of Chardonnay, and 1.5 acres of Pinot Gris spaced at the high density of 2,160 plants per acre. Riesling for icewine production will be planted in the near future. Drainage has been installed between every row and cover crops are grown alternate years between every second row to improve the soil structure, to increase competition for water, and to lessen soil compaction. Yields are exceptionally low for now but will increase to a maximum of 2 t. per acre at maturity. All vineyard treatments are organic and the plan is to certify the vineyard as such, and then to introduce bio-dynamic farming within a few years.

- **BRAE BURN ESTATE (Niagara-on-the-Lake, NP)** – In 1978, when Donald Ziraldo and Karl Kaiser purchased this 30-acre property as the site of their new Inniskillin winery, it was still a cornfield. It is situated on the south side of Line 3 west of the Niagara Parkway and surrounds the Inniskillin winery. The corner parcel closest to the intersection is composed of Jeddo clay loam till with some loamier Tavistock soil farther back. The vineyard is completely flat and fully tiled for better drainage. There are 21.5 acres under vine, with a tiny plot of Cabernet Sauvignon, 9 acres of Pinot Noir, 1 acre of Riesling, 3 acres of Shiraz, .5 acre of St. Laurent, and 5 acres of Vidal Blanc used to make the winery's famous icewines. Most reds are thinned by 30% at veraison for a harvest of 3 t. per acre, but Pinot Noir is slashed in half, yielding only 1.5 t. per acre. Neighbours include Albrecht Seeger on the north side of Line 3 and Peter Van de Laar to the south, next to the Frank Lloyd Wright barn, which is Inniskillin's logo and which houses the winery's retail space.

- **Braeburn Wines** – Label once used by Inniskillin for international blends, including Cabernet/Gamay and Chardonnay/Seyval. These were good-value serviceable wines but had little connection to the region and contributed little to the reputation of Inniskillin. After the merger with Vincor, the label was dropped entirely.

- **T.G. Bright & Co. Wines** – This major commercial winery established in 1874 produced every imaginable product over the course of its lifetime. It was the first to grow a varietal Chardonnay, and the first to give a vineyard designation on a bottle. The company was taken over by a group of shareholders and merged with Cartier-Inniskillin Vintners in 1993. Today, it is merely another brand name owned by Canada's biggest wine company, Vincor International Inc.

- **BUIS VINEYARDS (Niagara-on-the-Lake, NP)** – The Buis brothers, Peter and Kevin, farm several properties in the Niagara Peninsula including Glen Lake and Tobe vineyards. Fruit is sold exclusively to Hillebrand.

- **BURKHARDT VINEYARD (Niagara-on-the-Lake, NP)** – Walter Burkhardt bought a 40-acre vineyard on Lakeshore Road less than 400 ft. from Lake Ontario from Elmer Neufeld, brother of John, who runs Neufeld Farm next door. He added 2 contiguous properties, bringing his holdings to well over 120 acres. He grows Cabernet Franc, Gewürztraminer, Merlot, Pinot Noir, Riesling, and Vidal Blanc, which is sold to a variety of wineries, including Konzelmann, Legends Estates, Strewn, and Vincor International.

- **BUTLER'S GRANT VINEYARD (Vineland, NP)** – This outstanding vineyard just across the road from Stoney Ridge Estate Winery was assembled from 3 properties in the late 1970s by Jordan & Ste. Michelle Wines as an experimental vineyard. At the time it was considered one of the best sites in all of Niagara. The vineyard is composed of Chinguacousy clay loam till, and the northeast-facing slope of the land just below the escarpment provides air drainage as well. After T.G. Brights Wines acquired Jordan, the vineyard went up for sale, but at first the price was prohibitive. It sat on the market for more than a year. Late in 1987, when the first Free Trade Agreement was being negotiated with the U.S. government, there was much pessimism about the future of the wine industry, the price of the property dropped and St. Catharines lawyer Marvin Kriluck snapped it up. Kriluck grows Chardonnay, Gewürztraminer, Merlot, Muscat d'Alsace, Pinot Noir, and Riesling. The fruit is sold to several wineries, including Lakeview Cellars and Stoney Ridge, and the name of this vineyard often appears on labels.

- **BY CHADSEY'S CAIRNS WINERY AND VINEYARD** (17432 Loyalist Parkway [Highway 33], R.R.#1, Wellington, ON, K0K 3L0 / Phone: 613-399-5128 / Email: the.cairns@reach.net)

(Est. 1999) Richard Johnston was a New Democratic Party member in the Ontario Legislature from 1979 to 1990 and president of Centennial College from 1999 to 2004. In 1995, he and his wife, Vida Zalnieriunas, a practising psychotherapist, purchased a 215-acre property a few hundred metres from Lake Ontario in Hillier Township just west of the village of Wellington. With 3 distinct types of terroir, the couple speculate they have at least 60 acres of gravel and sandy loam, which they believe to be prime vineyard land. To date, they have planted 3.5 acres of Chardonnay, 1.2 acres of Chenin Blanc, 2.8 acres of Gamay Noir, 2 acres of Gewürztraminer, 1.3 acres of Muscat Oriental, 2.5 acres of Pinot Noir, 3.5 acres of Riesling, and 2.2 acres of St. Laurent. Grapes are cultivated at a vine density of 1,000 to 1,200 depending on the variety. The remaining 155 acres consist of heavy clay with limestone crumble, which would require extensive and expensive installation of a tile drainage system. Perhaps someday they will install it, but for now they have dedicated that part of the property to growing crops such as corn, wheat, and soybeans and as grazing land for their small herd of Cotswold sheep (some of which have found their way onto Toronto chef Jamie Kennedy's bistro menus). There is lake effect here, but, according to Johnston, it has its greatest impact early in the fall, not during the winter when it is most needed. As prevailing winds come in a southwesterly direction off the mainland, they are colder and drier than if they were to come in off the lake, just 400 m away. Winter temperatures can dip to below minus 30°C. Consulting with the proprietors in their first years of production was Martin Gemmrich, who, until last year, ran the Gemmrich grapevine nursery near Niagara-on-the-Lake.

Winemakers: Vida Zalnieriunas (2000-present); Martin Gemmrich (2000-2003, consulting) / Vineyard Manager: Richard Johnston

The following wines were tasted at the winery or quickly at a trade function.

Gamay [PEC, nonVQA] **2003** ★ ★ ↻ From estate-grown grapes. Lovely colour but lacks ripeness. Taste is a bit tart and finish a bit hard.

Gamay/Pinot Noir [nonVQA] **2003** ★ ★ ☆ → (Gam70/PN30) Grapes were purchased from Martin Gemmrich. Ruby-garnet colour with oaky, cherry aromas. Lovely flavour of black and red cherries with a fairly tart finish. Drink now-2006.

Gewürztraminer [PEC, nonVQA] **2002** ★ ★ ★ ☆ → From estate-grown grapes. Bright green-gold colour, wine-gummy lemon-drop nose, and slick finish. Drink now-2008.

Chambourcin [nonVQA] **2003** ☆ → Grapes are from Watson Vineyard. Deep black-cherry colour with a bouquet of cranberry, black tea, and charcoal. Tart, sharp taste.

Pinot Noir [PEC, nonVQA] **2003** ★ ★ ★ ↗ Pale ruby with a light, expanding bouquet of sandalwood, cherry, and earth. Balanced with a clean, fresh finish. Drink now-2009

Riesling [PEC, nonVQA] Grapes are from the estate vineyard. All 3 vintages have a bracing acidity reminiscent of Austrian wines. They're terrific with food but very hard to drink on their own. **2003** ★ ★ ☆ → A hint confected and bubblegummy on the nose. Beginning to demonstrate depth of flavours. Lemony. Fuller than one would expect for this variety but consistent with previous vintages. Drink now-2008. **2002** ★ ☆ → Lemony with thick texture and bracing acidity. Drink now-2008. **2001** ★ ☆ → Like unripe lemons, the acidity is high and startling. Drink now-2007.

C

• **CALAMUS ESTATE WINERY** (3100 6th Avenue, Jordan, ON, L0R 1S0 / Toll-Free: 1-888-225-9866 / Fax: 416-693-9894 / Email: calamus@sympatico.ca / Website: www.calamuswines.com)

(Est. 2005) Derek Saunders, a supervising video editor with CTV National News and long-time amateur winemaker, and his wife, Pat Latin, a buyer and senior manager in the fashion industry, purchased 2 benchland properties in 1999 and 2001 with the intention to start their own winery. By next year, the dream should have come true. The 2 parcels amount to 56 acres and, to date, 32 of them have been planted with vines. The winery, based in a renovated 75-year-old barn, will be built on the larger parcel, a gently sloped 42-acre property adjacent to the Ball's Falls Conservation Area. Here, the soil is a combination of Chinguacousy, Jeddo, and Oneida clay loam till. There are 21.5 fully underdrained acres planted with 4 acres of Cabernet Franc, 6 of Chardonnay, 3 of Gewürztraminer, 3.5 of Pinot Gris, and 5 of Riesling, all at a density of 1,360 vines per acres. The first crop from this site was slated to be harvested this year. The second property, purchase earlier, is situated much closer to the lake just east of Beamsville along Greenlane Road at Bartlett's Creek. This perfectly flat vineyard is composed almost entirely of Chinguacousy clay loam over a limestone base and is also fully underdrained. One acre of Cabernet Franc, 3.25 acres of Cabernet Sauvignon, 2.25 acres of Chardonnay, 1 acre of Merlot, 2 acres of Riesling, and .5 acre of Vidal Blanc were planted in 2000 and .5 acre of Gewürztraminer was added in 2001. Production is expected to reach 10,000 cases by 2007, although there is no Calamus wine just yet. Saunders has a manufacturing licence (required for winemaking) and is producing wine for sale in 2006, but intends to construct a retail space in a 130-year-old heritage barn on the property. Meanwhile, fruit has been sold to Featherstone Estate, Hernder Estate, Lakeview Cellars, Magnotta Wines, and Norman Hardie Wines in Prince Edward County.
   Winemaker: TBA / Vineyard Manager: Phil Clarke, Glen Elgin Vineyard Management Inc.

Wines not available for appraisal before press time.

- **Canadian Oak** – See Oak

- **CARALOU VINEYARD (Beamsville, NP)** – A top-notch 16-acre flat vineyard on the Lake Ontario shoreline next door to the Schuele vineyard. High-end Cabernet Franc, Chardonnay, Merlot, Muscat, and Pinot Noir was grown for Thirty Bench and Willow Heights in the mid-1990s. Today, the vineyard has been torn out and lies fallow. Pity.

- **Carbonic Maceration** – A process whereby whole clusters of red grapes (whites are not used) are gently placed in a tank or vat so as to neither crush nor bruise the berries. The tank is filled with carbon dioxide and sealed for several days. Fermentation occurs spontaneously without the involvement of yeast. The process takes place within the cells of the grape creating alcohol (specifically, ethanol) along with a bright red colour, wildly aromatic fruity flavours, and very little tannin. Wines produced by carbonic maceration do not have the capability to age and are best consumed young and fresh.

- **CARMELA ESTATES WINERY** (1186 Greer Road, R.R.#1, Wellington, ON, K0K 2J0 / Phone: 613-399-3939 / Toll-Free: 1-866-578-3445 / Fax: 613-399-3524 / Email: carmelaestates@bellnet.ca / Website: www.carmelaestates.ca)

(Est. 2002) The winery was originally named Peddlesden Winery, but after a falling out in 2003, majority partners Bob and Sherry Tompkins bought out their partners and changed the name to Carmela. The Tompkinses also own a construction company, a car dealership, and a business that sells all-terrain recreational vehicles for summer and winter fun. The 235-acre Carmela Estate Vineyard is composed entirely of Hillier clay loam with some shards of limestone on the surface and a fractured limestone base. It is essentially flat with a very slight southeast-facing tilt. To date, 28 acres have been planted with 5 acres each of Pinot Gris and Riesling and 6 acres each of Cabernet Franc, Chardonnay, and Pinot Noir. Early vintages were made entirely from grapes purchased in the Niagara Peninsula, but as estate grapes mature those purchases will decline. Winemaker Norman Hardie, a former manager of Truffles Restaurant in the Four Seasons Hotel, apprenticed at Bouchard Finlayson in South Africa and with Pascal Marchand at Domaine de la Vougeraie in Burgundy before coming to Carmela. He uses only French oak and applies a non-interventionist winemaking techniques. Production in 2004 was 2,000 cases and is expected to grow to 5,000 cases by 2006 and, ultimately, to between 15,000 and 20,000 cases. In addition to a tasting bar and retail shop, the winery offers restaurant and banquet hall facilities.

Winemaker: Norman Hardie / Vineyard Manager: Mike Traynor

Cabernet Franc [Ont]   **2002★★★➔** Very pale ruby-cherry colour. Light, fruity nose with soft, fruit flavour. Drink now.

Cabernet Sauvignon [Ont]   **2002★★★➔** Dark purple-garnet with a bouquet of black tea with raspberry syrup. Soft, light, balanced, and pleasant with an apple-skin finish. Drink now-2008.

Hubbs Creek Red [Ont]   **2003★☆↻** Garnet with rustic aromas of red fruit, sweat, and smoke. Fairly high acidity with some sweet cherry and green vegetal flavours.

Hubbs Creek White [Ont]   **2001⊠** It's sad when an upstart winery that buys grapes from a trusted grower in the Niagara Peninsula ends up with something as awful as this. Tasted twice. Reeks of Asian lady beetle.

Riesling, Dry [Ont]   **2002★★★☆➔** Big hit of sulphur to start followed by an aroma of fruit cocktail with nuances of pineapple, canned peach, canned pear, a hint of maraschino cherry, and a very exciting nuance of minerals in the background. Clean, dry finish. Drink now-2008.

- **CAROLINE CELLARS WINERY** (1028 Line 2 at Concession 3, Virgil, ON, L0S 1T0 / Phone: 905-468-8814 / Fax: 905-468-4042 / Email: carolinecellars@sympatico.ca / Website: www.lakeitfarms.com)

(Est. 2002) It was in 1978 that Rick Lakeit first expressed to Caroline, his mom, a deep desire to own a farm. Her generosity is the primary reason why he named the winery after her. Lakeit still works full-time at General Motors, but he and his wife, Elfriede, and their four children, Justine, Stephanie, Rick Jr., and Jaclyn, run a steadily growing winery operation. The 40-acre farm is situated on Line 2, halfway between the Niagara Parkway and the town of Virgil, where the soil is Chinguacousy clay loam till. In the early days, the family grew peppers and other green vegetables, planting fruit trees and grapevines much later. Today, three-quarters of the grape harvest is sold to Vincor, but the best grapes are held back for use in their own wines. Currently, production is just over 3,300 cases, but the winery's goal is to increase sales to about 11,000 cases annually by 2009.

Winemakers: Jordan Harris (2004); Jens Gemmrich (2002-2004)

The owners of Caroline Cellars would not provide vineyard information and did not want me to include their wines in this guide. The following tasting notes were scribbled under varying circumstances – at trade shows, over display tables, at wine functions – not the ideal conditions of my clinical tasting room.

Cabernet Franc Icewine [NP]   **2001★★★➔** Orange pekoe nose with an undertone of pine sap. Jarring note of bitterness in the finish. Drink now-2009.

Chardonnay [NP] **2001** ★ ☆ ➜ What it has is supple texture and decent balance. What it lacks is flavour and charm. Drink soon.

Pinot Gris [NP] **2002** ★ ★ ★ ➜ Soft, fullish, and spicy with a nice oily texture, and lovely flavours of peach and kiwi. Drink now-2006.

Riesling [NP] **2002** ★ ★ ☆ ➜ Pale green-gold with aromas of lemon and Granny Smith apple. Bracing but balanced acidity. Drink now-2007.

Sauvignon Blanc [NP] **2002** ☒ Hazy colour with a funky nose. Avoid.

• **Cartier Wines & Beverages** – This major commercial wine company was created in 1989 when a group of John Labatt Breweries Ltd. executives, led by Donald Triggs, Rick Thorpe (today the B.C. government's minister responsible for regulating the alcohol industry), and former winemaker Allan Jackson, conducted a management buyout of the brewery's wine division, Ridout Wines. *See* Vincor International for more details.

• **CAVE SPRING CELLARS** (3836 Main Street, Jordan, ON, L0R 1S0 / Phone: 905-562-3581 / Toll-Free: 1-888-806-9910 / Fax: 905-562-3232 / Email: info@cavespringcellars.ca / Website: www.cavespringcellars.ca)

(Est. 1986) As far back as he can remember, a young Leonard Pennachetti was beginning to develop an interest in grapes while walking the small labrusca vineyard his grandfather tended. Recognizing that passion for growing grapes, his father took him up in a plane in the early 1980s to scout the escarpment for a suitable site to create his own vineyard. Pennachetti Jr. chose a site with a gradual north-facing slope near the Cave Spring Farm. The original 71-acre parcel they purchased backs onto the Niagara Escarpment and consists primarily of stony Chinguacousy clay loam till over a sandstone and shale base. Leonard, his brother Tom, and school chum Angelo Pavan spent several summers planting Chardonnay, Chardonnay Musqué, Gamay, Pinot Noir, and Riesling at 1,250 vines per acre between 1978 and 1984. In the late 1980s, after establishing the winery, they added Cabernet Franc, Cabernet Sauvignon, and Merlot at 1,450 vines per acre. Recent plantings, including Chenin Blanc, Gewürztraminer, Sauvignon Blanc, and more acreage of the other varieties, have been more densely spaced at 1,900 vines per acre. Today, the Cave Spring Vineyard is 120 acres, enlarged over the years with the purchase of several adjacent blocks, including the former Shoreline, Etherington, and Shoemaker vineyards. There are some small sections of better-drained Oneida soils in the newer blocks. Nevertheless, the entire vineyard is tiled for drainage and dry-farmed without irrigation. Almost 50% of the winery's fruit comes from Cave Spring Vineyard (CSV on its wine labels). The winery is the exclusive buyer of grapes from Weis Vineyards, which, in addition to some Chardonnay, Pinot Noir, and Sauvignon Blanc, has the single largest planting of Riesling clone Weis-21 in the country. That's not surprising since this 65-acre property is owned by Tom and his wife, Anne Weis-Pennachetti, whose father, Hermann Weis, developed the clone at the family nurseries in Germany. Additional requirements are fulfilled through purchases from a number of growers throughout the Niagara Peninsula and, in years of crop shortages, from outside the province. The winery is located on Main Street in the village of Jordan, in the massive Jordan & Ste. Michelle Winery building dating back to 1871. Over the decades, Jordan sporadically enlarged the structure and added cavernous underground storage spaces, ultimately creating the largest (and oldest) wine cellar in the country. Today, the building houses the winery, a large wine retail outlet, On the Twenty restaurant, and several gift shops and antique stores. Leonard Pennachetti and his wife, Helen Young, also run Inn on the Twenty, a high-end hotel and luxurious spa across the road from the winery, and own numerous houses throughout the village. Cave Spring wines generally have tight structure, crisp acidity, subtle oak, and complex yet delicate fruit. The winery is so committed to quality that after discovering Asian lady beetle taint in some of its 2001 vintage, it dumped what remained unsold, almost 180,000 L of wine. In 2003, Cave Spring produced no estate-bottled reds. All were declassified. Older vintages are still aging exceptionally well, and recent vintages show the same potential for longevity. The winery also produces some late-harvest Vidal and Vidal icewine for export under a second label, Twenty Valley. Annual production averages 50,000 cases. The winery has grown slowly and steadily as consumer demand for its wines has increased. According to Tom Pennachetti, a reasonable production cap of about 75,000 cases may be achieved a few years hence.

Winemaker: Angelo Pavan (1999 Winemaker of the Year) / Vineyard Manager: Kevin Latter

Cabernet [NP] **1998** ★ ★ ★ ☆ → (CF60/CS40) Garnet with a sweet aroma and all the necessary taste components, but it is completely lacking in personality, complexity, or oomph. Drink now.

Cabernet/Merlot [NP] **2002** ★ ★ ★ ↗ *Best General List Red, Cuvée 2005.* Garnet with a raspberry, blackberry, and milk-chocolate bouquet. Light, but balanced, and it manages to hit the sweet spot. Drink now-2011. **2000** ★ ★ ☆ ↗ (CF52/CS29/M19) Very pale garnet with a sweet, minty, vanilla, oaky, herbal nose. Flavour of berries comes through, but there's an impression of underripeness. Drink now-2008.

Cabernet/Merlot, Beamsville Bench [NP] **1998** ★ ★ ★ ★ ☆ ↗ Garnet with hints of mahogany in the rim. Ripe black fruits, berries, mint, and dark chocolate. Undoubtedly the best red made to date at Cave Spring. Drink now-2013. **1997** ★ ★ ★ → Bright garnet with a mahogany edge. Green and vegetal with some pruniness in the nose. Has plenty of fruit on the palate, but the tannins are still aggressive. Fruits beginning to dry up. Drink now-2007. **1995 ★ ★ ★ ★ →** Good extract. Overpowering early hints of green pepper and asparagus now beginning to subside as fruit emerges. Drink now-2008. **1993 ★ ★ →** Supple and balanced but pruney. Drink up. **1992 ↓** Weedy and vegetal.

Cabernet/Merlot, Estate-Bottled Reserve [NP]   2002 ★ ★ ★ ☆ ↑ Dark garnet with blackberry flavours and sweet green pepper notes. More body than regular version and better balance. Drink 2006-2012. **1991 ★ ★ ★ ☆ →** Garnet with significant browning of the rim. Barnyardy nose with bouquet of prune plums. Sweet and mature. Drink now.

Chardonnay, Beamsville Bench [NP] 1994 ★ ★ ↘ Rich gold hue with an oxidative nose. Taste is beginning to crack up – the fruit has gone, but there is still a stemmy, tart bitterness in the finish. **1990 ★ ★ ★ ★ →** Pure gold with a nose that says "wow." Meursault-like bouquet, restrained and complex with creamy toasty nutty nuances. Aging gracefully with great depth and complexity, though significantly lighter than the Reserve wine of the same vintage. Drink now-2008.

Chardonnay, CSV [NP]   2002 ★ ★ ★ ★ ↗ Rich golden hue with a massive nose of fruit oak and citrus. There seems to be more of everything here. This is not a summer sipper. Save it for a cold winter's night with osso buco. Drink now-2012. **2000 ★ ★ ★ ↗** Deep gold with a strong aroma of tropical-fruit yogourt and toasted nuts. Palate is over the top – frankly, it's a monster – with more brawn and muscle than joy and charm. Hope it calms down soon. Now-2010. **1999 ★ ★ ★ ★ ↗** Gold with some spritz in the glass. Fresh aromas with fine oak, vanilla, and a sweetness I associate with buttered lobster. Sweet, spicy, still youthful, and full of verve. Drink now-2009. **1998 ★ ★ ★ ★ ↗** Bright gold with guava, spiced lemon, buttered fennel, and wet stone aromas. Fullish and potent, very ripe with mineral structure and refreshing lemony acidity. Supple, elegant, and long-lasting. Drink now-2012. **1997 ★ ★ ★ ★ ☆ ↗** Gold and glowing. Bouquet of pine, jasmine, and wildflower perfume, vanilla cream, honey, and clarified butter. Supple, delicate, smooth, exotic, and very fine. Drink now-2010.

Chardonnay, Estate [NP]   2000 ★ ★ ★ ↗ Pale gold with clean crisp notes of apple, pear, and lemon-lime. Good body, some depth, and a clean lingering aftertaste. **1998 ★ ↘** Has a dirty nose. High alcohol, low acid, cooked fruit. **1997 ★ ★ ★ ↗** Bright gold with a bouquet of lemon drops with hints of ginger. Still developing. Drink now-2007. **1996 ★ ★ →** *Best General List White, Cuvée, 1998*. Clean, light apple-pear flavours with citrus notes, medium body, and a balanced, lightly oaked, lingering aftertaste. Great value. Drink up.

Chardonnay, Reserve [NP] 2003 ★ ★ ★ ↑ Gold with a light aroma of butter, lemon, and very little oak. Still closed, hard, and reserved but perfect balance says it will go on for some time. Drink 2006-2010. **2002 ★ ★ ★ →** Golden hue with a powerful and concentrated bouquet of fruit and oak. Very potent at 14% alc./vol. and beginning to show a hot finish. Drink with food, now-2008. **1998 ★ ★ ★ →** Gold with a sweet, barnyardy nose of wet earth, mushrooms, composted leaves. Drink now. **1995 ★ ★ ★ ↘** Amber-gold with a maderized nose of cooked sugar. Drink soon. **1994 ★ ★ ↘** Amber-gold with a nutty, earthy, tarry nose. Drink now. **1993 ★ ★ ★ →** All power and elegance, beautifully balanced. Bouquet suggests fruit salad drizzled with caramel sauce. Nicely oaked and dense with flavours of stewed white fruits, lemon, nuts, toast. Drink in the next year or two. **1991 ★ ★ ★ ↘** *Grand Gold Award at VinItaly, 1993.* Barrel-fermented and barrel-aged. Rich gold, sharp nose of broiled pineapple and old apple cores. Breaks up quickly after opening, with sharp, oxidative, mushroomy flavours. Drink soon. **1990 ★ ★ ★ ★ ☆ →** Has lasted amazingly well and will continue to grow a few more years. Big, complex, and well balanced with well-integrated youthful and aged flavours. Graceful. Drink now-2010. This wine was highly praised by British wine icon Hugh Johnson during his 1994 visit to Ontario for its elegance, concentration, acidity, and fruit. Many of Cave Spring's older wines had higher acidity and lower alcohol in these early years, giving them finesse, better balance, and greater longevity. **1989 ★ ★ ★ ★ →** Rich gold hue with a lovely and delicate nose hinting at Earl Grey tea, orange marmalade, and candied ginger. Fully mature and still quite charming. Drink now-2008.

Chardonnay Musqué [NP] Until 1995, this unusual natural crossing or, possibly, mutation didn't qualify for VQA status. Nevertheless, it has always been one of my favourites with its exotic bouquet and flavour nuances reminiscent of Viognier. **2003 ★ ★ ★ ★ →** Pale gold with pink reflections. And an exciting, enticing, perfumed bouquet of wildflowers, freesia, hints of crisp apple, and ripe grapes. Terrific spritz on the palate, implicitly sweet, medium-bodied with racy acidity and wild, seductive flavours. The best musqué ever. Drink now-2006. **2002 ★ ★ ★ →** Lively and aromatic, Muscat-like with clean, fruit salad flavours. Hint of spritz but a touch overblown and alcoholic. Drink up. **1999 ★ ★ ↘** Lively nose of honeysuckle, orange candy, and perfumed hotel soap. Taste is tired and fading fast. **1998 ↓** Oxidized and dead. **1997 ★ ★ ★ →** Still has a hint of spritz, exceptionally high alcohol and the caramel-like flavours of maderized grapes and cognac, as in well-aged Pineau des Charentes. Drink soon.

Chardonnay Musqué, Late Harvest [NP] 1995 ★ ★ ★ → Yellow gold with a sweet, spirity Pineau des Charentes nose. Medium dry and full-bodied with flavours of butter cream, wild honey, baked nectarine, orange zest, and butterscotch. Only 275 cases produced. Fully mature; drink soon.

Gamay [NP] **2003**★→ Pale cherry-orange with a rubbery odour dominating the nose. Smelled better the second day, but taste turned sour. More of a miss than a hit. Drink now. **2002**★★★→ Soft, lively cherry and plum notes with fine texture and a clean finish. **1995**★★↘ Charming with loads of black and blueberry fruit. May be too late. **1994**↓ Once full of black raspberries, strawberries, blackberries, and plums. Finished. **1993**↓ Bright purple violet, concentrated strawberry-raspberry nose, dry, creamy texture, lively acidity, slightly short finish. Over the hill now.

Gamay Reserve [NP] **2002**★★★☆↗ A massive wine with 14% alc./vol. Full-bodied with firm structure and restrained black-cherry flavours. Fine now, but better next year. Drink until 2008. **1998**★★★☆→ Black-cherry Jello. Fully mature.

Gewürztraminer [NP] **2002**★★★↗ Rich gold hue with a hint of sulphur on the nose. Spritzy and vibrant with dense, closed citrus and honey flavours. Will improve. Drink now-2020. **1998**★★★☆↗ Pale gold colour and nose still closed and tight. Hard and austere but with dense texture and a solid mineral backbone. Lime flower flavours emerge very slowly. Drink now-2013. **1997**★★★☆→ Pale amber with rich floral notes and tropical flavours of caramelized peach and lemon drops. Drink now. **1996**★★★→ Brilliant yellow-gold with amber reflections. Clean, baked-apple nose with nuances of nutmeg and cinnamon. Lovely silk texture. Drink now.

Merlot [NP] **2000**★↘ Pale, watery, thin colour with an unripe, vegetal nose.'A bitter, unappealing wine from a cool vintage.

Merlot, Lenko Vineyard [NP] **1989**★★↘ (CS5/M95) An Italian-style merlot. Austere, clean, high acid, and layered with complexity. Time to drink up.

Pinot Noir [NP] **2003**★★★☆↑ Ruby hue with a pale rim. Juicy confected red-berry nose with mild herbal notes. Sweetish to start with a good level of ripeness, but flavours are undeveloped yet. Drink 2007-2011. **2002**★★★↗ Black-cherry colour and restrained nose that barely hints at black fruits. Opens to cherry and plum flavours. Drink now-2012. **1998**★★★→ Brilliant ruby with minimal change in colour to the rim. Playful aroma of red fruits and berries with an enticing cigar tobacco nuance. Sweet, deep, clean, and fresh with delicious strawberry-cherry flavours and a dry tannic finish. Drink now-2009. **1992**↓ Once hard, green, and bitter, now dead and decomposing.

Riesling, CSV [NP] Yield in this single vineyard is reduced to 2.5 t. per acre. **2003**★★★★☆↗ Silvery-gold with green reflections and a wonderful hit of spritz to arouse the palate. Classic citrus bouquet with ripe McIntosh apple sweetness and razor-sharp lime acidity. Already accessible but worth waiting for the real brilliance of this vintage to show through. The best Riesling to come from this vineyard. Drink now-2018. **2002**★★★☆↑ Straw-green in colour and beginning to show signs of petrol on the nose. Flavours are slightly candied with nuances of lemon, orange, and grapefruit. A bit clumsy at this stage. Drink 2007-2014. **2001** Not produced. **2000**★★★★↗ Bright gold with a hint of spritz and a deep, enticing mineral nose. Ripe and sweet with zippy acidity and rich, supple texture. Great stuff. Drink now-2015. **1999**★★★★→ Solid gold with a fresh and attractive floral nose of orange blossom and peach. Highly extracted with tongue-tingling acidity. Flavours linger. Drink now-2014.

Riesling, Dry [NP, nonVQA] **2003**★★☆→ A blend of domestic and imported juices due to crop shortages. Commercially good but lacks the Niagara signature. **2002**★★★↗ Golden colour with fine petrol notes. Clean, lemon-lime flavours and firm, dry mineral backbone. Drink now-2008. **2001** Not produced. **2000**★★★→ Spritzy with lively lemon-apple notes. Drink now-2009. **1999**★★★→ Lemon-lime bouquet, refined and elegant, beginning to develop classic petrol notes. **1998**★★→ Oxidative and untypical. Likely a poorly stored bottle. **1997**★★★→ Hints of petrol and lime. Fullish and soft. Drink now-2009. **1996**★★☆→ Lemon-lime, honeyed, and very flavoury but getting on. **1989**★★★↘ Lemony gold colour, honeyed citrus nose, hints of petrol, dry, full rich chewy texture, dry spätlese style, fully mature. A triumph!

Riesling, Icewine [NP] **2002** ★★★★★↗ Absolutely terrific. Complex with ripe pineapple flavours, hints of apricot, marmalade, and orange blossoms. Drink now-2020. **1998**★★★★★→ Tropical hints of banana, orange, peach, and pear. Like nectar. Ripe, fresh, juicy, sweet, lush, and more. Sensational! Drink now-2020. **1997**★★★☆→ Rich, concentrated, and pungent. Drink now-2015. **1996**★★★★→ *Best Dessert Wine, All Canadian Wine Championships.* A dollop of Gewürztraminer was added to spice things up. Very concentrated with a pungent honey and pear essence. High sugar and acidity. Going strong. Drink now-2012. **1995**★★★★→ A big vintage with ripe flavours. Drink now-2012. **1994**★★★★☆→ A wonderful and complete nectar. Fully mature but will hold for another decade.

Riesling, "Indian Summer" [NP] In earlier years it was a Late Harvest wine, more recently it has been bottled as a Select Late Harvest. **2003**★★★★→ Fruity and fresh with bright hints of pear reduction and dried fruit, and also yeasty with cake and custard nuances. High acidity, thick texture, long-lived. Drink now-2025. **2002**★★★★→ High-toned with aromas of dried apricot and fig. Solid, almost daunting texture. Clean, mineral-laden, and potent. Drink now-2020. **2000**★★★☆→ Pale amber-gold with a bright, peachy bouquet. Thick and luscious with a clean, lingering taste. Drink now-2010. **1998**★★★★☆→ If an aroma could hit "high C," this one would do it. It buzzes. Petrol notes, full, fat, thick, viscous palate with focused flavours. Drink now-2015. **1997**★★★☆→ Buttertart nose, pecan pie with a slightly bitter walnut-skin finish. Slowly passing its peak and sliding into a long, graceful decline. Drink now. **1995**★★★★→ Widespread botrytis in the vineyard resulted in a highly aromatic, concentrated wine with plenty of acidity. Honeyed, floral, and exotic with ripe white peach and raisin flavours. Drink now-2010. **1991**★★★☆→ No botrytis on this late-harvest wine. It was almost frozen at first picking. Delicately balanced, sweet, and ripe. Still drinking well. **1990**★★★↘ Ripe, full, soft. On the slide.

Riesling, Off-Dry [NP]   **2003**★★★☆→ *Best General List White, Cuvée 2005.* Pale gold with a lively hint of spritz. Peach and pear flavours with some apple, melon, and mineral notes. Will improve. Drink now-2010. **2002**★★→ Straw-gold with a lemony, tangerine nose and flavours of green apple. Clean and simple, it's an adequate quaffer. **2001** Not produced. **2000**★★★→ Spritzy with a zesty orange aroma and a kiss of sweetness. Drink now-2010. **1999**★★★→ Gold and spritzy with exotic mandarin fragrance and enticing flavours. Drink now-2010. **1998**★★★☆→ Deep gold with developing honey and petrol notes. Concentrated and solid with minerality and finesse. Drink now-2010. **1994**★★↘ Balanced and harmonious but tiring.

Riesling, Reserve [NP]   Estate-grown grapes are reduced to 3 t. per acre. **2004**★★★☆↗ (pre-bottling sample) Very pale with a youthful spritz. Bubblegum overtone for now with a nuance of boiled hot dogs with yellow mustard – typical for such a young wine. **2003**★★★★↗ Pale straw-gold with green reflections. Racy acidity and lovely citrus and lime flavours. Drink now-2015. **2002**★★★☆↗ Green-gold, with hints of lime and grapefruit. Big flavours, full-bodied. Can age for up to a decade. **2001** Not produced. **2000**★★★☆↗ Pale green-gold with aromas of lemon apple and wet stones. Clean and sturdy. Drink now-2012. **1999**★★★☆↗ Gold with honeyed pear and lemon flavours. Still stiff with good minerality and tight structure. Drink now-2012. **1998**★★★☆↗ Bright gold with a maturing petrol, honey, lime bouquet. Big and buxom for a Riesling. Viscous and mouth-filling. Drink now-2010. **1997**★★★☆↗ Tight, with a less developed bouquet and higher acidity. Lemon-lime and lasting. Drink now-2012. **1995**★★★☆↗ Dry, intense, tightly structured with petrol, lime, and spiced honey flavours. More submerged fruit waiting to develop. Drink now-2012. **1994**★★→ Firm and dry. Drink now. **1990**★★★→ Fully mature with flavours of broiled grapefruit and brown sugar. Drink now-2006. **1989**★★★☆→ Mature and holding well. Drink soon.

Rosé, Dry [NP]   Produced by the *saignée* method primarily from Cabernet Sauvignon and Cabernet Franc. **2002**★★★↻ Pretty pink colour with a fresh red berry aroma. Lively palate. A charmer.

Sauvignon Blanc [NP] **2002**★ ★ ☆ ↻ A simple wine. Not up to the standard of the rest of the portfolio.

Syrah [NP] **2002**★ ★ ★ ☆ ↗ The first vintage of this variety for Cave Spring. Exotic berries and spice nose with aromas of lead pencil, cedar, white pepper, and a hint of green pepper. Silky texture with chocolatey flavour. Has an exciting future. Drink now-2010.

Twenty Valley Label

Vidal, Icewine [NP] Sold primarily to restaurants. **2001**★ ★ ★ ★ → Pale amber hue with bouquet and flavours of honey, white peach, quince, and lemon oil. Thick honeyed taste with a nutty, peach-pit finish. Drink now-2009.

Vidal, Select Late Harvest [Ont] **2001**★ ★ ★ ☆ → Rich amber-gold colour with an aroma of boiled fruits and vanilla, like a pear marmalade. Lovely, light mouthfeel with a dry, pleasantly bitter finish. Drink now-2007.

• **CEDAR RIDGE VINEYARD** (Blenheim, LENS) – A 65-acre vineyard established in 1984 by London Winery Ltd. and located just west of Blenheim on Highway 3. Originally called Cedar Springs Vineyard, it is planted with Baco Noir, Cabernet Franc, Chardonnay, De Chaunac, Marechal Foch, Merlot, Riesling, Seyval Blanc, and Vidal. When the London Winery was purchased by Vincor in 1996, this property stayed in the hands of James Knowles, a descendant of the winery's founders.

• **Cedar Springs Wines** – An alternate label of London Winery Ltd., occasionally indicating vineyard-designated varietal wines but more often used for generic blends and "global selections." The label was put out to pasture when Vincor International took over the winery and its brands.

• **Chaptalization** – The addition of sugar or glucose to fresh grapes, grape juice, or grape must prior to or during fermentation. The purpose is to boost the level of alcohol and to give the wine more body. Wines that are chaptalized generally have more richness when young but often display artificial candied flavours once the wine has aged for a few years.

• **CHÂTEAU DES CHARMES** (1025 York Road, P.O. Box 280, St. David's, Niagara-on-the-Lake, ON, L0S 1P0 / Phone: 905-262-4219 / Toll-Free: 1-800-263-2541 / Fax: 905-262-5548 / Email: info@chateau descharmes.com / Website: www.chateaudescharmes.com)

(Est. 1978) Fifth-generation wine grower Paul Michel Bosc and his wife, Andrée, came to Canada from Algeria in 1963. Bosc worked as winemaker for the now-defunct Château Gai winery for 15 years before starting his own winery in partnership with St. Catharines lawyer Roger

Gordon. Bosc, always a trailblazer, was the first Ontario winemaker to plant an all-vinifera vineyard and, over the years, has pioneered the introduction of numerous varieties, including Aligoté, Auxerrois, Savagnin, and Viognier. He was also the first to produce Gamay Nouveau (in the style of Beaujolais Nouveau), the first to work with the Orthodox Jewish community to make kosher wines, the first to experiment with reverse osmosis, and the first to plant transgenic vines in a multiyear agricultural study with Guelph University and the National Research Council. In 1988, Paul Bosc Sr. was named Ontario's Grape King. Today, Château des Charmes is one of the larger estate wineries in the Niagara Peninsula, with 4 vineyards totalling 279 acres. Emphasis is placed on producing unique single-vineyard bottlings. The 85-acre St. David's Bench Vineyard (the entire property is 93 acres) surrounds the impressive châteaulike winery, completed in 1994 at a cost of $6.5 million. (Locals call it Bosca Loma after Toronto's Casa Loma.) Here, Cashel silty clay loam and Toledo silty clay gradually rise about 50 m to meet the St. David's section of the Niagara Bench. The land, purchased in 1987, was completely underdrained with 2.5 m spacing and planted in 1990 with Cabernet Franc, Chardonnay, Gewürztraminer, Merlot, Sauvignon Blanc, as well as Ontario's first Viognier, and Savagnin. Also planted here is an upright version of Gamay called Gamay "Droit" that Paul Bosc Sr. personally bred. It is unusual in that the vine grows straight up without the need for support wires. The Paul Bosc Estate Vineyard, located directly across the road from the winery, surrounds the family home. There are 60 acres planted on Beverly silty clay. Purchased in 1982, the vineyard was planted in the 2 following years with Cabernet Franc, Cabernet Sauvignon, Chardonnay, Gamay, Merlot, Pinot Noir, and Riesling. About 3 km north of the St. David's Bench and Paul Bosc Estate vineyards, south of the town of Virgil, lies the 60-acre Creek Road Vineyard. It has lighter soil of Vineland fine sandy loam and significantly older vines. This vineyard, developed in 1978 and 1979, was the first vineyard in Canada dedicated exclusively to vinifera grapes. It is planted with Aligoté, Auxerrois, Cabernet Sauvignon, Chardonnay, Gamay Noir, Pinot Noir, Riesling, and Sauvignon Blanc. There have been periodic replantings over the years. The Bosc family also owns the 100-acre Lepp Farm at Line 7 and Concession 7 in Niagara-on-the-Lake. This farm was planted in the early 1980s with Seyval Blanc, Vidal Blanc, and a few rows of Gamay. This vineyard is very productive, and is extensively planted with Chardonnay, Cabernet Franc, Vidal, and several experiment varieties. In 1999, Château des Charmes invested $750,000 to install 25 state-of-the-art wind machines in its vineyards to counter the devastating effects of severe cold weather. The investment paid off handsomely in years like 2003, when many other growers suffered dramatically reduced crops following spring frosts. The estate is currently run by sons Paul-André and Pierre-Jean (most people know him as Stéphane), although Paul Sr. remains active in the business. Annual production averages 90,000 cases, all of which is designated VQA.

Winemakers: Pierre-Jean Bosc (1993-present); Paul M. Bosc Sr. (1978-present, 1997 Winemaker of the Year) / Vineyard Manager: Paul M. Bosc Sr.

Château des Charmes labels are colour-coded as follows:
Silver Label – VQA (as of 2002), entry-level, vintage-dated, non-oaked wines from purchased grapes. Prior to 2002, these were nonVQA.
White Label – VQA, non-estate wines, including those estate lots that may be declassified and/or blended with purchased grapes. All production from the Nokara Estate was included here until 2002.
Black Label – VQA, 100% estate-bottled wines from owned vineyards.
Burgundy Label – VQA, 100% from the Paul Bosc Estate Vineyard.
Blue Label – VQA, 100% from the St. David's Bench Vineyard.

Aligoté, Estate-Bottled [NP] **2003**★★★↻ Silvery-gold colour with a ripe Granny Smith apple aroma and a clean, lemony taste. Rather fullish body. Makes a superb aperitif.

Auxerrois, Estate-Bottled [NP] Consumer acceptance of this hard-to-pronounce variety has been sluggish so this wine will soon be phased out. **2002**★★↻ Softer than the Aligoté with grape-fruity, lemon-lime hints. Makes a nice aperitif.

Brut Sparkling, Methode Traditionelle [NP] **NV**★★★★↻ *Gold, Ontario Wine Awards, 1999.* Latest bottles were elegant, complex, and a touch yeasty with biscuit, apple, lime, herb, and mint nuances with lovely sautéed pear and nut flavours . . . as good as some champagnes. But other bottles have been inferior. Inconsistent between batches means you should taste before buying in volume.

Cabernet [NP] **1996**★★→ (CF35/CS50/M15) Wines from the single vineyards and reserve lines were declassified, blended, and bottled under this label because of the lack of ripeness of the vintage. Clean black raspberry and black-currant flavours with nuances of crushed black pepper, tea, and green olive. Exceptionally good value. Drink now-2006. **1988**↓ Once very fine with a light berry nature, now tired and disappointing.

Cabernet, Paul Bosc Estate Vineyard [NP] A traditional Bordeaux blend of Cabernet Sauvignon, Cabernet Franc, and Merlot in varying proportions from year to year. **1996** Not produced. Declassified and blended into the White Label. **1995**★★★→ Rich and wonderful with black cherry, cassis, and chocolate flavours. 400 cases produced. Drink now-2010. **1994**★★★→ Very ripe fruit, lean, clean, tons of tannin combined with good extract. Developing well. Drink now-2008. **1991**★★★→ One of the great years of the past decade. Now fully mature. **1990**★★→ Ripe, balanced, and implicitly sweet, but lacking depth. Drink soon. **1988**★★↘ An excellent effort in a lousy year for Cabernets. Sweet, spicy flavours, fruit drying up a bit, pronounced acidity and long finish. Drink up.

Cabernet Franc, Estate-Bottled [NP]   **1999**★★★★↗ Deep garnet to the rim. Very clean, varietally pure aroma with interesting but as yet undeveloped fresh brambleberry nuances. There is a narrow range of flavours, but Bosc hits them very precisely. Drink now-2011.

Cabernet Franc, Paul Bosc Estate Vineyard [NP]   **1996** Not produced. **1995**★★★➔ *Gold, VinExpo.* 389 cases. Drink now-2010. **1991**★★★➔ *First Canadian red wine to win Gold at VinExpo.* Concentrated, ripe, intensely flavoured, and long-lived. Fully mature.

Cabernet Franc, St. Davids Bench Vineyard [NP]   **2001**☒ Opaque garnet shade with strong blackberry and raspberry notes at first. Asian lady beetle taint quickly appears and, unfortunately, stays, bringing on nuances of dill, pickles, and peanut shells. Very bitter finish. **1999** Tired, dull, musty. Tasted only once. May have been a badly stored bottle. **1998**★★★★↗ Deep garnet with an orange-brown rim. Bouquet of strawberries and gunpowder, i.e., a combination of charcoal, sulphur, and ashes. Solid taste and texture is still developing complexity. Drink now-2010. **1996** Not produced. **1995**★★★➔ Upfront fruity currant nose opens to a hint of veggies, especially green bean, dill, and tobacco. Soft, silky texture, deeply flavoured with good acidity. Dry, gritty tannins with a long, clean aftertaste. 930 cases made. Drink now-2010.

Cabernet-Merlot [NP]   **2002**★★★☆↗   (CF45/CS39/M16) Maroon-garnet hue with an undeveloped nose currently exhibiting wood, earth, some black-fruit aromas. Dry and well balanced with soft tannins and ripe black-currant fruit flavours. Drink now-2011.

Cabernet-Merlot, Estate-Bottled [NP]   **2001**★★↗ Deep garnet. Clean, fresh fruity and herbal flavours compete with Asian lady beetle odours. The wine puts up a good fight with tart apple flavours and apple-skin tannins. Drink soon. **1999**★★★★↗ Blackstrap-garnet colour with a subdued nose of black fruits and yeast. Concentrated strawberry, raspberry, and plum flavours with a lean, tannic finish. Drink now-2011.

Cabernet Sauvignon, Paul Bosc Estate Vineyard [NP] **2001**★★★↗ Opaque garnet. Dense closed black-fruit nose. After several hours, Asian lady beetle taint appears in the background. Strong flavours of black cherry and plum hide it for the most part, but there's a somewhat bitter finish. Drink now-2011. **1997**★★★★➔ Very tasty with complex nuances of smoke, tar, leather, cedar, tobacco. Drink now-2011. **1996** Not produced. **1995**★★★↗ *Gold, VinExpo.* 389 cases. Drink now-2011. **1991**★★★➔ *Jury Prize, Sélection Mondial.*

Cabernet Sauvignon, St. Davids Bench Vineyard [NP] **1999**★★★↗ Deep garnet with sturdy black cherry, plum, rose petal, black tea, smoke nose with solid oak toughness. Has the fruit to age well. Drink now-2014.

Chardonnay, Estate-Bottled [NP] 1996★★↘ Forward and elegant. Buttered toast with lemon marmalade. Drink up. 1994★↘ *Best General List White, Cuvée 1996.* Pleasant asparagus and green bean flavours. Fullish body with good acid balance. Drink up. 1992↓ Deep yellow-gold, with lactic/cheesy flavours, acid finish. Now over the hill. 1990★★★↘ A bold wine with rich buttery flavours livened up by lemony tartness and held together by a thin spine of oak. Drink soon.

Chardonnay Musqué [NP] 2002★★★↻ Solid gold with green reflections. Fullish pear and melon nose with hints of lime and wildflower honey. Big, gulpable palate with a slightly exotic twist. 486 cases made. Drink now.

Chardonnay, Paul Bosc Estate Vineyard [NP] 2001★★★↗ Gold and mildly spirity on the nose with floral notes and hints of apple butter. Soft, light, balanced, pleasant, and straightforward. For early drinking, now-2007. 2000★★★★☆↗ Old gold hue with a deep, concentrated, pungent though undeveloped bouquet, currently showing orange-citrus aromas. A honking-big wine with fabulous concentration and terrific balance of oak, fruit, alcohol, and acid. Drink now-2012. 1999★★★★↗ Old-gold colour with a lusty aromas of bacon fat, stewed white fruits, and sweat. Big, gutsy flavours to match with terrific complexity. Even at this age it still has youth and vitality. Drink now-2010. 1997★★★★→ Old-gold shade with a rich, nutty butter nose. Luscious and complex with a sweet flavour somewhat reminiscent of Italian smoked meats. Almost fully mature. Drink now-2009. 1995★★★★★→ Gold colour with an exotic bouquet of English wine gums in lemon lime and orange flavours. Flirts deliciously with the palate just as it does with the nose. Light yet powerful, delicate yet concentrated, and totally fascinating. 1,500 cases made. At its peak now but will hold at least till 2007. 1994★★★★→ *Best White, Cuvée 1996; Gold, Cellars of the World 1996.* Rich gold colour with smoky notes and whiffs of whole milk and wine gums. Rich, supple, implicitly sweet and very long in the finish. Lovely. Drink now-2006.

Chardonnay, St. Davids Bench Vineyard [NP] 2001★★★↗ Bright gold with an oaky nose of fresh-sawn planks, sweet vanilla, smoke, and herbs. Powerful oak flavours are balanced by full fruit, thick texture, and lingering aftertaste. Drink now-2008 but likely better sooner than later. 2000★★★★↗ Rich gold with amber reflections. Big, dense pungent nose with aromas of lemon butter, sautéed bread, and orange chutney. Concentrated flavours of oak, nuts, lemon, and custard. High but balanced acidity promises long life. Drink now-2010. 1995★★★★→ *Gold, International Wines & Spirits.* Nose slow to open but incredible depth and richness on the palate. Toasted nuts, baked pear, cream, and ripe apple pastry. 930 cases. Fully mature.

Chardonnay, Sur Lie/Non-Oaked [NP] **2001** ★ ★ ⟳ Lighter in flavour but fuller in texture than Chablis. Some lemony mineral hints. Drink.

Equuleus [NP] **2002** ★ ★ ★ ★ ↑ (CF25/CS50/M25) Even better than the 1998. Very deep garnet with a milk-chocolate nose spiked with raspberry and cassis aromas. Silky texture and lean fruity flavours that will need several more years to show their potential. Nicely balanced. Drink 2008-2016. **2001** ★ ★ ★ → (CF24/CS50/M26) Very deep garnet with a bouquet of cassis, red bell pepper, and a very subtle hint of Asian lady beetle. Lovely velvety texture is thicker than 2002 but has a hint of unexpected bitterness in the finish. Drink now-2012. **2000** Not produced. **1999** Not produced. **1998** ★ ★ ★ ★ ↗ (CF32/CS53/M15) Deep garnet with the beginnings of a brickiness to the rim. Well-developed nose of plum, rose, tobacco, earth, and boiled cabbage. Fruit is beginning to dry up as a thick tannic finish sets in. Drink now-2010.

Gamay Noir [NP] **2003** ★ ★ ★ ⟳ Fruity, youthful, energetic, and charming. Tastes like a bowl of cherries or a young Côtes du Rhône. Drink now while fresh and lively.

Gamay Noir "Droit," St. Davids Bench Vineyard [NP] A clone unique to this winery. **2002** ★ ★ ★ ★ → Ruby coloured with a fuller, ripe cherry aroma. Bright, lively palate, implicitly sweet and soft. Has good body and a lovely supple finish. Drink now-2007.

Gamay Nouveau [NP] ★ ★ ★ ⟳ Bosc's annual Beaujolais Nouveau–style wine, released each year on the third Thursday of November. The best in the country rivalling, and often surpassing, the French original. Drink from mid-November through Christmas in the year of release.

Gewürztraminer, St. Davids Bench Vineyard [NP] **2003** ★ ★ ★ ★ ↗ Very pale gold with a Germanic nose showing frosty notes of orange, peach, honeysuckle, and jasmine. Crisp yet fullish on the palate with an almost oily texture and lovely lanolin finish. Drink now-2013. **2002** ★ ★ ★ → Pale, silvery-gold with a classic honeyed, lemon bouquet. Tart, fresh, and frosty-tasting with nuances of lanolin and wildflowers. Drink now-2007.

Merlot, St. Davids Bench Vineyard [NP] **2000** ★ ★ ★ ↗ Deep mahogany-garnet with a bouquet that starts with vegetal notes but opens to aromas of raspberry concentrate, mocha chocolate, herbs, cedar bark, and fruitcake. Thick velvety texture and soft tannins. Very long. Drink now-2012. **1999** ★ ★ ★ ★ ↗ Very dark garnet, with hints of brick around the rim. Spirity and closed, very concentrated, with ripe berry fruit. Beginning to show signs of licorice, plum. Strong and lush. Drink now-2013.

Pinot Noir [NP] **2002** ★ ★ ★ → Nose is undeveloped at this point but promises plenty. Clean and fresh with good balance of acids and tannins and slowly emerging cherry and sandalwood notes. Drink now-2008. **2001** ★ ★ ↗ Pale black-cherry hue. Complex nose of sandalwood, earth, spice, and truffle. Clean, well balanced. Can be aged another 2 to 4 years but already drinking nicely. **2000**★★★➔ Ruby-tawny colour with a mahogany rim. Mildly candied nose at first with cherry notes and an oncoming maturity reflected in flavours of boiled cabbage, sweet stewed fruit, strawberry jam, and a hint of ginseng in the finish. Drink now-2008. **1996**★★➔ Included declassified estate vineyard grapes. At its peak now, drink up. **1995**★★★↘ Bottle variation. Some are terrific, others fading and tired. Drink up. **1994**★★↘ Dried-up fruit with hard, unpleasant tannins. **1991**★★★↘ Mahogany colour with a stewed radicchio and mushroom nose. A hint of sweet fruit left, but on its last legs. **1989**↓ Dried up. **1988**↓ Earthy, stewed fruit flavours with a tart finish.

Pinot Noir, Estate-Bottled [NP] **2001**★★➔ Despite a touch of Asian lady beetle, this wine has sufficient body and fruit to overcome the slight bitterness of the bug. **2000**★★★➔ Ruby-garnet with an orange tinge on the rim. Sweet, spicy cherry notes with a distinct Burgundian cabbagy twang. Ready to drink, now-2007. **1995**★★➔ Good level of complexity with characteristic Burgundian cherry hints. Aging well but drink soon. **1991**★★★★➔ Deep ruby with an orange-brown rim. Bouquet of dark, smoked cherries. Beefy and quite tannic but a nice piece of red meat will take care of any bitterness and let the fruit shine. Fully mature and damn good. Drink before 2006. **1988**★★↘ Bottle variation recently. Some have a charming stewed strawberry-cherry nose and good fruit followthrough while others are just earthy. Drink up.

Pinot Noir, Paul Bosc Estate Vineyard [NP] **1996** Not produced. **1995**★★★➔ Classic Burgundian cherry flavours. 500 cases. Drink now-2007.

Riesling, Estate-Bottled [NP] **2003**★★★↗ Brilliant gold hue with fresh notes of orange and tart lemon. Crisp, clean, and with a nice balance of racy acidity and fruit sugars. Drink now or leave up to 2010 to develop complexity. **2002**★★★↗ Austere nose but quality comes through. Lean, green, tough, and manly. Best after 2006. **1996**★★➔ Citrus and a hint of petrol. Drink up.

Riesling Icewine, Paul Bosc Estate Vineyard [NP] **2000**★★★★★↗ Gold, Ontario Wine Awards, 2004; Gold, Toronto Wine & Cheese Show, 2004. This is as good as it gets. Seductive botrytis nose with hints of petrol and minerals reminiscent of a classic Beeren-Auslese Eiswein from the high Mosel. Tremendous depth of flavours and perfect balance of sweetness and acidity. Clean, lively, intense, juicy, and superb. Drink now-2025. **1997**★★★★★↗ Gold, Ontario Wine Awards, 1999. Amazing concentration and depth. Drink now-2017. **1996**★★★★☆➔ Lovely. Concentrated peach and apricot nectar. 957 cases. Drink now-2012. **1994**★★★★☆➔ Gold, Séléctions Mondiales. Intense, balanced, complex. Drink now-2015. **1992**★★★★➔ Pineapple-y and perfect. My palate experiences a gustatory orgasm just thinking about it. Fully mature. Drink now-2010.

Riesling, Late Harvest, Estate-Bottled [NP] **1996** ★ ★ ★ → Golden, luscious, and balanced. A junior icewine. Drink now-2008. **1995** ★ ★ ★ ★ → *Gold, Ontario Wine Awards, 1997.*

Riesling, Totally Botrytis Affected, Paul Bosc Estate Vineyard [NP] **2001** ★ ★ ★ ★ ★ ↗ *Gold, Ontario Wine Awards, 2004.* Tasted only once at a trade table. Rich coppery colour, refined, sweet, light, and beguiling.

Rosé, Cuvée d'Andrée [NP] **2003** ★ ★ ★ ↻ *Gold, Ontario Wine Awards 2004.* Hot-pink colour with vibrant berry aroma. Residual sugar is perfectly balanced with fruity acidity. Mild strawberry and watermelon flavours and a lively finish.

Rosé, Vin de Nuit [NP] **1995** ★ ★ ★ ↻ An all-vinifera blend (CF/CS/G/PN/M) that receives one night of skin contact, ergo the name. Tavel-like but on its last legs now.

Sauvignon Blanc, St. Davids Bench Vineyard [NP] **2003** ★ ★ ★ ↗ Drink now-2008, but might surprise if aged up to a decade. **1995** ★ ★ ↘ Softer than the previous vintage, lacking acidity with light, cooked herbal flavours. Tiring. **1994** ★ ★ ★ → A clean and well-balanced wine with pleasant green herbal nuances. Drink now.

Savagnin [VQA] This rare French variety from the Jura has been discontinued. Many consumers misread the label, assumed it was a Sauvignon Blanc, and ended up not getting what they expected. It's tough being a pioneer. **2000** ★ ★ ★ → Richly textured with spicy, musky flavours. Drink now.

Sec Sparkling, Methode Traditionelle [NP] **NV** ★ ★ ★ ↻ *Gold, Ontario Wine Awards, 1997.* Floral aroma of apple blossoms with a squirt of lime.

Vidal Icewine [NP] **2001** ★ ★ ★ ★ → Pale amber-gold. Baked pear nose and flavours. Palate is like honey with a squirt of lemon. Drink now-2010. **1994** ★ ★ ★ → *Gold, Cellars of the World, 1996.* Softer, lighter, and more forward than the Riesling. Flavours are more honeyed, suggesting dried peaches or apricots.

Viognier, St. Davids Bench Vineyard [NP] **2003** ★ ★ ★ ↻ Pale straw-gold with an exotic honeysuckle, mandarin, wine-gum bouquet. Soft and flavourful; delicate and gulpable. Yum. **2002** ★ ★ ★ ↻ Light but with characteristic floral, peachy, wine-gum flavours.

• **CHERRY HILL VINEYARD** (Vineland, NP) – Wendy and Jim Theissen grow 6 acres of Chardonnay Musqué, much of which is sold to Lakeview Cellars.

• **CHERRYVAIL** (Vineland, NP) – This 5-acre vineyard owned by Vineland Quarries and situated immediately south of Ridgepoint Wines is leased to Roger Vail's company, Vailmont Vineyards. The north-facing

Oneida clay loam hillside, which has a variable 6%-15% slope, is fully underdrained. The only variety grown here, Baco Noir, planted in 1996, is harvested at 6.5 t. to the acre and sold to Henry of Pelham, Kittling Ridge, and Lakeview Cellars.

• **CHIARAMONTE VINEYARD (Niagara-on-the-Lake, NP)** — Ross Chiaramonte's 14-acre vineyard is on the East-West Line between Concession 6 and Town Line Road, more or less across the road from the junkyard. The flat vineyard is composed mainly of heavy Chinguacousy clay loam, but there are plenty of large rocks scattered irregularly throughout some sections of the vineyard. The benefit of having the rocks present is the additional heat generated back into the vineyard throughout summer nights, but the downside is the extreme difficulty of working the land with heavy machinery. Consequently, much of the harvest is gathered by hand. There's Cabernet Franc, Chardonnay Musqué, Merlot, and Sauvignon Blanc. Fruit is sold exclusively to Pillitteri Estates.

• **CHUDZIK VINEYARD (Jordan, NP)** — Owned by the Le Clos Jordanne winery, this property is situated above the escarpment on 17th Street at 7th Avenue. To date, 53 acres of Pinot Noir, 10.5 acres of Chardonnay, .5 acre of Pinot Gris, and 5 acres of Riesling (for icewine production) were planted at a very high density of 2,248 plants per acre in 2002. Drainage was installed between every row and cover crops are grown alternate years between every second row to improve the soil structure and to increase competition for water. Over-the-row tractors are used to lessen soil compaction. Yields are exceptionally low for now but will increase to a maximum of 2 t. per acre at maturity. All vineyard treatments are organic, and the plan is to certify the vineyard as such and then to introduce bio-dynamic farming practices within a few years.

• **CILENTO WINES** (672 Chrislea Road, Vaughan, ON, L4L 8K9 / Phone: 905-264-9463 / Toll-Free: 1-888-245-9463 / Fax: 905-264-8671 / Email: cilento@ica.net / Website: www.cilento.com)

(Est. 1995) If you are Italian, you make wine. Well, that's the way it used to be when Angelo and Grace Locilento started their juice business, Vin Bon Juice Co. They provided fermentable grape juice to home winemakers for many years. By 1995, though, they noticed that younger generations were more career-oriented with less free time to make their own wine. The emerging trend was to buy "ready-made" wine of good quality, so they decided it was time to start a winery. Since opening, the Locilentos have become recognized producers of VQA wines. They have found the Ontario market very competitive, despite the numerous awards they've picked up in domestic and international competitions.

They purchase grapes from trusted Niagara growers with whom they have had long relationships. Average annual production is 25,000 to 30,000 cases, most of which is sold through LCBO stores or at the retail shop at the suburban Toronto winery. A growing amount is being exported.

Winemakers:TBA (2004-present);Terence J. van Rooyen (1999-2004); Ann Sperling (1995-1999, 1998/1999, consulting)

Auxerrois [NP] **1997**★★☆↘ Interesting apple nose and pear palate. Past its peak.

Baco Noir-Foch, "Renaissance Classic Red" [Ont] **2002**★→ Cherry-garnet hue. Slightly sweet with a candied overtone. Drink up.

Cabernet Franc Reserve [NP] **2002**★★★☆→ Garnet with a blackberry nose, smooth, silky, supple texture and oaky, smoky taste. Drink now-2008. **1999**★★★→ Garnet with a mahogany rim and a soft, warm creamy, smoky nose. Ripe and fully mature.

Cabernet-Merlot [NP] **2001**☒ Hints of Asian lady beetle. **2000**☒ Dark garnet-ochre with a cooked nose and flavours of boiled cabbage and stewed fruits. Flawed and disappointing.

Cabernet Sauvignon [NP] **2001**★★★↗ Deep garnet colour with a cooked fruit nose. Drink now-2009.

Cabernet Sauvignon Icewine [NP] **2002**★★★→ Funky nose combines cooked fruit and weeds. Washed-out flavours with a short finish. Drink soon.

Cabernet Sauvignon Reserve [NP] **1999**★★★★↗ *Gold, All Canadian Wine Championships 2004.* Slightly vegetal and pruney to start, developing big cherry-berry, red currant, and cassis flavours with hints of chocolate, leather, and smoked nuts. With extended airing, notes of soy and mushrooms appear. Drink now-2009. **1997**★★★★→ *Gold, Ontario Wine Awards 1999.* Wonderful scent of black fruits. Ready to drink now.

Chardonnay, No Oak [NP] **2002**★★↻ Earthy, fullish, and best drunk young. Has pear and apple flavours and real Frenchness about it. **1997**★★☆↘ A simple wine now past its peak.

Chardonnay, Reserve [NP] **2003**★★★★↗ Gold with a light, sweet, ripe nose of lemon and vanilla. Delicate oaky structure, soft satiny texture, lovely fruit, and refreshing acidity. Really good. Drink now-2009. **2002**★★★★↑ Vibrant gold hue with concentrated aroma of oak, buttered toast, and warmed pear. Supple, vivacious palate with wonderful acid/fruit balance and a fine lingering after-taste. Drink 2006-2010. **2000**★★★★→ *Gold, Ontario Wine Awards 2002.* Brilliant gold hue with smoky aromas of toasted pinenuts and melted gruyère. Lovely texture and taste with flavours of coffee beans, hazelnut torte. Heavily oaked. Drink now-2008. **1999**★★★★→ Rich amber gold with a late-harvest smell hinting of sundried apricots and linden honey. Bigger, sweeter, and fuller than the 2000. A powerhouse. Drink now-2009.

Merlot, Cuvée du Domaine [NP] **2002**★★★➔ Light garnet with a sweet berry fruit nose. Clean, light, pleasant, and quaffable. Drink now-2007. **2001**★★➔ Garnet with a green herbal nose. A strange mix of sweet and green. Unexciting.

Merlot, Reserve [NP] **2002**★★★☆↑ Deep garnet with a nose of black cherries and charred oak. Deep black fruit flavours. Drink 2006-2009. **1999**★★★↑ Gold, Toronto Wine & Cheese Show 2004. Dark garnet with a closed nose. Hint of young black plums beginning to emerge on the palate. Full, rich, soft texture. Drink 2006-2012.

Pinot Noir-Gamay, Cuvée du Domaine [Ont] **2002**★★★↻ Ruby hue with a clean and fruity aroma. Simple, but has balance and good body.

Pinot Noir, Reserve [NP] **2001** The winery dumped its entire production of this wine because it had the dreaded Asian lady beetle taint. **2000**★★★★➔ Best Red Wine of the Year, All Canadian Wine Championships 2004. Forward-tasting with advanced development. Very ripe with flavours of cherry and sandalwood, strawberry jam and vanilla. Deeply oaked with potential to drink now-2007.

Riesling Brut [NP] **2000**★★★↻ Straw-gold with greenish reflections and big fat bubbles at first. Mousse continues to rise gently after 30 minutes. Clean and lemony with a fresh scent.

Riesling, Icewine [NP] **1999**★★★★↗ Gold, Concours Mondial, Brussels 2003; Gold, All Canadian Wine Championships 2003. Softening up but still shows some herbal nuances. Loads of complexity. Drink now-2010.

Riesling, Late Harvest [NP] **1997**★★★➔ Sold in 500 ml bottles. From botrytised, partially frozen grapes. More fruity than aromatic, a classic style for longer aging, though it drinks well now. Drink now-2010.

Riesling/Merlot, "Renaissance Classic Rosé" [NP] **2002** ★↻ A very strange combination. Not bad, but not to my taste.

Riesling Reserve [NP] **2003**★★★↗ Pale straw-gold with a grape-fruity aroma and a crisp, zesty finish. Perfect for casual sipping or a light fish dish. Drink now-2012. **2000**★★★➔ A slightly more substantial version, with candy-apple and pink grapefruit flavours and a hint of honey in the aftertaste. Drink now-2010.

Sauvignon Blanc Reserve, Cuvée du Domaine [NP] **2001**★★★➔ Gold, All Canadian Wine Championships 2002. Grassy nose with asparagus overtones. Granny Smith apple flavour with a mildly bitter finish.

Shiraz [NP] **2002**★★★➔ Garnet colour with mahogany reflections. Gamy nose of prune and smoked sausage, while the taste hints of chocolate yogourt. Drink now-2008.

Vidal, Off-Dry "Renaissance Classic White" [Ont] **2003**★★☆↻ Silvery-gold with a clean fruity nose and taste. Barely off-dry, closer to dry. **2002**★★↻ The hint of sulphur blows off, rapidly leaving mild bubblegum flavours. Good acidity.

Vidal, Select Late Harvest [Ont] 1997★★★→ Quite sweet
with apple, pear, and honey flavours. Fully mature. Drink soon.

Vidal, Special Select Late Harvest [NP] 1999★★★☆→
Amber with a rich caramelized apple and pear bouquet. Thick and
lush for drinking now-2007.

• **CLOSSON CHASE VINEYARDS INC.** (629 Closson Road,
Hillier, ON, K0K 2J0 / Phone: 613-399-1418 / Fax: 613-399-1618 /
Email: clossonchasevineyards@bellnet.ca / Website: in development)

(Est. 2004) Ownership includes filmmaker Seaton McLean and his wife,
actress Sonja Smits, lawyer Bill Fanjoy, documentary-maker Andy
Thompson, the chairman and CEO of Alliance Atlantis (which, among
others, owns Canada's FoodTV network) Michael MacMillan, and
Toronto-based financial adviser Gene McBurney. The property, a few
kilometres east of The Grange of Prince Edward, comprises 40 acres,
of which only 14 have been planted to date. There are 10 acres of
Chardonnay (first planted in 1998) and 4 of Pinot Noir (also from
1998), spaced at a high density of 1,864 vines per acre on a gentle,
south-facing slope. The soil here is composed of friable Hillier clay loam
over a bedrock of fractured limestone. There is no underdrainage
installed as natural drainage is considered sufficient. Supplemental
grapes have been purchased from the Niagara Peninsula, particularly
from Steve Kocsis's Mountain Road Vineyard and from Laundry-Mottiar
in Beamsville. An old barn was renovated, painted a gaudy purple, and
outfitted with 18,000 L worth of fermentation tanks and plenty of
French oak barrels. There is a tasting room but, pre-publication, there
was no wine available for tasting. The winery's goal is to produce 5,000
cases annually by 2010.

Winemaker: Deborah Paskus / Vineyard Manager: Deborah Paskus

Wines not available for appraisal before press time.

• **COLCHESTER FARMS LIMITED** (Colchester, LENS) – This proprietary vineyard of Colio Estate Winery slopes gently southward from
County Road 50 toward Lake Erie less than a kilometre away. Colio
purchased an 80-acre mature vineyard from Ron Moyer, its largest
grower in the mid-1980s. It then added a 60-acre property one section
over in 1999 and a 50-acre farm joining the properties in 2004. The
enlarged site now covers almost 200 acres. Currently, 160 acres are
being cultivated, although another 20 acres are to be planted in 2006.
The soil is Harrow sandy loam on a solid limestone base and the vineyard is tiled between every second row for better drainage. Although
there is no drip or overhead irrigation, young vines are hand-watered
during drought periods. Older plantings include Cabernet Franc, Merlot,

Riesling, and Vidal Blanc. Younger sections are dedicated to growing Chardonnay and Gamay Noir. The most recent additions, some which are just beginning to yield fruit and some which will come on stream in the next year or two, include more acreage of Cabernet Franc and Chardonnay, some Cabernet Sauvignon, Merlot, Pinot Gris, Sauvignon Blanc, Syrah, and Villard Noir. Older plantings are spaced at 1,210 vines per acre; newer ones at 1,140. Certain blocks, such as those varieties targeted for use in Colio's "Signature" series, are thinned to 2 t. per acre. Other viniferas bear up to 4 t. per acre, while hybrid varieties easily carry up to 6 t. per acre.

• **COLDWATER WINE COMPANY** (10 Trumpour Road, Hillier, ON, K0K 2T0 / Phone: Jonas, 416-524-3588, Vicki, 416-465-4633 / Email: coldwater@magma.ca / Website: in development)

(Est. 2004) Young Jonas Newman, a sommelier at Toronto's posh Scaramouche restaurant, and his partner, Vicki Samaras, whose back-ground is in botany, plant pathology, and environmental sciences, planned and saved for some time before jumping headlong into the winemaking cauldron. They bought a 100-acre piece of land close to Closson Chase, The Grange, and Little Creek Vineyard, where the shallow Hillier clay loam slopes southward in some sections, and southeastward in others, providing excellent exposure to the sun. To date, with advice from Niagara Peninsula winemaker Daniel Lenko, they've planted 1 acre of Pinot Noir in 2004 and added another 4 acres in 2005. They also put in 3 acres of Gewürztraminer and 2 acres of Chardonnay, all at a relatively high vine density of 1,650 plants per acre. This initial 10-acre section will provide them with their first harvest in 2008. Their objective is to produce 5,000 to 7,000 cases of wine by 2010.

Winemakers: Jonas Newman and Vicki Samaras / Vineyard Managers: Jonas Newman and Vicki Samaras

Wines not available for appraisal before press time.

• **COLIO ESTATE WINES** (1 Colio Drive, Harrow, ON, N0R 1G0 / Phone: 519-738-2241 / Toll-Free: 1-800-265-1322 / Fax: 519-738-3070 / Email: cheers@coliowinery.com / Website: www.coliowines. com / *Administrative address:* 2300 Haines Road, Mississauga, ON, L4Y 1Y6 / Phone: 905-896-8512 / Toll-Free: 1-800-263-0802 / Fax: 905-896-8790 / Email: cheers@coliowines.com)

(Est. 1980) The first winery to be established in Essex County after Prohibition and still the largest winery in the Lake Erie North Shore viticultural area, Colio Estate Wines is expected to surpass production volumes of 275,000 cases by 2006. The company is, essentially, a product of failure, in the most fortuitous way. In the late 1970s, members of the Mascarin, Belardo, and DeLuca families travelled to Italy to try to set up a wine importing business. When relaying the facts of the Canadian market and describing the excessive bureaucracy of the LCBO to their Italian hosts and potential suppliers, they became convinced that a better route would be to start their own winery in Canada. After all, they already had optimal conditions of soil and climate, considering a thriving industry had existed in Essex County prior to Prohibition. Upon their return, they set up strategic alliances with local grape growers, convinced master winemaker Carlo Negri of the Collavini winery in Italy to emigrate to Canada with his family, and built a huge, state-of-the-art winemaking facility in Harrow, one of the province's southernmost villages. Today, with 14 winery-owned stores and a respectable number of listings in LCBO outlets, the winery is focusing on growing its business in the premium range. In 1999, it introduced its CEV line of estate-grown varietals. Colio owns 3 contiguous vineyards under the banner of Colchester Farms Ltd., with almost 160 acres under vine. In Harrow, immediately behind the winery, 1 acre of Vidal Blanc is cultivated for use in the production of icewine. These vineyards provide up to 40% of the winery's needs. The remainder is purchased from growers in all 3 designated viticultural regions. This year marks Colio's 25th anniversary.

Winemaker: Carlo Negri (1980-present – 2005 Winemaker of the Year) / Vineyard Manager: Kevin Donohue

Colio's wines are marketed under several labels:

Colio – NonVQA blended wines produced from domestic and/or imported grapes.

Colio Estates – Formerly called Harrow Estates. This line features VQA varietals produced from grapes purchased within the 3 designated viticultural areas. However, because of the short crop in 2003, the line also included premium nonVQA wines blended from imported juice or grapes in that vintage.

Colio Estate Vineyards – Labels carrying the CEV moniker are VQA varietals produced from Colio's own estate vineyards in the heart of the Lake Erie North Shore viticultural area. Super-premium bottlings now carry an additional Carlo Negri Signature designation.

Colio Label

Bianco Secco [nonVQA] **NV★↻** Simple white offering good value.

Chardonnay [nonVQA] **NV★☆↻** Decent single varietal with good acidity and some simple apple nuances.

Extra Dry [nonVQA] **NV★↻** Simple and straightforward white.

Rosso Secco [nonVQA] **NV★↻** Banquet quality. Fine with most food.

Viva Spumante [nonVQA] **NV★★↻** From domestic and international grapes. Grassy, floral, crisp nose with a semi-dry, tutti-frutti taste.

Colio Estates (formerly Harrow Estates) Label

Cabernet Franc [LENS] **2002★★★→** *Best General List Red Wine, Cuvée 2004.* Pale ruby-cherry with a delightful light nose of fruit, herbs, and spice. Has depth, satiny texture, and balance. Drink now-2007. **1996★★☆↘** *Best General List Red Wine, Cuvée 1998.* Light, clean, and true to the variety. Some spicy nuances. Drink soon. **1994★★★↘** *Gold, World Wine Championships, Chicago, 1996; Best Red, Royal Agricultural Winter Fair, 1996;* and subsequently chosen to be the "Queen's Park House Wine." Early tasted samples were tough, with deep, lean flavours and a short finish. Recently, the wine has softened up, developing creamy, blackberry flavours. Still has palate-cleansing acidity and plenty of oaky-smoky tannin. Drink up. **1993★★★→** Mahogany hue with significant brick and orange along the rim. Aging into flavours of soy, balsamic. Soft and peaking. Drink up.

Cabernet/Merlot [Ont] **2002★★★↗** Ruby-cherry colour with a full aroma of strawberry, cherry, and plum. Silky texture, supple mouthfeel, and a vibrant, tart finish. Drink now-2009.

Gamay Noir [Ont] **2002★★★→** Lovely aroma of strawberry and cherry. Fruity and Beaujolais-like. Good acidity and great structure. Drink now.

Marechal Foch [LENS] **1994↓** Black cherry; some hybrid odours, candied red-berry fruit, grapey with no subtlety; firm, tart, and a bit too dry on the palate; short sour finish.

Marechal Foch [nonVQA] **NV★★↻** Cherry hue with purple-pink edges. Light berry nose has a rustic nature to it. No depth but a fun wine nevertheless.

Merlot [LENS] **1994★★↘** Mid-weight, lean black fruit flavours, balanced. Beginning to tire.

Merlot [nonVQA] **NV★★☆↻** Mid-weight, black fruit flavours, simple but balanced.

Orchard Blush [nonVQA] **NV★★↻** Pink hue with a strawberry-like aroma. Simple, decent, ordinary.

Pinot Blanc [Ont] **2002★★↻** Nondescript nose; citrusy flavour.

Pinot Gris [LENS] **2002★★☆→** Pale gold with an earthy and wild nose. Aroma changes and grows minute to minute with hints of gooseberry and white plum. Long, crisp and clean.

Riesling [LENS] **2002★★★→** Green gold with a bouquet of fruit, wildflowers, and apple cider. Zippy taste with a slightly dusty, gritty finish. Drink now-2007. **1994★↘** Perfumed, soapy nose, creamy palate with soft texture and caramelized fruit flavours. Drink soon. **1990↓** Grapefruit, wildflowers, perfume, and petrol nose; now past its peak. **1988↓** Oxidized.

Riesling-Traminer [LENS]   Not a blend but a vinifera crossing. **2002★★→** Hint of sulphur at first, but blows off to exhibit crisp flavours of citrus, spice, and honey. **1995★★→** Bright and lively clove and orange flavours with the slightest nuance of petrol. **1994★★★↘** *Gold, Vinexpo.* Gewürz-like spicy notes; off-dry with racy acid.

Sauvignon Blanc [LENS]   **2002★★→** Pale gold with a subdued nose, hinting of grass and passionfruit. Tart and refreshing. Drink now.

Vidal, Icewine [LENS]   **2002★★★☆→** Amber hue with a syrupy, caramelized pear aroma. Low acidity and soft, sweet taste for immediate gratification. Drink now-2007. **1992★★★★↘** *Platinum, World Wine Championships.* Pineapple, honey, and apricot flavours; lively acidity balances the high residual sugar.

Vidal, Late Harvest [Ont]   **2002★★★☆→** Deep gold with a nose of pear concentrate. Thicker texture than 2001 with deeper flavours. Drink now-2009. **2001★★★→** Gold hue with aromas of poached pear and lemon, light taste and a clean, dry, pleasantly bitter finish. Balanced. Drink now-2007. **1997★★★→** *Gold, Ontario Wine Awards, 1999.* Lovely drinking right now.

Colio Estate Vineyards (CEV) Label

Cabernet Franc, Barrel-Aged Reserve [LENS]   **2002★★★☆↑** Deep garnet colour and lush, juicy fruit nose, but tough, woody tannin overpowers the fruit. Drink 2007-2013.

Cabernet Franc Icewine [LENS]   **2002★★★★↗** Lovely, pleasant strawberry-jam aroma with flavour of cherry-pie filling. Mouth-cleansing acidity and good structure. Drink now-2012.

Chardonnay, Aged without Oak [LENS]   **2002★★★→** Pale gold with a lovely aroma of baked pear and white peach. Light, doughy flavours with a clean, crisp finish. Short-lived. Drink before end of 2006.

Gamay Noir, Barrel-Aged [Ont]   **2002★★★→** Light ruby colour with a bouquet completely dominated by new oak. Very pleasant though unlike any Gamay I've tasted. It's more like a Rioja Reserva with its characteristic cedar pencil shavings smell and soft, creamy oak taste. Drink now.

Gewürztraminer [LENS]   **2002★★☆→** Rich gold. Aroma has a plastic overtone. Dry with the implicit sweetness of a late-harvest wine. Fullish though a bit hollow mid-palate. Drink now.

Lily (Sparkling) [Ont]   **2002★★☆↻** *Gold, Ontario Wine Awards, 2004.* Delicate pale pink hue with a single bead of very slow, fine bubbles. Elusive hints of candied grapefruit on the nose. Has a kiss of sweetness and a clean, simple, pleasantly astringent aftertaste.

Meritage, Barrel-Aged [LENS]   **2002★★★☆↗** Garnet with a brick-coloured rim. Oaky with some complex aromas beginning to show through. Earth, dried herb, cedar, and violet bouquet with the flavours of a black-fruit cocktail. Soft, sweetish palate is supple and forward. Drink now-2010.

Merlot, Barrel-Aged Reserve [LENS] **2002★★★☆↗** Garnet-black hue with powerful aroma of black fruits, mint, and chocolate. Intense flavour, supple texture, and balanced tannins. Drink now-2010.

Pinot Grigio [LENS] **2002★★★→** Pale gold with a light, vinous aroma. Fuller and softer than the Harrow Estate version with a big heavy mouthfeel.

Carlo Negri Signature Wines:

Cabernet-Merlot, Signature [LENS] **1999★★★☆↗** Garnet with a hint of orange setting in at the rim. Expansive, inviting nose with cherry, charred oak, and coffee notes. Velvety supple texture with plenty of sweet fruit and balanced oak structure. Drink now-2014.

Cabernet Sauvignon, Signature [LENS] **2002★★★★↑** Deep garnet with a solid opaque centre. Powerful black fruit and berry notes, rich, creamy, and slightly nutty and tarry with great depth, subdued complexity, as well as a long and elegant future. Drink 2009-2018.

Meritage, Signature [LENS] **2002★★★★↑** Solid garnet to the rim. Dense smoky, oaky, licorice, blackberry, raspberry aroma with clear hints that much more will soon emerge. Rich, supple, sweet, and wild, with black currant flavours. Drink 2007-2014.

Specialty Wines:

Nobile, VinSanto [LENS] By VQA rules, this is called a *Vin de Curé*. Sadly, it is no longer produced. **NV★★★★→** This dessert wine produced in 1988 combined Riesling with Vidal Blanc grapes. Some were affected by the natural grape mould, *Botrytis cinerea*, while the remainder were air-dried and raisined over a period of months prior to fermentation. Deep golden-brown colour with sweet, rich, raisiny flavours.

• **COUNTY CIDER COMPANY** (657 Bongards Crossroad at County Road 8, R.R.#4, Waupoos, ON, K0K 2T0 / Phone: 613-476-1022 / Toll-Free: 1-866-476-1022 / Fax: 613-476-1022 / Email: county cider@reach.net / Website: www.countycider.com)

(Est. 1996) Someone once said, "When life hands you a lemon, make lemonade." Grant Howes must have been listening. With the price of fresh Ontario apples in a rapid tailspin, he took the family apple orchards and turned them into a successful and growing cidery. To make cider in the province of Ontario, you need a winery licence. So as more and more winelovers began to move into the County to grow grapes, Howes, too, began to consider the idea. On the 70-acre home farm that supports his orchards, he planted 5 acres of vines and called it Shingle Ridge. Just 275 m from the lake, the vineyard moderately slopes southward and consists of Brighton gravel over limestone. Howes has 1.5 acres of Gamay, 2 acres of Geisenheim, and .75 acres each of Pinot Noir and Zweigelt. Yields are reduced at veraison to 2 t. per acre and, although some is used to produce his own wines, much of the harvest is sold to a variety of local wineries. Howes has started to plant a second vineyard just across the water of the Bay of Quinte in the county of Lennox and Addington. Called the Loyalist Vineyard, it is a 60-acre property on the south side of Highway 33 near Adolphustown. This site is very gently sloped southward toward the shore of Adolphus Reach just 15 m away. It has alluvial glacier deposits over a limestone base and is fully underdrained and irrigated. In 2002, just 10 acres were planted with 2 acres each of Castel, Chardonnay, and Pinot Noir, and 1 acre each of Cabernet Franc, Chambourcin, Pinot Gris, and some miscellaneous rootstock varieties, all spaced at 1,200 vines per acre. This year provided the first crop, which was thinned down to 2 t. per acre. Although most of County Cider Company's volume is regular, hard, and sparkling apple cider, grape wine production reached 1,500 cases this year and is expected to grow to 2,000 cases by the end of 2006.

Winemaker: Jenifer Dean / Cidermaker: Grant Howes / Vineyard Manager: Grant Howes

Cabernet Franc [nonVQA] **2001** ☒ Cloudy, with sediment. A sick bottle.

Geisenheim, Shingle Ridge Vineyard [nonVQA] **2002** ★☆→ Silvery-gold with a bitter, herbal, perfumed nose. Lemon-apple flavours, but bitter finish puts me off.

Pinot Noir, Shingle Ridge Vineyard [nonVQA] **2002** ★★★☆→ Ruby with a cherry cough syrup nose. Bouquet improves dramatically after lengthy aeration. Lovely, supple, silky texture with nuances of ripe strawberry, raspberry compote, sweetened milky coffee, and milk chocolate. Drink now-2008.

<u>Ciders:</u>

County Premium Cider – 1 L plastic bottles, 6.5% alc./vol. **NV** ★★☆↻ Clean, crisp, dry, light-flavoured.

Feral Cider – 1 L plastic bottles, 6.5% alc./vol. **NV** ★★↻ Bright neon orange-pink colour. Candied, red-pop aroma. Riper flavours, but there is an artifice here.

Iced Cider – 375 ml glass bottles, 10.3% alc./vol. **NV** ★★★↻ Amber colour with a smell of old-style cloudy apple cider but with a sweet luscious taste.

Peach Cider – 1 L plastic bottles, 6.5% alc./vol. **NV** ★☆↻ Blended with peach concentrate. Slightly candied and artificial for my palate.

Waupoos Premium Cider – 500 ml glass bottles, listed in LCBO stores. **NV** ★★★↻ Clean, crisp, semi-sweet.

• COYOTE'S RUN ESTATE WINERY (485 Concession 5, near Line 7, St. David's, ON, L0S 1P0 / Phone: 905-682-8310 / Fax: 905-682-1166 / Email: dsheppard@coyotesrunwinery.com / Website: www.coyotesrunwinery.com)

(Est. 2003) Hi-tech wizard Jeff Aubry had a dream of starting a winery and the money to finance it but lacked the know-how. He and his dad, Gerald, enlisted former Inniskillin winemaker David Sheppard to produce vinifera wines from estate-grown grapes as well as those from grower-partner Steven Murdza. The 59-acre estate vineyard (formerly called Crysler Farm) is situated on a predominantly west-facing slope of the St. David's section of the Bench, south of Frogpond Farm, east of Maleta Estate, and north of Château des Charmes. In 1996 and 1998, 19 acres were underdrained and planted with 2.2 acres of Cabernet Franc, 5 acres of Chardonnay, 3 acres of Pinot Noir, and 8 acres of Vidal Blanc, all spaced at 1,400 plants per acre. Last year, the winery added 2 acres each of Merlot, Pinot Gris, Pinot Noir, and Shiraz, as well as 1 acre each of Cabernet Franc and Malbec. In this ancient lakebed location, the soil is composed of heavy limestone clay with some uncharacteristic glacial deposits of granite, quartzite, gneiss, and pyrite. There's a dividing line across the property with mostly dark brown clay on one side and lighter red clay on the other. Areas of the property were once used by the Bernstien Brick Co. to produce building materials. Sheppard is experimenting with a wide variety of barrels, including the usual French and American oak, as well as several Canadian and Hungarian casks. The winery bottled 2,500 cases in their first year of production, but projections are to grow to 15,000 cases by 2010.

Winemaker: David Sheppard / Vineyard Manager: Steve Murdza

Cabernet Franc [NP] **2003** ★ ★ ★ ↑ Still juvenile with primary fruit flavours and baby-fat texture. Big, lively, with a lot of potential for development. Drink 2007-2012.

Chardonnay [NP] **2003** ★ ★ ★ → Silvery gold with a soft, clean aroma of Anjou pears. Uncomplicated and quaffable with ripe flavours. Drink now.

Chardonnay, Reserve [NP] **2003** ★ ★ ★ → Bright pale gold with an oak, vanilla, and crème Anglaise bouquet. Soft, clean, and nicely structured with lasting caramel and Brazil nut flavours. Drink now-2007.

Chardonnay, Old Vines [NP] **2003** ★ ★ ★ ↗ Pale green with gold reflections and a lovely, delicate bouquet. Nuances of cinnamon toast, fresh creamery butter, and solid mineral notes. Drink now-2009.

Pinot Noir [NP] **2003** ★ ★ → Lovely juicy, youthful, fruity aroma and classic flavours of cherry and strawberry. Light and balanced. Drink now-2006.

Pinot Noir, Reserve [NP] **2003** ★ ★ ★ ★ ↑ Big and bold with toasty, oaky, solid structure. Tart and healthy with restrained flavours of sandalwood, spice, rose, hazelnuts, and much more to come. Drink 2006-2012.

Pinot Noir, Rose [NP]   **2003** ★ ★ ★ ↻ Pale salmon colour with a lovely fruit salad nose. Tart, refreshing taste of strawberries, cherries, and crisp apples. Fab with food. Drink now.

Riesling [NP]   **2003** ★ ★ ↗ Silvery-gold. Nose and palate show more muscle than bones. Fullish, brawny palate with stiff, severe flavours. Ripe with a tough finish. May soften. Drink now-2008.

Vidal Icewine, Barrel-Fermented [NP]   **2003** ★ ★ ★ ★ → Thick, oily, yellow-gold with a fresh, frosty smell of baked pear and toasted almonds. Concentrated, intensely rich, and balanced. Drink now-2013.

• **CREEKSIDE ESTATE WINERY** (2170 Fourth Avenue, P.O. Box 55, Jordan Station, ON, L0R 1S0 / Phone: 905-562-0035 / Toll-Free: 1-877-262-9463 / Fax: 905-562-5493 / Email: info@creeksideestate winery.com / Website: www.creeksideestatewinery.com)

(Est. 1998) Laura McCain-Jensen and Peter Jensen, who already owned a small winery in Nova Scotia's Annapolis Valley, added the former V.P. Cellars, a 3,000-case boutique winery, to their holdings. They quickly modernized the production facility, adding a new crush pad, a gentle bladder press, temperature-controlled fermentation tanks, and a modern bottling line, thus increasing capacity to 30,000 cases. The following year they added a 500-barrel underground cellar and an offsite warehouse. The 20-acre vineyard on the east bank of Sixteen Mile Creek was partially replanted to increase the acreage of Cabernet Sauvignon, Sauvignon Blanc, and Shiraz. Here, the soil is primarily Peel lacustrine silty clay over clay loam till. The vineyard is underdrained and planted 1,200 vines per acre. In 1999, the Jensens acquired a second property, a 50-acre block on Queenston Road in the St. David's area, where, from 2000 to 2002, they planted 40 acres of Cabernet Sauvignon, Chardonnay, Merlot, Pinot Noir, Shiraz, and Viognier, also at 1,200 vines per acre. This site has mainly Beverly lacustrine silty clay. It is flat and fully tiled for drainage. Yields on both sites are reduced by thinning as much as half the fruit at veraison to keep crop levels down to 2 t. per acre. These properties provide Creekside with about one-quarter of its fruit requirements. Grapes are purchased from numerous Niagara growers, including Lowrey Vineyard, Hunter Farms, Maroudas Vineyard, Fruithaven Farms, and Chardonnay Lane. Total production in 2004 was 24,000 cases. By the end of this year, the Jensens expect to increase that to 30,000 cases.

Winemakers: Craig McDonald (2002-present); Rob Power (2002-present); Marcus Ansems (1998-2002) / Vineyard Manager: Bryson Waind

Cabernets [NP] 2002★★★☆↗ Garnet with a creamy, mocha-chocolate, raspberry and plum bouquet. Lively flavours with a lingering finish. Drink now-2010.

Cabernet Sauvignon, Signature [NP] 2001★★★↑ Deep garnet with raspberry, oak, and milky notes. Sweet, ripe, soft, and supple at first, then the mouth-drying tannins show up. Drink 2006-2011. **2000★★★↑** Dark garnet with dense oak and full fruit nose. Flavours of plum, blackberry, black olives, cedar, and freshly sawn oak planks. Full-bodied and tannic. Drink 2005-2015.

Chardonnay [NP] 2001★★★→ Rich gold with a nose of buttered nuts and crème caramel. Full-bodied but a bit flabby with a breadcrust flavour in the finish. Drink now. **2000★★→** Deep yellow-gold colour with a buttered corn nose. Full bodied with good acidity and a clean, long finish. Drink now.

Chardonnay, Signature [NP] 2000★★★→ Gold, Cuvée 2003. Rich golden hue with a dense oaky aroma. Concentrated flavours are just beginning to find direction. High acidity but deft balance. Drink now to end of 2006.

Gamay [NP] 2001☒ Strong odour of Asian lady beetle.

Meritage, Laura's Blend [NP] 2001★★★↗ Garnet with aromas of smoke, charred oak, raspberry, and blackberry. Clean, light, balanced, with some complexity. Drink now-2007.

Meritage, Signature [NP] 2002★★★☆↑ Deep garnet with an overtly herbaceous nose at first, later exhibiting cedar, pencil lead, and black fruit aromas. Fullish, thick texture but with strong, dusty tannins. Aftertaste lingers nicely. Anticipated maturity 2006-2012. **2001★★★↗** Garnet with a creamy nose of oak, raspberry, and black currant. Fresh, youthful, vibrant, and deeply flavoured. Drink now-2010.

Merlot [NP] 2002★★★↗ Garnet with a warm nose that hints of plum and blackberry. Good fruit, velvety texture, and a lingering aftertaste. Drink now-2008.

Merlot, Signature [NP] 2002★★★↗ Gold & Best Merlot, Cuvée 2004. **2001★★★↗** Deep garnet with browning edges. Black tea, ripe apple, and green plum nuances in the bouquet. Fairly tannic. Drink now-2009.

Pinot Gris [NP] 2003★★★→ Has aromas of white peach and Bartlett pear along with a spicy palate that is balanced, clean, well structured, and medium-full. Drink now-2006. **2001** Gold, Ontario Wine Awards 2002.

Pinot Noir [NP] 2001★★★→ Ruby with a lovely oak, cherry sandalwood nose and forward, dried-fruit flavours. Slightly soapy finish. Drink now-2007.

Pinot Noir, Signature [NP] 2001★★★→ Ruby-cherry hue with light sandalwood and coffee aromas. Maturing (prematurely, I suspect), with dried fruit, herbal, and earthy notes. Drink before the end of 2006. **1999** Gold, All Canadian Wine Championships 2002.

Rosé [NP] **2001** ★★★☆↻ Salmon-flesh colour with a light nose hinting of oranges and cherries. Relatively flavourless, but well balanced with solid texture.

Sauvignon Blanc [NP] **2003** ★★★☆↻ Very pale gold, like bleached straw. Aromas of asparagus and cut grass and taste of tart apples. **2002** ★★↻ Silvery-gold with a crisp, Granny Smith apple nose. Clean and straightforward. **2001** *Gold, All Canadian Wine Championships 2002; Gold, Ontario Wine Awards 2002.* **2000** ★★★→ Pale straw-gold with a light, grassy gooseberry nose. Big, full fat texture with earthy undertones. Drink now.

Shiraz, Signature [NP] **2002** ★★★☆↗ *Gold & Best Shiraz, Cuvée 2004.* Inky, deep purple colour with an array of aromatics including blackberry, crème fraiche, cocoa, toast, oak, nuts, and black licorice. Rich, supple palate and lively acidity. Drink now-2010. **2000** ★★★→ Dark colour but little depth. Dry and oaky with some black fruit flavours and distinct hints of black licorice. Drink now-2006.

Vidal, Icewine [NP] **1999** ★★★★→ Amber-gold with a concentrated, herbal, walnut skin nose. Very sweet, thick, and clean with hints of orange pekoe tea and fruit syrup. Drink now-2008. **1998** ★★★★☆→ Deep amber hue with a bouquet of dried fruits, spiced fruitcake, and marmalade. Sweeter than sweet. Not cloying but extremely rich. Drink now-2008.

Vidal, Select Late Harvest [NP] **2000** ★★★☆→ Amber-yellow with a spirity nose. Baked pear purée with golden syrup topping, and hints of orange peel and spice in the finish. Drink now-2008.

• **CROWN BENCH ESTATES** (3850 Aberdeen Road, Beamsville, ON, L0R 1B7 / Phone: 905-563-3959 / Toll-Free: 1-888-537-6192 / Fax: 905-563-3441 / Email: winery@crownbenchestates.com / Website: www.crownbenchestates.com)

(Est. 1999) For an older married couple to choose caring for a vineyard and operating a winery as a "quiet retirement project," Peter Kocsis and his wife, Livia Sipos, make me wonder how hard they must have worked before slowing down to this pace. They left the life of business and academe in Ottawa returning to the same lot and concession where Peter was born and grew up. The 25-acre parcel the couple purchased in 1996 was already a working vineyard with some of the oldest vinifera plantings on the Beamsville Bench. Composed of Jeddo clay deposited over a limestone base, the property has a gently sloped amphitheatre shape and is one of the very few vineyards on the Beamsville section of the bench to have both north- and south-facing exposures. Twenty acres are under vine, including 1.5 acres of Cabernet Franc planted in 1975 and 1 acre planted in 2001, 1 acre of Cabernet Sauvignon from 2001, 6 ancient acres of Chardonnay planted way back in 1969, 2 acres of Furmint, 2 acres of Merlot from 1970 and 2 more planted in 2001, 1.5 acres of Pinot Noir planted in 2001, and 3 acres of Vidal Blanc from 1970. All vines are spaced at 1,000 plants per acre and thinned at veraison to yield 2 t. per acre. Here, though, the grapes cropped at veraison are not just dumped on the ground like elsewhere. They are carefully gathered and pressed to make verjus, a sour, green grape juice often used in place of lemon. Crown Bench is the only winery in Canada making verjus. Peter and Livia also experiment with wine infusions and have developed a number of unusual and exotic concoctions from their wines. They shun French and American oak in favour of barrels coopered from Hungarian oak. Currently, they are producing at capacity using only their own estate grapes. Despite the fact that the winery was completely frozen out in 2003, they keep to their policy of not purchasing grapes from other vineyards. Crown Bench produces 4,000 cases in an average vintage.

Winemakers: Peter Koscis (1999-present); Deborah Paskus (1999-2000, consulting) / Vineyard Manager: Livia Sipos (2004 Grape King)

Cabernet Franc, Beamsville Bench, Vintners Reserve [NP] **2001** ☒ Unpleasant odour of geranium and sour milk. Likely a victim of Asian lady beetle. **1999** ★ ★ ★ ↗ Garnet with violet edges and a soft, fullish aroma of black tea, mint, and raspberry syrup. Lush and balanced. Drink now-2009.

Cabernet Franc Icewine [NP] **2000** ★ ★ ★ → Hints of baked bread give way to aromas of strawberry jam and cherries stewed over an open fire. Smoky, toffee notes. Drink before 2008.

Cabernet Sauvignon, Vintners Reserve [NP] **2001** ★ ★ ★ ☆ ↗ Light garnet with a green pepper nose that also hints of Asian lady beetle. Ripe fruit on the palate is somewhat marred by a bitter herbal finish. Drink now-2009.

Chardonnay [NP] **2001** ★ ★ ☆ → Gold hue with aromas of apples, herbs, hints of bread and lemon juice. Light, dry, and straightforward, but a smidgen too alcoholic for the depth of fruit. Drink now.

Chardonnay, Vintners Reserve [NP] **2001** ★ ★ ★ → Gold with an herbal applesauce aroma. Good fruit, a bit doughy in the finish. Drink now. **2000** ★ ★ ★ → Gold with a nutty, oxidative nose of brown butter. High alcohol and high acidity with a lively finish. Drink now.

Chardonnay, Livia's Gold, Botrytis Affected [NP] Produced from early harvested botrytis-affected Chardonnay grapes. **2002** ★ ★ ★ ★ → *Gold, International Wine & Spirit Challenge 2003; Gold, Chardonnay du Monde 2003.* Brilliant pale gold with a richly perfumed, custard cream bouquet. Well balanced with delicious white fruit flavours. Drink now-2010. **2000** ★ ★ ★ ★ ☆ → Rich, yellow-gold with amber highlights. Bouquet of wild peach blossom honey with a sweet, elegant palate that, thankfully, is not as tart as most icewines. Drink now-2008.

Meritage [NP] **2000** ★ ★ ★ ↗ Garnet with a red fruit nose supported by plenty of vanilla oak. Maturing well. Lean texture and some pleasant woody notes in the finish. Drink now-2010.

Merlot, Vintners Reserve [NP] **2001** ★ ★ ★ ↗ Deep garnet with a soft, dusty fruit aroma. Has plenty of fruit and lots of supporting oak but is disjointed for now. Drink 2006-2010. **2000** ☒ Pale ruby with a watery rim. Sick nose and hard, dirty taste.

Vidal Icewine [NP] **1999** ★ ★ ★ ☆ → Amber-gold with aromas of dried peach, dried apricot, and caramelized pear. So sweet it hurts. Drink up.

Vidal Icewine, Barrel-Fermented [NP] **2000** ★ ★ ★ ★ → Deep amber-gold with a powerfully caramelized nose and a pungent overtone of white truffle. Taste stretches in the realm of glazed peach strudel with toasted almonds.

Vidal Icewine, Vintner Select [NP] **2002** ★ ★ ★ ★ → Gold with amber reflections, and lightly caramelized peach and candied pineapple aromas. Sweet, peach flavours with very high acidity. Drink now. **2001** ★ ★ ★ ★ → Amber-gold with a bouquet of caramelized brown sugar over poached pear. Concentrated and viscous, intensely sweet and powerful. Drink now.

Specialty Products:

Altair [nonVQA] Combines maple syrup with Vidal icewine. **NV** ★ ★ ★ ↻

Ambrosia [nonVQA] Chocolate-infused Vidal icewine. **NV** ★ ★ ★ ☆ ↻ *Grand Gold, Selections Mondial 2004.* A truly decadent dessert in a glass.

Berry Trio [nonVQA] Blueberry-, cranberry-, and raspberry-flavoured icewines presented in a uniquely designed, stacked, and shrinkwrapped 3-bottles-in-1 package. Fun for dinner parties where a variety of flavours can be offered. Individual wines are reviewed below.

Blueberry Ice [nonVQA] Combines blueberry essence with Vidal icewine. **NV** ★ ★ ★ ↻ Intense flavour of liquid blueberry pie filling. My favourite in the Berry Trio.

Cranberry Ice [nonVQA] Vidal icewine has been flavoured with cranberry essence. **NV** ★ ★ ☆ ↻ Clean, zippy varietally correct cranberry flavour. Well balanced.

Hot Ice [nonVQA] Combines Vidal icewine with an infusion of hot jalapeno peppers. **NV** ★ ★ ★ ↻ It's fire and ice. Ouch, and I want another glass. The flavour is of sweet, dried peaches and cream with the finish of chipotle.

Raspberry Ice [nonVQA] Raspberry essence in Vidal icewine. **NV** ★ ★ ★ ☆ ↻ *Gold & Fruit Wine of the Year, All Canadian Wine Championships 2002.* Has both concentrated raspberry flavour and icewine richness. Makes a spectacular pairing with chocolate desserts.

Verjus – The pressed juice of green grapes picked at veraison. Unfermented, so there's no alcohol. **NV★★★★↻** Owners say you can drink this, but I find the taste too green and tart for my palate. Its best use is in the kitchen and especially in a vinaigrette used to dress a wine-friendly salad. Try in place of lemon or vinegar.

Vanilla Ice [NP] Vidal icewine was flavoured with pure Bourbon vanilla. **NV★★☆↻** Like crème anglaise over poached pears.

Wild Ginger Ice [NP] Vidal icewine was flavoured with ground root of wild ginger. **NV★★★↻** Has a candied ginger flavour, a hint of spice, and nuance of orange zest.

- **CSETS VINEYARD (Beamsville, NP)** – Situated next door to Malivoire's estate vineyard, Csets supplies Chardonnay and Merlot to Henry of Pelham.

- **CUESTA VINEYARD (Twenty Valley, NP)** – A 30-acre farm adjacent to McGrade Vineyard to the south and Butlers Grant to the West was purchased in 1998 by Stoney Ridge Estate Winery. Over the next 2 years it was graded and planted with Cabernet Franc, Cabernet Sauvignon, Merlot, and Pinot Noir at 1,300 vines per acre. The vineyard has a north-facing slope, is fully underdrained, and is composed of sand and clay. There is excellent resistance to winter damage at this site as deep ravines on either side of the vineyard draw cold air away from the vines. All fruit is processed by Stoney Ridge.

- **Culotta Wines** – Pietro Culotta started as a wholesaler of grapes imported from California for the home winemaking community. In 1979, his grandson, Peter, founded the wine company to produce wines by blending imported juices with Ontario juice. The winery got its provincial licence in 1984. In December 1995, the winery licence, all wine stocks, brand names, and the six retail stores were sold to Kittling Ridge Wines & Spirits.

- **CULP VINEYARD (Niagara-on-the-Lake, NP)** – This 35-acre vineyard on the north side of Greenlane Road between Bartlett and Sann comprises 3 parcels, 2 of which are owned by Don and June Culp and a third is listed in the name of their son, Kevin. The property was deeded to the family in 1869, and grape growing has been practised for several generations. The soil is almost entirely reddish-hued Jeddo clay loam supporting 32 acres of Auxerrois, Cabernet Sauvignon, Chardonnay, De Chaunac, Merlot, Seyval Blanc, and a small patch of Concord grapes that are sold off every year to a Toronto processor. The Culp Vineyard Chardonnay was given the highly esteemed single-vineyard designation a few years ago by Inniskillin Wines. Today, the grapes are all sold to Vincor International.

D

- **D'ANGELO VINEYARDS ESTATE WINERY** (5141 Concession 5, R.R.#4, Amherstburg, ON, N9V 2Y9 / Phone: 519-736-7959 / Toll-Free: 1-888-598-8317 / Fax: 519-736-1912 / Email: info@dangelowinery.com / Website: www.dangelowinery.com/ontario.html)

(Est. 1989) With wineries in 2 provinces, Sal D'Angelo is simply following in the footsteps of many earlier generations of family winemakers. Sal's grandfather tended grapes in Italy, teaching him during his visits how to nurture the soil. His dad made wine in the family's cantina, showing him how to turn healthy grapes into tasty wine. As a very young man living in Essex County, Sal found his calling. After pondering the purchase of a lakeshore property, he chose an inland location instead, where during the summer the temperature rises about 5 degrees higher than at the nearby lakeside town of Amherstburg. It was 1983. Sal bought the 50-acre parcel of land 6 km east of the Detroit River and 9 km from the mouth of Lake Erie and planted his first acre of vines. By the end of 2004, vine coverage had steadily grown to more than 40 acres, including Baco Noir, Cabernet Franc, Chambourcin, Chardonnay, Marechal Foch, Pinot Noir, and Vidal Blanc at 1,150 vines per acre. The relatively flat property, composed of Brookston clay loam, is fully tiled to provide adequate drainage. D'Angelo uses a divided canopy training system and practises heavy leaf-thinning right after bloom to maximize sunlight and to improve air circulation. He thins about 30% of the fruit at veraison to achieve crop levels of 3.5 t. per acre. Sal's first crush was in 1989. Today he sells much of his 200 t. of grapes to Colio Winery, retaining about one-third of his fruit to produce 3,000 to 5,000 cases under his own label. He tends to release his reds much later than most wineries. Currently, the winery retail shop is stocked with 1998 and 1999, and several vintages from the beginning of the 1990s also are available. He and his family operate a second winery in British Columbia's Okanagan Valley together with a bed and breakfast and a bistro-style restaurant. Situated on the Naramata Bench on the east side of Lake Okanagan, it is within walking distance of the Kettle Valley Trail. His first B.C. crop was harvested in 2004. His motto is: "We make wine the natural way – we grow it."

Winemaker: Sal D'Angelo (1999 Ontario Grape King) / Vineyard Manager: John Klassen

Cabernet [LENS] **1996** ★★→ (CF77/CS10/Gam9.5/M3.5) Clean fruit, oaky coconut flavours. Drink before end of 2006.

Cabernet Franc Reserve [LENS] **1999** ★★★↗ Ruby-garnet with sweet, ripe, black raspberry aroma. Fruit taste is overpowered by mouth-drying tannins. Going strong. Drink 2006-2010. **1998** ★★★→ Ruby-garnet with black raspberry, strawberry, and camembert bouquet. Vibrant black-fruit flavours with a hot, alcoholic finish. Drink now.

Cabernet Franc, Viewpointe Vineyard [LENS] **2000** ★★★↗ Brilliant black-cherry hue with a dense and quite closed nose. Chunky and tannic for now. Could become terrific once the fruit is permitted to peek out. Drink 2006-2010.

Cabernet-Merlot [LENS] **1993** ★★↘ (CS43/Gam15/M42) Cigar-box nose. Ample acidity, fruit still overpowered by oakiness and beginning to dry up.

Marechal Foch, Old Vines Reserve [Ont] **1999** ★★★→ Inky colour and strong minty chocolate nose. Full-flavoured but lacks definition at this point. Drink now-2009. **1996** ★★★↘ Some of the best flavoured, juicy, blackberry fruit I've tasted from this region. High acidity will continue to preserve this wine, even as the fruit begins to dry up. **1993** ★★★↘ Cherry-garnet; overdone oak nose completely masks the fruit; rich, oaky complexity combines nuts, toast, and vanilla but oak-dominated finish persists. Drink up.

Pinot Noir [LENS] **1991** ★★★→ Taking on mature ruby-mahogany colour. Minty, minty, minty, with nuances of tiger balm and old cedar closets. Plenty of fruit left, good acidity, and spicy fruit flavours. Drink now-2008.

Vidal [Ont] **1990** ↓ Yellow-gold with caramel nuances on the nose. Lively melon and green apple flavours. Dead.

Vidal Icewine [LENS] **1996** ★★★★→ Exceptional. **1995** ★★★★→ Very fine. **1994** ★★★★→ Luscious yet restrained.

• **DANIEL LENKO ESTATE WINERY** (5246 King Street, Beamsville, ON, L0R 1B3 / Phone: 905-563-7756 / Fax: 905-563-3317 / Email: oldvines@daniellenko.com / Website: www.daniellenko.com)

(Est. 1999) Bill and Helen Lenko's vineyard once provided some of the best grapes in the province to commercial wineries, such as Angels Gate, Cave Spring, Stoney Ridge, and Willow Heights, as well as to dedicated home winemakers. Bill was chosen Ontario's Grape King in 1990. Now the grapes stay home since son Daniel bought the property and chose to turn it into an estate winery. Of the 30 acres owned by the family, 29 are planted with some of the oldest vinifera vines in the province. There are 2 acres of Cabernet Franc (planted in 1985), 3 acres of Cabernet Sauvignon (1985), 10 acres of Chardonnay (the oldest in the country, planted in 1959), 6 acres of Merlot (1975), .5 acre of Pinot Noir (1985), 4 acres of Riesling (1980), .5 acre of Syrah (2000), 1 acre of Vidal Blanc (1983), and 1.5 acres of Viognier (1992). Vine density is set at 1,200 plants per acre, and crops are thinned to a maximum of 2 t. per acre. The clay loam soil is fully tiled between the rows as it sits on a base of limestone and shale. Cover crops are grown between the rows and turned in to provide green manure. Fertilization with composted cattle and chicken manure is also practised. There is a 7% north-facing slope to the land, which lies 2 km south of the Lake Ontario shoreline next door to Thirty Bench. In 2002, Daniel, too, was named Ontario Grape King. Production hovers around 5,000 cases, most of which goes out through the tasting-room door to knowing regulars.

Winemaker: Daniel Lenko / Vineyard Manager: Daniel Lenko (2002 Grape King) / Chief Piemaker: Helen Lenko

Cabernet Franc [NP] **2002**★★★★↗ Garnet with a dense, taut, vital, restrained scent that's itching to show off. Mint, oak, and subtle but complex flavours and satiny texture. I predict it will develop great finesse. Drink 2006-2012.

Cabernet Sauvignon [NP] **2002**★★★★↗ Purple-black colour with a concentrated nose of black tea, plum, and mulberry. Lean, hard, secretive palate for now. Needs time. Anticipated maturity, 2008-2018.

Chardonnay, Unoaked [NP] **2003**★★★★→ Pale straw-gold with a fullish, apple-peach-lemon aroma. Ripe fruit, not exceptionally complex but so pleasant and quaffable I'd advise having a second bottle at the ready. Drink young for its freshness.

Chardonnay, Old Vines, French Oak [NP] **2002**★★★★→ Rich shade of old gold. Fine balance of sun-ripened white fruit and toasty oak in the bouquet along with a big, soft, full taste that charms and lingers. Drink now-2008.

Chardonnay, Signature [NP] **2002**★★★★☆↗ The cadillac of Lenko Chardonnays. Brilliant gold colour. Restrained but rich nose of poached Anjou pears with crème anglaise and pralines. Plenty of oak but perfectly balanced with fruit, cream, caramel, and coconut flavours. A triumph. Drink now-2009.

Merlot, Old Vines [NP] **2002**★★★★↗ Deep garnet-mahogany with a smoky, earthy, somewhat medicinal nose. Soft, supple palate has herbal flavours and dense undeveloped fruit beneath. Nicely balanced and already drinking well. Drink now-2014.

Pinot Noir [NP] **2002**★★★↗ Brilliant ruby hue. Big, dense, highly extracted nose with flavours of dark fruits, plum, lead pencil, black licorice, earth, and a hint of mint. Has promise. Drink 2006-2012.

Riesling [NP] 2003 ★ ★ ★ → Light, confected aroma with balanced sweetness and acidity. Drink now-2009.

Riesling, Reserve [NP]   2003 ★ ★ ★ ★ ↗ Silvery with gold reflections. Lime and kiwi nose with hints of honeydew melon and a smidgen of greengage plum. Ripe white-peach flavour with fullish body, tremendous depth, and solid structure. Drink now but best 2007-2015.

Vidal Icewine [NP] 2001 ★ ★ ★ ★ ★ ↗ Their last vintage of icewine from this variety. The vines were replaced the following year with Riesling. Bright yellow-gold with an intense sweet/tart refreshing aroma reminiscent of poire william eau-de-vie. Thick, luscious, honeyed palate with clean, pure, distinct flavours of pears poached with bitter orange peels and drizzled with warmed butter. Drink now-2011.

Viognier [NP] 2003 ★ ★ ★ ★ → Silvery-gold with the slightest hint of blush. Peach, pear, and lanolin bouquet with a delicate spritz of lemon. Good body, balance, supple texture, and refreshing acidity are overshadowed by sheer charm. Drink now for youth and freshness. **2002 ★ ★ ★ ★ →** *Best aromatic white, Cuvée, 2004.* Delicately perfumed with honeysuckle and wine gums. Silky palate and exceptionally well balanced. Drink often, before 2007.

White Cabernet [NP] 2003 ★ ★ ★ → (CS100) Colour of salmon flesh with a bouquet of barely ripened strawberries spritzed with lemon. Fullish mouthfeel with big flavours of stewed strawberries. Good body and length. Drink now.

• **DANIELS FARM (Niagara Parkway, NP)** – The home farm for Howard Alexander Staff.

• **DEJONGE VINEYARD (Pelham, NP)** – Larry DeJonge owns this 10-acre former cherry farm, but it is currently managed by Matthew Speck for Henry of Pelham. It lies on the corner of 9th Street Louth and Regional Road 81 across the road from the Molek Vineyard. There are 8 acres of Chardonnay and a small amount of Chardonnay Musqué, plus some Seyval Blanc, Vidal, and Merlot planted at a density of 1,000 vines per acre on sandy gravel. The soil here has such good drainage that underdrainage tiles are unnecessary. In fact, if anything, vigour is a bit of a problem, but this is being dealt with through leaf-plucking and careful management of the trellis system.

• **DELAINE VINEYARD (Niagara Parkway, NP)** – In 1998, Vincor chairman and CEO Don Triggs and his wife, Elaine, both of whom grew up on farms in Manitoba, purchased a 95-acre apple orchard called Riverscourt Farm. It's a long, narrow strip of land that runs from the Niagara Parkway to Concession 1 on the south side of Line 4, which is an unopened dirt road. Renaming the property with a blend of their first names was the easiest part. They took detailed terrain measurements, extensive soil samples, reviewed weather and rainfall patterns, and measured morning, midday, and evening temperatures in different areas on a daily basis for an entire season. They discovered that temperatures vary significantly from east to west as a result of the moderating effects of the Niagara River. The western end of the vineyard is 2 degrees hotter in summer and 2 degrees cooler in winter. A triangular northwest corner has heavier Chinguacousy clay loam till, while the southeast end tends to have moderately sandier soil with a patch of Vineland reddish-hued lacustrine fine sandy loam somewhere in the middle. The vineyard is higher at both opposite corners and slopes down very gently toward a line running lengthwise across the middle. Based on the research, the Triggses subdivided the entire vineyard into 36 north-south strips and planted different combinations of fruitstock and rootstock at either end. There are 11 vinifera varieties cultivated, including Cabernet Franc, Cabernet Sauvignon, Chardonnay, a thin strip of Chardonnay Musqué, Gewürztraminer, Merlot, Pinot Noir, Riesling, Sauvignon Blanc, Semillon, and Syrah. Vine spacing is 1,360 per acre on rows of 2.5 m, with drainage tiles installed between every row. All the fruit is processed at Jackson-Triggs Niagara Estate winery under the supervision of winemaker Tom Seaver.

- **DE SOUSA WINE CELLARS** (3753 Quarry Road, Beamsville, ON, L0R 1B0 / Phone: 905-563-7269 / Fax: 905-338-9404 / Email: desousa@desousawines.com / Website: www.desousawines.com / *Toronto Winery*: 802 Dundas Street West, Toronto, ON, M6J 1V3 / Phone: 416-603-0202)

(Est. 1990) John De Sousa Jr.'s grandfather earned his living making and selling wine to the local bars in his homeland in the Azores, a tiny collection of Portuguese islands in the middle of the Atlantic Ocean. His father, John De Sousa Sr., wanted to follow in his dad's footsteps but, after emigrating to Canada, opened a small jewellery store instead. Over the years, the business flourished and he opened another jewellery shop, then another and another, and eventually added a restaurant and a banquet facility to his portfolio of businesses. In 1977, De Sousa Sr. and his wife, Maria, purchased a 100-acre farm with a working vineyard. Years later, under a government replacement program, he pulled out the labrusca varieties and began to replace them with hybrid and vinifera vines. To date, 75 acres have been replanted with Baco Noir, Cabernet Sauvignon, Chardonnay, De Chaunac, Marechal Foch, Riesling, Seyval Blanc, and Vidal Blanc, at 1,500 vines per acre. The property is relatively flat around the winery itself, but has north-facing slopes of 15 degrees nearby. In 1998, John Jr. opened a second winery, a small storefront operation in downtown Toronto in the heart of the

Portuguese community his father had served first as a jeweller, then as a winemaster. About three-quarters of their 18,000-case production is red. The winery plans to boost volume to 25,000 cases by 2006.

Winemaker: Andrzej Lipinski (2001-present); John De Sousa Jr. (1990-present); John De Sousa Sr. (1990-1997) / Vineyard Manager: John De Sousa Jr.

Baco Noir [Ont] **2002**★★★↗ Deep garnet with a very berry aroma and hints of forest floor, earth, and mushrooms. Tart and juicy with more flavour than body. Drink now-2009.

Cabernet Franc, Reserve [NP] **2002**★★★★↗ Dark garnet with a big oaky, spirity nose of raspberry, vanilla, and blackberry. Tannic and tasty. Drink now-2010.

Cabernet-Merlot, Reserve [NP] **2002**★★★☆↗ (CS50/M50) Dark garnet with a plummy nose. Tannic with flavours of cherry and black pepper. Drink now-2010.

Chardonnay, Reserve [NP] **2002**★★★☆↗ Bright gold with candied nose of apple, orange, and lemon drops. Subtle oaky structure slows the wine down from opening up. Drink now-2007. **2001**★★★☆↗ Brilliant gold with a dusty nose of oak, smoke, ginseng, vanilla, caramel, pralines, mint, roots ashes, and burning frankincense. If nothing else, it is certainly complex. Drink now-2006.

Dois Amigos [NP] A blend of Baco Noir and Marechal Foch. **2003**★★↻ Ruby-garnet with a clean, fresh, soft, and simple fruit aroma. Rustic flavours, but well balanced with decent body.

Merlot, Reserve [NP] **2002**★★★↗ Opaque garnet hue and oaky, coconutty, walnut-skin aromas. Intensely tannic, maybe even so much so as to overshadow the fruit. Drink now-2009.

Sauvignon Blanc, Reserve [NP] **2002**★★★→ Brilliant gold with an oxidative note in an otherwise apple-butter nose. Nutty taste with tropical fruit flavours. Drink now.

• **DIM VINEYARD, IVAN & SONS (Jordan, NP)** – Martin Dim, who is the nephew of Vladimir Dim, manages this 30-acre property at 2703 King Street (Highway 8) in Jordan. There are 25 acres under vine with tiny amounts of Baco Noir, Cabernet Franc, Chardonnay, Gamay Beaujolais, Gamay Noir, Gewürztraminer, Merlot, Riesling (planted in 1977), Sovereign Coronation, SV-23-512, and Zweigelt. Vines are evenly distributed at 1,000 per acre in a clay loam soil. Grapes are sold to Andrés Wines, Stoney Ridge Estate Winery, and Thirty Bench Wines.

• **DIM VINEYARD, VLADIMIR (Jordan Station, NP)** – Vladimir Dim grows 21 acres of grapes, including Cabernet Franc (3 acres), Chardonnay (4-5 acres), Merlot (3 acres), Riesling (1 acre), and Vidal Blanc (1 acre), all planted around 1990. Harvest was sold exclusively to

Henry of Pelham during the early years. More recently, crops have been sold to Kittling Ridge Estates and Stoney Ridge Estate Winery. The vineyard is north-facing with a 6%-8% slope. Soils are typical of the area – light sandy loam and small, round gravelly stones. Replanting has been undertaken in the past few years. The property is across the road from Lake Edge Vineyard.

• **DOMAINE CALCAIRE** (854 Danforth Road, Hillier, ON, K0K 2J0 / Phone: 613-476-5339 / Email: calcaire@kos.net)

(Not yet licensed) Dan and Carrie Taylor have high hopes, but no winery yet. The wine they have produced to date has been made under their own label on the licence of Black Prince winery. Their 18-acre farm is located about 2 km from Lake Ontario, to the north of By Chadsey's Cairns, south of Closson Chase and west of Hubb's Creek. Since 2001, they have planted 1.5 acres each of Pinot Noir, Pinot Meunier, and St. Laurent at very high densities, ranging from 2,200 to 3,600 plants per acre in order to encourage low vigour in the south-facing clay/limestone soil. The Taylors have been using bio-dynamic vineyard practices since day one, although they are not certified as such.
   Winemaker: Dan Taylor / Vineyard Manager: Dan Taylor

Wines not available for appraisal before press time.

• **Domaine D'Or** – Brand owned by Andrés Wines. NonVQA generic reds and whites produced from imported wine, juice, or grapes.

Tasting notes listed under Andrés Wines.

• **DOMAINE LA REINE VINEYARDS & WINERY** (Station Road, Hillier, ON, K0K 2J0 / Phone: 613-394-0236 / Email: ghein@reach.net / Website: www.domainelareine.ca [in development])

(Not yet licensed) Pioneering winemaker Geoff Heinricks's dreams and antics have become familiar to literary winelovers through his bestselling book, *A Fool and Forty Acres*, published in 2004 by McClelland & Stewart. He and his wife, Lauren Grice, purchased a virgin 40-acre parcel in Prince Edward County in the fall of 1994. Heinricks uses organic practices to cultivate his vines in the typical Hillier soil – heavy clay loam and limestone rubble sitting on thin beds of well-fractured limestone and shale. Most of his ungrafted vines, planted in 1995, 1996, and 1997, have been lost to phylloxera, summer drought, and root rot. Those vines grafted onto local riparia rootstock still survive, despite the punishing winters. Heinricks now has 1.3 acres of 18 different clones of

Pinot Noir along with some Pinot Gris and Pinot Meunier interspersed, and .5 acre of St. Laurent, all planted between 2002 and 2004 at the very high density of 3,630 vines per acre. There also is an 8-year-old test plot of Syrah, which Heinricks has decided to expand over the next 2 years, .75 acre of Pinot Noir on an adjacent property owned by Toronto chef Jamie Kennedy, as well as another 1.25 acres on contract at Little Creek Vineyards. Heinricks has propagated a white mutation of Pinot Noir, which he has dubbed Pinot Lauren, and is cultivating 400 plants in his own vineyard. Another 1,000 plants are being tested at 3 other vineyards, Dan Taylor's Domaine Calcaire, Jamie Kennedy's Hillier Bluff Vineyard, and a vineyard owned by Jeff Connell. Heinricks plans to start construction on his own winemaking facility in 2006 or 2007. Meanwhile, he is a "tenant winemaker" at Closson Chase Vineyards, where he sold his first 22 cases of Pinot Noir this past spring. Heinricks's first wine (according to his book, he has 1 bottle left) was produced in 1998, the best vintage on record in Ontario.

Winemaker: Geoff Heinricks / Vineyard Manager: Geoff Heinricks

Pinot Noir, "Grand Hiver" [nonVQA] From grapes grown at Little Creek Vineyard with 15% barrel top-up provided by Long Dog Vineyard & Winery and bottled at Closson Chase Vineyards. **2003 ★ ★ ★ ☆ ↗** Light ruby hue with an aroma that starts a little shakily then genuinely impresses. The first whiff suggests acetone along with high-toned floral and delicate fruity notes. Two minutes later, it's leafy, herbal, and minty, with a hint of volatility still; but after 10 minutes, the bouquet is billowing with preserved Bing cherries, nutmeg, wildflowers, and sandalwood. Palate is both sweet and tart, with enticing flavours that linger for some time. Drink now-2010.

• **DOM VAGNERS WINERY** (1973 Four Mile Creek Road, R.R.#3, Niagara-on-the-Lake, ON, L0S 1J0 / Phone: 905-468-7296 / Email: mvagners@scottlabsltd.com)

(Est. 1993) Wine lover Martin Vagners is the Canadian head of Scott Laboratories, a company that has extensive involvement with the wine industry, selling yeast strains, fermentation, and processing compounds and a variety of other products. Having purchased a 7-acre section surrounded by peach orchards in 1990, he immediately planted 2.5 acres of traditional Bordeaux varieties (Cabernet Franc, Cabernet Sauvignon, and Merlot) adding a little over an acre of Gewürztraminer, Pinot Gris, and Riesling in 1993. In 1995, he planted 1.2 acres of Pinot Noir, and in 2001 filled in a tiny section with .10 acre of Muscat Ottonel. He also planted about 500 Pinot Gris plants and 100 Pinot Blanc vines to make sparkling wine, but these are not very cold-hardy. All varieties are cultivated at the relatively high density of 2,000 vines per acre. The vineyard is flat, with sandy soil, and situated 20 m above and 2 km south of Lake

Ontario just west of the sparsely populated suburbs of Niagara-on-the-Lake. Vagners is not a member of the VQA, although all of his wines are produced exclusively from his own estate-grown grapes. As a result, he does not have the legal right to call them "estate-bottled." He uses only 10%-20% of his yield, selling the rest of the crop to other local wineries. His own average annual production is about 200 cases of wine with a long-term goal of growing to 1,000 cases. No wine was produced in 2003, as Vagners sold his entire harvest. As the years have passed, Vagners says he realizes that Cabernet Franc and Pinot Noir are the 2 varieties best suited to his site. In future, he plans to put more emphasis on those grapes, eventually uprooting the other varieties.

Winemaker: Martin Vagners / Vineyard Manager: Martin Vagners

Creek Road Red [nonVQA] **2002**★★★➜ (CF60/CS10/M30)
Silver, All Canadian Wine Championships. Mahogany-garnet with a bouquet of black-currant berries, plums, and a hint of prune. Warm, advanced flavours of raisin and prune, with hints of dried apricot. Ready to drink now.

Pinot Noir [nonVQA] **2002**★★★☆➜ Pale ruby-orange with hints of brick red along the rim. Floral, barnyardy, with lovely nuances of sweaty underpants. Flavours are subtle, delicate, and perhaps a bit fragile, but seductive and charming. Drink now-2006.

• **DVA** – See Viticultural Area

E

- **E. & F. FARM (St. Catharines, NP)** – Owners Eric Polcin and Fred Hernder are brothers-in-law. The flat 22-acre farm lies between 9th and 11th Streets Louth from 4th Avenue to Glass Avenue, just around the corner from the Jackson-Morgan Farm. Except for about an acre of headlands, the entire property is planted to vines. There are 8 acres of New York Muscat and 6 acres of Vidal planted in sandy soil. On a clay patch in the middle, they grow 4 acres of Seyval Blanc and 5 acres of Cabernet Franc.

- **EASTDELL ESTATES** (4041 Locust Lane, Beamsville, ON, L0R 1B2 / Phone: 905-563-9463 / Fax: 905-563-1241 / Email: winery@ eastdell.com / Website: www.eastdell.com)

(Est. 2000) When international business consultants Susan O'Dell and Michael East purchased the Walters Estate Winery in 1999, the first thing they did was to dump much of the previous vinegary production and thoroughly scrub down the buildings. Next they began to tear out some of the existing grape varieties and to relandscape the property to combine commercial vineyards with a full range of natural Carolinian plantings, waterfalls, ponds, and wildflower fields. The couple also rejigged the on-site dining room, creating The Bench Bistro, with a spectacular view across the lake to Toronto and seasonal menus to highlight their wines. At one point, the wine country "dream" almost turned into a nightmare. It was 2001 and the entire industry was being hit hard with the scourge of Asian lady beetle. EastDell had the unfortunate experience of being the first winery to be publicly identified with a tainted wine. They quickly replaced the product with another wine that now is its fastest-growing brand. The estate comprises 110 acres, of which 50 are planted at a spacing of 1,000 vines per acre with Cabernet Franc, Cabernet Sauvignon, Chardonnay, Gewürztraminer, Merlot, Pinot Noir, Riesling, and Vidal Blanc. The vineyard is laid out in several blocks, most with north-facing slopes composed of grey-brown Chinguacousy silty clay loam, but one, the Walnut Grove Block, faces southeast and has the slightly redder Oneida clay loam till. The property is bordered on 3 sides by forested ridges and laced with pretty walking trails and ravines among the Carolinian trees. Production in 2003 was 12,000 cases.

Winemaker: Scott McGregor (2004-present); Jason James (2004-present);Tatjana Cuk (2000-2003) / Vineyard Manager: KCMS Consulting

Black Cab [Ont] **2003★★★➜** (BN36/CF45/CS19) Garnet with aromas of plum, black cherry, and the slightest hint of Asian lady beetle. Balanced, with good concentration and structure. Drink now-2007. **2002★★★➜** (BN44/CF36/CS20) Deep garnet colour with hints of chocolate. Clean, simple, and light but well balanced and easy-drinking.

Cabernet-Merlot, "Escarpment" [NP] **2002★★★➜** Deep garnet with a big oaky nose. Nuances of strong coffee, game, and leather. Richly textured and supple with flavours of plum, smoke, nuts, and cedar resins. Tarry tannic finish. Drink now-2010.

Chardonnay, Barrel-Fermented [NP] **2003★★★➜** Straw-gold with green reflections. Despite a minor reek of Asian lady beetle, it has ripe, implicitly sweet fruit with a vinous flavour. Drink now-2007. **2002★★➜** Deep gold with a cider or apple-butter aroma. Light, with a washed-out middle palate and an artificial, candied taste. Drink now.

Chardonnay, Unoaked [NP] **2003★↻** Gold colour with bubbles forming inside the glass. Canned asparagus nose with residual sugar in the taste. Sweetish, with flavours of overboiled asparagus. Tasted twice. Not to my liking. **2002★★★↻** *Gold, All Canadian Wine Championships 2004.* Rich straw-gold with oaky, smoky, herbal notes and a subtle nuance of boiled cream. Supple, simple, and very pleasant for immediate drinking. **2001☒** The first Ontario wine to be publicly identified with the dreaded Asian lady beetle taint.

Pinot Noir [NP] **2003★★★↗** Brilliant ruby with clean, tart, fresh, and ripe fruit. Silky texture, charming flavours, and a lovely "have another sip" finish. Drink now-2008.

Red Cab [Ont] **2003★★★➜** (CF54/Gam46) Ruby-garnet with surface aromas of red cherry, raspberry, and apple and a minor undertone of Asian lady beetle. Soft, ripe fruit flavours. Drink now-2006. **2002★★➜** There's bottle variation here. Some have a funky nose and unpleasant bitterness in the finish. Others are lean and juicy with raspberry and red-cherry flavours and a balanced but dusty, tannic finish.

Riesling [NP] **2002★★↻** Green-gold hue with sharp lemon-orange notes. Not much to it. Clean, easy-drinking.

Riesling, "Escarpment" [NP] **2003★★➜** Pale green-gold with a hint of spritz. Perfumed, floral, grapefruity aromas. Refreshing with balanced acidity and residual sugar. Drink now-2008.

Summer Rosé [NP] **2002★★☆↻** From a blend of Riesling and Cabernet Franc. Pale cherry-pink with a strawberry aroma and a lean, fruity taste. Best young.

- **EAST LAKE VINES (Cherry Valley, PEC)** — This small vineyard of 8.5 acres borders the south shore of East Lake. John Fricker and Marianne Sanders bought the property early in 1999 and immediately planted a small test-plot vineyard. It includes high-density parcels of .10 acres each of Chardonnay, Pinot Blanc, Pinot Gris, Riesling, Syrah, and Vidal Blanc, plus 2 small sections of Pinot Noir on different rootstocks. In subsequent years, they added a second vineyard of just over an acre lower on the property closer to the water. Here, they cultivate Landal and St. Laurent spaced at a density of 1,400 vines per acre. The soil is a mix of Brighton gravelly sand and Ameliasburg clay loam over fractured limestone. East Lake Vines is less than a kilometre north of Robert Thomas Estate Vineyard.

- **EASTMAN VINEYARD (Vineland, NP)** — Don Eastman purchased a 13.4-acre property nestled between the Mertens and Rosomel Vineyards in the heart of the Beamsville Bench section of the Niagara Bench. When he bought the vineyard, it was half-planted with young viniferas, but the rest were old non-vinifera varieties such as Concord, Niagara, and Veeblanc. Over the course of several years, the labruscas were removed, a new drainage system was installed between every second row, and premium viniferas were planted. Today, roughly 9 acres are under vine with more than half of the acreage devoted to Chardonnay, some of which is 30 years old. The rest is planted in .75-acre sections of Cabernet Franc, Gamay (old vines), Gewürztraminer, Merlot, and Riesling. The vineyard has a slight north-facing slope with a clay-based soil that includes some loamier areas. It is generally more pliable than the redder clay across the road. Much of the crop went to Stoney Ridge in the early years. Much like the wines from Rosomel Vineyard next door, Eastman Chardonnays tend to have more elegance in their flavours and lasting power, even when the bouquet seems forward. Today, the Chardonnay grapes go to Tawse Winery and Temkin-Paskus, while the remainder of the varieties are doled out in small amounts to home winemakers and other local wineries, depending on availability.

- **EDGE ROCK VINEYARD (Vineland, NP)** — Considering what this property looked like less than a decade ago, this experimental vineyard that backs onto Vineland Estates is one of the more exciting projects in the Niagara Peninsula today. This is a quarry reclamation project. It was conceived by John Walker of Walker Industries, a diversified company that owns Vineland Quarries and operates a wide spectrum of heavy industry, including highway construction and waste management, all a far cry from their recent foray into viticulture. Generally speaking, quarries are unattractive places, but this one has been made quite beautiful. After excavating all the gravel there was to take, the original overburden of Halton and Wentworth tills (clay loams with a matrix of up to 20% gravel) was carefully replaced and seeded to give the pit the appearance of a luxuriant valley. Next, 12 acres on the south-facing slope were planted over with vines starting in 1999, and as many as 200 south-facing acres remain available for planting. The vineyard is tiled between every row for perfect drainage, and a state-of-the-art drip irrigation system has been installed. Grapes, currently being tended by Claus Wolf and Custom Farm Services, include the finicky Pinot Noir and several heat-loving varieties like Cabernet Sauvignon, Malbec, Merlot, Petit Verdot, Sangiovese, and Syrah. Thirteenth Street Winery has produced small amounts of very promising Syrah, Merlot, and Meritage from the first crop (2002).

- **ELLER FARM VINEYARD (Jordan, NP)** – Owned by Howard and Wendy Staff, this 120-acre property slopes down from an 8-degree north-facing grade at the south end to flat land at the opposite end. Standing among the 40 acres of vines, one can get a fabulous view of the north shore of Lake Ontario and the city of Toronto. On the clay-loam soil there are 20 acres of Concord (sold to U.S.-based Welch's juice company), 10 acres of Fredonia, a tough-skinned table grape sold to grocery stores in Quebec, as well as 5 acres each of Cabernet Franc and Cabernet Sauvignon (both planted in 1997) and 3 acres of Marechal Foch (1983) harvested for Vineland Estates.

- **EMERALD SHORE VINEYARD (Jordan, NP)** – In 1997, Marcus and Diane van Bers purchased this 48-acre property off King Street, between 13th and 15th Streets. The vineyard is relatively flat with a less-than-1% north-facing slope. Soil composition is clay loam till over a bedrock of interbedded limestone and shale. In the year following the purchase, the van Bers tore out the existing Concord and Niagara grapes that had been grown to supply the now-defunct Jordan & Ste. Michelle Winery, and began to plant viniferas. The last 5-acre block was planted earlier this year. The vineyard now has 44 acres planted, including 6.3 acres of Cabernet Franc, 7.3 acres of Cabernet Sauvignon, 3.9 acres of Chardonnay, 8.3 acres of Gewürztraminer, 2.8 acres of Merlot, 5.2 acres of Pinot Noir, 6.5 acres of Riesling, and 3.6 acres of Semillon, all spaced at 1,210 vines per acre. Commercial fertilizers are shunned in favour of green manure and composted manures. Leaf-plucking is carried out on the east side of each row to allow more sun exposure on the grape bunches and to improve air circulation, and the fruit is thinned at veraison to keep yields down to between 2.5 and 4 t. per acre. Grapes are sold to Angels Gate Winery and Thirty Bench Wines.

- **EPP VINEYARD (Jordan, NP)** – This north-facing farm is owned by Harold Epp, but it has been under the viticultural control of The Malivoire Wine Company since 2000; consequently, the fruit qualifies as Malivoire's "estate" production. Of the 12 plantable acres on the farm, there are 3.8 acres of Marechal Foch planted in 1975 at a density of 850 vines per acre, all used in Malivoire's concentrated Old Vines Foch. The remaining varieties, 3.4 acres of Chardonnay, 2.5 acres of Cabernet

Franc, and 0.4 acres each of Gamay and Pinot Gris, all were planted in 1998 at 1,200 vines per acre.

- **ERIE SHORE VINEYARD** (410 County Road 50 West, R.R.#3, Harrow, ON, N0R 1G0 / Phone: 519-738-9858 / Fax: 519-738-9714 / Email: alma@erieshore.ca, harvey@erieshore.ca / Website: www.erie shore.ca)

(Est. 2002) Owners Alma and Harvey Hollingshead, both of whom have a background in agricultural finance, purchased this 40-acre property situated 3 km west of the lakeside village of Colchester in 1993. They planted their first patch of grapes in 1997 (a few rows of Vidal Blanc) and added the rest of their 15 acres of vines with vinifera and hybrid varieties in 1999 and 2000. Further plantings are scheduled for 2006. The vineyard soil is Perth clay loam and drainage tiles are installed between the rows. The gently sloped vineyards – there are 2 sections, one facing southeast, the other southwest – are just 600 m from the shoreline of Lake Erie. The Hollingsheads grow Baco Noir, Cabernet Franc, Chardonnay, Chambourcin, Riesling, Vidal, and Zweigelt plus tiny amounts of several test varieties. All wines are produced from estate-grown grapes, although for now, most of their harvest is sold to other wineries as well as to local amateur winemakers. Average annual production is 2,000 cases. Their ultimate goal is to produce 5,000 cases by 2010.

Winemaker: Harvey Hollingshead / Vineyard Manager: Alma Hollingshead

Baco Noir [Ont] **2003**★☆➔ Opaque garnet with a smoky, herbaceous nose. Tart, tough, and green flavours best consumed with red meat. Drink now-2007. **2002**★★➔ Dark garnet with aromas of black fruit. Juicy, tart palate with an herbal finish. Drink now-2007.

Cabernet Franc [LENS] **2000**★★➔ Mahogany-garnet with a toasted sesame-seed nose. Mildly aggressive taste with a hint of bitterness in the finish. Drink soon.

Chardonnay [LENS] **2003**★☆↻ Gold hue with a water nose completely lacking personality. Sweetish, caramel flavours.

Riesling [LENS] **2003**★★↻ Straw-gold colour with a nondescript nose barely hinting of lemon. Good body, balance, alcohol, and acidity. All it needs now is personality.

Vidal [Ont] **2003**★★★➔ Silvery with a dry aroma of grapefruit pith. Clean, pleasant, and quaffable but unexpectedly sweetish on the palate. (Perhaps a note on the label to indicate this would be in order?) Drink now-2006.

Vidal Icewine [LENS] **2000**★★★☆↗ Deep gold with a clean, light, honeyed orange and lemon-peel aroma. Tastes of molasses and marmalade. Drink now-2009.

Zweigelt-Cabernet [Ont]   **2001** ★ → (CF15/Z85) Pale ruby-cherry with a pale ink rim. Cardboardy nose with a leafy, stemmy taste.

• **EURO NURSERY & VINEYARD INC. (Harrow, LENS)** – This 100-acre property was originally established in 1993 as a grape-grafting operation and demonstration vineyard. There are 57 different cultivars, clones, and rootstock varieties available, and ongoing experimentation in conjunction with a Swiss company may provide additional varieties in the future. There are 87 acres under vine with Cabernet Franc, Cabernet Sauvignon, Chardonnay, Gewürztraminer, Hibernal, Merlot, Pinot Noir, Regent, Riesling, and Viognier all planted at an average spacing of 1,666 vines per acre. The site offers an intense mix of soils from clay loams to gravelly sands over a limestone base. Fruit is harvested at an average of 4.7 t. per acre and sold to Colio Estate Wines, Pelee Island Winery, Sanson Estate, and Viewpointe Estate.

F

- **FALK FARM (Niagara-on-the-Lake, NP)** – Bill Falk manages 14 properties from Line 2 to the lakeshore. This site, located just east of John Neufeld's Palatine Estate Winery, is his home farm.

- **FEATHERSTONE ESTATE WINERY & VINEYARDS** (3678 Victoria Avenue, Vineland, ON, L0R 2C0 / Phone: 905-562-1949 / Fax: 905-562-3989 / Email: contact@featherstonewinery.ca / Website: www.featherstonewinery.ca)

(Est. 2000) This winery is owned and operated by the husband-and-wife team of David Johnson and Louise Engel, whose culinary expertise was already well known in the Guelph area after they established the Guelph Poultry Gourmet Market in the mid-1980s. David's amateur winemaking hobby of those early days led to his studying viticulture at the University of Guelph and to the viniculture programs at Niagara College and Brock University. His philosophy is to run a one-man winery with a hands-on approach to producing small lots of quality estate-bottled wines. Louise does the books and the marketing, and together they run the on-site store. The house, retail shop, and winery sit on 23 acres with 19 under vine. Varieties cultivated include 2.5 acres of Riesling planted in 1978 and an additional 1.4 acres planted in 1996, 3 acres of Cabernet Franc, and 1.75 acres of Chardonnay dating back to 1991. Recent plantings include 1 acre each of Gamay Noir and Pinot Noir, 2 acres of Sauvignon Blanc, 2.5 acres of Gewürztraminer, and 3 acres of Merlot. In 2004, Vidal grapes were uprooted with the intent to make future vintages of icewine from Cabernet Franc and Riesling. Soil is heavy clay, moderately limiting potential yields. David annually adds paper fibre to his vineyards at a rate of about 15 t. per acre to promote aeration during wet spells and for moisture retention during dry periods. His efforts at vineyard improvement culminated with his being chosen Ontario's Grape King in 2003. The hilly farm enjoys natural air and soil drainage and a winding creek provides a constant source of water. Current production averages 3,000 cases, although only 1,500 were produced in 2003. The couple plans to increase production to 4,000 cases per year once all plantings have matured.

Winemaker: David Johnson / Vineyard Manager: David Johnson (2003 Grape King)

Cabernet Franc [NP] **2003** ★ ★ → Ruby-garnet colour. Nose is inviting at first with a milky nuance, but evolves into a yogourty odour. Taste has a disturbing sour-cream flavour I believe will turn cheesy in time. Drink now. **2002** ★ ★ ★ → Fresh and juicy flavours with deep and lasting black currant, blackberry, and mocha notes. Lovely texture. Drink now to 2008. **2001** ☒ Asian lady beetle detected. **2000** ★ ★ ★ → Pale cherry-garnet with a gently oaked nose of nuts, dark rye, and charred oak. Clean, medium-bodied palate with flavours of raspberry and blackberry. Drink now-2007. **1999** ★ ★ → Pale black-cherry hue with fuller, more developed nose. Showing hints of complexity on the palate – fruit salad – though somewhat austere. A respectable first effort. Drink now.

Cabernet Franc, Cherry Barrel [NP] **2003** ★ ★ ★ ↗ Black-cherry-garnet colour with an elegant, fruity, fresh raspberry aroma. Tastes of concentrated black fruits, tight balance, lean texture, and an exciting future. Drink now-2009.

Cabernet Rosé [NP] **2000** ↘ Pale salmon-flesh colour. Has a slightly eggy, dirty nose with hints of sulphur, wet earth, and musty cardboard.

Chardonnay, Barrel-Fermented [NP] **2000** ★ ★ ★ → Pale straw-gold with an inviting, even enticing nose. Vanilla, nuts, toasted bread, hints of peach jam, and fruit cocktail all come to mind. Big-bodied, fleshy mouthfeel with some complexity, but best to drink now.

Chardonnay, Canadian Oak [NP] **2003** ★ ★ ★ ↗ Gold with an elegant, nutty, vanilla, crème brûlée bouquet. Finer and more subtle than the estate-bottled version. Has lovely soft, supple texture and promise of deeper flavour as it develops. Drink now-2008.

Chardonnay, Estate-Bottled [NP] **2003** ★ ★ ★ → Pale gold with an aroma of roasted coffee and toasted hazelnuts. Big, fat, oaky, and dry. Drink now-2007.

Gamay, Unfiltered [NP] **2003** ★ ★ ★ ↗ Deep ruby-purple with a youthful, winy, black-cherry nose. Fresh-apple acidity, deep red and black fruit flavours, and fine balance. Drink now-2007. **2002** ★ ★ ★ → *Gold, Ontario Wine Awards, 2004.* Deep garnet hue with flavours of mocha and warm strawberries in crème fraiche. Clean finish. Drink now. **2001** ☒ Asian lady beetle detected.

Gemstone Red [Ont] **2002** ★ ★ ★ (BN85/CF15) Inky garnet colour with a chocolate-milk nose. Taste is a bit gamy with stewed fruits. Tart, juicy finish.

Gemstone White [Ont] **2000** ★ ★ → Pale colour, vinous nose, light body, and straightforward off-dry taste. Pleasant.

Gewürztraminer [NP] **2003** ★ ★ ★ ↗ Pale straw with a light spritz. Classic peach, honeysuckle, lime, and lychee nose with a dry, thick, oily, crisp, and balanced palate. Drink now-2008. **2002** ★ ★ ★ →

Brilliant gold hue with a bouquet of white peach, greengage plum, herbs, and honey. Clean, tart, refreshing palate. Drink now-2008. **2001** ☒ Asian lady beetle detected.

Pinot Noir [NP] 2001 ☒ Tainted with Asian lady beetle.

Pinot Noir Rosé [NP] 2001 ☒ Tainted with Asian lady beetle.

Riesling, Estate-Bottled [NP] 2003 ★ ★ ★ ↗ Pale straw hue with a touch of spritz. Fresh, floral, fruity bouquet with kiwi, lime, honeydew melon, and cedar notes. Light, crisp, lean, and dry. Drink now-2010.

Riesling, Off Dry [NP] 2000 ★ ★ ★ → Pale straw with a tart, green lemon-lime nose. Solid structure, fine balance, with real potential for future vintages.

Riesling, Reserve [NP] 2002 ★ ★ → Yellow-gold. Nose reminiscent of hard apple cider and ginger ale. Some mineral notes but low acid level, leaves the taste a bit flabby.

Vidal Blanc [Ont] 2002 ★ ★ ↻ Straw-gold with a bouquet of fresh-cut grass, gooseberry, and grapefruit. Slightly off-dry, medium-bodied, balanced acidity, and a clean finish. **2001** ☒ Asian lady beetle detected. **2000 ★ ★ →** [nonVQA] Pale-straw with a mildly spicy nose – hints of pine or juniper. Crisp, ripe apple flavours. Off-dry start with a dry finish.

• **FIELDING ESTATE WINERY** (4020 Locust Lane, Beamsville, ON, L0R 1B2 / Phone: 905-563-0668 / Fax: 905-563-0664 / Email: contact@fieldingwines.com / Website: www.fieldingwines.com)

(Est. 2004) As a master franchisor in the fast-food industry, Ken Fielding intends to use his hospitality and business experience to make the new family winery a winner. In 2000, he purchased a 20-acre property southwest of the village of Beamsville to establish a home for himself, his wife, Marg, and son Curtis, and to build a winemaking facility. The rolling land has both north- and south-facing slopes with mixed Chinguacousy and Oneida clay loam soils. This site has 1 acre each of Cabernet Sauvignon, Gewürztraminer, Riesling, Sauvignon Blanc, and Viognier, plus 4 acres of Merlot and 3 acres of Syrah. Closer to the lake, on the east side or Beamsville near the intersection of Greenlane and Tufford Road, Fielding purchased a second property. This 40-acre vineyard is flat with smooth terrain composed of Chinguacousy clay loam till with washed and sorted stony material mixed in. Several acres of ancient labrusca and hybrid grapes were torn out and replaced. There are 15 acres of vines now cultivated here, with 1 acre each of Cabernet Sauvignon, Chardonnay, Merlot, and Pinot Gris, plus 2 acres of Riesling and 9 acres of Pinot Noir. Average vine spacing on both sites is 1,350 per acre. In its first year of production, the winery produced 550 cases of wine. The master plan is to grow to 10,000 cases by the end of the decade.

Winemaker: Andrzej Lipinski / Vineyard Manager: Duarte Oliveira

Cabernet-Merlot [NP] **2002**★★★☆↗ (CS50/M50) Solid garnet with a thick, warm nose of plum and baked plum, licorice allsorts, and sweet pepper. Chunky texture with fruit boxed in by big tannic structure. Hint of char in the finish. Drink now-2012.

Chardonnay [NP] **2003**★★★★↗ Gold with an inviting and enticing Burgundian nose that combines strong lemon, cream, and toasted nut aromas with profound elegance. I thought it was verging on brilliance until I tasted the 2002. Drink now-2009. **2002**★★★★☆↗ Pale gold with a soft, sweet, delicate vanilla, caramel cream, and baked pastry dough bouquet. There's also a crisp, wet stone nuance of minerality. Lighter and softer than the 2003, but with more subtle complexity. Has fabulous ripeness, intensity, and harmony. Drink now-2009.

Pinot Gris [NP] **2004**★★★☆→ Pretty pale pink. Good concentration with strawberry nuances. Solid structure, good acidity, and nice bitter finish. Drink now-2008.

• **FIELDSTONE ESTATE VINEYARDS (Hillier, PEC)** – Purchased in 2000 by Dick Singer and his son, Steven. Dick is a wine writer and international wine adjudicator with more than 30 years experience – tasting, that is, not farming. The 155-acre property has a terroir of Hillier mixed-clay loam with limestone shards throughout. There are some patches of sandy loam and the whole vineyard faces south with a 3% slope. The bottom of the property runs into a marshy area where Hubb's Creek turns south and runs into Huyck's Bay on Lake Ontario. The vineyard has a light but constant breeze from the west. About 120 acres are plantable. By spring 2004, 9 acres were planted at a density of 1,200 vines per acre with 6 varieties, including 2 acres each of Chardonnay, Pinot Noir, and Riesling and 1 acre each of Cabernet Franc, Pinot Gris, and Syrah. The Singers dry farm the vineyard, although, with the creek on the property, irrigation is possible in a pinch. The vines survived severe frost in their first winter by being hilled up and experiencing good snow cover. In 2002, Singer harvested 300 pounds of grapes to make an experimental 140 bottles, but, in 2003, all the grapes were removed mid-season to help the vineyard recover from the previous winter and to build reserve strength for the next. Primary challenges in the area include leaf hoppers, Asian lady beetles, birds, and deer.

• **FLAT ROCK CELLARS** (2727 Seventh Avenue, Jordan, ON, L0R 1S0 / Phone: 905-562-8994 / Fax: 905-562-9162 / Email: info@flat rockcellars.com / Website: www. flatrockcellars.com)

(Est. 2003) Situated high above the Jordan section of the Niagara Bench with a panoramic view of the peninsula and the Golden Horseshoe across the water, this 98-acre jewel of a property is buttressed by the vineyards of Le Clos Jordanne on its north and south borders and by

Cave Spring to the west and Howard Staff vineyards to the east. Proprietors Ed and Nadja Madronich have focused on top quality every step of the way. The business end of the winery is built into a hill providing a 5-level gravity flow operation minimizing machine-handling of the wines. The 150,000 L winery is outfitted with state-of-the-art equipment, exclusively French oak barrels, and production is bottled in screw caps to avoid any possibility of tainted corks. There are 75 acres under vine with 35 acres of Pinot Noir, 25 acres of Chardonnay, and 15 acres of Riesling, of which a tiny 2.5-acre section has been isolated for its unique attributes. These are the 3 varieties Madronich believes are best suited to Niagara's climate and terroir, and I couldn't agree more. Every row is underdrained and vines are spaced at the above-average density of 1,350 plants per acre. The vineyard itself is shaped somewhat like a large south-facing ski-jump. It starts high on the upper bench of the Peninsula, dips sharply to a large flat section in the middle, and rises up on the other side, providing both south- and north-facing slopes with a small flat valley in the centre. The variation in topography is matched by a wide distinction in soil types. The vineyard is a mixture of stratified silt, silt on clay loam, and sand on a gravel subsurface. The winery's name, Flat Rock, was chosen while the underdrainage work was being completed. Thousands of large flat rocks had to be moved to make way for the drainage tiles. The vines are green-harvested in August to limit yields to a maximum of 2.5 t. to the acre, ensuring full ripeness and higher fruit concentration. Grapes are hand-harvested and hand-sorted. Pinot Noir is destemmed before fermentation, while Chardonnay and Riesling are whole-bunch pressed. Winemaker Darryl Brooker, an Australian with experience at Mountadam Winery in the Barossa Valley and Villa Maria Wines in Marlborough, New Zealand, started in August 2003 just before the winery's first crush. His philosophy is minimal interference to preserve the wine's natural fruit flavours. Current production is 6,500 cases, with projected annual production expected to reach 12,000 cases by the end of 2007. All bottles are finished with the modern Stelvin screwcap.

Winemakers: Vicky-Louise Bartier (2005-present); Darryl Brooker (2003-2004)

Chardonnay [NP] **2003** ★ ★ ★ ➔ Straw-gold with a delicately oaked nose. Wood provided support but allows the fruit to star in this production. Also has nuances of crème anglaise and custard. Palate seems light at first, but kicks in with more depth and complexity. Drink now-2008.

Pinot Noir [NP] **2003** ★ ★ ★ ➔ Brilliant ruby hue with sweet, floral, berry, sandalwood aromas along with some red and green veggie notes. Delish. Could do with more texture to the fruit and less wood. A very good first effort. Drink now-2011.

Riesling [NP] **2003** ★ ★ ★ ➔ Very pale straw-gold with a fine, delicate, and quite light floral, fruit-cocktail aroma. Has a solid kiss of sweetness to balance the high citrusy acidity. A very pleasant if simple drink. Peak is now-2007.

Riesling, "Nadja's Vineyard" [NP] 2003 ★ ★ ★ ★ → Very pale straw-gold. Hugely different from the regular Riesling. Crisp, deeply floral, honey, and lime-oil bouquet. Hints of petrol beginning to show. Slightly spritzy palate with juicy, mouth-watering acidity, good structure, minerality, and tons of flavour. A very classy wine. Drink now-2015.

Vidal, Icewine [NP] 2003 ★ ★ ★ ★ ☆ → Brilliant gold with soft, sweet pear and clover honey flavours. Lush and balanced. Drink now-2012.

• **Fleur de Niagara** – Brand name owned by Inniskillin. A non-vintage fortified wine (like Pineau des Charentes) produced by blending 33% unaged grape distillate with 67% partly fermented grape juice. The mixture was aged in oak casks for 2 years. If you come across a sample labelled Fleur d'Ontario, it was produced and bottled prior to 1997. Canada's best aperitif wine at the time. Regrettably, no longer produced.

• **FORRER FARMS INC. (Niagara-on-the-Lake, NP)** – Four contiguous farms running east from East-West Line to the suburbs of Niagara-on-the-Lake. The original farm was purchased by Jack Forrer, a welder, and his wife, Helga, in 1960. He worked the land evenings and weekends until he could afford to quit welding. Over time, Forrer purchased adjoining properties and pioneered the planting of European hybrids and vinifera grape varieties. One of his highest honours came in 1972 when he was chosen Ontario's Grape King. Today, there are 3 generations actively working the 200 planted acres of this 230-acre farm. Jack continues to tend the vines along with his son, Don, son-in-law, Ray Duc, and Ray's son, Jeffery, who recently completed the winery and viticulture program at Niagara College. The entire property is flat, composed of sandy loam soil, underdrained and irrigated. Its location, less than a mile from Lake Ontario and directly behind the Jackson-Triggs and the new Stratus wineries, provides excellent access to its two main customers, Jackson-Triggs and Inniskillin. Key varieties grown here include Baco Noir, Cabernet Franc, Cabernet Sauvignon, Chardonnay, Gamay, Merlot, Pinot Noir, Riesling, Sauvignon Blanc, and Vidal, all planted at 1,000 vines per acre. The oldest hybrids were planted in the mid-1960s; viniferas were added from the mid-1970s. Crops are thinned up to 50% at veraison to limit yields to 4 t. per acre.

• **Fox Vineyard, Foxcroft Vineyard** – See Wismer Vineyards

• **Frank Pohorly Vineyard** – See Riverbend Vineyard

• **French Cross** – Brand owned by Andrés Wines. Generic nonVQA varietals produced from imported wine, juice, or grapes.

Tasting notes listed under **Peller Estates.**

• **French Oak Vineyard** – See Thirty Bench Wines

• **FROGPOND FARM** (1385 Larkin Road, R.R.#6, Niagara-on-the-Lake, ON, L0S 1J0 / Phone: 905-468-1079 / Fax: 905-468-5665 / Email: jens@frogpondfarm.ca, heike@frogpondfarm.ca / Website: www.frogpondfarm.ca)

(Est. 2001) After immigrating from Stuttgart, Germany, in 1994, Jens Gemmrich, a cooper and winemaker by trade, and his wife, Heike Koch, a teacher, settled in the Niagara Peninsula near the home of Jens's brother, Martin. Jens worked as assistant winemaker at Stonechurch Vineyards until 2000, after which he remained as a consultant. After 2001, he also made wine for and consulted with Caroline Cellars. Soon after moving into the region, the couple found a neglected 10-acre property with an old mixed-fruit orchard on Larkin Road near Concession 1, began to clear the flat land, repaired the drainage system, and planted a vineyard in the sandy loam soil. Heike and Jens also farm a 4-acre section of brother Martin's Gemmrich Vineyard nearby. Of the total 11.5 acres planted, 3.6 acres are Cabernet Franc and 1.2 acres are Merlot planted in 1998. In 1999, they added 2.7 acres of Riesling and, in 2004, 2 acres each of Chambourcin and Vidal. The vines are spaced at a density of 1,200 plants per acre. By 2001, they were ready to bottle their first vintage. All wines are estate-bottled and certified organic, complying with Canadian, European, and Japanese organic agricultural standards. Thus, no insecticides, herbicides, synthetic fungicide, or chemical fertilizers are used at any time. The vineyard is fertilized with natural composted sheep manure, soil erosion is prevented with cover crops that include wildflowers and weeds, and all grapes are hand-harvested to ensure the delicate fruit is not damaged before processing. Wines are fermented in stainless-steel tanks and given full malolactic fermentation. Reds are aged 6 to 8 months in 2,500 L oak casks and bottled unfined after 1 light filtration. Sulphur levels are significantly lower than those permitted by the LCBO. Current production is just under 2,500 cases (12 × 500 ml) and projected volume is expected to rise to almost 5,000 cases annually by 2007.

Winemaker: Jens Gemmrich / Vineyard Manager: Jens Gemmrich

Cabernet-Merlot, Organic [NP]   Bottled in 500 ml size.
   2002 ★ ★ ★ ☆ ➔ (CF70/M30) Light garnet with violet edges. Hints of earth, leather, and red fruits like cherry, plum, and pomegranate.

Softer and more approachable than the 2001 with equally good balance. Drink now-2010. **2001** ★ ★ ★ → (CF75/M25) Rich, garnet-purple solid to the rim. Big, full, juicy, and ripe with aromas of black fruits, especially blackberry, black currant, and black cherry. Exceptional balance and luscious body. Drink now-2012.

Riesling, Organic [NP] Bottled in 500 ml size. **2002** ★ ★ ★ → Straw-gold colour with clean, full, hearty petrol nose. Flavours of orange citrus and honeyed pears. Concentrated, mouth-watering acidity, solid body. Drink now-2009. **2001** ★ ★ ★ ☆ → Overwhelming freshness combined with heartiness. Ripe, green lime-oil fragrance and stiff-upper-lip structure. A real mouthful. Drink now-2007.

• **Funk Vineyard** – See G.H. Funk Vineyard

G

- **GEMMRICH VINEYARD (Niagara-on-the-Lake, NP)** – This vineyard, located on Line 4 near the Niagara Parkway, is owned by Martin Gemmrich and farmed organically by his brother, Jens, owner of Frogpond Farm. In 2004, a 4-acre parcel of winter-damaged viniferas was uprooted to make room for hardier hybrid varieties, Chambourcin and Vidal Blanc. The vineyard is flat with a few minor dips and rises, and the soil is Chinguacousy clay loam.

- **GEORGE II FARMS (Beamsville, NP)** – Bill George, the 2001 Ontario Grape King, and his wife, Lesliann, are the sixth generation to farm grapes on this 80-acre farm, which has been in the family since 1796. It is fairly flat, sloping ever so gently toward the shoreline below Beamsville, where the lake's moderating effect is at its maximum. Here, the soil is Chinguacousy clay loam and the vineyard is both irrigated and fully tiled for drainage. Located next door to Schuele Vineyard, George grows primarily vinifera varieties, including Cabernet Franc (planted in 1997), Cabernet Sauvignon (from 1993), Chardonnay (1988), Merlot (1988), Riesling (with plantings dating to 1970 and 1993), and Sauvignon Blanc (1995) plus one hybrid variety, Vidal Blanc (planted in 1980). Depending on the variety, yields average from 2.5 to 4 t. per acre and are sold to Vincor's Jackson-Triggs winery.

- **GHETTI ESTATE (Niagara-on-the-Lake, NP)** – Telvido Ghetti, Ontario's 1965 Grape King, sold grapes to T.G. Bright & Co. for many years. The vineyard was one of the first ever to be named on a label for his Late Harvest Baco Noir. The property was sold to Craig Honsberger, who sells his fruit to Kittling Ridge.

- **G.H. FUNK VINEYARD (Jordan Station, NP)** – In 1983, Marion and Gunther Funk bought a 9.3-acre flat patch of land on Thirteenth Street near Jordan, planted with a few acres of Riesling and Ehrenfelser. They added Cabernet Sauvignon, Chardonnay, Merlot, and Pinot Noir in their first year, adding Cabernet Franc, Sauvignon Blanc, and more Cabernet Sauvignon, Chardonnay, Pinot Noir, and Riesling in later years. They also planted Nebbiolo and Zinfandel but, after several disappointing crops, uprooted them along with the Ehrenfelser. The tender, loving care they gave their vines soon led boutique winemakers such as John Marynissen, Eddy Gurinskas, and Jim Warren to feature the vineyard name on the labels of Marynissen Estates, Lakeview Cellars, and Stoney Ridge, at a time when grape growers received very little recognition. And in 1995, winemaking's dynamic duo, Temkin-Paskus, made the finest sparkling wine ever produced in Canada from Funk Pinot Noir. The vineyard has 3 distinct soils: silty sand for the Pinot Noir, sandy loam where the Cabernets are planted, and silty clay where the majority of the Merlot and Riesling grow. The bedrock is an impermeable glacial till known locally as fractured Queenston sandstone. Vines are planted at a density of 1,000 plants per acre and trained no more than 12 in. off the ground to provide more heat to the fruit. The crops are thinned to about 2.5 t. per acre to ensure concentration and even ripeness. Although today some of the crop is sold to amateur and commercial winemakers, most of the harvest goes to Thirteenth Street Winery, in which the Funks are partners.

- **GLASS FARM (St. Catharines, NP)** – This 68-acre site, situated on Glass Avenue 3 km south of the lake, has been the property of Fred Hernder since 1967 and, naturally, the grapes all go to his Hernder Estates Winery. Forty acres are planted to a density of 1,400 vines per acre in the deep, sandy loam soil. The land was laser-levelled to a slope of only 1 in. per 100 ft. to prevent water from sitting on the surface, and underdrained between every second row in 1993. It was later planted with 12 acres each of Cabernet Franc, Cabernet Sauvignon, and Merlot, plus 4 acres of Gewürztraminer.

- **GLENBROOK VINES (Hillier, PEC)** – Fourth-generation farmer Mike Foster and his wife, Dana, planted 4 acres of Cabernet Franc in 2001 at a density of 968 vines per acre. They chose a section with a south-facing slope on their 100-year-old, 100-acre farm, just north of Carmela Estate. It is neither underdrained nor irrigated, as the Hillier clay loam is quite friable. The fruit is destined to go to The Grange of Prince Edward Estate Winery.

- **Glen Elgin Vineyard** – See Wismer Vineyards

- **GLEN ELGIN VINEYARD MANAGEMENT (Beamsville, Jordan, Vineland, NP)** – A vineyard management company under the direction of Phil Clarke. Vineyards include Calamus Estate Vineyard, as well as 7 vineyard blocks grouped under the name Wismer Vineyards.

- **GLENLAKE VINEYARDS (Niagara-on-the-Lake, NP)** – Located on Lakeshore Road adjacent to the Willow Lake Ventures vineyard of Monica Froese, this 80-acre vineyard is owned and managed by Peter and Kevin Buis. Lakeshore vineyards generally have lighter sandy soils, which gradually get heavier as one moves back from the lake and closer to the river. The cooling influence of the lake delays spring bud-break by as much as 2 weeks but also results in later ripening at harvest. Renowned for its Chardonnay, as well as its Cabernet Sauvignon, Cabernet Franc, and Merlot, this vineyard also yields premium Riesling, Gamay, Gewürztraminer, and Seyval Blanc. Grapes are sold exclusively to the Hillebrand winery. Glenlake wines are full, firm, and plump.

- **GOTHIC COTTAGE VINEYARD (Langton, LENS)** – Civil engineer Lewis Balogh seriously considered Prince Edward County before choosing to buy a property 10 km north of Long Point in the Lake Erie North Shore region instead. When he planted the 100-acre farm in 1990, it was the first commercial vineyard in Norfolk County. Today, there are at least a dozen. Balogh grows 6 acres of hybrid varieties, including Baco Noir, Chambourcin, Léon Millot, Marechal Foch, Vidal Blanc, and Villard Noir. He used to cultivate several acres of vinifera grapes but lost most of them to crown gall. The problem came to him with the original stock purchased from the nursery, but even after uprooting the diseased vines, he had to leave the land fallow for a minimum of 4 years. The glacial nature of his soil – called Norwich moraine – permits him to plant his viniferas on their own rootstock since, as he says, there is no danger of invasion by *Phylloxera vastratix*, the vine louse that cannot survive in such high concentrations of sand. All that's left of his European vines today is a small number of Chardonnay plants, which once went into the wines of Meadow Lane. His fruit is sold to a number of local wineries and to home winemakers.

- **THE GRANGE OF PRINCE EDWARD ESTATE WINERY** (990 Closson Road, Hillier, ON, K0K 2J0 / Phone: 613-399-1048 / Toll-Free: 1-866-792-7712 / Fax: 613-399-2164 / Email: info@the grangewines.com / Website: www.thegrangewines.com)

(Est. 2002) Robert Granger, a Toronto lawyer, purchased 50 acres of rolling land in the mid-1960s as a family retreat. Now, daughter Caroline, a former runway and catalogue model in Paris and New York, lives here year-round. They have converted an old Loyalist barn (*circa* 1830) into a charming winery, barrel cellar, and tasting/retail space. The driveway leading up to the buildings winds past a small vineyard and a picturesque pond, all set among trees. The vineyard is planted with Cabernet Franc, Chardonnay, Gamay, Pinot Gris, Pinot Noir, and Riesling. Surface soil is Hillier clay loam with some gravel deposits over a fractured calciferous limestone base. Current annual production is 3,600 cases, but projected annual production will reach up to 25,000 cases once the vines are fully mature.

   Winemaker: Jeff Innes

Chardonnay, Trumpour's Mill [nonVQA] **2003** ★ ☆ ➔ Pale gold with a nutty, woody nose. Drink now.

Gamay, Trumpour's Mill [nonVQA] **2003** ★ ★ ↻ Ruby-garnet colour with an aroma of blackberry, wildflowers, and tea. Fruity, but there's a very slight bitterness in the finish.

Gamay Noir, Trumpour's Mill [Ont] **2003** ★ ☆ ↻ Ruby-purple colour with a simple, fruity taste.

Riesling, Trumpour's Mill [Ont] **2003** ★ ★ ☆ ➔ Pale green-gold with a lemon-lime aroma and too much sulphur. Peachy, sweetish taste. Drink now-2008.

• **GRAPE LANE FARMS** (Jordan, NP) – Herb and Mona Morrison tended beef cattle and chickens in the early 1950s. In 1963, they planted their first Concord and Niagara grapes for processing into juices and jams. In the mid-1980s, hybrid varieties Baco Noir, Marechal Foch, and Vidal Blanc were added and, from 1996, Cabernet Franc, Chardonnay, and Riesling have come into play. The 48-acre family farm now is owned and run by Jim and Maureen Morrison, who planted the first viniferas less than a decade ago. The original labrusca grapes still comprise one-third of the planted area and, although the cattle are long gone, chicken farming is still a major part of the operation. The "chicken coop" holds 45,000 birds at a time, which are sold to KFC. Morrison says that 70% of his labour goes into tending the grapes, while 70% of his income comes from the chickens. The rolling property, located at 21st Street and 7th Avenue, is composed of clay loam, very gently sloped, north-facing, fully underdrained, and planted 800 vines to the acre. Fruit is shared between Harbour Estate and Lakeview Cellars.

• **Green Harvest** – See Veraison

• **GREG SLINGERLAND VINEYARD** (Niagara-on-the-Lake, NP) – This 20-acre property on Four Mile Creek Road north of Line 6 has 14 acres dedicated to grapevines. The soils are heavier here with more clay in the mix. Cabernet Franc and Vidal Blanc are sold to Pillitteri Estates.

• **GURINSKAS VINEYARD** (Vineland, NP) – The name was changed to Lakeview Vineyard after new investors were brought in. See Lakeview Cellars Estate Winery for details.

H

• **HARBOUR ESTATES WINERY** (4362 Jordan Road, Jordan Station, ON, L0R 1S0 / Phone: 905-562-6279 / Fax: 905-562-3829 / Email: info@hewwine.com / Website: www.hewwine.com)

(Est. 2000) Three generations of tender-fruit farmers have partnered to turn this 38-acre family farm into a destination winery. Fraser and Darlene Mowat, their 3 children, Angela, Cassie, and Kenneth, and Fraser's parents, Bill and Nedra, planted their first few grapes in 1997. Today, all the nectarines, peaches, pear, plums, raspberries, and strawberries have been pulled in favour of *Vitis vinifera* grapes. There are 30 acres planted in the Vineland fine, sandy loam soil with 6 acres of Cabernet Franc, 16 acres of Cabernet Sauvignon, and 8 acres of Merlot, all thriving at the low density of 960 vines per acre. The property has 1,800 ft. of frontage and a 50-ft.-high vista overlooking Jordan Harbour. Thus the Mowats have opted to develop an event-oriented program taking advantage of the lovely vistas. Several grassy acres have been left open for a series of annual events, including concerts featuring rock bands like April Wine, summer picnics with wagon rides, rib roasts, and fundraisers for local charities. Harbour Estates also has a strong private label program, so wines may be found in restaurants under proprietary names. Production was 3,500 cases in 2001 and grew to 10,000 cases the following year. To supplement their own harvest, the Mowats buy grapes from local growers including Grape Lane Farms, Kelta Vineyard, and others. The winery's objective is to reach the 20,000-case level by 2015.

Winemakers: Ken Mowat (2002-present); Jeff Innes (1999-2002) / Vineyard Manager: Fraser Mowat

Baco Noir [Ont] **2003**★★☆↻ Vibrant purple garnet with a creamy, lactic, smoky, beeswax nose. Sweetish berry flavours and distinct residual sugar.

Cabernet [NP] **2002**★★★→ Garnet with a scented nose that reminds me of perfumed hotel soap bars. Subdued fruit flavours with a mildly bitter finish. Drink now-2007.

Cabernet Sauvignon Icewine, "Red Ice" [NP] **2002**★★★★→ Pale burnt-sienna colour with a kirsch nose of stewed cherries and strawberries. Lush, soft and intensely sweet with a pleasant hazel-nut-skin dryness in the finish. Drink now-2009.

Premier Vintage [NP] A Bordeaux-style blend of Cabernet Franc, Cabernet Sauvignon, Malbec, Merlot, and Petit Verdot. **2002 ★ ★ ★ →** Deep garnet with mixed aromas of red and black fruit. Fairly tannic taste, with deep fruity flavours and moderately high acidity. Drink now-2010.

Riesling [NP] **2003 ★ ★ ☆ ↻** Light straw-gold with a lemon-lime aroma. Clean, light, and grapefruity.

Sauvignon Blanc [NP] **2003 ★ ★ ↻** Pale gold with apple and lemony flavours.

• **HARVEST ESTATE WINES** (1179 Fourth Avenue, St. Catharines, ON, L2R 6P7 / Phone: 905-682-0080 / Fax: 905-682-0640 / Email: wine@harvestwines.com / Website: www.harvestwines.com)

(Est. 2000) Sharing space with the Harvest Barn country fruit market at Exit 51 on the south side of the QEW, this seems more like a retail operation than a winery. Owners are Fred Hernder and his family, who also own Hernder Estate Wines and are one of the largest farmland owners in the peninsula. Harvest purchases all its grapes from Hernder Farms and uses the same winemaker. Production was almost 6,000 cases of grape and fruit wines in the company's first year of operation. No figures were provided for current production.

Winemaker: Ray Cornell (2000-present)

Autumn [NP] A blend of Cabernet Franc, Cabernet Sauvignon, and Zweigelt. **2002 ★ ↻** Some fruity notes, but there is a cooked nuance and too much oak.

Baco Noir, Reserve [NP] **2002 ★ ★ ★ →** Blackstrap colour with a nose of dark chocolate, roasted coffee, and stewed black cherries. Long, tart, dense taste.

Cabernet Franc [NP] **2000 ★ ★ ☆ →** Lovely, creamy, dark-chocolate nose. Hard, stiff pruney palate suggests mild oxidation. Drink soon.

Chardonnay, Barrel-Fermented [NP] **2001 ☒** A victim of Asian lady beetle taint.

Chardonnay, Unoaked Sur Lees [NP] **2002 ★ ★ ☆ →** Green-gold with aromas of condensed milk, vanilla, and caramel. Soft, supple taste with low acidity and a light, leesy finish. Drink now.

Riesling, Dry [NP] **2003 ★ ★ ★ →** Pale straw with lemon, orange, and apricot notes. Drink now-2010. **2002 ★ ★ ★ →** Pale gold with an apple sweetness balanced by grapefruity bitterness. Hints of quince in the finish. Its charm is only beginning to emerge. Drink now-2010.

- **HENRY OF PELHAM FAMILY ESTATE WINERY** (1469 Pelham Road, St. Catharines, ON, L2R 6P7 / Phone: 905-684-8423 / Toll-Free: 1-877-735-4267 / Fax: 905-684-8444 / Email: winery@ henryofpelham.com / Website: www.henryofpelham.com)

(Est. 1988) The first time I spoke with the Speck boys, who run this very successful winery, I jokingly asked them to show me some identification to prove they were old enough to be inside a licensed venue. They've come a long way since then. Paul, Matthew, and Daniel Speck planted, posted, thinned, and nurtured the land that has been in the family since 1794. In that year, a 33-year-old United Empire Loyalist by the name of Henry Smith, a former bugle boy and soldier with Butler's Rangers, founder of the villages of Niagara-on-the-Lake and St. Catharines, colonel in the local constabulary, settled down to farm his 1,600-acre land grant with his wife and 14 children. The property stretched along the escarpment from Power Glen to Rockway. Family records indicate that the Smith family were some of the first to introduce domesticated grapes to the Niagara Peninsula. In 1842, Henry's son Nicholas, who operated a toll gate where the road crossed his property, built an inn and tavern at the northwest corner of Pelham Road and 5th Street where, today, the winery's retail shop and administrative offices are to be found. In the early 1900s, Nicholas's grandson, George Smith, the Speck boys' great-grandfather, quarried red sandstone off the farm to build St. Mary's Church on St. Paul Street West. The church, a landmark today, was completed in 1912. Paul Speck Sr., the boys' father, purchased the 175 remaining Smith-owned acres in 1983 to ensure the land would stay in the family. There are 90 acres given over to vines on the property, the remainder are forested or arable but unplanted. The Specks also purchased a 44-acre property to the west of their own farm, which they named Short Hills Vineyard. It is entirely planted. Fruit from owned vineyards satisfies up to 60% of the winery's needs. The remainder is brought in from neighbouring vineyards. Production in 2004 reached 78,000 cases of which less than 15% will leave the province. Export sales are highest in Japan, Taiwan, and in the greater Manhattan area. Henry of Pelham was the first Canadian winery to sell wine in cyberspace and the first to bottle a VQA wine with a screwcap closure. Paul, the oldest, administers the winery, Matthew manages the company vineyards and grower relations, while youngest brother, Daniel, looks after sales.

Winemaker: Ron Giesbrecht (1990-present, 2001 Winemaker of the Year); David Hulley (1989); Rob Summers (1988) / Vineyard Manager: Matthew Speck

Baco Noir [Ont] **2002**★★➔ Purple-black colour with simple, fruity black-cherry, blackberry taste. Drink now-2006. **2001**☒ Overpowering smell of Asian lady beetle. **1997**★★➔ Quite tart with strong dill notes. Drink up. **1996**★↘ Oaky, smoky, toasty, tart, black cherry and black currant. Drink up. **1995★★➔** Inky-purple with tart blackberry flavours. Tart finish. **1994★◄** Far less interesting than previous years. With the vintage, the Specks began to set aside the best barrels for their Reserve. **1993★★★◄** Inky purple-black with a powerful nose of fruit, cream, nuts, oak, smoke, jam, chocolate, and vanilla. Huge fruity palate with lots of lively acidity and a short, rich dry finish. **1992▼** Lousy vintage. Thankfully, now dead. **1991★★★◄** Canada's first "highly acclaimed" Baco. Still hanging in, but barely. Drink soon.

Baco Noir, Reserve [Ont] **2002★★★➚** Deep purple-garnet with a smoky, slightly cooked nose that combines aromas of both fruits and veggies. Flavours include sweetened milk, vanilla, black fruits, and charred leather. Drink now-2010. **2000** *Gold, Ontario Wine Awards 2002.* **1999** *Gold, Ottawa Food & Wine Show 2001; Best Red Hybrid, Cuvée 2001.* **1997★★★➔** Big. Not unlike the 1993 but a hint lighter. Drink soon.

Brut, Cuvée Catherine [NP] **NV★★★★↻** The first time I tasted this, it was served side by side with Pol Roger Brut. This was better. It continues to be one of the finest bubblies in Canada. Very fine mousse with tiny, fast-paced, and lingering bubbles. Light mineral nose with an elegant, sweet, pastry dough flavour and hints of russet apple, lemon drops, and key lime pie. Dry and medium-bodied. This wine will improve with a couple of years aging but, since there is no vintage date, place a tag on the bottle with date of acquisition to know when a couple of years have passed.

Brut Rosé, Cuvée Catherine [NP] **NV★★★★↻** *Winemakers' Selection Award, Cuvée 2004.* Pale onion-skin colour with a lively mousse of tiny bubbles. Crisp acidity, dry, ripe cherry-berry flavours and superb balance.

Cabernet [NP] A blend of Bordeaux varieties. *(After 1997, this wine was labelled "Cabernet-Merlot, Meritage.")* **1997★★★◄** (CF63/ CS22/M15) A lighter red wine, in the Loire style. Drink soon. **1995★★★➔** Good depth and concentration. Drink now-2007.

Cabernet-Baco [Ont] Formerly sold under the brand name Loyalist. **2002★★➔** Cherry-purple colour. Closed and brooding nose at first, opens after half an hour to aromas of sour cherries, but palate retains its sharp edge and bitter finish. Drink now-2007.

Cabernet-Merlot [NP] After 1996, this wine was labelled Unfiltered. **1995★★★➔** Concentrated fruit with immense complexity. Coffee, dark chocolate, cedar, spice, tobacco, flowers, cassis, raspberry. Outstanding and long-lived. Drink now-2015. **1993★★★➔** Sweet, confectioner's sugar, berry, and cream bouquet, ripe and charming. Drink now-2008.

Cabernet-Merlot, Meritage [NP] **2002★★★➚** Garnet-purple hue with solid, oaky nose. Flavours of smoke, blackberries, spice, and herbs are concentrated and still undeveloped. Drink 2008-2015.

1999★★★➔ Herbaceous aroma with a taste of raspberries and milk chocolate. Accentuated tannins in the finish. Drink now-2009.

Cabernet-Merlot, Speck Family Reserve [NP] 1998★★★★↗ Deep garnet to the rim. Complex nose of blackberry, plum, flowers, and milky Ovaltine. Sweeter, riper, and fruitier than the regular Unfiltered version. Decant before serving. Drink now-2015.

Cabernet-Merlot, Unfiltered [NP] 2000★★★➔ Some bottle variation. I've recently encountered bottles with advanced colour of mahogany-garnet with browning rim. Oxidative with maturing flavours of cabbage, stewed prunes, cherry compote, smoke, mushrooms, and tar. Drink now. **1999★★★★☆➔** Deep garnet with a big, full, and multilayered bouquet of black fruits and lightly toasted nuts. Lighter than the 1998. Drink now-2010. **1998★★★☆➔** *Gold, All Canadian Wine Championships 2001.* Deep garnet with a dense, closed, herbal, oaky nose. Balanced acidity and tremendous complexity for drinking now-2012. **1997★★★★➔** *Gold, Ontario Wine Awards, 1999.* (CS51/M49) Big, full, rich, and complex with black fruit and toasted nut flavours. Full-bodied and long-lived. Drink now-2009. (*Prior to 1997, this wine was labelled without the Unfiltered moniker. See later vintages above.*) **1995★★★➔** Fullish, viscous, and soft. Drink now before the fruit dries up.

Cabernet Rosé [NP] For freshness, drink youngest vintage available; for complexity, cellar up to 4 years. **1996↓** (CF+CS) Implicitly sweet with seductive apple, plum, and strawberry flavours. **1995★★★↘** (CF only) Pretty salmon-pink hue with good sweet-tart balance and a charming nose of sugared strawberries. Had a nice spritz in its youth.

Cabernet Sauvignon-Cabernet Franc [NP] 1994★★↘ (CF45/CS50/M5) Deep garnet to the rim with a young, thick herbal nose and dense, juicy flavours of blackberry and tart plum. Tannic and long-lived. Drink now-2006.

Chardonnay, Non-Oaked (Sur Lie) [NP] 2003★★★↻ Young and vibrant with lovely body, dry, full fruit with hints of apple and peach and decent length. Drink now. **2001☒** Overpowered by Asian lady beetle. **1994★★★↘** Ripe, fruity nose and heavy, thick taste reflecting a heavier clay soil. Muscular, with a long, lingering, featherweight aftertaste. Drink now.

Chardonnay, Barrel-Fermented [NP] 2003★★★↗ Pale straw-gold with a fresh mountain-air impression with hints of wildflowers and pear. Packed with clean, ripe fruit flavours and plenty of new oak. Drink 2006-2011. **2002★★★↗** With this vintage, H-of-P became the first Canadian winery to bottle a VQA wine under screw cap, although 70% of the run was bottled with the traditional cork. Golden hue with billowing toasty, smoky, warmed-butter aroma. Big-bodied and tasty with apricot-butter flavour. Somewhat gritty tannins when it was young; they've softened substantially since then. Drink screw-cap-finished wine now-2009; cork-finished, now-2007. **1999** *Gold, All Canadian Wine Championships 2001.* **1995** ★ ★ ★ ↘ Crisp, oaky, toasty, brown-butter flavours. Good acidity for this hot vintage. **1994** ★ ★ ★ ↘ Austere nose with green acidity with some cheesy flavours developing. Drink soon. **1990** ★ ★ ★ ★ ↘ Amber gold with a nose of baked, if not over-baked, pastry. Buttery and full, it rapidly takes on nutty, toasted flavours. Holding well but fully mature. Drink up.

Chardonnay, Reserve (Prior to 1997, it was called "Proprietors Reserve.") [NP] **2002** ★ ★ ★ → Pale gold with a light poached pear and crème anglaise nose. A simple pleasure with mild fruit and nut notes. **1996** ★ ↘ Declassified to [Ont] in this feeble vintage. Clean, lemony flavours with a slight spritz, high alcohol, and a nuance of cream cheese. **1994** ★ ★ ↘ Rich, complex, flavoury, and charming. Drink now. **1990** ★ ★ ★ ↘ Nutty, with caramelized flavours of baked peach, molasses, shepherd's pie. Drink up.

Chardonnay, Speck Family Reserve [NP] **2002** ★ ★ ★ ★ → Brilliant gold with a thick, oily look. Aromas and flavour of warmed butter, toast, oak, nuts, caramel, lemon, and baked pears. Already wonderful, though it still has a long way to go. Drink now-2010. **1999** ★ ★ ★ ★ → Old gold colour with an intense, smoky, peaty, oaky toasty nose. A big mouthful with vanilla, caramel, and apple-butter flavours. Smooth, supple, strong, and long in the finish. Drink now-2009.

Gamay [NP] **2003** ★ ★ ★ → Ruby-cherry colour with an aroma of pencil shavings (more graphite, less cedar). Fresh, crisp, and tart with strawberry and cherry flavours and some red-currant nuances. Drink now-2006. **2002** ★ ★ ★ → Flavours are simple, joyful, and exuberant. More of a young Côtes du Rhône style than Beaujolais. Drink now-2006. **1996** ★ ★ ↘ Good colour, tart cherry aroma, and a lean finish. Tumbling rapidly.

Gewürztraminer [NP] **1999** ★ ★ ★ ↗ Deep yellow-gold with a youthful, spritzy palate. Bright, crisp, and vibrant with years of devel-opment ahead. Drink now-2012. **1998** ★ ★ ☆ → Deep yellow-gold with an assertive if not dull nose of sweat, honey, beeswax, and motor oil. Thick texture and relatively balanced palate. Can age but has nowhere to go. Drink now.

Merlot [NP] **2001** ★ ★ ★ ↗ Maroon garnet with a big nose of plum, oak, and pencil shavings. The nose is powerful enough to overpower the Asian lady beetle taint in the background. Plum, apple, and sour cherry flavours and a bitter rosemary-thyme flavour. Drink now-2010. **2000** ★ ★ ★ ↗ Garnet to the rim. Austere, oaky nose with plenty of fruit for the future. Lush, fullish, with mouth-cleansing acidity. Drink now-2012. **1999** *Gold, All Canadian Wine Champi-onships 2001.* **1998** ★ ★ ★ ★ → Screaming with complexity and rich flavours. Drink now-2008. **1997** ★ ★ ★ → *Gold, Ontario Wine Awards 1999.* A powerhouse in its youth, but not tasted since then.

Probably near its peak, so drink up. **1991★★★→** Loaded with ripe, plummy fruit, with chocolate, coffee, cedar, and spice. Marvellous, thick, California-style. Fully mature. Drink up.

Pinot Noir, Unfiltered [NP] **2002★★★→** Ruby-garnet with an elegant scent of strawberry, red cherry, and spice. Richly layered, soft flavours, and an enticing, earthy, tannic finish. Drink now-2010. **1998** *Gold, All Canadian Wine Championships 2001*. Fruit is predominantly from Reimer Vineyard. More concentration than previous vintages with good grip and some nice raspberry tones. Drink soon. **1992↓** A good effort in a poor vintage. Now over the hill. **1991↓** Once a big, bruisin' California-style wine, thickly textured and deeply flavoured with toasty, coffee/chocolate nuances, plum butter, and orange biscuit. Recently deceased.

Pinot Noir, Speck Family Reserve [NP] **2002★★★↗** Dark ruby-cherry colour with a dense bouquet of black fruits, dried cherries, sandalwood, saddle leather, earth, and sweat. Tannic, herbal, concentrated fruit flavour and enticing finish. Drink 2006-2010.

Riesling, Dry [NP] **2002★★★→** Pale gold with a light lemon-petrol nose. Crisp acidity and tart, grapefruity taste. Drink now-2007. **2001☒** Asian lady beetle detected. **1999★★★→** Fullish bouquet of honeyed apple with a hint of prickle on the palate. Ready to drink. **1996★★★↘** Crisp with citrus flavours and strong scents of honey and petrol. **1994★★★→** Complex lemony flavours with a strong spine of acidity.

Riesling Icewine [NP] **2002★★★★↗** Rich, dense, and intensely sweet honeyed nose. Lemon-lime flavours, mildly herbal with rosemary nuances. Drink 2007-2017. **2000** *Gold, VinExpo 2003; Gold, Challenge International du Vin 2003; Gold, Japan Wine Challenge 2002.* **1999** *Gold, Japan Wine Challenge 2001; Gold, All Canadian Wine Championships 2001.* **1996★★★★→** Intense with flavours of pear and applesauce. High, refreshing acidity. Drink now-2012. **1995★★★★→** Very rich, unctuous. Drink now-2010. **1994★★★★→** Terrific acidity, amazing balance. Drink now-2015. **1991★★★★→** Lovely with flavours of caramel and raisins like a fine Tokaji Aszu. Drink now. **1989★★★★→** Still delicious. Drink now-2010.

Riesling, Off-Dry [NP] **2003★★★→** Pale gold with an even paler pink reflection. Crisp orange-apricot nose with balanced acids and residual sugar. Light but pleasant. Drink now-2009. **2002★★★↗** Straw-gold with aromas of apple, honeysuckle, and hints of petrol. Zesty lemon taste with some apple fruit sweetness. Drink now-2008.

Riesling, Reserve [NP] **2002★★★★↗** Very pale, silvery green-gold colour. Green, grapey, leafy, herbal, petrol, and lime notes. Great structure, clean flavours, mouth-wateringly delicious. Drink now-2010. **2001☒** Asian lady beetle detected. **2000★★★↗** Silvery-gold with fine bubbles forming on the inside of the glass. Lemon-grapefruit nose with hints of pith. Orange-grapefruit flavours and hints of white currant. Zippy acidity and clean, lingering finish. Drink now-2009. **1999** ★ ★ ★ ↗ *Gold, All Canadian Wine Championships 2001*. Gold with a pear, apple, and honey bouquet and developing hints of petrol. Very lemony taste. Drink now-2009. **1997** ★ ★ ★ ☆ → Gold colour with apple and pear aromas. Tart, lemony taste with good body. Drink now-2009. **1995** ★ ★ ★ ★ → Bone dry with a stunning petrol nose, lovely texture, and a long aftertaste. Drink now. **1994** ★ ★ ★ → Deep gold with an unexpected Burgundian reek. More like Meursault than Alsace at first. Honey and oak flavour. Has lemony snap on the palate. Drink now-2007. **1992** ★ ★ ★ ☆ → Deep gold with apple, honey, pear, and petrol notes. Lemony. Seems more youthful than the '04, but drink now.

Riesling, Special Select Late Harvest [NP] **2000** ★ ★ ★ ★ ↗ Old gold with a bouquet of caramelized lemon slices and orange zest. Rich, fresh, sweet, and juicy with pure, elegant mineral flavours. Drink now-2020.

Riesling, Speck Family Reserve [NP] **2002** ★ ★ ★ ★ ↗ Bright gold with a fullish, oily, petrol nose and rich nuances of lemon and white peach. Big, bold, and, for now, brusque. High alcohol, solid body, and structure. Needs time to mature. Drink 2006-2015.

Rosé, Dry [NP] **2004** ★ ★ ★ ☆ ↻ (Gam24.5/PN18.5/Z57) Violet-pink hue with a tart cherry and cranberry aroma. Fullish palate, dry, and vinous. Chill well. **2003** ★ ★ ★ ↻ [Ont] Declassified appellation suggests inclusion of a hybrid, perhaps Baco Noir. Flavours have a candied but generally pleasant overtone. Good acidity and solid mouthfeel. **2002** *Rosé of the Year, All Canadian Wine Championships 2003*.

Sauvignon Blanc [NP] **2003** ★ ★ ★ ★ ↻ Yowza! Even I love it! Pale silver-gold colour, tremendous, fresh gooseberry aroma and crisp, spritzy texture. A fabulous summer sipper or winter aperitif. **2002** ★ ★ → ↻ Clean peachy-lemon flavours with a hint of passionfruit. **2001** ☒ *Best White, Cuvée 2002*. If this was the best, with its overpowering Asian lady beetle taint, I cringe to think what it competed against.

Seyval Blanc, Select Late Harvest [Ont] **1994** ★ ★ ★ ↘ Balanced, rich, sweet, elegant, charming, and complete. **1989** ★ ★ ★ ↘ Rereleased in 1995 honouring the 200th anniversary of patron Henry. Fully mature with a superb raisiny nose, but fruit beginning to dry up.

Vidal, Select Late Harvest [Ont] **2003** ★ ★ ★ ☆ ↗ Straw-gold with fresh pear and lemon aromas, hints of mint and green, leafy notes. Surprisingly sweet. Nose does not betray the level of residual sugar. Fresh flavours but best to drink now. **1994** ★ ★ → Cardboardy nose in its youth but very sweet with balancing acidity. Drink now-2009.

Vidal, Special Select Late Harvest [Ont]   **2001** *Gold, All Canadian Wine Championships 2003.* **1999** *Gold, All Canadian Wine Championships 2001.* **1998** ★ ★ ★ ★ → Terrific still.

• **HERNDER ESTATE WINERY** (1607 8th Avenue, St. Catharines, ON, L2R 6P7 / Phone: 905-684-3300 / Fax: 905-684-3303 / Email: wine@hernder.com / Website: www.hernder.com)

(Est. 1993) The Hernder family has been growing grapes since 1939, when Gottfried Hernder purchased a mixed farm with a small acreage of native labrusca grapes. After his death in 1968, son Fred bought the farm and began to acquire others. In 1977, he was crowned Ontario Grape King, the youngest farmer to be so named. By 1988, when the government was paying farmers to pull out labrusca grapes, Fred began the switch to the more desirable vinifera and hybrid varieties. That same year he purchased a large cattle barn and converted it into a winemaking facility. Expansion has continued at a rapid pace, with the building of a picturesque visitor centre featuring an entrance through a covered bridge over a small lake with a fountain, a banquet facility that is a popular venue for weddings, and a large tasting room and retail shop. Hernder owns 9 farms encompassing about 650 acres, and almost 400 of them are dedicated to grapevines. Production in 2004 was 24,000 cases.

Winemaker: Ray Cornell / Vineyard Manager: Chris Hernder

Baco Noir [Ont]   **2001** ★ ★ → Soft, maturing flavours. Plain and decent BBQ material. **1996** ★ ★ ↘ Powerful coffee, licorice, and sour-cherry nose with very high acidity. Drink soon.

Baco Noir, Reserve [Ont]   **2002** ★ ★ ★ ☆ ↗ Inky-garnet with an aroma of blackberries mushed up in table cream. Big, juicy flavours of raspberry, black cherry, and tart apples. Needs time to soften up. Drink now-2010.

Cabernet Franc [NP]   **1999** ★ ★ → Brick colour. Soft, herbal balance and fully mature. Drink now.

Cabernet Sauvignon, Reserve [NP]   **2000** ★ ★ ★ ↗ Dark garnet with an aroma of red and black fruits. Taste is of red currants. Needs time. Drink 2006-2011.

Chardonnay, Icewine [NP]   **2002** ★ ★ ★ ★ ↗ Rich green-gold colour with a soft herbal nose. Softer on the palate than most icewines and a smidgen more complex, with unusual nuances of butterscotch and toasted hazelnut. Drink now-2009.

Chenin Blanc [NP]   **2002** ★ ★ ☆ ↻ Gold with a crisp nose that hints of lemon-scented disinfectant. Clean and correct with simple flavours.

Foch, Old Vines [Ont]   **2002** ★ ★ ★ ↗ Opaque inky-garnet shade with a smoky nose of chocolate milk, plum pudding, custard, and caramel. Spirity with strong rustic flavours. Severe finish for now. Drink now-2008.

Gewürztraminer [NP]   2002★★→ Yellow-gold colour with a bright, spicy tangerine-peel aroma. Crisp, sweetish, honeyed palate but bitter grapefruit pith flavours spoil the finish.

Meritage, Estate Unfiltered [NP]   2000★★★→ Inconsistent. Some bottles seemed unknit with an eggy nose, while others were oaky, smoky, and toasty with nut, plum, and black-cherry flavours. Drink now-2010.

Merlot [NP]   2002★★★★↗ Purple-garnet with an undeveloped nose. Dense, juvenile plummy fruit, very tannic. Drink 2007-2012.

Morio Muscat [NP]   2002★★★↺ Sweet and wild with flavours of white plum, apples, perfume, and lanolin. Clean, dry finish.

Riesling [NP]   2003★↺ Sweetish and candied with a processed applesauce nose.

Riesling, "Millennium" [NP]   2000★★★★→ Deepening amber-gold hue. Very aromatic with spicy eucalyptus flavours. Honeyed, fruity, floral, and luscious. Drink now-2012.

Riesling, "Mockingbird" [NP]   2002★↺ Yellow-gold with a non-descript nose. Simple and quaffable.

Riesling, Reserve [NP]   2003★★★→ Pale silvery gold with a sweet grapefruit taste and excellent texture. Drink now-2011.

• **HERNDER FARM (St. Catharines, NP)** – Half of the 96-acre Masterson Farm was purchased by Fred Hernder in 1997. (The other half went to the Speck brothers, who renamed their portion Short Hill Vineyard.) The 43-acre property lies between 8th Avenue and Pelham Road and between 3rd and 5th Streets Louth. The Hernders have laser-beamed the land to a slope of 1 in. per 100 ft. toward the middle of the site, with a central culvert installed to prevent water accumulation. The soil is a reddish sand with some clay patches. Once the acreage is planted with Chardonnay and Riesling grapes, the entire section will be underdrained between the rows.

• **HERON POND BENCHLAND ESTATES (Vineland, NP)** – Located next to the Kew Vineyard, this gently sloped, north-facing property includes open fields, bushlands, ponds, and 48 acres of grapes. Owner Graham Rennie grows Chardonnay, Merlot, Cabernet Sauvignon, Cabernet Franc, and Pinot Noir, which is sold to Stratus Winery.

• **HIDDEN BENCH WINERY** (4152 Locust Lane, Beamsville, ON, L0R 1B2 / Phone: 905-563-8700 / Fax: 416-231-4403 / Email: hthiel@ hiddenbench.com / Website: www.hiddenbench.com)

(Est. 2003) In 2002, Harald Thiel, a Toronto businessman in the audio-visual field, traded in his shares in the company and bought the 33.5-acre Locust Lane Vineyard on the Beamsville Bench just across the road from EastDell Estates. At that time, it had 15.3 acres of grapes planted since 1998, including 5 acres of Chardonnay, 1.7 acres of Cabernet Franc, 1 acre of Cabernet Sauvignon, 2.5 acres of Merlot, 2.5 acres of at least 5 clones of Pinot Noir, 2.1 acres of Riesling, and 1.5 acres of Syrah. In 2004, Thiel added .5 acre of Malbec, 3.75 acres of 5 additional Dijon clones of Pinot Noir, 2.75 more acres of Syrah, and an acre of Viognier. Older plantings are spaced at 1,200 vines per acre while the more recent ones are more densely planted at 2,700 vines per acre. Thiel believes the more densely planted vines will give better fruit, especially in the case of the Pinot Noir. Last year he was evaluating his Riesling and considered replacing it with Pinot Noir. That may have been done by now. The vineyard is approximately 1.6 km south of the lake and between 25-30 m above it. It has a 5% east-facing slope and is composed of typical middle-bench Chinguacousy clay loam with a fair amount of loose stone. It is both tiled for drainage and drip-irrigated. Grapes are thinned 10%-25% at veraison, depending on the vintage, with an objective of harvesting between 2.5 and 3 t. per acre. There were 1,800 cases of wine made in 2004 with an eye to increasing production to as much as 8,000 cases by 2009. In 2004, Thiel also purchased the highly acclaimed 26-acre Rosomel Vineyard nearby, and signed on its former owner, Roman Prydatkewycz, as his vineyard manager.

Winemaker: TBA / Vineyard Manager: Roman Prydatkewycz

Wines not available for appraisal before press time.

• **HILLEBRAND** (1249 Niagara Stone Road [Hwy 55], Niagara-on-the-Lake, ON, L0S 1J0 / Phone: 905-468-7123 / Toll-Free: 1-800-582-8412 / Fax: 905-468-7123 *or* 905-468-4789 / Email: info@hillebrand.com / Website: www.hillebrand.com)

(Est. 1979) Founded by Vineland-born engineer Joseph Pohorly as Newark Wines. Joe planted a 35-acre vineyard with hybrid and vinifera grapes at Virgil, then a one-traffic-light-town on the highway to Niagara-on-the-Lake. The wines weren't terribly complex or even consistent, but they were better than much of the dreck being produced at that time by the Big Six. However, sales were slow and Pohorly's pockets were fast becoming empty. In 1982, a German company, Scholl & Hillebrand, purchased a large chunk of the operation. Pohorly stayed on and even helped to develop the company's first icewines, but by 1984 he cashed out entirely. The winery went through a series of winemakers until it finally settled on the very talented J-L Groux, who helped solidify Hillebrand's reputation as a superior producer. Groux believed in the importance of vineyards to achieve quality and, by respecting his growers, was able to draw the best out of his Lakeshore, Queenston Heights, and Beamsville Bench suppliers. In 1994, Andrés Wines purchased the winery. Today, Hillebrand produces everything from Canadian Chablis and other bulk blends, a line of VQA "fighting varietals," as well as premium and super premium wines. Under the Showcase and Trius labels, the winery bottles many vineyard-designated Chardonnays, Cabernets, Merlots, Rieslings, and a decent méthode champenoise sparkler. In fact, trying to stay on top of the numerous experimental bottlings has been a challenge, even for geeks and gazetteers like me. In 2002, for example, I tasted 7 different Chardonnay bottlings in the Showcase series alone. They explored different vineyards, different oaks, and different aging regimens. Groux's work has contributed immensely to a better understanding of the Niagara region and its subappellations. In 2004, Groux left Hillebrand to join another winery, but by press time a new winemaker had not yet been named. The winery has received accolades from the music world, for its annual music festivals – Hillebrand Jazz and Blues at the Winery – as well as from the world of gastronomy for its excellent on-site restaurant operated under the direction of master chef Antonio de Luca. Total production in 2004 was 180,000 cases.

Winemakers: Natalie Reynolds (2001-present); J-L Groux (1987-2004, 1998 Winemaker of the Year); Benoit Huchin (1987-1991); Andreas Gestaltner (1984-1987); Jurgen Heldig (1983); Peter Gamble (1982); Bruno Criveller (1982); Joseph Pohorly (1981) / Vineyard Manager: Walter Horr

Collector's Choice Label

Chardonnay, Barrel-Aged [NP]   Part barrel fermented, part stainless-steel fermented, and all aged in barrels for less than a year. **2001 ★ ★ ★ ↗** Ripe apple and pears-in-syrup nose. Rich butter, oak, vanilla, and lemon flavours, well balanced with a hint of bitterness in the finish. Drink now-2006. **1999 ★ ★ ↘** Amber hue. Seems over the hill and over-oaked with a hot finish. Drink up. **1994 ★ ★ ↘** Amber hue. Some butterscotch and pineapple flavours remaining. Drink up.

Cabernet-Merlot, Barrel-Aged [NP]   **2001 ☒** This would have been a lovely wine if not for the Asian lady beetle taint that overwhelms the nose and leaves a very bitter taste. **1999 ★ ★ ★ ↗** Still tight with hard tannins and a raw spine of acidity. There is plenty of fruit, but the question is will it outlast the mouth-drying tannins. Drink now-2010. **1998 ★ ★ ★ ↗** Lovely bright ruby-garnet hue with the slightest brick red around the edges. Ripe, smooth, plenty of fruit, and a wonderful, soft, supple texture, thanks to more delicate oaking. A great vintage well executed. Drink now-2013. **1995 ★ ★ ★ →** Deep ruby-garnet with significant mahogany reflections. Over-oaked with new wood, giving it a dry texture and a strong, smoky cigar-box nose. Lots of fruit, but can it break surface with all that wood? Drink now. **1993** ★ ★ ★ ↘ Ruby-brown colour. Fruit fully mature with a lively balance of acid and tannin. Drink soon. **1992** ↓ A very poor vintage that never got past first base. Heavy chaptalization could not bring any fruit into this bitter, cabbagy, unforgiving wine. Now, it's gone. **1989** ★ ★ ★ → Ruby garnet with a very brown core. Fully mature, healthy fruit with lovely flavours of smoked nuts, sweetmeats, and fruitcake. Drink now.

Harvest Label

Cabernet-Merlot [NP] **2002** ★ ★ ★ → Light garnet colour and soft fruitbread nose. Clean, pure, varietal flavours are light and straightforward with both black and red berry notes. Can be aged for up to a year or 2 at most.

Cabernet Sauvignon [NP] **2003** ★ ★ → (NonVQA in this vintage) Garnet colour and odd, hybrid, grapey nose. Juvenile-tasting fruit, but there's an old butter nuance I find disturbing. **2002** ★ ★ ★ → Lively garnet with pink edges. Fruity bouquet with cherry/plum aromas and some tobacco/veggie notes. A well-made, straightforward quaffer that may improve over the next year.

Chardonnay [NP] Cool-fermented in stainless steel with partial oak aging for complexity. **2002** ★ ★ ★ → Pale gold with ripe pear and apple flavours and a kiss of oak. Implicitly sweet and easy-drinking with a clean finish. **2001** ★ ★ → Very strong nuances of oak and butter. A particularly woody style.

Gamay Noir [NP] **2003** ★ ★ → (NonVQA in this vintage) Deep ruby colour with full body and dried berry notes. Somewhat tough at first sip. **2002** ★ ★ → Ruby-cherry hue with a clean, juicy strawberry taste. Light but lovely flavour. Drink soon while still fresh and fruity.

Gewürztraminer [NP] **2002** ★ ★ ★ → Soft peachy, lanolin aroma with a honeyed taste. Yummy with Asian food.

Merlot [NP] **2003** ★ ★ ★ → (NonVQA in this vintage) Garnet with lean and clean wood notes in the bouquet. Some blueberry and Damson plum flavours and a well-structured if short finish. Drink now. **2002** ★ ↻ Vegetal, green, and unripe.

Muscat Reserve [NP] Includes Muscat Ottonel, Muscat Gelber, and Muscat Canelli. **2002** ★ ★ ★ → Wonderfully refreshing with sweet, floral hints. Perfectly balanced acidity and residual sugar. A superb summer sipper and especially suited to matching with salads.

Pinot Noir Rosé [NP] **1994** ↓ Lovely strawberry aroma; medium-full body; juicy, fruity taste.

Riesling [NP] **2002** ★ ★ ★ → Straw-gold hue, zippy lemon-lime aroma, and clean, soft mouthfeel. Drink now-2007. **1994** ★ ↘ Sweetish with high acidity and a candied lime flavour.

Hillebrand Estates Label

Eiswein [preVQA] **1986** ★★★★→ Deep brown, caramelized-raisin flavours, high acidity, and excellent balance. Excellent acid balance suggests it may continue to keep for a few more years, but why wait? It's fully developed now. **1983** ★★★→ This first vintage was picked in October and held in cold storage until December temperatures dropped to -12°C. The grapes were then taken outside and left overnight to freeze solid. It was all in the name of experimentation and learning.

Marechal Foch [Ont] **1993** ↓ Deep black cherry; gamy nose of smoke, sweat, and leather; sweetish at first but lean and tart, short finish.

Vidal Icewine, Barrel-Aged [NP] Hillebrand was the first to barrel age its icewines, at first to the derision of critics. They have proven to be softer and more complex than stainless-steel tank-held wines. **2002** ★★★★

Vidal Icewine, Zabek Vineyard [NP] Hillebrand's icewines generally tend to be rich, thick, and syrupy. **1996** ★★★★→ Best Dessert Wine, Cuvée 1998. I have a special fondness for this vintage, as it's the only icewine I ever helped to harvest. Having done it once, I have no desire ever to do it again. The wine is luscious and lingering. Fully mature but will hold for at least another decade. **1995** ★★★→ Like concentrated pear syrup. Drink now-2015. **1994** ★★★→ Soft, creamy, thick, and forward with apricot, raisin, and honey. Fully mature. Drink now-2010.

Vidal, Late Harvest [Ont] **2002** ★★★→ Gold, Ontario Wine Awards 2004. Peach and, especially, pineapple aromas with a lovely gentle sweetness, perfect for casual sipping or pairing with desserts. It may seem blasphemous, but I'd happily sit on a shaded summer terrace with a glass of this chilled with an ice cube.

Showcase Label

Cabernet Franc, Glenlake Vineyard [NP] **2001** ★→ Plenty of red berry fruit but marred by stink of Asian lady beetle. **2000** ★★★↗ Deep garnet with a predominantly herbal bouquet showing additional aromas of black cherry, spice, leather, and old cream. Juvenile fruit flavours are still slightly fat and sweetish, but crisp acidity and balance suggest slow development. Drink now-2008. **1999** ★↘ Prune colour and nose. Fruit is drying up while tannins persist. Drink up. **1998** ★★★★↗ Gold, All Canadian Wine Championships 2000. Solid garnet to the rim. Nose is particularly elegant, with mature Bordeaux-like nuances of cranberry, raspberry, dried cherry, wet earth, and decaying leaves. Supple and round in the mouth with balanced, mature fruit flavours. Drink now-2010. **1997** ★★★→ Pale garnet with a thinning and browning rim. Hints of pencil shavings and eraser, mildly vegetal, like sage and oregano. Advancing flavours and a tough, lean core. Drink soon. **1995** ★ ★ ★ **➔** Maturing and delicious. Drink now-2007.

Cabernet Franc, Icewine [NP]   **2002** ★ ★ ★ ★ ★ **↗** Brilliant pale ruby-garnet colour with a subtle bouquet of raspberry, black cherry, lemon rind, and even a hint of black pepper. Ravishing. Drink now-2020.

Cabernet Sauvignon, Glenlake Vineyard [NP]   **2001** ★ **➔** Some complexity but spoiled by smell of Asian lady beetle. **2000** ★ ★ ★ **↗** Deep garnet with a bouquet of ripe black fruits along with some green pepper notes. Lush and silky palate turns dry and dusty. Needs time to relax. Drink 2006-2012. **1997** ★ ★ ★ **↗** Deep garnet, looks younger than the 2000. Taut and dense with an aroma of pencil shavings, deeply submerged black fruits, and a tough, bitter tannic finish. Just a bit short of excellent. Drink now-2010. **1995** ★ ★ ★ **➔** Gold, Cuvée 2000. Peaking. Drink now.

Chardonnay, Glenlake Vineyard [NP]   **2002** (See below) A year of wild experimentation on the part of winemaker J-L Groux – numerous barrels were bottled individually to identify subtle nuances of oak. I had a tough time distinguishing them. **2000** ★ ★ ★ **➔** Bright gold with tiny bubbles adhering to the inside of the glass. Elegant bouquet of toasted nuts, lemon butter, and stewed pears. Good acidity and fine balance. Can still improve. Drink now-2008. **1999** ★ ★ ★ **↘** Light gold colour with signs of age beginning to creep into a bouquet of roasted coffee beans, warmed milk, fresh churned sweet butter, custard, and nuts. Some bitterness in the finish. Fully mature. **1998** (See below) Three experimental versions were aged in Allier, Vosges, and American barrels for wine geeks to explore and understand cask influence. **1995** ★ ★ ★ **↘** Clean, rich, deeply scented with notes of butter, pineapple, lemon, caramel, nuts, vanilla, and new French oak. Medium-bodied with creamy texture and balance, but not high in acidity. Past its peak.

Chardonnay, Glenlake Vineyard, Allier Oak [NP]   **1998** ★ ★ ★ ★ **➔** Restrained, elegant, poached pear and crème anglaise flavours, balanced and beautifully structured. Drink soon.

Chardonnay, Glenlake Vineyard, American Oak [NP] **1998** ★ ★ ★ ★ **↘** Fat, buttery, coconut-macadamia flavours, now starting to taste oxidized. Rapidly becoming flat and flabby.

Chardonnay, Glenlake Vineyard, Vosges Oak [NP] **1998** ★ ★ ★ ★ **➔** Soft, creamy, vanilla-caramel flavours, peaking, will begin to tire soon.

Chardonnay, Glenlake Vineyard, Barrel 2190, Nevers Oak [NP]   **2002** ★ ★ ★ ☆ **↗** Power and delicacy in this version. Drink now-2008.

Chardonnay, Glenlake Vineyard, Barrel 3116, Vosges Oak [NP]   **2002** ★ ★ ★ ☆ **↗** Powerful with subtle, nutty flavours. Drink now-2008.

Chardonnay, Glenlake Vineyard, Barrel 4138, Tronçais Oak [NP] **2002** ★ ★ ★ ☆ ↗ I found this indistinguishable from the Nevers oak bottling. Drink now-2008.

Chardonnay, Glenlake Vineyard, Barrel 7048, Jupilles Oak [NP] **2002** ★ ★ ★ ↗ Closer to Nevers and Tronçais than to Vosges. But there is a hint of nuttiness. Drink now-2008.

Chardonnay, Glenlake Vineyard, Unfiltered, Bottled with the Lees [NP] **2001** ★ ★ ★ ★ → Cloudy gold colour (from the lees) with tiny bubbles adhering to the inside of the glass. Bouquet of buttered nuts. Sweet, supple, and thick with a slight bitterness in the finish. At its peak. Drink now-2006.

Chardonnay, Mori Vineyard, Barrel 2230, Nevers Oak [NP] **2002** ★ ★ ★ ☆ ↗ Lighter, more delicate, and slightly more floral in nature than the Glenlake version. Sweeter nose than the Jupilles barrel. Drink now-2008.

Chardonnay, Mori Vineyard, Barrel 7041, Jupilles Oak [NP] **2002** ★ ★ ★ ☆ ↗ Paler in colour and more delicate in flavour than the Glenlake barrels. A hint creamier than the Nevers barrel. Drink now-2008.

Merlot, Glenlake Vineyard [NP] **2001** ★ → Nice lush texture but nose is spoiled by Asian lady beetle. **2000** ★ ★ ↘ *Gold, All Canadian Wine Championships 2002*. Garnet with a brick colour settling in at the rim. Excessive tiny bubbles form in the glass with time. Some burnt-rubber notes along with charred popcorn and diesel oil. Tart and unknit with lovely texture but no charm. Must have been a sick bottle. **1999** ★ ★ ★ ★ → *Gold, All Canadian Wine Championships 2000*. **1998** ★ ★ ★ ↗ Garnet with a pale brick edge and minuscule bubbles forming along the rim. Maturing nose of earth, cedar, and fruit compote. Balanced with a tannic core. Drink 2006-2012. **1995** ★ ★ ★ → A lovely expression vintage of a lovely vintage. Drink soon.

Pinot Noir, Glenlake Vineyard, Barrel-Aged [NP] **2002** ★ ★ ★ ↗ Bright ruby hue with a pink rim. Shy but inviting nose and sweet, ripe, clean, balanced flavours with good acid grip. Drink now-2009. **2000** ★ ★ ★ ★ → Good balance and now at its peak. Flavours include cherry, strawberry, and a smidgen of plum. Drink now-2008. **1999** ★ ★ ★ → Bright ruby with a hint of tile on the edge. Big cigar-box nose. Vibrant red-fruit flavours with higher alcohol and higher acidity than the 1998. Drink now-2011. **1998** ★ ★ ★ → Ruby colour with tile at the rim. Mature fruit nose hints also at earth, decaying leaves, and strawberry compote. Lovely texture and a clean, light finish. Drink now-2009.

Riesling, Icewine [NP] **2003** ★ ★ ★ ★ ☆ ↗ Gold with a clean, concentrated aroma of honeyed pears, boiled and strained. Thick and unctuous apple and pear purée. **2002** ★ ★ ★ ★ ★ ↗ Astonishing, rich, and delicious while vibrant and snappy. Pear purée, pineapple, honey, and lemon drops. Nectar. Drink 2010-2025.

Vidal, Icewine, Barrel-Fermented [NP] **2003** ★ ★ ★ ★ ↗ Gold shade with aromas of plastic, pear essence, eau-de-vie, and caramel custard. Very sweet and very rich with an orange-lemon acidity. Drink now-2013. **2002** ★ ★ ★ ★ ★ ↗ *Gold, Concours Mondiale, Belgium 2004.* Close to perfection. Soft, lovely crème brûlée nose. Balanced acidity and fabulous apricot, mango, butternut flavours. Drink now-2015.

<u>**Trius Label**</u>

Brut, Methode Classique [NP] **NV** ★ ★ ★ ↻ *Gold, Cuvée 2003; Best Sparkling Wine, Cuvée 2000 & 1998.* Some batches are better than others. I've had great bottles and merely good ones. Without a vintage date, there's no way to tell.

Cabernet Franc [NP] **2002** ★ ★ ★ ↗ Deep ruby-garnet hue with a big bouquet of ripe blackberries, black cherry, licorice, and pink bubblegum. Terrific balance, lovely supple texture, and pure fruit flavours. Drink 2006-2010.

Cabernet Sauvignon [NP] **2002** ★ ★ ★ ↗ Deep black-red colour with a peppery, smoky, and black-currant nose. Concentrated plum and cedar flavours with thick, luscious texture. Needs a long wait. Drink 2008-2016.

Chardonnay [NP] **2002** ★ ★ ★ ↻ Pale gold with a mellow, pears-in-cream bouquet. Then, "Pow!," high alcohol. Best drunk young.

Chardonnay, Barrel-Fermented [NP] **2002** ★ ★ ★ → Glorious gold hue with a gently oaked bouquet of lemon zest, ripe pear, and buttered toast. Sweet flavour, supple and potent. Drink now-2007.

Chardonnay, Barrel-Fermented, Lakeshore Vineyards [NP] **2001** ★ ★ ★ → Produced from free-run juice, barrel-fermented, and aged 3 months on the lees. Rich gold hue. Sweet vanilla nose with a thick palate-coating texture and a long, supple, earthy taste. Hint of bitterness in the finish. Drink now-2006. **1995** ★ ★ ★ ↘ Rich gold, enticing fruit, and crème caramel nose, well structured with pure, if not intense, flavours. Drink up. **1994** ★ ★ ↘ Balanced with some vanilla notes but tired and oxidizing.

Chardonnay, Barrel-Fermented, Niagara-on-the-Lake [NP] **2001** ★ ★ ★ → Has a slightly sharper nose than the Lakeshore Vineyards version. Lighter, fruitier, finer, and leaner with flavours of baked pear, oak. Drink before the end of 2006.

Grand Red [NP] **2001** ★ ★ ★ ★ ↗ *Prestige Trophy, Citadelles du Vin, Bordeaux 2004.* (CF55/CS40/M5) Big, rich, closed up, with subdued black currant and dark-chocolate flavours. Thick texture and a long finish. Drink 2008-2016. **2000** ★ ★ ★ ★ ↗ (CF16/CS50/M34) More than just the price is grand. After tasting more than a thousand barrels of wine, then winemaker J-L Groux chose the best 30 casks to create his first vintage of this "super-Niagaran."

Merlot [NP] **2002** ★ ★ ★ ↗ Clean, fruity, and full-bodied with a rich plum, blackberry, and spiced-cream bouquet. Supple, balanced, and tannic. Drink now-2010.

Red [NP] A blend of the 3 most common Bordeaux grapes – Cabernet Franc, Cabernet Sauvignon, and Merlot – in varying proportions from year to year. **2002** ★ ★ ★ ★ ↗ (CF67/CS18/M15) A complete, dense, and wonderful bottle with loads of plum, cherry, and cedar flavours. Very complex and moderately long-lived. Drink 2006-2012. **2001** ★ ★ ↗ A most difficult wine to assess. On the one hand, this concentrated red has smoky, toasty, hazelnutty, floral, tangerine-peel aromas, plummy flavours, and a rich, satiny texture. Unfortunately, it also lets slip some occasionally overpowering odours of Asian lady beetle. Drink now-2010. **2000** ★ ★ ★ ★ ↗ *Gold, All Canadian Wine Championships 2003*. Garnet with a ruby rim. Has a faraway nose, still locked up deep in the bowl. Black cherry, black currant, and lightly charred oak aromas with the fruit dominating. Ripe, silky, yet sinewy texture with a mouth-drying, tannic finish. Drink now-2012. **1998** ★ ★ ★ ★ ↗ Brilliant black-cherry-garnet hue. Full, dense fruit nose is beginning to open up, introducing some earthy notes. Thick, ripe, and lush, goes down like liquid velvet. Soft, supple, round, and persistent. Drink now-2015. **1997** ★ ★ ★ → *Gold, All Canadian Wine Championships 2000*. Garnet with some brick reflections along the edge. High-toned fruit smell, like black-raspberry candies. There's plenty of lean fruit but the woolly tannins deliver a very dry finish. Drink now-2008. **1995** ★ ★ ★ ★ ↗ *Best Red, Cuvée 1998*. Peppery with fine acidity, floral hints, exotic smoky-oaky nuances, flavours of coffee and spiced vanilla cake, rich, blackberry-fruit flavours. Drink now-2012. **1994** ★ ★ ↘ (CF53/CS46/M2) Hint of cough medicine, lean, with hints of licorice and violet. Drying up, drink soon. **1993** ★ ★ ★ ↘ (CF10/CS40/M50) Strong, vibrant, perfumed nose when young, now completely settled down, with plenty of tannin, high acidity, and good fruit extract. Drink now-2006. **1992** Not produced. **1991** ★ ★ ★ ★ → *Pichon-Longueville Trophy, International Wine & Spirits Competition; Best Red, Cuvée 1995*. (CF30/CS66/M4) Peppery with earthy, humus aromas. Plummy taste. Very rich with good extract and balanced acid and tannin. Drink now-2009. **1990** ★ ★ ★ → (CF25/CS50/M25) Refined, sweetish bouquet. Fully mature, drink now. **1989** ★ ★ ★ ↘ (CF16/CS70/M14) Black-currant, black-cherry flavours, with minty, licorice, meaty flavours and vegetal notes. Fully mature. Drink up.

Riesling [NP] **2003** ★ ★ ★ ★ ↗ Silvery-gold with a clean, lemon/grapefruit nose. The taste is loaded with zing. Lovely, crisp, lemony acidity with sweet apple and mandarin flavours. Drink now-2015. **2002** ★ ★ ★ ★ ↗ *Gold, All Canadian Wine Championships 2002*. Pale, straw-gold hue. Bouquet is undeveloped but showing hints of petrol and Meyer lemon. Taste has fresh flavours of ripe apple and grapefruit. Racy acidity and deep mineral flavours suggest a long,

slow, brilliant development. Drink 2007-2015. **1999**★★★☆→
Brilliant gold with a fullish lemony nose with mild petrol notes.
Good body and balanced acidity. Drink now-2009. **1992**★★→
Extremely high in acidity when young. The question was not, Would
the wine last? but, Would it ever be drinkable? By 1999, it was still
"developmentally challenged"; more recently, it has become more
complex, although the dryness and high acidity suggest longer cellaring may be required. Try again after 2007.

Vidal Icewine [NP] **2002** ★ ★ ★ ★ ★ ↗ Gold, Concours Mondiale,
Belgium 2004; Gold, Cuvée 2004. Intense, clean, and luscious.
Flavours stretch from fresh pear to orange peel to dried apricot.
Drink now-2012. **1999** ★ ★ ★ ★ ★ ↗ Gold, Sélection Mondial,
Brussels 2002; Gold, All Canadian Wine Championships 2000. Rich,
honeyed, lovely flavours of dried white peach, boiled pears. Drink
now-2010. **1998** ★ ★ ★ ★ ★ ↗ Gold, Vinltaly 2000. Powerful, rich,
intense, sublime. Drink now-2010.

Vidal Icewine, Zabek Vineyard [NP] **1996**★ ★ ★ ★ ★ ↗ My first
(. . . and last! Brrr!) winter harvest. Extremely high in acidity when it
was young. This was also the first vintage (as I recall) where J-L
Groux used oak barrels in the production of an icewine. It softened
the sharpness and added a creamy nature to the wine. Drinking
well now, will hold at least to 2011.

Vineyard Select Label

Chardonnay [NP] **2001**★↻ Gold with an aromatic nose of buttered corn on the cob and yogourt. Clean and refreshing, but there
was something about this wine that left me with an uneasy feeling
on the palate.

Gamay Noir Rosé [NP] **2003**★★↻ Baked pastry nose with off-
dry strawberry and cranberry flavours. A delicious break from very
dry red wines.

Gewürztraminer [NP] **2002**★★↻ Off-dry (lightly sweetened
with sussreserve), spicy, hints of talcum powder and flavours of ripe
russet apple.

Muscat Reserve [NP] Morio Muscat in some vintages; in others it's
blended with Muscat Ottonel. **2002**★★↻ Sweetened with sussreserve. Seductive fragrance of tropical fruit and lanolin, clean, fruity
marmalade finish. **2001**☒ Tainted by Asian lady beetle.

Pinot Gris [NP] **2002**★★↻ Pale colour, but good depth to the
aroma. Taste combines tropical fruit and spice. Dry, medium-bodied,
brisk finish.

Pinot Meunier, Barrel-Aged [NP] **2000**★★★↘ Erotic, sweaty,
sweet cherry nose, very delicate and beginning to crack. Drink soon.

Riesling, Semi-Sweet [NP] **2001**☒ Asian lady beetle detected.

Sauvignon Blanc [NP] **2002**★★↻ Dry with mild, grassy notes
and gooseberry flavours, much improved by a dish of steamed
asparagus and marinated salmon.

Other Hillebrand Labels

Brulé Blanc [nonVQA] **NV**★✧ Better than drinking water.

Brulé Rouge [nonVQA] **NV**★✧ Nice base for summer sangria.

Chablis [nonVQA] **NV**☒ The name alone is a crime.

Cuvée 1812 Red [nonVQA] **NV**☆✧ Tasted like vintage 1812.

Cuvée 1812 White [nonVQA] **NV**★☆✧ This could start a war.

Eagle Ridge Sauvignon Blanc [nonVQA] **NV**☆✧ Sauvignon bland.

Eagle Ridge Zinfandel [nonVQA] **NV**★☆✧ Leave for serious zin fans.

Harvest Cuvée Red [nonVQA] **NV**★✧ Taste-free but inoffensive.

Harvest Cuvée White [nonVQA] **NV**★✧ Hint of lemon Pledge.

Schloss [nonVQA] **NV**☒ Blech. Should be renamed Schlop.

Stone Road Country Red [nonVQA] **NV**★☆✧ An international blend with a tiny bit of residual sugar. Candied nose, decent fruit flavour, short jammy finish.

Stone Road Country White [nonVQA] **NV**★☆✧ International blend with residual sugar for suppleness. Straightforward, apple-citrus flavour.

Stone Road Sauvignon Blanc [nonVQA] **NV**★✧ Quite ordinary.

- **HILLIER BLUFF VINEYARD (Hillier, PEC)** – Toronto super-chef Jamie Kennedy purchased this 115-acre property on Station Road, next door to Geoff Heinricks's Domaine La Reine, in 2001. There is an old home that Kennedy plans to refurbish and open in 2007 as a seasonal tavern, featuring local wines and fresh foods. Since buying the property, he has planted 1,500 Pinot Noir vines each year at the very high density of 4,000 vines per acre. The vineyard has a moderately steep south-facing slope and is composed of Hillier clay loam, with granite cobbles and plenty of glacial rubble throughout. The long-range plan is to make a high-end, low-volume Pinot Noir and to serve it in the tavern.

- **HIPPLE VINEYARD (Vineland, NP)** – This vineyard owned by Larry Hipple sells all its grapes to Lakeview Cellars Estate Winery. Hipple is a part-owner of the winery.

- **HONSBERGER VINEYARD (Jordan, NP)** – This vineyard, owned by veteran grape grower Craig Honsberger, sold some of its excellent Riesling to The Malivoire Wine Company for its icewines. From 2004, grapes went to Vincor International.

- **HUEBEL VINEYARD (Niagara-on-the-Lake, NP)** – This 60-acre vineyard owned by Otto Huebel and managed by Matthew Oppenlander is located in the Queenston/St. David's area at the base of the Niagara Escarpment. It is one of the earliest-budding vineyards in the area, so it is susceptible to spring frost damage. On the other hand, it is also one of the earliest ripening in the peninsula so the chances of achieving high sugar levels are consistently high. Soil is heavy clay and yields are quite low, giving wines with good body and longer life. Pinot Gris, Pinot Noir, and Chardonnay are grown. Otto Huebel recently planted an additional 100 acres on land adjacent to Hillebrand.

- **HUFF ESTATES INC.** (2274 County Road #1 [at Hwy 62], Bloomfield, ON, K0K 1G0 / Phone: 613-393-5802 / Fax: 613-393-2428 / Email: karen@huffestates.com / Website: www.huffestates.com)

(Est. 2000) Frank Orlando "Lanny" Huff is a chemical engineer who has been involved in the plastics industry for 40 years. He hails from a family of United Empire Loyalists that settled the county in 1825. The location of the winery was once known as Huff's Corners. Huff owns 2 properties with a combined area of 203 acres of land, but only 33 are planted to date. The main vineyard surrounding the winery is a 43-acre south-facing property of Hillier clay loam soil over limestone, with 16 acres planted. Here, 7 acres of Castel, Chambourcin, and Vidal were planted in 2002 and 4.5 acres each of Chardonnay and Pinot Gris were added in 2004. A second, more gravelly, southeast-facing property of 160 acres is located in South Marysburgh on South Bay. There, 6.5 acres of Cabernet Franc, Cabernet Sauvignon, and Merlot were put into the ground in 2001, 4.4 acres of Chardonnay and Pinot Gris were added in 2002, and an additional 6.5 acres of Cabernet Sauvignon, Merlot, and Chardonnay were planted in 2003. Both vineyards are fully tiled to ensure good drainage. When I toured the cellar in 2004, there were 50 new French oak barrels – all empty – in the newly built cellar. Production in 2003 was 2,100 cases, and the plan is to grow that to 8,000 cases by the end of 2006. Some wines tasted were made from grapes purchased locally (Chardonnay from Lighthall Vineyard) or from the Niagara Peninsula (Riesling from Fox, Merlot from Palatine Vineyards), until estate vines begin to produce a crop. After 2007, the winery intends to focus solely on estate-grown grapes. Other plans call for a hotel and amphitheatre. Burgundy-born winemaker Frédéric Picard aims for lean, elegant wines to pair with food. He is particularly impressed by the higher acidity in Ontario wines, saying they make better food wines. Tasting notes below show a winery in its infancy. My sense is that the wines, already good, will improve dramatically in a very short time. This is one to watch.

Winemaker: Frédéric Picard / Vineyard Manager: Mike Traynor

Cabernet Sauvignon-Cabernet Franc [Ont]   2003 ★ ★ →
(CF20/CS80) Bright garnet with a pale rim. Weedy nose reminiscent of crushed tomato stems. Lean, tart, and slightly underripe. Drink now-2010.

Chardonnay [Ont] **2003** ★ ★ ★ ↗ Lightly oaked buttery nose with good concentration and bracing acidity. Distinctly "French-styled." Drink 2006-2009.

Gamay [Ont] **2003** ★ ★ → Vibrant black-cherry hue with a sweet, berry fruit nose. Very tart, black-cherry taste. Drink now-2010.

Riesling [Ont] **2003** ★ ★ ↗ Pale, green-gold colour with a strong sulphur and lime nose. Extreme acidity reminds me of unripe lemons. Drink 2006-2010.

South Bay Blend [Ont] Produced entirely from estate-grown grapes. **2003** ★ ★ ★ ↗ (CF40/CS40/M20) Purple-garnet with lifted aromatics reminiscent of European bitters – spice, roots, herbs, and concentrated fruits. Taste shows ripeness not often encountered in the county, along with palate-cleansing acidity and a pleasant, balanced finish. Drink now-2011.

• **HUGHES VINEYARD (Beamsville, NP)** – This 24-acre vineyard owned by Ed and Caroline Hughes is entirely under vine. Situated next door to Myers Vineyard on Greenlane Road less than 1 km from the lake, it is composed of deep red Jeddo clay and gravel over Queenston shale. The vineyard is fully drained and, by 2007, also will be irrigated. The Hugheses grow Baco Noir, Cabernet Franc, Cabernet Sauvignon, Chardonnay, Gamay, Gewürztraminer, Merlot, Pinot Gris, Pinot Noir, and Riesling. Vine density varies from 700 plants per acre for Baco Noir to 1,330 for Pinot Noir. Grapes are sold to Featherstone Estate, Tawse Winery, and Willow Heights Estate. Ed Hughes, a graduate of oenology and viticulture from Brock University's Cool Climate Oenology and Viticulture Institute (CCOVI), is also a certified chef and pastrymaker who runs Niagara Cuisine Catering. (www.niagaracuisine.com)

• **HUNTER FARMS LTD. (Niagara-on-the-Lake, NP)** – Ken Hunter's 50-acre tract is located on Hunter Road near Nevin Road, just west of the town's suburbs and north of Highway 55. The terrain is significantly sloped, with sandy loam on the surface and lacustrine silty clay below. The vineyard is irrigated between every row and has overhead irrigation. Hunter uses bio-dynamic farming practices and yields about 2.5 t. per acre. He sells Syrah to Creekside Estate.

I

- **Icewine** – Ontario's hottest wine starts with its coldest grapes. If ever we needed an excuse to be thankful for winter, icewine is it. Icewine – in the early days of discovery and experimentation, we called it *eiswein* after the original German stuff – is produced in the dead of winter from grapes that have naturally frozen while they still hang on the vines. Because of their very high sugar content, the shrunken, partially dehydrated berries freeze solid after the temperature drops below -7°C. Brave pickers gather during the coldest time of the night, just after 2:30 a.m., to start the harvest of grapes. They continue picking till dawn, when the sun comes up and the temperature begins to rise. The grapes are as hard as marbles, and so fragile they may fall to the ground if clumsily touched with thickly gloved hands. Throughout the night and well into the morning the grapes are gently squeezed in powerful bladder presses. Only the gooey, concentrated fruit extract is removed. Squeezing too hard might heat up the press, melting the frozen water crystals, and that would just dilute the finished wine. Only a few drops are extracted from each grape. The predictability and the severity of our winters means that Ontario can produce icewine every year. In fact, we make more icewine more often than any other nation on the face of the earth. And because our winemakers get such a regular workout, they have gained an abundance of expertise over the years and maintain a low failure rate. Since the first major international honour – the Grand Prix d'Honneur – was awarded to Inniskillin in 1991 for its 1989 Vidal Icewine, Ontario icewines have racked up so many medals, trophies, awards, and certificates, we've stopped counting. Winemakers still enter the wines each year – the promotional value of a win is always useful in the foreign markets – but they tend only to ho-hum unless some mention is made of their dry wines. You know you've become a success when international counterfeiters start producing fake wines to take advantage of your name and reputation. In recent years, there has been a huge growth in icewine counterfeiting in Asian countries, so much so that some Canadian winemakers estimate as much fake icewine is sold as the genuine thing. It's a major concern for Ontario producers. They now are actively developing strategies to combat the crooks.

- **IL VIGNETO (Grimsby, NP)** – A 180-acre vineyard purchased in 2003 by the Speranzini family to supply their Willow Heights Estate Winery. The name means, simply, The Vineyard. It is 180 acres of flat clay lime-stone soil planted prior to 1980, with 6.5 acres of Chardonnay, 7.8 acres of Riesling, and 12.5 acres of Vidal Blanc. In 2004, Speranzini planted an additional 5 acres of vinifera grapes, including small amounts of Pinot Gris, Pinot Noir, and Syrah.

- **INNISKILLIN WINES INC**. (Niagara Parkway at Line 3, R.R.#1, Niagara-on-the-Lake, ON, L0S 1J0 / Phone: 905-468-2187 / Toll-Free: 1-888-466-4754 / Fax: 905-468-5355 / Email: inniskil@inniskillin.com / Websites: www.inniskillin.com)

(Est. 1975) Canada's first modern estate winery was founded by Donald Ziraldo, a Guelph-trained agronomist whose family owned a fruit nursery, and Karl Kaiser, an Austrian-born immigrant who could not stomach the awful sludge being produced by the big wineries in the early 1970s. Together, the partnership revitalized, reinvented, and refor-matted Canada's wine industry with Kaiser making exceptional wines and Ziraldo accomplishing feats of marketing. Their earliest wines were made from French-American hybrids such as Chambourcin, Chelois, De Chaunac, Leon Millot, Marechal Foch, Seyval Blanc, and Vidal, at a time when the mainstream wineries were still manufacturing ports, sherries, and labrusca-based pop-wines. Each time the industry came close to catching up to them by following in their footsteps, the pair raced ahead with innovation and panache. Although the 1980s proved difficult for the wine industry, Inniskillin flourished thanks to the rising quality of their wines and highly publicized small successes, including a big "sale" of wines to France and Germany, the introduction of new products, such as Heuriger, Fleur d'Ontario, and a sparkling wine. Bigger (and also highly publicized) triumphs included the introduction of the company's first Vidal Icewines, its Pinot Noirs, single-vineyard bottlings, a territorial foothold in California's Napa Valley, and the establishment of the Vintners Quality Alliance (VQA), of which Ziraldo was appointed founding chairman. The 1990s, on the other hand, saw major changes and additional achievements at Inniskillin. In 1991, Kaiser was awarded the most prestigious wine industry trophy in the world, the VinExpo Grand Prix d'Honneur, for making the 1989 Vidal Icewine, a feat that focused the eyes of the world on the tiny Niagara winery. Within a decade, Inniskillin would become the world's leading producer of icewine. In 1992, Ziraldo merged the winery with Cartier Wines & Beverages to create Cartier-Inniskillin Vintners, providing financial resources and stability to the winery as never before. The following year, he signed the first Canada-France joint-venture deal with the renowned Burgundy winemaking firm of Jaffelin. In 1994, Inniskillin initiated a wine collaboration with the Okanaquen Indian Band at Inkameep to create a beachhead in British Columbia. In a 1995 co-venture, Key Porter Books published Ziraldo's *Anatomy of a Winery*, an illustrated exploration of the Niagara winery's self-guided tour, while Kaiser was voted "wine-maker of the year," twice, by separate organizations. In 1996, they estab-lished Inniskillin Okanagan Vineyards, a 22-acre hillside property on one of the region's most favoured slopes. Ziraldo was honoured with the Ontario Grape Growers' Award of Merit in 1997, an Order of Canada in 1998, and, to round out the decade, a Lifetime Achievement Award from the Canadian Wine Institute in 1999. Kaiser added the Queen's Silver Jubilee medal to his honours in 2004 and the charter Tony Aspler Award of Excellence the following year. Today, the winery owns 2 vineyards: Brae Burn Estate, on which it stands, and Montague Vineyard in one of the warmest corners of the Peninsula, next to the Niagara Airport. Annual production averages 150,000 cases of VQA wine. Currently, wines are bottled at Vincor's Dorchester Road plant in Niagara Falls.

Winemakers: Karl Kaiser (1974-present); James Manners (2004-present, table wines); Philip Dowell (1999 to 2003, table wines) / Vineyard Manager: Gerald Klose

Inniskillin table wine labels are tiered as follows:

Black Label – Entry-level, non-oaked, single-varietal, vintage-dated, VQA wines made from grapes purchased from a wide variety of growers throughout the Niagara Peninsula. In years of short crops, such at 2003, fruit is imported and nonVQA wines are bottled. This line is produced in large volumes and is available in general distribution.

Pearl Label – Reserve-level, single-varietal, vintage-dated, VQA wines from purchased grapes from favoured vineyards and harvested at a higher level of ripeness. Except for the Riesling, all wines are barrel-aged.

Silver Label – Distinctive varietals from named single vineyards of exceptional quality.

Gold Label – The "Founders' Series." Chardonnay and Pinot Noir pro-duced in a Burgundian style from a strict selection of the best barrels available of each vintage. Wines spend more time in oak to extract richer flavours.

Auxerrois [NP]   **2002**★ ★ ★↻ Grapey aroma with ripe lemon/ apple taste.

Cabernet Franc [NP]   **2002**★ ★ ★↗ Violet-garnet with a light, fresh, undeveloped nose of black tea with raspberry syrup. Juicy, sweet, and balanced. Drink 2006-2010. **1998**★ ★ ★↗ Garnet with a light, ripe, berry-fruit bouquet. Soft and pleasant. Drink now-2007. **1997**★ ★ ★→ Garnet with a sweet smell despite some green notes. Leaner and tougher than the 1998. Also peaking. Drink now-2006. **1994**★ ★ ★↘ Garnet with a brick rim. Nose is cracking with sour, unripe, cabbagy notes. Past its peak. **1991**★ ★ ★↘ Two bottles tasted recently. A 375 ml size was well past its ability to provide any pleasure other than curiosity. Like an Eastern European "port" or a bual Madeira in a mid-life crisis. The 750 ml was pruney and pleasant but starting to fade.

Cabernet Franc Icewine [NP] **2002**★★★↗ Nose of red cherry with hints of orange and spice. Terrific balance of sweetness and acidity promises a long life. Drink now-2016.

Cabernet Franc Reserve [NP] **2002**★★★☆↗ Garnet hue with a soft and light nose and palate of crushed raspberries and blueberry jam. Drink now-2010. **2001**☒ Spoiled by Asian lady beetle. **2000**★★★↘ Ruby hue with mahogany hints. Herbal nose to start with powdered sugar, green pepper, and red fruit aromas. Lean, tart, well structured with soft tannins and a good lingering aftertaste. Drink now-2009. **1999**★★★↗ Mahogany-garnet. Spicy, minty, medicinal, black-cherry cough-syrup nose with sweet flavours of ripe apple and a finish of bitter apple skin. Drink now-2009. **1998**★★★★↘ From the Seeger and Van de Laar vineyards. Garnet with a ripe, dense, roasted-coffee aroma and black-cherry, plum, and mint notes. Muscular but starting to show some tone and complexity. Drink now-2010. **1997**★★★↘ From Bethune, Wiley, and Marianne Hill vineyards. Sweet fruit nose, thick, supple texture, with plenty of tannins in the finish. Drink now-2007.

Cabernet Franc-Merlot [NP] **1994**★↘ (CF60/M 40) Purple-black colour but nose was pure dill pickle at the end of 1996. Not much future, drink up. **1993**★★★↘ Garnet with a browning edge. Bouquet of iodine and mint with a smoky, tarry plum flavour. Drink soon; it's fading. **1991**★★★→ Dark garnet with a pruney, dried-cherry nose. Fruit is drying up. Has a tasty, toasted hazelnut-skin finish. Drink up. **1988**★★★→ Soft, ripe, cooked cherry and prune nose, hints of black tea and tobacco. Senile but fascinating.

Cabernet-Merlot [NP] **2000**★★☆→ Dull garnet with a cabbagy, roasted-coffee stink. Drink now. **1991**★★★↘ Black-cherry fragrance is subtle but pleasant. In decline.

Cabernet Sauvignon [NP] **1993**★★★→ Deep and brooding garnet hue, green, leafy, herbal nose, fullish body, and long finish. Coming around.

Cabernet Sauvignon, Founders' Reserve [NP] **1995**★★★★→ Ripe and ready.

Chardonnay [NP] The biggest-selling VQA white wine in the country. Consistently appealing, youthful, and fruity. Typically, apple, melon, pear, or lemon flavours with occasional hints of mango, papaya, and pineapple. Well balanced and good value. Tastes best at 2-3 years. **2003**★★★↻ **2002**★★★↻ **2001**☒ Asian lady beetle. **2000**★★★↻ **1999**★★★↘ Earthy with mineral notes. Too old for some tastes. Drink up.

Chardonnay, Alliánce [NP] Produced in consultation with winemaker Bernard Repolt of Maison Jaffelin in Beaune. Burgundian palate was apparent as Repolt and Kaiser would taste every cask of

Ontario Chardonnay, then select 6-8 of the best barrels. Lasted only a few years as consumers misunderstood the product, thinking it was a "blend" of French and Canadian grapes. **1997★★★↘** **1996** Not produced. **1995★★★↘** Once very good, now fading rapidly, **1994↓** (Klose-25%/Seeger-75%) It had a touch more elegance than the previous vintage despite its lower level of ripeness. Over the hill. **1993↓** *Best Canadian White, Toronto Wine & Cheese Show 1995 & 1996.* Almost entirely Klose Vineyard. Exotic, wildly fruity, hints of fermenting fresh-cut grass, implicitly sweet, rich, and full-bodied. Oozed charm and suppleness in its youth.

Chardonnay, Founders' Reserve [NP]   **2001★★★→** *Gold, Chardonnay du Monde 2004.* Gold hue and clean bouquet of fruit and butter, but this wine tastes fat with an oxidative nose. It's toasty, oaky, nutty with flavours of glazed pastry dough and brown butter. Drink sooner rather than later. **2000★★★→** Deep yellow-gold with a fat, buttery nose. Hints of lemon and spice on the palate, as well as nuances of bacon fat and roasted coffee beans. Drink now.

Chardonnay, Klose Vineyard [NP]   **2002★★★→** Pale silvery-gold with a ripe, implicitly sweet bouquet. Flavours include lemon, white peach, pear, pastry dough, toast, and hints of oak. Subtle but complex. Drink now-2008. **2000★★★→** Pear fruit flavours of its youth are gone, now replaced by toasted hazelnut, brown butter, sourdough, and mushroom notes. Drink soon.

Chardonnay, Montague Vineyard [NP]   One of the warmest sites in the peninsula, according to winery bumph. **2002★★★→** Pale gold with a bouquet of vanilla, oak, and honeyed lemon. Taste leans to spiced tropical fruit. Good body and balance. Drink now-2007. **2000★★→** Deep yellow-gold with an overpowering, corn-on-the-cob nose. Flavours of brown butter, honey, and beef drippings. Drink up. **1989★★★→** It's alive! High toned with a light fruit nose. Austere and crisp with delicate structure. Its lightness is its appeal. Drink soon. **1988★★★→** Lighter and more delicate than the 1989 but feistier. Drink now.

Chardonnay, Reserve [NP]   **2002★★★↗** The standard-bearer for mid-priced Chardonnay. Brilliant gold hue with a subdued nose of toast with lemon butter. Clean, almost crisp palate of medium body, satiny texture, and supple mouthfeel. It has the peachy sweetness that comes with ripeness without any detectable residual sugar. Careful though, at 14% alc./vol., it packs quite a punch. Drink now-2007. **2001☒** Asian lady beetle taint detected. **1997★★★→** Peanut-brittle nose on top with undertones of mushrooms and beef stew. Best drunk soon. **1995★★★↘** Grapes predominantly from Seeger Vineyard. Rich, well rounded, with subtle nuances of vanilla and spice. **1994★★★↘** Aroma of cream puffs with lemon custard. Some oxidative notes but holding. Drink soon. **1993★★★↘** Bouquet of candied fruit, flowers, herbs, and old cork. Drink up. **1991★★★★→** Butter-pecan pie nose is rich, mature, and appealing. Great balance suggests it will continue to hold in a good cellar for a few years yet. Drink now-2009.

Chardonnay, Seeger Vineyard [NP] **1989**★★★➔ Full-bodied and muscular. Fully mature. **1988**★★★↘ Nutty with brown butter and molasses flavours. Time to drink up.

Chardonnay, Schuele Vineyard [NP] **2002**★★★↗ Pale straw-gold with a balanced nose that hints of fruit as well as oak. Some power and a fair degree of elegance. Drink now-2007.

Fleur de Niagara [Ont] **NV**★★★➔ A local variation of Pineau des Charentes. Grape brandy (from Kittling Ridge) was added to fresh grape juice before it had a chance to ferment. The sweet wine cocktail is then left to age in barrel for a period of time until the flavours have melded. Prior to 1998, it was called Fleur d'Ontario. Sadly, it was discontinued in 2000.

Gamay (Black Label) [NP] **2001**☒ Asian lady beetle taint detected.

Gewürztraminer [NP] **1993**★★↘ Delicate, perfumed soap aroma and sweet, candied fruit taste. Yummy but drink up. **1992**★★★↘ Unusually pale colour for this age of wine. Straw-gold, it has lost its freshness but still has a huge acid bite. **1991**★★★★➔ Amber with reddish-brown reflections. Nose reminds me of caramelized apple, clear tea, soy, Bovril, and a good Speyside malt whisky. Drink up. **1980**★★★★➔ [preVQA] Deep amber gold. Very aged but ridiculously good with flavours of taffy apple, butterscotch candy, orange pekoe tea, and lemon drops. Like an old vintage Madeira. Fully mature and holding.

Marechal Foch [Ont] **1993**★★★➔ Black inky purple-garnet with subtle fruit and cream nose. Early vegetal notes have become earthy and mushroomy like a disturbed forest floor. **1992**↓ Dead. Ontario's worst vintage ever. **1991**★★★↘ Still hanging in but fading. **1990**★★↘ Fading. [preVQA] **1982**↓ **1980**★★★↘ **1978**↓ **1974**★★★↘ More than 30 years old and it's still hanging on. Last tasted in 2004.

Meritage, Reserve [NP] **2002**★★★☆↗ Garnet with a clean and balanced but somewhat shy nose. Good raspberry and plum flavours, but lean and a touch hot in the finish. Drink now-2012. **2001**★★★↗ Brilliant garnet with a bouquet that starts with sweet veggies and charred wood, developing rich black-cherry and plum notes. Good structure with sharp acidity and terrific potential. Drink 2006-2012. **2000**★★★↗ Garnet hue with mahogany reflections. Big and full-bodied with plum, charred walnuts, leather, and boiled cabbage nuances. Maturing well. Drink now-2008. **1999**★★★↗ Dark mahogany garnet with a toasty, oaky, smoky, tarry, chocolate bouquet. Dense dark plum and black pepper flavours, supple texture, and dusty tannins. Drink now-2012. **1998**★★★★↗ Very dark garnet shade with a plump, plummy nose and big, solid, and concentrated palate. Marred slightly by a bitter charred finish. Drink now-2010. **1997**★★★↘Leafy nose. Now taking on a tart edge. Drink soon.

Merlot [NP] **2002**★★★↗ Garnet with a pink rim. Hints of berry beginning to appear, sweet as raspberry jam. Silky, smooth, with soft tannins. Drink 2006-2010. **1999**★★★→ Brilliant garnet with some brick in the rim. Dense, closed nose with oaky, herbal over-tones. Blackberry and plum flavours offer balance, youth, and exu-berance. About to peak, Drink now-2008. **1993**★★★↘ Garnet with an orange-brown rim. Porty with sharp, balsamic, prune juice flavours. Dying in the glass.

Merlot-Cabernet Franc [NP] **1995**★★★→ (CF40/M60) Garnet with a browning edge. Soft, lovely, lean flavour tending to black-berry. Fully mature. Drink now.

Merlot, Schuele Vineyard [NP] **1999**★★★★↗ Garnet with a spicy nose of rosemary, thyme, smoke, plums, and raspberries. Thick, velvety, and lush, developing well with years to go. Drink now-2013.

Petite Sirah, Kew Vineyard [NP] Alas, these vines were uprooted in the spring of 1994 after suffering from crown gall, a vine disease that chokes the plant at the graft. **1993**★★★↘ Dark, tough, and tannic, richly textured, subdued, and closed in 1995 with blackberry fruit, pepper, and coffee tones. Has developed a velvety texture and rich, gamy nuances. Long finish. 275 cases produced. Drink soon. **1992**↓ One of the best reds of this dreadful vintage. Drink up.

Pinot Grigio [NP] **2002**★★★↺ Ripe and balanced with refresh-ing melon flavours. Drink while young and fresh. **2001**☒ Tainted by Asian lady beetle.

Pinot Gris, Montague Vineyard [NP] From the silver label series sold mainly to restaurants. **2002**★★→ Crisp and clean with a ripe nose but beginning to take on a bitter edge from too much time in oak.

Pinot Noir [NP] 1997 ★★★↘ Chestnut-brown with a nose of stewed cabbage, caraway, and strawberry compote. Hints of bitter chocolate and cherry fruit, but this wine is on the slide. Drink soon.

Pinot Noir, Alliánce [NP] See also Alliánce Chardonnay. The Pinot suffered a similar fate. **1995**★★★↘ Had a lovable, old, Burgundian "stink." Sliding now with tart flavours, drink soon with cheese. **1994** Not produced in this cool vintage. **1993**↓ Once notable for its elegance and a floral, fruity bouquet of violets, strawberry, cherry, plum, nuts, and coffee flavours. That's all changed to apple skin, cedar shavings, and pencil eraser. Can still be used as a marinade.

Pinot Noir, Founders' Reserve [NP] **2000**★★★★↗ Pale garnet-brown with classic bouquet of ripe fruit and barnyard. Well balanced and beautifully structured with classic, youthful, Burgundian flavours of licorice, smoke, sandalwood, truffles, coffee, cedar, tobacco, earth, and plum. Only 800 cases made. Drink now-2009. **1999**★★★→ Ruby with an orange rim. Aromas of cherry, herbs, and Virginia tobacco. Showing some complexity but drink soon. **1998★★★★→** Deep ruby-garnet with a toasty, smoky, spicy, pipe tobacco and dried currants bouquet. Smooth, soft, velvety, and supple. There is a note of bitterness in the finish but some red meat would fix that. Drink now. **1997★★★↘** Smoky, sharp, and beginning to tire. Drink up. **1995★★★★→** Ripe, mature, delicious.

Pinot Noir, Montague Vineyard [NP] **2002★★★★↗** Ruby-cherry with a minty, candied-fruit aroma. Soft fruit flavours leaning to plum, red cherry, and golden raspberry. Tough but well-structured finish. Drink now-2010. **2001★★★↗** Ripe fruity nose hints of sandalwood, oak, and cherry pie. Big body, still-tough structure, but ooh, those lo-ong, lingering, complex, sexy flavours. Drink now-2007. **2000★★★↗** Dense, dusty nose of charred wood, but palate has a good balance of fruit and oak. Drink now. **1999★★★→** Ruby-cherry hue with a delicate fragrance of wild-flowers, raspberry, strawberry, and red cherry. Aging gracefully with clean, soft flavours of plum, spice, and orange bitters. Drink now. **1998★★★★→** Ruby with an orange rim. Complex bouquet of incense, jasmine, sandalwood, spice, coffee, and sweet bacon fat. Rich, soft, full, ripe, and sweet, with complexity, elegance, and delicacy. Drink now-2008.

Pinot Noir, Murray Vineyard [preVQA] **1984★★↘** Inniskillin's first commercial release of Pinot Noir. At first, I noted it to be light, almost feeble, but with correct Pinot Noir flavours. When last tasted, in Dec. 2002, it was still alive with gamy nuances and sour cherry flavours, though the balance had become quite fragile. Some bottles still exist.

Pinot Noir, Puddicombe Vineyard [preVQA] **1980★★★↘** This was Kaiser and Ziraldo's first experimental batch and was never released to the public. Total production was just over a barrel (± 35 cases). Sherrylike, pruney, and drying up.

Pinot Noir Reserve [NP] **2002★★★☆↗** Bright ruby with a sweet, ripe, light aroma and balanced, strawberry-cherry flavours. Drink now-2008. **2001★★★→** Ruby-garnet colour with enticing coffee/mocha aromatics. Well knit with good structure and ripe flavours of cherry and plum. Terrific now but will continue to improve for another 5 years. **2000★★★→** Ruby with an orange rim and a barnyardy, toasted sesame-seed nose. Zippy acidity, restrained fruit, and dusty tannins in the finish. Drink now-2007. **1995★★★↘** Aromas of green pepper and green banana. Still has some sweetness but fruit is drying up. **1994★★↘** Lean but silky and elegant with cooked cherry, spice, and mint flavours. **1993★★★↘** Cherry-brown hue with cheesy nose and tart, herbal apple-skin flavours. **1992↓** Deep mahogany with a smoky, burnt-rubber nose and minty finish. **1991★★★☆↘** *Gold, VinItaly 1993.* Once a big bruiser of a wine, the muscles are sagging now.

1989↓ Gone. **1988**★★★↘ Concentrated plum butter and orange-peel flavours. **1987**↓ Pale ruby-orange with a charred, candy floss bouquet. Some fruit left but tart and rapidly cracking up. Fascinating afterglow.

Riesling [NP] **2002**★★★→ *Best Value White, Canadian Wine Awards 2003.* Full of ripe, lively flavours of melon, lime, pink grapefruit. Balanced and luscious. Drink now-2006. **1992**↓ Austere gummy nose, hints of spice. Tart, dried up.

Riesling B.A. [preVQA] **1986**★★★☆↘ Golden brown with faint aromas of caramel, white raisins, prunes, and orange marmalade. Balanced with relatively little acidity. Past its peak and spinning in a slow freefall.

Riesling, Icewine [NP] **2002**★★★★☆↑ One of the best balanced and most exciting wines ever to emerge from this winery. Lively and luscious, with complex nuances of pine needles, applesauce, pear nectar, marmalade, pineapple, and spiced fruit. Drink 2007-2022. **1998**★★★★☆→ Pale amber-gold with a youthful, fresh nose of pear and mango. Layer upon layer of flavour slowly emerges. Supple texture, very sweet with great natural acid balance. Drink now-2020. **1997**★★★★→ Amber-gold with an advanced petrol nose. Nuances of browned butter, corn syrup, and vanilla custard. Tart finish. Drink now-2015.

Riesling, Late Harvest [NP] **1996**★↘ Sold in burgundy-shaped bottles to take advantage of the Chardonnay-drinking mass market. Lighter than previous vintages.

Riesling, Reserve [NP] **2002**★★★↗ Pale straw-gold with lime flavours and slowly emerging petrol nose. Severe palate (for now) with racy acidity and mouth-drying structure. Needs a couple years to settle down. Drink 2006-2012. **2000**★★★★↗ Brilliant, deep golden hue with an enticing meaty, sausagelike smell. Lemon-lime and petrol flavours and a lovely, classic, perfectly balanced mineral structure. A keeper. Drink now-2020.

Riesling, Seeger Vineyard, Old Vines [NP] This wine, from the Silver Label series, is made available only to restaurateurs. **2002**★★★↗ Very fresh tasting with a sprightly prickle on the tongue. Green fruit and confectioner's sugar aromas, lemon and lime on the palate.

Riesling, Special Select Late Harvest [NP] **1999**★★★★↗ Bright gold with a sweet petrol nose. Juicy, light, and clean, but finishes short at this stage. Should benefit from further patience. Drink now-2014.

Shiraz, Brae Burn Estate Vineyard [NP] **2000**★★★↗ Big oaky nose with subdued fruit. Dense fruit beneath heavy oak holds more promise but little immediate pleasure. Drink now-2010.

Vidal Icewine [NP] **2002**★★★★☆↗ *Citadelles du Vin, VinExpo 2004.* Yellow-gold with youthful, undeveloped flavours. High-toned with aromas of lemon, ripe pineapple and pear. Drink now-2018.

1998★★★★☆→ Amber-gold with thick, concentrated consistency. Very sweet with flavours of orange pekoe tea, pear, and dried mango. Drink now-2015. **1997★★★★→** Developing well. Drink now-2012. **1995★★★★→** A classic botrytis year resulted in complex flavours of pineapple, mango, peach, apricot, and passion fruit with rich texture and excellent acidity. Delicate structure. Drink now. **1994★★★★→** Lean, clean, elegant, and balanced with deep and long but restrained flavours. Drink now. **1993★★★☆→** Gold, All Canadian Wine Championships 1995. Amber-gold with tired flavours of dried apricot and prune. Drink up. **1992** Gold, VinItaly 1993. **1990★★★☆→** Coppery-gold with nuances of soy and roasted nuts. Disjointed taste with volatile aromatics. Drink up. **1989★★★★★→** Grand Prix d'Honneur, VinExpo 1991. A stunner. Its win in Bordeaux put Canadian wines firmly on the map. Bouquet includes white truffle and marmalade of pears, white plums, and apricots. Drink now-2015. **1988★★★☆→** Cognac colour with a strong, smoky, herbal nose of soy, vegemite, black bean paste, and Asian spices. There's a sharpness in the finish. Drink now. **1987★★★★☆→** Old cognac hue with aromas of dried apricot and musty apples. Flavour turns to sautéed apple and banana chunks drizzled with thick molasses. Drink now-2012. **1986★★★★☆→** Old cognac colour with a smoky nose of roasted apples and caramel sauce. Supple, harmonious, and rich. Drink now-2010. **1985★★★★↘** Coppery colour with a nose of caramelized sugar. Tart as orange juice with a dusty, austere finish. Drying up, drink soon. **1984★★★★☆→** I'm always sad to open this vintage. The wine is no longer as exciting as it once was, although it still has much to offer. Amber-gold, reminiscent of turned autumn leaves. Slightly sharp aroma of dried apricots, prunes, and raisins. Sweet and sour, dried fruit flavours, still in balance. Drink now-2009.

Vidal Icewine, Oak Aged [NP] **2002★★★★↗** Gold, Canadian Icewine Trophy, Sweet Wine Trophy, International Wine Challenge, 2004. Still juvenile with candied pineapple and pear flavours and a hint of vanilla cream. Drink now-2015. **1997★★★★→** Copper colour with a bouquet of smoke, peanut brittle, dried apricot, and roasted Brazil nuts. Drink now. **1996★★★★→** Coppery-gold with a smoky nose of tea, fruitcake, and a splash of balsamic vinegar. Drink now.

Vidal, Select Late Harvest [NP] **1997★★★☆↗** Old-gold colour with a lively pear essence. Supple texture, medium weight, clean, and balanced. Tastes of overripe Red Delicious apples. Drink now-2012. **1994★★★★↗** Drink now-2014.

Vidal, Sparkling Icewine [NP] If you like "regular" icewine, you'll love this. **2002★★★★★→** Gold, Ontario Wine Awards 2004. Rich as whipped cream. Drink now-2012. **2001★★★★☆→** A light mousse bursts into sweet fruitiness, then bright acidity rinses away the creamy nectar leaving a cleansed palate. Scrumptious! Drink now-2010. **1998**★ ★ ★ ★ ★ ➔ Inviting nose with concentrated apricot and honey flavours. Fluffy texture, creamy taste. Long, sweet, rich, clean aftertaste. Drink now.

Vin Nouveau [preVQA] Touted, at the time, as the "future" of premium wines in Canada. Much better than what was available, but one of the lower rungs on the ladder of modern wineries. Produced from 1974 to 1978. Most now over the hill. **1978**★ ★ ★ ◅Now vegetal and tired. **1977**↓ **1976**↓ **1975**↓ **1974**★ ★ ★ ◅ The company's inaugural wine. Still kicks ass.

Viognier, Servos Vineyard [NP] **2002**★ ★ ★ ↻ Pale gold with a marvellous bouquet of flowers, crushed grapes, wine gums, and white peach. Supple and seductive.

Welschriesling, Late Harvest, Klose Vineyard [NP] **1993** ★ ★ ★ ◅ Bright yellow-gold with an oxidized nose of new plastic, cheap sherry, and old apples. Drink up.

Zweigelt [NP] Young wines show strong bramble and black-currant notes. **1997**[Ont]★ ★ ◅ Pale cherry with a browning rim. Advanced nose of sweet red fruits and fading roses. Holding, but just. Drink up. **1994** [NP]★ ◅ Bright tawny colour, tantalizing nose, lively acidity, lean texture, and sharp finish. Drying up, drink soon.

J

- **JACK FORRER VINEYARD (Niagara-on-the-Lake, NP)** – This 6-acre teaching and demonstration vineyard was donated to the Glendale Campus of Niagara College by Jack Forrer, a long-time grape grower and Ontario's 1972 Grape King. It is used by students in the school's Winery and Viticulture Technician program to teach future winery technicians about Canada's top-12 *Vitis vinifera* grapes, rootstocks varieties, vine spacing, and trellising systems and provides much of the raw material for the award-winning wines produced by Niagara College Teaching Winery.

- **JACKSON-MORGAN VINEYARD (St. Catharines, NP)** – Kerry Morgan purchased this property from Fred Hernder in 1997 and continues to sell exclusively to Hernder Estates. Of the 30 acres, 27 are planted with Chardonnay (18 acres), Chardonnay Musqué (2 acres), and Vidal (8 acres) on mostly clay loam. The vineyard is completely underdrained every second row.

- **JACKSON-TRIGGS NIAGARA ESTATE WINERY** (2145 Niagara Stone Road [Hwy 55], R.R.#2, Niagara-on-the-Lake, ON, L0S 1J0 / Phone: 905-468-4637 / Toll-Free: 1-866-589-4637 / Fax: 905-468-4673 / Website: www.jacksontriggswinery.com)

(Est. 1993) What started off as a marketing department brand name has, over the past dozen years, become the largest-selling Canadian label in Vincor International's collection of operations. The brand Jackson-Triggs Vintners is named after the 2 original founders of the corporation, chairman and CEO Donald Triggs and executive winemaker Allan Jackson. Since the early days it has been a vehicle for moving imported and domestic varietals and blends under the banner of "Product of Canada." It still sells huge amounts of these bulk wines but also has become a significant player in the VQA wine business, with the opening, in 2001, of a state-of-the-art Niagara-based winery dedicated to producing premium, super-premium, and ultra-premium VQA wines. Indeed, the quality is indisputable and substantiated by many international awards. The new 47,000-sq.-ft. winery, designed by the architectural firm of Kuwabara Payne McKenna Blumberg, utilizes advanced winemaking equipment and techniques. There are 3-tiered, gravity-flow-assisted systems to minimize mechanical manipulation of wines, traditional open-top fermenters and modern roto-fermenters, gentle bladder presses, and numerous stainless-steel storage and filtration units. There are 2 barrel cellars, an area for making bottle-fermented sparkling wines, and a substantial wine library. The 26 acres of vineyards focus on 3 vinifera varieties, Chardonnay, Pinot Noir, and Riesling, all planted in Beverly lacustrine silty clay soil, although there is a demonstration vineyard at the front of the winery with other varieties. Additional grapes are purchased from a wide variety of independent grape growers all around the Niagara Peninsula. Also provided are hospitality, tasting, and retail areas, and an outdoor amphitheatre where many concerts, films, and other events are scheduled during the warmer months. Annual production tops 100,000 cases.

Winemakers: Rob Scapin (1993-present); Tom Seaver (1993-present) / Vineyard Manager: Martin van der Merwe

Jackson-Triggs wines are labelled as follows:

White Label – "Proprietors' Selection" wines are entry-level, nonVQA wines produced from imported grapes blended with the legally required percentage of domestic fruit. They are produced in huge volumes and widely available.

Black Label – "Proprietors' Reserve" wines are premium VQA table wines from purchased vinifera grapes, as well as icewines from vinifera and hybrid varieties.

Gold Label – "Proprietors' Grand Reserve" wines are limited edition, ultra-premium VQA table wines produced from purchased vinifera grapes, as well as icewines from vinifera and hybrid varieties.

Charcoal Label – Single varietals and blends produced from vinifera grapes grown in the Delaine Vineyard, owned by Vincor founder Don Triggs and his wife, Elaine.

Delaine Vineyard (Charcoal Label)

Cabernet-Merlot [NP] **2002** ★ ★ ★ ★ ↗ (CF33/CS47/M20) Deep garnet with a tough, closed, charred oak nose reminiscent of mesquite hardwood or a briar pipe. Taste hints at black cherry and black currant, but fruit is submerged and hiding behind some strong tar and licorice flavours at this time. Concentrated texture, balanced acidity, and a tough, tannic finish. Drink 2007-2014. **2001** ★ ★ ★ ↗ (CF30/CS40/M30) Lovely ruby-garnet hue with deeply imbedded flavours of black fruits. Needs time. Drink after 2009.

Chardonnay [NP] **2002** ★ ★ ★ ★ ↗ *Gold, Canadian Wine Awards 2004*. Even better than previous vintage. Spirity but enticing bouquet of apple butter, vanilla, caramel, toast, and oak. Rich, ripe and implicitly sweet. Long-lived too. **2001 ★ ★ ★ ↗** Inviting nose with sweet floral, pear notes underpinned by honey, vanilla, and oak flavours. Balanced, beautiful, and easy to drink.

Gewürztraminer [NP] **2002 ★ ★ ★ ★ ↗** Pale straw-gold with a very ripe, very sweet nasal impression. Palate is dry with flavours of wine gums, lovely soft fruit notes, and a lasting and beguiling complex finish. Drink now-2007.

Merlot [NP] **2002 ★ ★ ★ ★ ↑** Garnet with an oaky nose of charred cedar, stewed plums, mint and black-cherry cough syrup. Tart and clean with juicy, blackberry flavours, medium body, and soft tannins. A complex and elegant bottle. Drink 2006-2011. **2001 ★ ★ ★ ↗** Young and green with strong veggie characteristics when first tasted. Herbal now – thyme and rosemary. Tons of tannin still overpower deeply submerged sweet plum and spice flavours. Will improve with patience. Drink now-2009.

Pinot Noir [NP] **2002 ★ ★ ★ ★ ↗** Ruby-garnet with a thick aroma of dried cherries, prune compote, and hints of soy, herbal notes, sandalwood, and earth. Mouth-drying tannins. Drink now-2012. **2001 ★ ★ ★ ↗** Cherry-garnet colour with a fine fruity and woody aroma. Ripe fruit flavours and soft, lush texture. Drink now-2009.

Riesling [NP] **2002 ★ ★ ★ ↗** Nose hints of candied fruit. Clean, dry, balanced, and supple with delightful flavours of grapefruit, lime, and white peach. **2001 ★ ★ ★ ★ ↗** Classic, Mosel-like, wildflower, pine, and petrol notes with firm mineral undertones. Flavours of lemon, lime, kiwi, and spearmint. Razor-sharp acidity promises a long life.

Proprietors' Grand Reserve (Gold Label)

Cabernet Franc Icewine [NP] **2002 ★ ★ ★ ★ ★ ↗** Deep pink hue. Concentrated and pungent with fine flavours of strawberry, raspberry, and red cherry. Thick, rich, syrupy, and unctuous. Drink now-2020. **2000 ★ ★ ★ ★ ↗** Deep pink, intensely sweet with beguiling strawberry-rhubarb aroma. Concentrated and pungent with slightly candied fruit flavours. Drink now-2015. **1999 ★ ★ ★ ★ ★ →** Gorgeous! Very fine strawberry and raspberry flavours in a luscious syrup. Drink now-2019.

Chardonnay [NP] **2001 ★ ★ ★ ★ ↗** Rich golden hue with big tropical pear and vanilla flavours punctuated by notes of fired oak, roasted coffee, toasted walnuts, caramel, and fresh-baked bread. A terrific wine, with complex, elegant, and lingering flavours. Drink now-2009. **2000 ★ ★ ★ ★ ↗** Big, buttery style (though lighter than 2001) with tasty, toasted-hazelnut croissant flavours. Opulent, if not over the top. Drink now-2007. **1999 ★ ★ ★ →** From old vines. Deep gold with a fine buttered-oak nose and concentrated honeyed pear flavour. Drink now. **1998 ★ ★ ★ ★ →** Deep golden colour with a rich bouquet reminiscent of wild mushroom risotto. Great balance. Fully mature.

Gewürztraminer [NP] **2002** Not produced. **2001**☒ Mildly tainted with Asian lady beetle. **2000** ★ ★ ★ ➔ Lovely, oily, honeyed, spicy character not often found in local Gewürz. Deeply aromatic with terrific body, off-dry with balanced acidity and great length. Drink now-2006.

Gewürztraminer Icewine [NP] **2002** ★ ★ ★ ★ ➔ Rich, dense, and honeyed with nuances of tangerine, lemon extract, and spice. An outstanding wine to be drunk over the next 5 years. **1999** ★ ★ ★ ★ ★ ➔ *Gold & Best of Class, Ontario Wine Awards 2001; Gold, All Canadian Wine Championships 2001; Gold, Concours Mondial, Brussels 2001.* Fabulous flavours of tropical fruits and exotic spices. Drink now-2011.

Meritage [NP] **2002** ★ ★ ★ ☆ ↗ Deep garnet with aromas of charred oak, vanilla, raspberry, and cassis. Youthful bite has softened. Has a lingering fruit finish. Drink now-2013. **2001** ★ ★ ★ ↗ Deep garnet colour and initial aromas of black fruits and charred oak. Lean, strong fruit flavour, but hints of Asian lady beetle surface after extended aeration. Drink now-2010. **2000** ★ ★ ★ ☆ ↑ (CF20/C$40/M40) Dense garnet hue. Austere, closed at first with oaky, vegetal, earthy, leafy undertone. Deep down black currant and plum flavours overshadowed by the wine's rigid structure. 1,000 cases made. Drink 2007-2012. **1999** ★ ★ ★ ↗ *Gold, Cuvée 2002.* (CF14/CS50/M36) Lean, elegant, well structured. Not as big and overripe as the 1998. Silky, with soft tannins and delicious cassis bouquet. Drink now-2011. **1998** ★ ★ ★ ★ ↗ *Best Meritage, Canadian Wine Awards 2001; Best Red Wine, Cuvée 2001; Best Red Trophy, All Canadian Wine Championships 2000.* (CF36/CS27/M37). A big bruiser. Full-bodied, warm fruit flavours, with smoky, chocolate, fruitcake aromas. Strong, solid core and fleshy, supple texture. Drink now-2018.

Merlot [NP] **2002** ★ ★ ★ ☆ ↑ Garnet with a purple-pink rim. Closed nose is dense with pepper and oak notes. Lovely, thick texture, clean, tart, balanced. Drink 2007-2014. **2001** ★ ★ ☆ ↗ Bright garnet hue with brick-coloured edges. Fullish texture and jovial berry flavours. Signs of Asian lady beetle appeared when the bottle was open for more than a few hours. Drink now-2008. **2000** ★ ★ ★ ↗ Garnet hue with a bouquet full of joy. Plummy with soft, velvety texture and a lingering finish. Drink now-2009. **1998** ★ ★ ★ ↗ Deep garnet with a dark brick rim. Dense smoky, oaky nose with black fruits, nuts, mint, eucalyptus, and juniper berry notes. Taste is sturdy with resiny flavours and mouth-drying tannins. Needs time. Drink 2006-2011.

Méthode Classique (Sparkling Wine) [NP] **2001** ★ ★ ★ ☆ ↺ Pale straw-gold with a crisp lemony nose and Granny Smith apple flavours. Refreshing taste. **2000** ★ ★ ★ ↺ Pale straw-gold with fine bubbles that last well. Nutty-sweet aroma reminiscent of vanilla halvah. **1999**★★★↻ (67%C-33%PN) Clean, crisp, and varietally balanced. Not very complex but plump, with firm, ripe fruit flavours.

Riesling [NP] **2000**★★★☆↗ Bright yellow-gold shade and gorgeous honey, lime, and petrol nose. Big, fat, thick mouthfeel. Pair with rich food. Drink now-2008.

Riesling Icewine [NP] **2002**★★★★↑ Intensely sweet, concentrated, and shy. Components are there, but not working together just yet. Taste has painfully sharp acidity for now. Needs time to tone down. Drink 2008-2016.

Proprietors' Reserve (Black Label)

Cabernet Franc/Cabernet Sauvignon [NP] **2002**★★★↗ Garnet with a rich cherry and plum scent. Lean, delicate, and elegant. Drink now-2008. **2001**★★★↗ This well-made wine started with a lovely scent of rich red and black fruits with good tannin balance. The following day, though, the same bottle showed hints of Asian lady beetle. Drink now-2006.

Cabernet Franc/Merlot [NP] **1997**★★★→ Brilliant ruby-garnet hue. Fragrant, inviting bouquet with raspberry and black-currant aromas. Silky, smooth mouthfeel. A luscious gulp. Drink now-2008.

Chardonnay [NP] **2003**★★★→ Pale gold with an aroma of coffee with cream. Nice balance of fruity and bitter notes. Drink now-2007. **2002**★★★→ *Best General List White Wine, Cuvée 2004.* Pale straw-gold with a clean, light, citrus, peach, and vanilla cream aroma. Shy but charming taste of fruit macerated in condensed milk. High alcohol (13%) leaves a hot, spirity finish. Drink now through 2006. **2001**☒ Overwhelming Asian lady beetle taint. **2000**★★★→ Rich gold with a warm bouquet of baked pastry, pear tart, and nut bread. Drink now. **1999**↓ Kaput. Oxidized.

Gewürztraminer [NP] **2002**★★★→ Deep gold with fresh, candied fruit notes. Clean and refreshing with a pleasant bitterness in the finish. **2001**☒ Taste ruined by Asian lady beetle. **2000**★★★→ Rich gold hue with hints of maderization on the nose. Interesting oily, honeyed fruit nuances. Drink up. **1999**★★★→ Pale watery-gold with amber reflections. Starting to oxidize. Still has wonderful flavours of baked apple, stewed peach, and wine gums. Drink soon.

Meritage [NP] **2002**★★★↗ Garnet with oaky overtones and a bouquet of mocha, black currant, plum, and blackberries. Big and tough with medium full body and a lovely bitter finish. Drink now-2010. **2001**☒ Spoiled by Asian lady beetle. **2000**★★★→ (CF30/CS36/M34) Deep garnet with rich bouquet of black currant and raspberry. Big on ripe flavours, short on complexity, and there's a hollow spot mid-palate. 8,000 cases. Drink now-2010. **1999**★★★→ (CF30/CS45/M25) Elegant with ripe cassis flavours. Silky texture, like warm berry compote. Drink now-2009. **1998**★★★↗ (CF32/CS52/M16) Solid garnet colour to the rim.

Generous nose of stewing berries. Macho-bodied, smoky, dry, rich, and supple. Drink now-2012. **1997**★★★→ (CF37/CS39/M24) Garnet with warm, inviting aroma of cherry pie and cookies. About to hit its peak. Drink now-2009. **1995**★★★★→ (CF40/CS49/ M11) Warm, mahogany-garnet hue with a simmering bouquet that touches on fennel, licorice, dark chocolate, brewed coffee, and more. Peaking. Drink now-2007.

Merlot [NP] **2002**★★★↗ Garnet with a blueberry and plum aroma. Soft and plush with apple-skin flavours and a long, satiny finish.

Méthode Cuve Close Sparkling Wine [NP] **2001**★↻ Brilliant gold colour, several beads of fine bubbles. Dusty nose and dull palate. Lacks charm.

Pinot Noir [NP] **2000**★★★→ Grapes from the Theissen vineyard. Clean, taut, light, with nuances of sandalwood and boiled beets. Developing well with fine fruit and oak balance. 350 cases. Drink now-2006.

Riesling [NP] **2002**★★★→ Bright gold with a bit of spritz. Austere grapefruity taste with nuances of apple, lemon, and herbs. Drink now-2008. **2001**☒ Has Asian lady beetle taint.

Riesling, Dry [NP] **2003**★★★→ Pale straw colour with a clean and sweetish grapefruity aroma. Honeyed lemon-orange flavour with a crisp finish. Drink now-2007. **2001**☒ Taste ruined by Asian lady beetle.

Sauvignon Blanc [NP] **2001**★↻ Grapes from the George vineyard. Tasted twice. One bottle was crisp and clean in the Sancerre style, the other showed clear signs of Asian lady beetle. Drink up.

Vidal Icewine [NP] **2002**★★★↗ Intensely sweet. Straightforward with some pear and apricot flavours. Drink now-2008. **2001**★★★★↗ Super-concentrated with lovely acidity. Drink now-2010. **1999**★★★★★→ *Gold & Best of Class, Ontario Wine Awards 2001.* Very concentrated. Full of lovely peach and pineapple nuances. Drink now-2007. **1994**★★★↘ Simple and yummy. Drink soon.

<u>**Proprietors' Selection (White Label)**</u>

Cabernet-Merlot [nonVQA] **2002**★★★→ Plush, velvety texture with nicely developing fruit, solid mouthfeel, and good balance. Drink now-2008.

Cabernet Sauvignon [nonVQA] **2002**★★★→ Garnet colour with a soft, plummy, black-currant nose and nuances of pencil shavings. Dry, balanced, and well structured. Decent drinking, now-2008.

Cabernet-Shiraz [nonVQA] **2002**★★★→ Black-cherry colour with soft, plummy, black-currant bouquet. Clean, pure fruit flavours. Relatively unidimensional but highly satisfying.

Chardonnay [nonVQA] **2002**★★➜ Good light flavours in a simple and straightforward white. Washed-out pear, lemon, and grapefruit nuances.

Merlot [nonVQA] **2002**★★★➜ Varietally pure and clean with some strawberry and blueberry aromas. Soft flavours, juicy acidity, and solid structure. Drink now-2007.

Pinot Noir [nonVQA] **2002**★★➜ Sweet, ripe, and intensely flavoured with a candied overtone. Soft, light, and short.

Riesling [nonVQA] **2000**★➜ Gold with an oxidative, candied nose. Unexciting, but passable.

Sauvignon Blanc [nonVQA] **2002**★★➜ Clean with a light, pithy, lemon aroma. Unexciting, but sound.

Semillon-Chardonnay [nonVQA] **2001**★★➜ Some grassy nuances but dry, oxidative, resiny overtones dominate somewhat tired fruit flavours. Match with bland food.

Shiraz [nonVQA] **2002**★★★➜ Black-cherry colour with a lean blackberry and black raspberry aroma and taste. Balanced, dry, and crisp.

White Merlot [nonVQA] **2002**★★★➜ Pretty pink, pretty sweet, and pretty good.

• JÄGGER FARM (St. Catharines, NP) – This 27-acre property belonging to Fred Hernder is on 3rd Avenue at 3rd Street Louth. It's flat and the soil is quite sandy with some pebbly sections. Hernder grows 2 acres of Vidal, 5 acres of New York Muscat, and 10 acres of Niagara and Concord, which he sells to a large producer of kosher wines in the United States. The remaining 15 acres were planted with Chardonnay and Riesling in 1998, and subsequently underdrained every second row.

• JAMIE SLINGERLAND VINEYARD (Niagara-on-the-Lake, NP) – Jamie Slingerland is the son-in-law of Gary Pillitteri and vineyard manager for Pillitteri Estates Winery. His own vineyard, on the south side of Line 1 between Concessions 2 and 3, is a mere 4 acres of Chinguacousy clay loam planted entirely to Cabernet Sauvignon. All fruit goes to the family winery.

• JORDAN & STE. MICHELLE CELLARS – Established in 1926, it was bought out by T.G. Bright & Co. in 1987. Its 2 primary contributions to the wine industry include the development of an experimental vineyard, known today as Butler's Grant Vineyard, and the construction of one of Canada's largest underground cellars, currently owned by Cave Spring Cellars.

- **JOSEPH'S ESTATE WINES** (1811 Niagara Stone Road [Highway 55], R.R.#3, Niagara-on-the-Lake, ON, L0S 1J0 / Phone: 905-468-1259 / Toll-Free: 1-866-468-1259 / Fax: 905-468-3103 / Email: info@ josephsestatewines.com / Website: www.josephsestatewines.com)

(Est. 1996) In 1979, Joe Pohorly, a native of Vineland, a farmer's son, high-school teacher, civil and architectural engineer, and admitted workaholic, founded the Newark Winery, the third boutique winery to be licensed in Ontario since Prohibition. Three years later, he sold a majority interest to German investors Scholl & Hillebrand, which renamed it Hillebrand Estate Winery and retained him as a consultant winemaker. The following year, after helping Hillebrand to produce one of Canada's first icewines, Pohorly sold his remaining shares and purchased a half-interest in The Colonel Butler Inn in Niagara-on-the-Lake. He and his wife, Betty, ran the inn for several years, but the urge to make wine persisted. In 1992, he bought 20 acres of orchard and fruitland and immediately began to convert most of it to grapes. The Pohorly vineyard is virtually flat with a drop of 14 ft. from its western limit to the opposite border on the East West Line. It is well-drained Vineland lacustrine sandy loam with the additional benefit of drainage tiles every 40 ft. Today, the estate is planted 1,000 vines to the acre with 1.5 acres each of Baco Noir, Cabernet Franc, Chancellor, Chardonnay, Pinot Noir, Riesling, Vidal Blanc, and 5 acres of Pinot Gris. Current wine production averages 32,000 cases annually. Pohorly also cultivates .5 acres each of strawberries, peaches, and pears. In 1998, he discovered the health benefits of grape seed oil and began work on developing a process for cold-pressing high-quality Canadian oil from the region's grape pomace and, recently, began production of Dr. Joseph's Grape Seed Oil. A year earlier, Pohorly received his Ph.D. in environmental engineering from Columbia University. He has won The National Research Council's Regional Innovation Award and, last year, was named Niagara-on-the-Lake's Businessman of the Year. Also in 2004, the winery was chosen as one of the top-10 Canadian wineries in a *Toronto Star* readers' poll.

Winemakers: Joseph Pohorly (1996-present); Katherine Reid (1996-present) / Vineyard Manager: Joseph Pohorly

Cabernet Franc [NP] **1999** ★ ★ ➔ Ruby-garnet with a vague, vinous nose. Functional but uninteresting. Drink now-2006.

Cabernet Franc, Icewine [NP] **2001** ★ ★ ★ ★ ➔ Tawny colour with a rich strawberry custard aroma and a nuance of orange pekoe tea. Very intense with flavours of strawberry syrup and stewed cherries. Drink now-2009.

Chancellor, Grand Reserve [NP] **2001** ★ ★ ☆ ➔ Opaque garnet shade with oak, cream, milk chocolate, blackberry, wild goldenrod, and milkweed aromas. Clean and deeply flavoured, but distinctly hybrid. Drink now-2007.

Chardonnay [NP] **2002**★☆↻ Gold colour with a yeasty, bread-dough aroma and a fullish unfiltered aftertaste.

Gamay, Caroline's Rosé [NP] **2002**★★↻ Very pale orange-red hue with a candied fruit-cocktail bouquet. Sweetish with a clean, melted candy taste. Chill well.

Gewürztraminer [NP] **2001**★☆↻ Straw-gold with a boiled-down fruit aroma. Light, candied lemon flavour.

Merlot, Reserve [NP] **2002**★★☆→ Deep garnet with an aroma of stewed plum butter. Flavour starts well but finishes tart. Drink now-2008.

Petite Sirah [NP] **2001**★★☆→ Ruby garnet with a nose of sweet canned cherries. Tart, clean vinous flavour. Drink now-2006.

Pinot Grigio [NP] **2002**☆↻ Straw-gold with tiny bubbles forming inside the glass. Lemony with a slight chemical nuance. Balanced acid and sweetness, but there's an unclean yeasty aspect to the aftertaste.

Pinot Noir [NP] **1999**★★★→ Cherry-amber with mahogany reflections. Lovely aromatic hints of licorice, plum, and faded rose. Drink now, it's mature.

Riesling [NP] **2000**★☆↻ Straw-gold with bubbles forming inside of the glass. Odd ginseng nuance with a lemon-grass overtone. Clean lemony taste.

Vidal, Icewine [NP] **1999**★★★★→ *Best Commercial Dessert Wine, Indy International Wine Competition 2004; Double Gold, All Canadian Wine Championship 2003.* Deep gold with a bouquet of crème brûlée drizzled with sweet pear liqueur. Sweet, balanced, heady, and delicious. Drink now-2011. **1998**★★★★→ *Best Commercial Dessert Wine, Indy International Wine Competition 2001.* Amber-gold with a honeyed lemon, crème caramel, and poire william eau-de-vie. Opulent, complex, and lingering. Drink now-2012.

Vidal, Late Harvest [NP] **1996**★★★→ Fullish body; fruit now leaning toward caramelized pear and white peach.

Vidal, Special Select Late Harvest, "Winter Harvest" [NP] **1999**★★★☆→ Bright gold with a lightly honeyed poached-pear aroma. Light, soft, sweet, and balanced. Drink now-2009.

Zweigelt, Reserve [NP] **2001**★★→ Deep garnet with violet-purple reflections. Mildly floral nose with a taste of wild blackberries. Hard tannins and relatively high acidity. Drink now-2007.

K

- **KACABA VINEYARDS** (3550 King Street, Vineland, ON, L0R 2C0 / Phone: 905-562-5625 / Fax: 905-562-1111 / Email: info@kacaba.com / Website: www.kacaba.com)

(Est. 1999) Mike Kacaba is a Saskatchewan farm boy of Ukrainian heritage who became a successful Bay Street litigation lawyer. He and his wife, Joanne, a systems administrator at the University of Toronto, purchased a 33-acre tract of land that was about to be turned into a subdivision. The couple immediately began developing the moderately sloped, north-facing Oneida clay loam till into a vineyard. Today there are just under 20 acres of the Bordeaux varieties, Cabernet Franc, Cabernet Sauvignon, and Merlot, plus some of the oldest Syrah in the peninsula. Despite economizing, he has sunk more than $3 million into this tiny gravity-flow operation. The wines are of very high quality. Last year, Ukrainian president Viktor Yushchenko came to see the winery he had heard great things about and was completely enamoured of the winery's icewines. Current production is approximately 7,000 cases and is targeted to grow to 10,000 cases by 2009.

Winemakers: Beth Mischuk (2002-present); Jim Warren (2000-present, consulting); Rob Warren (2000-2004); Sue Ann Staff (1999) / Vineyard Manager: Beth Mischuk

Cabernet Franc Icewine, "Joanne's Rouge" [NP] **2002**★★★★☆↗ Pale carmine with an onion-skin shade approaching the rim. Aromas of strawberry shortcake and taste of strawberry-cherry syrup with cranberry acidity. Luscious. Drink now-2010.

Cabernet Franc Reserve [NP] **2002**★★★★↗ Lovely, concentrated, and complex nose of plum, spice, gingerbread, and licorice. Lush, supple, and delicious. Drink now-2012.

Cabernet Sauvignon Reserve [NP] **2002**★★★★↗ Opaque garnet with a dense, closed nose. Black-currant and licorice aromas emerge after many hours. Concentrated ripe fruit taste, sweet texture, and tough, new-oak tannins. Drink 2008-2016.

Chardonnay [NP] **2002**★★★★→ From Lenko Vineyard old vines. Concentrated and deeply aromatic with a light, bready flavour in the finish. Drink now. **2000**★★★★→ From Bebenek Vineyard old vines. Big, oaky nose with Burgundian minerality and spiciness. Drink now. **1999**★★★↘ This first vintage was pale, light, and clean with an oaky, buttered melba nose. If you have any, drink up.

Gamay Noir [NP] **2002**★★★★↗ Ruby-garnet with a bumbleberry bouquet. Huge for a Gamay, with oaky structure, creamy texture, sweet, ripe, multidimensional flavours. Drink now-2008.

Gewürztraminer Icewine, "Jennifer's Jade" [NP] **2002**★★★★↗ Yellow-gold with a concentrated, sweet, spiced peach nose with a whiff of French fry oil. High-toned pear and pineapple flavours. Drink now-2012.

Gypsy [NP] **2000**★★↻ A light and aromatic patio wine made from Muscat, Riesling, Vidal Blanc, and Viognier.

Meritage [NP] **2002**★★★↗ Deep garnet with a dense, juicy, fruity bouquet marred briefly by an eggy odour. Yummy taste, though the fruit is somewhat unfocused at this early stage. Hide until after 2006. **2000**★★★↗ Gold, Cuvée 2003, Gold & Best Red, Ottawa Wine & Cheese Show 2002. (CF70/CS25/M5) Fullish and tough in its youth with some vegetal nuances. Thick and viscous texture and long aftertaste. Drink 2006-2010.

Merlot [NP] **2002**★★★☆↗ Gold, Ottawa Wine & Cheese Show 2003. Dark garnet with a bit of brownness along the rim. Soft blueberry and black-currant notes. Rich, supple, with concentrated fruit flavours and a soft tannic finish. Drink now-2012. **2001** Not released because of Asian lady beetle taint.

Pinot Noir [NP] **2002**★★★☆↗ Bright ruby with a restrained nose. Fruit is hidden for now as oak dominates releasing only nuances of sandalwood, vanilla, and field flowers. Sweet, ripe, and balanced. Drink 2006-2010. **1999**★★★→ Pale ruby-cherry with a light cherry aroma and flavour. Drink up.

Syrah [NP] **2002**★★★★↗ Bright purple-garnet with an intense blackberry aroma. Mildly herbal taste with hints of chocolate, licorice, spice, and dusty ginseng. Tongue-prickling alcohol. Desperately needs aging. Drink 2007-2015. **2001** Not released after Asian lady beetle taint was detected. **2000**★★★→ Purple-black in Sept. 2002, with a big, alcoholic nose. Tannic and closed with nuances of blackberry, spice, and pencil lead.

• **KELTA VINEYARD (Beamsville, NP)** — Steven and Rebecca Drotos farm this flat, underdrained property located on Greenlane Road at Merritt Road below the Escarpment, about 2 km from the lake and just east of the Culp Vineyard. They have a bit more than 13 acres, of which 8.5 are planted on Jeddo and Chinguacousy clay. Their oldest grapes come from a single acre of Vidal planted in 1980. The couple added 2 more acres of Vidal, 2 acres of Chardonnay, and 1.75 acres of Baco Noir in 1995, soon after purchasing the property. In 1997, they added 1.75 acres of Riesling. From 1997 to 2000, all grapes were sold to Henry of

Pelham. In 2001, everything went to home winemakers and, since 2002, grapes have been sold exclusively to Harbour Estates Winery.

- **KEW VINEYARD (Beamsville, NP)** – This 60-acre property has been witness to most of the history of Ontario's wine industry. First planted with labruscas in the mid-1950s by a German immigrant, it was eventually purchased by Dieter Guttler, who planted vinifera varieties in the late 1970s. His Riesling (Weis clone 21B), as well as some Chardonnay and a small amount of Chenin Blanc – which was later lost to crown gall – helped establish a quality reputation in 1985 for the emergent Vineland Estate Winery. Property ownership was transferred to Guttler's wife, who sold it to John Belanger while he was part-owner of Stoney Ridge Estate Winery. Today the vineyard is owned by Cuesta Estates & Winery Corp., and has 54 acres planted with Baco Noir, Cabernet Franc, Chardonnay, Gewürztraminer, the hybrid GR7, Merlot, Riesling, Sauvignon Blanc, Vidal Blanc, and Zweigelt at an average density of 1,300 vines per acre. Fruit is sold to various wineries.

- **KINZAT VINEYARD (Niagara-on-the-Lake, NP)** – Joseph Kinzat's vineyard is on Line 2 at Town Line Road, across the street from the Turek Vineyard. The flat property is composed of Chinguacousy clay loam and is fully tiled for drainage. Pillitteri buys seriously frozen Cabernet Sauvignon, Riesling, and Vidal Blanc for icewine production; the rest of the fruit is sold to Vincor.

- **KIRKBY VINEYARD (Niagara-on-the-Lake, NP)** – John Kirkby's vineyard is situated just west of the Lailey Vineyard. He recently planted Gamay and Riesling, which will find their way into Lailey's wines once the vines have matured.

- **KITTLING RIDGE ESTATE WINES & SPIRITS** (297 South Service Road, Grimsby, ON, L3M 4E9 / Phone: 905-945-9225 / Toll-Free Toronto Line: 416-777-6300 / Fax: 905-945-4330 / Email: admin@kittlingridge.com / Website: www.kittlingridge.com)

(Est. 1991) John Hall, a 23-year veteran winemaker, first with Parkdale Wines, then as executive vice-president for Rideout and Chateau-Gai, and his wife, Eileen, purchased the Rieder Distillery (founded by Otto Rieder). After running the business as it was for several years, they decided to add a winery licence and renamed the operation. In 1996, they bought out Culotta Wines, primarily to acquire that company's 6 retail licences. The winery owns no vineyards, preferring to leave the grape growing to grape growers and focusing on what it does best, vinifying and distilling.
    Winemaker: John Hall / Stillmaster: John Hall

Baco Noir [Ont] **2002**★↻ Ruby-garnet with a brick rim. Light but sharp nose of red fruits. Unexciting.

Cabernet [NP] **2002**★★↻ Light ruby with a red-brick rim. Nose hints at milk chocolate and red fruits. Light taste is balanced, clean with varietal decorum.

Cabernet Sauvignon, Proprietor's Cuvée [nonVQA] **NV**★★↻ Clean, lean, balanced, and easy-drinking. Soft, black fruit flavours.

Gamay-Cabernet [NP] **1994**★★↘ (CS45/Gam55) Brilliant ruby-purple colour, plummy with a mellow finish. Drink up.

Marechal Foch [Ont] **2002**□↻ Deep garnet colour, thick to the rim. Troubling nose is earthy, dirty, fungal, and hinting of dung. Bitter with a profound lack of charm.

Merlot, Proprietor's Cuvée [nonVQA] **NV**★★↻ Clean, sweet, candied fruit. Easy-drinking with plush, strawberry flavours.

Old Vines Foch [Ont] **2003**□↻ Ruby-garnet with a red-brick shade at the rim. Herbal notes with a hint of black-cherry cough syrup. Not to my taste. Weedy, vegetal, bitter, and sappy.

Riesling [NP] **1995**★★→ 2,200 cases made, using grapes from Vailmont and Mertens vineyards. Pale silvery hue, grapefruity nose, bland finish. Drink up.

Riesling-Gewürztraminer [Ont] **2002**★★↻ Pale gold with tiny bubbles forming on the inside of the glass. Some honey and petrol notes with barely off-dry pear and apple flavours.

Riesling-Gewürztraminer [NP] **1994**★↘ (Gew40-*Mertens Vineyard*/R60-*Vailmont Vineyard*) More dimension than plain Riesling but a touch softer. Fading fast.

Shiraz-Cabernet, Proprietor's Cuvée [nonVQA] **NV**★★↻ Dark purple colour with soft, candied, lightly spicy blackberry taste.

Trillium Red [Ont] **2002**★↻ Garnet with a pale purple rim. Light nose of red fruits. Sharp, tart, almost sour taste of underripe apples. Hint of veggies.

Vidal [Ont] **1994**★★↘ From the Shoemaker and Jakiniew vineyards. Slightly oaked but drink up.

Vidal Icewine [NP] **1991**★★★★→ *Grand Gold, VinItaly, 1994.* Golden and brilliant. Round and fullish with an excellent level of citrusy tartness.

Vidal, Late Harvest [Ont] **2001**★★★★→ I call this "Icewine Lite" as it has all the appeal and none of the intense sweetness of the frozen version. Candied pear flavours add to the charm. Drink now-2007.

White Zinfandel-Vidal, Proprietor's Cuvée [nonVQA] **NV** ★↻ Pale pink with a sweetish, candied flavour and a bitter almond finish.

Symmetry Collection

Chardonnay, Sur Lie, American Oak [NP] **2002**★★→ Pale gold with a lean, slightly oaky nose. Taste hints at apples sautéed in

browned butter. Light flavour, full body, high alcohol, and a somewhat bitter finish. Drink now.

Late Harvest Vidal [Ont] 2002★★★★➔ Deep gold hue with a
concentrated fruit syrup aroma. Flavours are reminiscent of vanilla-
pear ice cream and crème brûlée. Sweet, ripe, fresh, and balanced.
Drink now-2007.

Riesling [NP] 2001☒ Asian lady beetle detected.

Distilled Products

Icewine & Brandy NV★★★★↻. A blend of icewine and 7-year-
old brandy. The icewine lowers the brandy's alcohol level to 17 %,
while the brandy lowers the high sweetness level of the icewine
and adds a kiss of oak flavour. Dismissed and despised by the wine
industry as a bastardization of "true icewine," it is nevertheless very
popular with the drinking public. No wonder. It is absolutely delicious with its rich, not overly sweet flavour of poached pears and
lightly roasted walnuts. Stylistically, like an aged Pineau des Charentes
with higher residual sugar.

Vidal Icewine Grappa 30% alc./vol., produced in a small pot-still
from lightly pressed icewine grapes. 1991★★★★↻ Distinctly
sweet icewine nose, dry fiery palate, long lovely aftertaste.

• **KLOSE VINEYARD (Niagara-on-the-Lake, NP)** – This 15-acre property, which belongs to Inniskillin's vineyard manager, Gerald Klose, is
located at the corner of Niagara Parkway and Line 2, between Reif's
Estate Winery to the immediate south and Zabek Vineyard on the
north side of Line 2. Its proximity to the Niagara River provides the area
with some tempering influences during both summer and winter. This
moderating effect delays bud-break by several days in the spring but also
allows for later picking at harvest time. The soil is heavy Chinguacousy
clay loam with loose pea gravel in equal proportions sitting on a deep
bed of shale. The high percentage of pea gravel plays a key role in heat
retention, extending warmth and adding ripeness to the fruit throughout the growing season. The property is essentially flat with a very gentle
slope toward the middle. Underdrainage has been installed between
every row and the vineyard is not irrigated. There are 1.5 acres of
Cabernet Sauvignon and 10 acres of Chardonnay, most of it planted in
1986 at 1,300 vines per acre. An acre of Welschriesling was torn out
recently and left fallow for future planting. Grapes are sold exclusively to
Inniskillin. Klose employs minimal soil tillage, very little fertilization, and
lots of leaf removal to reduce vegetative growth. He thins about 40%-
50% of his Cabernet Sauvignon 1 month before harvest to ensure complete ripeness. Reds are hand-picked; whites are mechanically harvested.

• **Kocsis Vineyard** – *See:* Steve Kocsis Vineyards; Mountain Road Wine
Company

• **KONZELMANN ESTATE WINERY** (1096 Lakeshore Road, R.R.#3, Niagara-on-the-Lake, ON, L0S 1J0 / Phone: 905-935-2866 / Fax: 905-935-2864 / Email: wine@konzelmannwines.com / Website: www.konzelmannwines.com)

(Est. 1988) In 1982, having sold off a small family property in Stuttgart, Germany, Herbert and Gudrun Konzelmann settled on 40 acres just west of the town of Niagara-on-the-Lake. The primarily sandy loam soil of the lakefront property was reinforced against severe erosion with a rock wall in 1994. Since 1997, Herbert also owns 2 contiguous vineyards, Boldt and Gunter, just 5 km south of the home vineyard providing the winery with an additional 45 acres as loam. Until a few years ago, the winery used exclusively owned grapes, but as the business grows, more grapes have been purchased from neighbours. Currently, Konzelmann is able to supply 75%-80% of its needs with estate fruit. About 70 acres are planted with Cabernet Sauvignon, Chardonnay, Gamay, Gewürztraminer, Merlot, Pinot Blanc, Pinot Noir, Riesling, Riesling-Traminer, Shiraz, Vidal, and Zweigelt, all at an average of 1,509 vines per acre. The water's edge vineyard is early budding and susceptible to unexpected spring frost. Konzelmann used to make a much-loved peachwine, but the peach orchards have been taken out and replanted with vines. Production in the short-crop year of 2003 was 29,000 cases, of which about 10% is exported. In an average year, volume is closer to 40,000 cases.

Winemaker: Herbert Konzelmann (1996 Winemaker of the Year) / Vineyard Manager: Matthias Boss

Cabernet-Merlot Reserve, Unfiltered, Barrel-Aged [NP] **1998** ★ ★ ★ ★ ➔ *Gold, All Canadian Wine Championships 2002.* Opaque garnet with a dense, closed, oaky nose that slowly begins to reveal the rich fruit of plums and the wild perfume of cassis. Great balance and growing complexity. Drink now-2012.

Cabernet Sauvignon-Merlot Reserve, Barrel-Aged [NP] **1997** ★ ★ ★ ↘ Dark mahogany with an orange-brown rim. Candied black-fruit nose with an aroma of kirsch. Fruit is drying up. Drink now. **1995** ★ ★ ★ ➔ Light mahogany shade with a pale orange rim. Soft, candied red-fruit nose with hints of milk chocolate. Fully mature, holding well but ready to fade. Drink up.

Cabernet Sauvignon, Reserve, Barrel-Aged [NP] **2003** ★ ★ ★ ➔ Garnet with a dense, closed blackberry aroma. Lean and tart with an excellent balance of ripe, fruit sweetness and bitter tannins. Drink now-2011. **2000** ★ ★ ★ ➔ Garnet coloured with a closed, dense, ripe fruit nose. Still backward and undeveloped. Drink 2007-2014.

Cabernet Sauvignon Icewine [NP] **2002** ★ ★ ★ ★ ➔ Coral colour with an herbal note at first, followed by fruity hints of strawberry and black currant. Light in flavour with intense jammy sweetness. Drink now-2010.

Chardonnay [NP] 2002★★★➜ Fresh and balanced with enticing poached pear and vanilla flavours. A lovely quaffer for early consumption.

Chardonnay, Barrel-Fermented [NP] 1994★★★↘ Still charming but drink soon. 1993★★★↘ Complex and superb with lively acidity, big oaky oxidative flavours, and high-extract fruit. Drink up.

Chardonnay, Grande Reserve [NP] 2003★★★★↗ Gold with a big, oaky, buttery nose. Soft, full, ripe, nutty, creamy vanilla flavours with depth and fine balance. Drink now-2009. **2000** *Gold, VinItaly 2003; Gold, All Canadian Wine Championships 2003.*

Gewürztraminer, Late Harvest [NP] 2003★★★★➜ Pale gold with a bouquet of lychee, lime, and honey. A terrific wine, surprisingly dry. Taste reminds of broiled grapefruit. Classic. Drink now-2009. **2002**★★★➜ Deep yellow-gold with a subdued nose. Rich flavours of honey and lanolin surface, but acidity is low. Drink early. **1996**★★★➜ *Best Aromatic White, Cuvée 1998.* **1994**★★★↘ Absolutely yummy with sweet, spicy flavours of honey and lychee. Drink up. **1993**★★★↘ Soft, sweet, fruity, and balanced with roasted peach/apricot flavours. Drink up.

Merlot, Barrel-Aged [NP] 2001★★★↗ Deep garnet with a spirity nose. Palate locked tight. Drink now-2009.

Merlot, Grand Reserve Classic [NP] 1999★★★★➜ *Best Limited Edition Red Wine, Cuvée 2005.* Deep garnet with a brick-red rim. Oaky, smoky, and bursting with black currant, black cherry, raspberry, spiced apple. Soft and ready but strong tannins will subside slowly. Drink now-2010.

Merlot, Reserve [NP] 2002★★★↻ Ruby-cherry with a pale orange rim. Dusty, perfumed nose and light body. A quickie, for drinking now-2006. **2001**★★★➜ Pale garnet with a fresh, medicinal, slightly herbal nose. Juicy, fruity taste for drinking now-2006. **2000**★★★↗ Ruby-garnet with a full, candied aroma of sweet red fruits, strawberry-rhubarb compote. Ripe, lush taste with a dusty, smoky finish. Drink now-2008. **1998** *Gold, All Canadian Wine Championships 2000.*

Pinot Blanc [NP] 2003★★★↻ Silvery gold with a clean, light, vinous aroma. Ripe and crisp with a pleasant personality for a simple wine. Drink now with gusto.

Pinot Noir (Spätburgunder) [NP] 2002★★★★➜ Pale ruby with mahogany reflections. Nose reminds me of an Alsace Pinot Noir with its delicacy and sweet fruit notes. A light-bodied wine with more flavour than the aromas would suggest. Drink now-2007. **1998**★★★➜ *Gold, All Canadian Wine Championships 2000.* Lovely, aging mahogany/cherrywood hue with a rich, ripe, sweet, and fully mature cabbage and plum nose. Marvellous drinking right now. **1993**★★★➜ Balanced fruit and oak now fully integrated. Has some complexity. Drink up.

Pinot Noir Reserve, Barrel-Aged, Unfiltered [NP] 1998
★ ★ ★ ★ ★ → Deep ruby-garnet with hint of pale brick beginning
to show up on the rim of the glass. Spectacular, concentrated, ripe,
balanced, and beguiling nose, like only a Pinot can provide. Tremendous depth with layer upon layer of flavour slowly being revealed
over a number of hours. Sandalwood, incense, spice, berries, plums,
boiled beets, black cherries, smoked sausage, tar, and licorice. And,
there's more to come. Drink now-2012.

Riesling [NP] 2003 ★ ★ ★ ↺ Pale gold with a lovely spritzy character. Clean, light, fresh-tasting, uncomplicated, and charming. Drink
now. 1989 ★ ★ ★ → Has 3% sussreserve. Deep, honeyed, spicy,
petrol nose. Fruity and elegant. Drink up.

Riesling Reserve, Winemaster's Collection Grand Reserve
[NP] 2000 ★ ★ ★ ★ ↗ Brilliant green-gold hue with rich petrol
overtones. Slightly over-sulphured. Excellent balance and great
flavours with a nice, bitter mineral undertone and an earthy finish.
A terrific food wine.

Riesling, Late Harvest [NP] 2001 ★ ★ ★ ★ ☆ → Gold, Toronto Wine
& Cheese Show, 2004. Deep gold with a concentrated pear syrup,
brown sugar, caramel, and vanilla cream nose. Sweet, luscious, and
perfectly balanced, with tremendous complexity of flavours. Drink
now-2016.

Riesling, Select Late Harvest [NP] 2001 ★ ★ ★ ★ → Gold & Best
Sweet Wine Trophy, Cuvée 2004; Gold & Best Value Sweet Wine Trophy,
Toronto Wine & Food Show 2004. Clean, with applelike acidity,
poached pear flavours, and a deep, wonderful light finish. Drink
now-2015.

Riesling-Traminer, Icewine [NP] 1994 Best Canadian Sweet Wine,
Toronto Wine & Cheese Show, 1996.

Riesling-Traminer, Late Harvest Dry [NP] 2002 ★ ★ ★ ☆ →
Gold, Ontario Wine Awards, 2004. Pale gold with amber highlights
and a ripe apricot, lime, orange, and mango nose with deep, flinty
minerality. The nose has sweetness, but the taste is herbal and
grapefruity. Drink now-2010.

Riesling-Traminer, Special Select Late Harvest [NP] 1997
★ ★ ★ ★ ↗ Gold, All Canadian Wine Championships 2000; Gold,
Concours Mondial 2000. Pale amber-gold with a honeyed and
buttery nose. Developing complexity with notes of tea, caramel,
orange juice, and apricot nectar. Good body and pleasant bitter
finish of tea and grape skins. Drink now-2015.

Vidal Icewine [NP] 2000 ★ ★ ★ ★ → Gold, International Wine &
Spirit Competition 2003; Gold, Cuvée 2003; Gold, All Canadian Wine
Championships 2002; Gold & Best Vidal Icewine Trophy, Canadian
Wine Awards 2002. Pale gold with a highly aromatic, floral, and
perfumy nose. Taste is of spiced fruits, citrus, vanilla, and honey.
Drink now-2010. 1998 ★ ★ ★ ★ ☆ ↗ Gold, Concours Mondial 2000;
Gold, All Canadian Wine Championships 2000; Best Dessert Wine,

Cuvée 2000. Amber-gold with a bouquet of apricot fruit leather. Mouth-watering, rich, supple, smooth, and satisfying. Drink now-2012. **1997** ★ ★ ★ ★ ➔ *Gold, Ontario Wine Awards, 1999.* **1994** ★ ★ ★ ★ ➔ Luscious and intensely fruity, almost perfumed. **1993** ★ ★ ★ ★ ➔ Intense, balanced, delicious. Drink up.

Vidal Select Late Harvest [Ont] **1994** *Gold, Toronto Wine & Cheese Show 1996.*

Zweigelt Reserve [NP] **2003** ★ ★ ★ ↗ Garnet with a fresh nose of mulberries and pencil lead. Fresh and quaffable. Easy to like, it is packed with light flavours of black cherry and finishes with a wallop of alcohol. Drink now-2008.

• **KUGLER FARM AND KUGLER VINEYARD (Niagara-on-the-Lake, NP)** – Thomas Kugler's 2 flat properties lie less than 1 km apart. The 13-acre "farm" is situated on the north side of Line 1 just west of Concession 3. Here the soil is very sandy. Kugler cultivates Merlot, Pinot Gris, Syrah, and Vidal Blanc for Konzelmann Estate Winery, as well as a tiny amount of Seyval Blanc that he turns into his own family's house wine. Neighbouring vineyards include Konzelmann's Boldt and Gunther Vineyards to the north and east, Mori Nursery to the south, and 1 of the vineyards belonging to Caroline Cellars to the west. The 17-acre "vineyard" site, where Kugler's home is located, lies just north of Line 2 at Concession 3. The soil closer to the road is sandy loam, and becomes sandier toward the back of the property. Baco Noir, Cabernet Sauvignon, Chardonnay, Gewürztraminer, Pinot Noir, and Vidal Blanc are cultivated for Konzelmann Estate, while 3 rows of Riesling-Traminer are sold off elsewhere. This tract is sandwiched between Caroline Cellars and Erv Willms's Sandstone Vineyard. Both properties are underdrained and irrigated, with vine spacing at about 1,200 plants per acre. Yields average 3-3.5 t. per acre for viniferas and 7-8 t. per acre for hybrids.

L

- **LAILEY VINEYARDS** (15940 Niagara Parkway, Niagara-on-the-Lake, ON, L0S 1J0 / Phone: 905-468-0503 / Fax: 905-468-8012 / Email: tonya@laileyvineyard.com / Website: www.laileyvineyard.com)

(Est. 2000) The 20-acre home farm that now supplies the raw material for some of Ontario's most exciting wines was first planted with hybrid grape varieties and fruit trees in the early 1950s by William and Nora Lailey. In 1970, their son, David, and daughter-in-law, Donna, bought the farm, which is situated on the Niagara Parkway, 2 km south of Niagara-on-the-Lake next door to Reimer Farm and not far from the Zabek Vineyard. Donna and David started D&D Farms selling juice and grapes from their own vineyard and, eventually, sourcing from other Niagara growers, to supply commercial wineries as well as amateur winemakers. Over the years, they began to convert their own property to classic European varieties. By 1991, Donna was honoured as Ontario's first female Grape King – she insisted on being called Queen – for having the best-looking vineyard in the province. (Curiously, Donna is allergic to grapes.) For most of her professional life, Donna has been a grower and a negotiant, and it was in this context that she met Derek Barnett, then winemaker at Southbrook Farm. In 2000, Donna and David, their daughter Tonya and her husband, Yves Starreveld, joined with Derek and his wife, Judith, to establish a new estate winery, Lailey Vineyard, with Derek as manager and winemaker. The winery now comprises 24 acres – the original 20-acre property plus an adjoining 4-acre parcel. All of the larger property is flat land with a few troublesome dips where frosty air tends to pool during sudden freeze-ups. The soil is foot-deep, sandy loam over limestone and shale with significant amounts of gravel in some areas. Varieties grown here include Cabernet Franc, Cabernet Sauvignon, Chardonnay, Merlot, Pinot Noir, Riesling, Sauvignon Blanc, Seyval Blanc, Vidal Blanc, and Zweigelt. The newer property has a rolling aspect with two hills that have a gradient of about 20% and somewhat heavier soil, although both sites are completely tiled, providing excellent drainage. It is planted predominantly with Pinot Noir but also has a few rows of Malbec, Petit Verdot, and Semillon for blending with the classic Bordeaux grapes. Lailey is not yet organic, but has eliminated all herbicide use in the vineyards and is moving determinedly in that direction with the help of a Burgundian viticulturalist. In the cellar, a majority of the wines have been aged in French oak barrels; however, the winery was the first in the country to carry out trials with Canadian oak, and is dedicating greater percentages of its production each year to aging in Canadian barrels. Currently, the winery produces an average of 8,000 cases. Production should peak at 9,500 cases by the end of 2006.

Winemaker: Derek Barnett (2000-present, 2000 Winemaker of the Year) / Vineyard Manager: Donna Lailey

Cabernet Franc [NP] **2002**★★★★↗ Deep garnet colour with smoky, charred oak notes and rich black-fruit aromas. Very complex with layers of lovely fruit, nut, and wood flavours that last and last. Long-lived. Drink 2006-2018. **2001**★★★★↗ Brilliant garnet colour with a profound nose of cigar tobacco, cedar, herbs, spice, iodine, oak, and French fry fat. Great depth and complexity with lean texture, lush flavours of plums, blackberries, and chocolate, and balanced, soft tannins. Drink 2006-2014.

Cabernet Franc, Canadian Oak [NP] **2002**★★★★↗ Deep garnet colour with herbal, tobacco, seaweed notes that open to dense, lovely black-fruit and wild herb flavours. Implicitly sweet with a delicate vegetal undertone. Drink 2008-2016.

Cabernet-Merlot [NP] **2002**★★★↗ Deep garnet with pale pink edges. Dusty nose of earth and paper filter pad. Lacks the depth of the single varietals but is balanced and has soft, red-fruit flavours. Drink 2008-2018. **2001**★★★↗ (CF40/CS45/M15) Lavender-perfumed nose with a vegetal note in the background. Velvety mouthfeel and long lingering taste. Just beginning to open up. Drink 2006-2015.

Cabernet Sauvignon [NP] **2002**★★★★↗ Deep garnet hue with a concentrated and complex nose of caramel, licorice, herbs, spice, and mint. Thick, rich texture, solid structure, with perfect balance of flesh to bones. Drink 2008-2020. **2001**★★★★↗ Powerful textbook nose and lush palate with flavours of plum and black currant. Drink 2006-2016.

Cabernet Sauvignon, Canadian Oak [NP] **2002**★★★★↗ A triumph. Powerful, oaky nose with massive, plummy spiced fruit. Palate still closed up, but balance of dense fruit, high acid, and nutty tannins is excellent. Drink 2008-2020.

Chardonnay [NP] **2003**★★★↗ Gold colour with an inviting nose of concentrated lemon butter and oak aromas. High acidity and powerful, smoky-oaky-nutty flavours. Big. Drink now-2008. **2002**★★★↗ Brilliant gold hue. Oaky nose with nuances of roasted coffee beans. Perfectly integrated fruit and oak. Drink now-2008. **2001**★★★→ Rich gold colour with a full, toasty nose and a rich buttery texture. Seamless fruit and oak balance. Drink now-2006.

Chardonnay, Canadian Oak [NP] **2003 ★ ★ ★ ↗** Pale gold with a bouquet that's both refined and reserved. Slowly, aromas of coconut, hazelnut, and lemon custard emerge. Seems fragile at first, but it's just the wine's fineness, delicacy, and graceful delivery of flavours. Drink now-2009. **2002 ★ ★ ★ ★ →** Rich gold with an oaky, herbal aroma and nutty, vanilla nuances. Rich, seductive flavours of butter, toffee, and pear tart. Long finish. Drink now-2009. **2001 ★ ★ ★ →** Gold with interesting nuances of apple blossom, licorice, coconut butter, and toasted biscuits. Lean but firm core. Only 25 cases made. Drink now-2007.

Chardonnay, Limited Edition [NP] **2002 ★ ★ ★ ★ ↗** *Gold, Ontario Wine Awards, 2004.* Deep gold with rich, oaky, toasty nose of roasted almonds and hazelnuts. Fruit still locked in by oak. Drink 2006-2010.

Chardonnay, Old Vines [NP] **2002 ★ ★ ★ ★ ↗** Has an oily look. Rich gold with amber reflections. Nose is undeveloped but already showing apple, peach, pear, mango, and pineapple flavours. So ripe it seems sweet, which it's not. Thick, lush, superbly oaked. Drink now-2010 **2001 ★ ★ ★ ★ →** Gold with a lively, even passionate nose of white fruit, flowers herbs, butter, spice, and nuts. Tart, hot, vibrating with flavour and eager to please. Drink now-2009. **2000 ★ ★ ★ ★ ↗** Old gold hue that's starting to turn amber. Bouquet is losing its youth, but hasn't yet evolved into maturity. Big, fat, and complex flavours of honey, herbs, spice, and cereal. 75 cases made. Drink now-2008.

Gamay [NP] **2003 ★ ★ →** Pale cherry with an earthy aroma and hints of strawberry. Taste is a touch severe for a wine that should be friendly, jubilant, and easy-drinking. Drink now.

Gewürztraminer [NP] **2002 ★ ★ ★ ↗** Gold with a strong whiff of diesel fuel and sulphur that gives way to herbal notes of rosemary and sage with a grapefruit pith undertone. Austere and severe with solid backbone and good acidity. Needs time to relax. Drink 2006-2012.

Merlot [NP] **2002 ★ ★ ★ ★ ↗** Deep garnet with a dense nose of herbs, chocolate, coffee, cream, and spice. Very ripe, sweet fruit and soft tannins. Rich, supple, and lovely. Drink 2008-2016.

Pinot Noir [NP] **2003 ★ ★ ★ ☆ ↗** Ruby with clean aromas of berries and bacon fat. Sweet, ripe, and dense with plenty of new flavours to develop in years to come. Drink 2006-2013. **2002 ★ ★ ★ ★ ↗** Ruby-garnet hue with a soft cherry, strawberry, and fresh-sawn oak bouquet. Pure, varietal flavours of cherry, sandalwood, mushroom, earth, and dried autumn leaves. Yumsters. Drink 2006-2012. **2001 ★ ★ ★ →** Lovely aromas at first but a smoked rubber nuance sets in after a few minutes. Has body but lacks charm. Drink now-2009.

Pinot Noir, Canadian Oak [NP] **2003 ★ ★ ★ ↑** Ruby with an assertive nose that is significantly more perfumed than the regular

Pinot Noir. It, too, is sweet and ripe but has somewhat more aggressive tannins. Drink 2007-2014. **2002★★★★↗** Earthy, leather notes with tart cherry fruit flavours. More forward fruit than the regular version. Drink now-2010.

Riesling [NP] **2002★★★↗** Pale straw with spritzy bubbles appearing in the glass. Crisp, grapefruity, with hint of lemon and peach. Juvenile and undeveloped fruit with solid mineral core. Taut. Drink 2006-2011.

Riesling Dry, Late Harvested [NP] **2002★★★↗** Lovely confected nose hints at face powder. Surprisingly taut at first, opens to flavours of honey and petrol after a few minutes. Drink now-2015.

Riesling Icewine [NP] **2002★★★★↑** Concentrated with sweet, poached-pear notes. Thick, rich body with a long life ahead. Drink 2007-2017.

Rosé [NP] **2003★★★↻** Usually made from Gamay, this vintage is primarily Vidal Blanc with a splash of Chambourcin. Pale cherry-pink with a strawberry-rhubarb compote nose and an undertone of pink grapefruit. Cheery and quaffable.

Sauvignon Blanc [Ont] **2002★★★→** Gold with a subdued nose of grass and herbs. Taste is more grapefruit with a hint of passion-fruit peeking through. Lovely balance, lemony finish. **2001★★★→** Good herbal nose with mildly earth flavours. Big acidity and a hint of residual sugar to balance. Drink up.

Syrah [NP] **2003★★★☆↗** Opaque purple garnet with a nose that starts off eggy, moves to pencil lead, then mulberry fruit. Tart blackberry and mulberry flavours with a nuance of black-cherry compote. Squeaky-clean palate with a somewhat dusty finish. Drink 2006-2009.

Vidal (Black Capsule) [Ont] Fermented dry. **2003★★★↻** Pale gold with a peachy-apricot nose. Crisp and lemony. Fresh tasting with mouth-watering acidity.

Vidal (White Capsule) [Ont] Fermented off-dry and kept on the lees for 2 months. **2003★★★↻** Pale straw with a peachy-grapefruit aroma. Slightly fuller bodied with a lemony, vibrant, refreshing taste.

Vidal Icewine [NP] **2002★★★★→** Delicate, spicy vegetal nose of spruce buds, lime, and broiled grapefruit. Drink now-2010. **2001★★★★→** Fresh, tropical mango flavours. Rich, lush, intense, and incredibly sweet. Drink now-2010.

Vidal Icewine, Canadian Oak [NP] **2002★★★★↗** Amber-yellow with a Cognac-like, oaky bouquet and spicy hints of nutmeg, licorice, and anise. Lively, balanced, and very tasty. Beginning to develop some nutty flavours. Drink now-2015.

Zweigelt [NP] **2003★★★↗** Garnet with a pink rim. Blackberry, black cherry, and wood bouquet with a lean, austere taste. Good balance says it will be more interesting in a year. Drink now-2008. **2002★★→** Purple pink with nondescript aroma. More tannin and acid than fruit; however, this juicy wine is ready now to wash down burgers. **2001** ★ ★ ★ → Now coming out of its shell. Creamy texture with blackberry and mulberry flavours. Drink now-2007.

- **LAKE EDGE VINEYARDS (Jordan, NP)** – This vineyard belonging to Dave and Mary Wiley is on the south side of Regional Road 81, between 15th Street Louth and Jordan Road. Although the terrain has a moderate north-facing slope, there is a deep ravine on either side of the site, leaving the plantable area a plateau of sorts. Consequently air drainage is exceptional and all varieties tend to weather the coldest winters. As with many bench vineyards, the soil here is Chinguacousy clay loam till with some glacial deposits, over a deep bedrock of limestone. Sixteen acres are planted, including 1 acre of Cabernet Sauvignon, 2 acres each of Cabernet Franc, Chardonnay, Pinot Noir, and Sauvignon Blanc, 3 acres each of Gamay, Merlot, and Riesling, and .5 acres of Gewürztraminer. Vines are spaced at 1,360 plants per acre, with the oldest ones dating back to 1989. Fruit has been sold to Henry of Pelham.

- **LAKE ERIE NORTH SHORE** [LENS] – This designated viticultural area includes all the land within the boundaries of Essex, Kent, and Elgin Counties, except the part of Kent County lying to the north of the Thames River. The region is surrounded by water on 3 sides, with Lake Erie to the south, the Detroit River to the west, and Lake St. Clair to the north. As one of Canada's southernmost viticultural regions (the other is Pelee Island 2 km farther south), this area enjoys a growing season which is 10 days longer, with more hours of sunshine and the highest heat units of any other region in the country. Latitudinally, it is on a par with northern California, the French Riviera, and Madrid, Spain. However, the region can also depend on severe winters to ensure a healthy production of icewine every year. There are 3 well-established operations and as many as 10 growing boutique wineries with approximately 1,000 acres/400 ha of cultivated vineyards. Despite all the publicity around Prince Edward County, this is the region to watch.

- **LAKELODGE VINEYARDS (Niagara-on-the-Lake, NP)** – Owned by Ed Werner and managed by Peter Buis. Grapes from this vineyard are included in Hillebrand's Trius Lakeshore Chardonnay. Morio Muscat is also planted and sold exclusively to Hillebrand.

- **LAKEVIEW CELLARS ESTATE WINERY LIMITED** (4037 Cherry Avenue, R.R.#1, Vineland, ON, L0R 2C0 / Phone: 905-562-5685 / Fax: 905-562-0673 / Email: lakecell@lakeviewcellars.on.ca / Website: www.lakeviewcellars.on.ca)

(Est. 1991) The Gurinskas Vineyard was established as a retirement project by amateur winemaker Eddy Gurinskas and his wife, Lorraine, in 1986. They tended the vineyard, hand-harvested the grapes, eventually made some wine, hand-labelled the bottles, and opened a small retail store in the garage. In 1996, to increase production and financial stability, they brought in Larry Hipple and Stu Morgan as equal partners. Hipple, a grape grower, and Morgan, a former Canadian fighter pilot and member of the elite Snowbirds aerobatic team, each brought a new skill set to the operation. At that time, the vineyard name was changed to Lakeview Cellars Estate Vineyard. In 2001, the partnership sold a majority interest to Diamond Estates, which also owns the nearby Birchwood Estates Winery. Situated on the first plateau of the escarpment just below Vineland Estates, it is composed of Oneida and Chinguacousy clay loam over hardpan clay. Varieties include Baco Noir, Cabernet Sauvignon, Chardonnay, Merlot, Pinot Gris, and Vidal. Hybrid varieties (spaced at 650 vines per acre) were planted in 1986, viniferas (at 1,000 vines per acre) in 1989. The winery sows grass between every second row to help the tractors go through on rainy days. They leaf-pluck manually on the east side of each row for greater sun exposure to the fruit, and harvest an average of 4.5 t. per acre. Fermentation of the reds tends to be long, to extract as much flavour as possible. Lakeview continues to buy grapes from vineyards owned separately by Hipple and Morgan and over the years has purchased from B&V Vineyards, Butler's Grant, Cherry Hill, Funk, Misek, Vinc, and other vineyards in the region.

Winemakers: Tom Green (2002-present); Eddy Gurinskas (1991-2003, 2003 Winemaker of the Year)

Baco Noir Reserve [Ont] **2002**★★★➔ Garnet with a maroon rim and a smoky nose of charred oak, dark chocolate filled with kirsch liqueur. Tart, oaky, vanilla taste with sour-cherry flavours. Drink now-2007. **2001**★★★➔ Deep garnet with a sharp, smoky nose with plummy, vanilla notes. Tannic and tough. Drink now-2009. **2000**★★★☆↗ *Gold, All Canadian Wine Championships 2003; Gold, Cuvée 2003; Gold, Ontario Wine Awards 2003.* A big bruiser that needs time to soften up. Drink 2006-2010. **1997**★★★➔ *Gold, Ontario Wine Awards, 1999.* Oaky, dense, concentrated with a big blackberry nose. Very tart core that's unlikely to diminish. Drink now-2007. **1994**★★↘ Rich with extract but hard and tart. **1993**★★★☆↘ Black as Kalamata olives with a vibrant black-fruit nose. Complex hints of oak, spice, and smoked sausage, and beautifully balanced with lively acidity, fullish body, firm tannins, and a long finish. Slowly passing its peak. Drink soon.

Cabernet-Merlot [NP] **1997**★★➔ Smoky-vegetal nose, slightly gamy with a tart finish. Drink now.

Cabernet Sauvignon Reserve, Lakeview Vineyard [NP] In earlier years, this was labelled Gurinskas Vineyard. **2002**★★★★↑

Garnet with a bouquet of oak, vanilla cream, chocolate, baked pastry, and licorice allsorts. Condensed viscous fruit with gritty tannins. Needs time. Drink 2008-2014. **2001** ☒ Asian lady beetle taint present. **1998** ★★★★☆↗ Incredibly dark, deep garnet colour from the centre to the rim. Big, developing plummy nose of chocolate, rose, tobacco, and cedar. Lush, thick, and beautifully balanced. An outstanding wine with a long, luscious life ahead. Drink now-2020. **1994** ↓ Long gone. **1993** ★★★☆→ Deep, complex, and profound flavours of tobacco and spice. Drink soon. **1991** ★★★★→ By far the best wine made in Lakeview's early years. It was Eddy's favourite and is one of mine too. Harvested from third leaf vines. Concentrated oak and blackberry flavours. Fully mature, drink up.

Chardonnay [NP] **2002** ★★★→ Gold, Cuvée 2004. Full-blown nose of ripe fruits, citrus, ripe melon, peach, and vanilla cream. Clean, with balanced acidity and a pleasant finish.

Chardonnay Reserve, Lakeview Vineyard [NP] **2002** ★★★☆→ Rich golden hue with a subdued but dense oaky nose. Packed with sweet, toasty, nutty, custard-cream flavours, this wine is B-I-G. Drink often, now-2008. **2000** Gold, Cuvée 2003; Gold, Canadian Wine Awards 2002.

Gamay/Zweigelt [NP] **1997** ★ ↘ Awkward, bittersweet, and tired.

Gewürztraminer [NP] **1998** ★★★→ Exotic, perfumed, lanolin bouquet with an oily texture and grapefruity taste. Drink now-2008.

Gewürztraminer Icewine [NP] **2002** ★★★★→ Pungent bouquet of orange peel, spice, and herbs. Profoundly complex with flavours of caramel, spice, and fresh and dried fruits. Drink now-2010. **2001** ★★★★→ Gold, All Canadian Wine Championships 2003. Concentrated aromas and flavour of caramelized pear and apple. Not cloying but extremely rich, thick, and sweet. Drink now-2010.

Kerner, Morgan Vineyard [NP] **2003** ★★★→ Gold colour with a floral, lemon-blossom aroma. Fresh, tart, and lively palate with flavours of Granny Smith apple. Drink now-2008.

Marechal Foch [Ont] **1997** ★★☆→ A dark, black/brown version of garnet. Nose combines fruit, veggie notes, earth, and roast-beef drippings. Tart palate with a still-tannic finish. Drink now-2007.

Merlot [NP] **1997** ★★☆↘ Still has the somewhat bitter green pepper and veggies taste of its youth. The tannins have diminished, but the acidity has not. Drink soon.

Meritage [NP] **2002** ★★☆→ Garnet with a soft, plummy nose. Tough palate with a tannic finish. Drink now-2009. **2000** ★★★☆↗ Deeply coloured, dense, and juicy. Drink 2008-2016.

Pinot Noir, Funk Vineyard [NP] **1995** ★★★☆→ Ruby-tawny colour with a rye toast and dried cherries nose. Some apple-y acidity, but it's holding. Drink up.

Pinot Noir Reserve, Butler's Grant Vineyard [NP] **2002**★★★☆↗ Ruby-cherry with a classic, fullish, sweet, ripe, slightly confected red-cherry and sandalwood nose. Has good body, supple texture, deep mineral underpinnings, and a fine, dry, tannic finish. Drink now-2010.

Riesling [NP] **2000** *Gold, All Canadian Wine Championships 2002.* **1997**★★★→ Amber-gold with a simple, grapefruity nose. Drink up.

Riesling Reserve, Butler's Grant Vineyard [NP] **2003**★★★→ Gold hue with lime and mandarin aromas. Taste is of broiled grapefruit dusted with sugar. Drink now-2008.

Rosé [NP] **2002** *Gold, All Canadian Wine Championships 2004.*

Vidal, Icewine [NP] **2000** *Gold, All Canadian Wine Championships 2002; Gold, Canadian Wine Awards 2001.* **1997**★★★★→ Terrific. Concentrated honey and pear flavours, with the texture of boiled-down sugar syrup. Drink now-2009.

Vidal, Icewine, Barrel Aged [NP] **1994**★★★☆→ Rich and full, with coffee notes.

Vidal, Late Harvest [Ont] **1994**★★☆↘ Pale gold, soft, sweet, and grapey with a candied-fruit nose.

Vintage Starboard [NP] Fortified, vintage-dated, sweet red dessert wine produced from Cabernet Sauvignon. **2000**★★★→ Deep garnet with an orange tint along the rim. Bouquet of stewed plums, slightly nutty with an undertone of bitters. Tasty, sweet flavours, but there's a spirity finish. Drink with fruit, nuts, and blue cheese.

Soaring Ridge Cellars Label

Wines were not ready for appraisal before press time.

• **LAMBERT VINEYARD (Niagara-on-the-Lake, NP)** – This relatively flat property is located on both sides of Line 1 between Concessions 6 and 7, north of Highway 55 and west of Creek Road. Owner Dave Lambert grows Auxerrois, Baco Noir, Cabernet Franc, Cabernet Sauvignon, Chardonnay, Merlot, Pinot Gris, Riesling, Seyval Blanc, Verdelet, Vidal Blanc, and Zweigelt as well as Castel, Concord, Elvira, and Niagara. Grapes are sold exclusively to Vincor.

• **LASTIWKA VINEYARD (Grimsby, NP)** – Joseph Lastiwka grows Kerner and Welsh Riesling for Andrés and its subsidiary, Hillebrand.

• **Late Harvest** – Wine produced from fresh grapes, of which a portion has been left on the vine late into the season to desiccate under natural conditions and to concentrate the sugars.

- **LAUNDRY-MOTTIAR – COOKE FARM (Beamsville, NP)** – This 24-acre Sandy Cove Drive vineyard is owned by the Laundry family. There's a minimal north-facing slope to the lakefront property, which is composed of washed Chinguacousy clay loam till. Nineteen acres are dedicated to grape growing, of which 13 are contracted to several wineries. A 6-acre parcel is leased to daughter Heather and son-in-law Shiraz Mottiar. The couple use organic practices for their 3 acres of Cabernet Franc, .5 acre of Merlot, and 2.5 acres of Pinot Noir, all planted at 1,210 vines per acre. On that parcel, fruit is reduced by half at veraison, providing yields that average 1.8 t. per acre. Grapes are sold to Tawse Winery in the Niagara Peninsula and to Closson Chase in Prince Edward County.

- **LAUNDRY-MOTTIAR – LISTER ROAD VINEYARD (Beamsville, NP)** – Heather Laundry and Shiraz Mottiar's farm on Lister Road comprises 7 acres, of which 5.5 are planted at an exceptionally low density of 660 vines per acre. This lakeshore property lies just east of Csets Vineyard and is composed of sandy loam over a bed of shale. It is completely underdrained. The couple grows only 1 variety here, Pinot Gris, having planted an average of 1 acre every second year since 1993, with a 5-year hiatus from 1999 and the last acre planted in 2004. They cut off about one-quarter of the fruit at veraison to limit yield to 3-4 t. per acre, which is sold in part to Hillebrand Estates, Kacaba Winery, Lakeview Cellars, and Malivoire Wine Company, where Shiraz works as an assistant winemaker to Ann Sperling.

- **LAUNDRY-MOTTIAR – QUARRY ROAD VINEYARD (Beamsville, NP)** – Purchased only last year by Heather Laundry and her husband, Shiraz Mottiar, a winemaker at Malivoire Wine Company, this 13.5-acre property will only begin to provide fruit in 2008, having been planted only this year. This is the couple's home farm. Two acres of Riesling and 3.5 acres of Chardonnay are planted with a spacing of 1,394 vines per acre, while 3.5 acres of Pinot Noir are planted at a higher density of 1,848 vines per acre. The vineyard is north-facing with a 5% grade almost 3 km away from the lake and 100 m above it. The soil is Tavistock clay loam till over a bed of limestone and fully tiled for better drainage. It is cultivated with organic practices and is on the way to being certified as such. First fruit has been promised to Tawse Winery.

- **LE CLOS JORDANNE (2540 South Service Road, Jordan, ON, L0R 1S0 / Phone: 905-562-9404 / Fax: 905-562-9407 / Email: info@ leclosjordanne.ca / Website: www.leclosjordanne.ca)**

(Est. 2000) A joint venture of Mississauga-based Vincor International Inc., Canada's largest wine company, and La Famille des Grand Vins Boisset of Burgundy, the third-largest wine merchants in France. The first wines are being made in a temporary facility rented from Lakeshore Growers, but in time, the partners plan to build one of Canada's most attractive and innovative wineries designed by the internationally renown architect Frank O. Gehry. Four tracts of land have been acquired, including 2 owned outright and 2 that have been leased on a long-term basis. The vineyards have been planted and are being tended with organic practices. Once organic certification has been achieved, the owners plan to work toward bio-dynamic certification within a few years. The estate vineyard is a 35-acre parcel on the south side of King Street (Regional Road 81) at the end of Jordan Road, and is enclosed on 3 sides by forests. The vineyard has a slight north-facing slope and is composed of Chinguacousy clay loam and Oneida silty clay, peppered with limestone particles resting on glacial till. So far, 20 acres of Pinot Noir and Chardonnay have been planted at a high vine density of 2,160 plants per acre. Drainage tiles have been installed between every row. Special cover crops selected for their rooting characteristics are grown between every second row and alternated every year to improve the structure of the soil and to increase competition for water. European over-the-row tractors are used to avoid compacting the soil. A generous space has been left open in the middle of the vineyard for the construction of the winery, which promises to be an architectural masterpiece of global significance. The 3 additional vineyards providing fruit are Bowen, Chudzik, and Neudorf, and are listed separately. First production will be released in 2006, and annual volumes are projected to reach under 20,000 cases.

Winemakers: Thomas Bachelder (2003-present); Pascal Marchand (2001-present, consulting) / Vineyard Manager: Thomas Bachelder

Wines not available for appraisal before press time.

- **Lees** – The sediment of dead yeast cells, grape skins, pulp, seeds, and, occasionally, stems that are left to settle in the bottom of a tank or barrel. *See also* Sur lie.

- **LEGENDS ESTATE WINERY** (4888 Ontario Street North, Beamsville, ON, L0R 1B3 / Phone: 905-563-6500 / Fax: 905-563-1672 / Email: info@legendsestates.com / Website: www.legendsestates.com)

(Est. 2000) Winemaking is a recent endeavour for this long-time farm family. Patriarch John Lizak established a 10-acre tender fruit farm in Grimsby in 1946. John's son, Ted, and daughter-in-law, Diane, expanded the operation to more than 200 acres, and in 1985 purchased a parcel on the south shore of Lake Ontario. In the mid-1990s, Ted's son, Paul, proposed the idea of establishing a fruit winery to process some of the harvest into fruit wine, and took on the further challenge of making wine from estate-grown grapes. In 1999, the Lizaks planted their first vines. The farm is 110 acres, but only 35 are planted with grapes, including 4 acres of Cabernet Franc, 1 acre of Cabernet Sauvignon, 2 acres each of Malbec, Syrah, and Pinot Gris, 4.5 acres of Chardonnay, 9 acres of Merlot, 8 acres of Sauvignon Blanc, along with 2.5 acres of Petit Verdot. The most fragile varieties are planted closest to the lakeside in soils of Vineland fine sandy loam and Tuscola lacustrine silty loam at a density of 1,100 vines to the acre. Total volume in 2004 was 15,000 cases of wine, and up to one-third of the production was sent into the export market. By 2010, Legends intends to grow to the 30,000-case level. For now, the home vineyard produces 50% of the winery's needs. The balance comes from fruit purchased from other Niagara area vineyards, including Burkhardt, Frontier, and Wismer vineyards.

Winemakers: Andreea Botezatu (2004-present); Paul Lizak (2000-present); Andrzej Lipinski (2002); Jim Warren (2000-2001, consulting on fruit wines) / Vineyard Manager: Shawn Souter

Baco Noir [Ont] **2002**★★→ Purple-garnet colour with a light, superficial nose of cherry, blackberry, and crushed apple. Intense aroma, simple taste. Drink up.

Cabernet Franc [NP] **2003**★★★↑ Brilliant garnet with violet reflections. Fresh aroma with some green notes. Undeveloped taste still showing little character, but has the potential to grow into a soft, lush wine within 3 years. Drink 2006-2011. **2002**★★★↗ Clean, ripe, soft black-fruit aroma with nuances of blackberry and iodine. Very elegant mouthfeel with deep, undeveloped flavours. Should age gracefully for several years. Drink 2006-2012.

Cabernet Franc Icewine [NP] **2002** ★★★★★↗ Yummy. Pretty pink with a fresh-baked bread bouquet to start, and soft, lovely, fullish strawberry jam flavours to finish. Drink now-2012.

Cabernet Franc Reserve [NP] **2002**★★★↗ Deep purple with strong black fruit aromas and hints of spice. Nice flavours but tannins currently overpower the fruit in a dusty, mouth-drying finish. Needs at least 3 years to soften up.

Cabernet-Merlot Reserve [NP] **2002**★★★★↑ Purple-garnet with a rich black-fruit nose. Big, complex taste with hints of toasted bread, nuts, and oak. Slow to open, so it should be slow to develop. Drink 2008-2018.

Cabernet Sauvignon Reserve [NP] **2002**★★★★☆↑ Dense purple-garnet colour with textbook balance and structure. Tough yet lush. Hard yet sublime. Simmering with concentrated flavours that will take years to unveil. Drink 2010-2025.

Chardonnay, Oaked [NP] **2002**★★★→ Straw-gold with a closed nose. Taste still tight and unrevealing but texture is solid and well balanced. Drink now 2006-2009.

Chardonnay, Musqué [NP] **2002** *Gold, Ontario Wine Awards 2003.*

Chardonnay, Reserve [NP] **2002**★★★★→ *Gold, Ottawa Wine &*

Cheese Show 2003. Pale gold with a light fruit nose supported by strong, toasty, oaky nuances. Soft, clean, and lemony with a myriad of flavours and a rich finish. Taste after taste, it just gets better. Drink now-2010. **1998** Gold, VinItaly 2000. Not tasted.

Chardonnay, Unoaked [NP] **2002** ★ ★ ★ → Pale straw-gold with bright aromas of pear, apricot, and lemon. Fruity, fullish, and well balanced. Drink now through 2006.

Chenin Blanc [NP] **2002** ★ ★ ★ → Silvery hue with an undeveloped nose showing little more than sulphur at first. There are crisp fruit nuances of apple and citrus and sufficient tension in the palate to warrant aging.

Gewürztraminer [NP] **2003** ★ ★ ★ ★ ↗ Gold, Ontario Wine Awards 2004. From the Burkhardt Vineyard. Pale gold and quite aromatic with fresh, grapey, orange marmalade aromas. Thick, almost oily palate with a spicy flavour. Outstanding. Drink now-2020. **2002** ★ ★ ★ ★ ↗ Gold, Ottawa Wine & Cheese Show, 2003. From the Wismer Vineyard. Gold hue with pink reflections. Fresh, apple, peach, greengage plum, and lychee bouquet. Flavour grows and grows. Drink now-2020.

Meritage, Reserve [NP] **2002** ★ ★ ★ ★ ↗ Deep opaque garnet, with an exceptionally dense nose of cassis, clove, black cherry, rose, oak, and smoke. Very juvenile palate of ripe fruit with undeveloped flavours, strong tannins, and perfect balance. Needs light-years to age properly. Drink 2008-2017.

Merlot [NP] **2002** ★ ★ ★ ↗ Terrific balance and texture with a soft fruity finish. Drink now-2012.

Merlot Reserve [NP] **2002** ★ ★ ★ ★ ↑ Purple-garnet hue with a fabulously rich, lush bouquet. Flavourful, juicy, sweet, and loaded with dark-berry nuance. Long, dense finish. Drink 2007-2017.

Muscat Ottonel [NP] **2002** ★ ★ ★ → Floral and spicy like a semi-dry Riesling. Clean with racy acidity, a hint of lemon-lime, muted perfume, and a balanced, tasty, refreshing finish. Drink now-2007.

Pinot Gris [NP] **2002** ★ ★ ★ ★ ↗ Brilliant pale salmon hue. Fruity nose hints of Russet pear, citrus, and strawberry. Profound palate is supple, round, big, bold, and full of rich flavours. Can age and will improve. Drink now-2010.

Pinot Noir, Reserve [NP] **2002** ★ ★ ★ ★ ↗ Pale garnet colour with an elegant, penetrating nose. Bitterly tough at first, but depth and charm slowly emerge as the wine opens. It's there even more so the next day. Full-bodied, with deep and elegant flavours of raspberry, cherry cola, stewed plum, warm moist earth, spice, and Spanish cedar. Drink 2006-2010.

Riesling, Dry [NP] **2003** ★ ★ ★ ↗ Pale straw-gold with a hint of spritz. Ripe with a kiss of sweetness and perfectly balanced acidity. Drink 2006-2015. **2002** ★ ★ ★ ★ ↗ Brilliant gold with an amazing, complex bouquet of petrol, honey, citrus, and wild, frosty, floral, and fruity aromas. Tastes dry, with flavours of greengage plum and perfect balance. Drink 2006-2018.

Riesling, Rosomel Vineyard Reserve [NP] 2003 ★ ★ ★ ★ ↗
Brilliant gold hue with tiny bubbles forming on the inside of the glass. Clean, bright, fresh nose of orange, lemon drops, and apricot. Razor-sharp acidity with excellent balance and long and, undoubtedly, interesting life ahead. Drink 2007-2025.

Riesling, Semi-Dry [NP] 2002 ★ ★ ★ ★ ↗ Brilliant gold colour with a bouquet that starts with the smell of the coloured sugar in licorice allsorts. Has hints of violet and rose. Taste vibrates between Kabinett and Spätlese in residual sweetness, with deep-set flavours that linger for some time. Yum. Drink now-2020.

Sauvignon Blanc Reserve [NP] 2003 ★ ★ ★ ↗ Bright straw-gold. Fresh but subdued nose. Good balance of fleshy fruit, minerality, and structure. Drink now-2009.

Vidal, "Heritage House" [Ont] 2003 ★ ★ ★ → Amber gold with pink reflections. Soft, full nose with hints of orange and peach. A big wine with solid structure and a refreshingly tart taste. Quaffable.

Vidal, Icewine [NP] 2002 ★ ★ ★ ★ → Brilliant deep gold with a restrained nose that hints of pear. Malty flavours and a very sweet, rich finish. Only 8.1% alc./vol. Drink now-2010.

• **LEPP VINEYARD (Niagara-on-the-Lake, NP)** – Owner Arnie Lepp was named 1998 Grape King. Three vineyards (Wagg Road, Wall Road, and Line 1) lie more or less between Caroline Cellars and the Stonechurch Winery. Lepp grows Merlot, Pinot Gris, and Sauvignon Blanc, some of which he sells to Stoney Ridge Estate Winery, to Hillebrand Estates for its premium, ice, and sparkling wines, and to several other wineries.

• **LIGHTHALL VINEYARD (Picton, PEC)** – Peter and Alice Mennacher have 100 acres on County Road 13 just west of Long Dog Vineyard & Winery. They tend 5 acres of Chardonnay planted in 2001 and 3 acres of Pinot Noir added in 2005. Cultivation is labour-intensive as they hand-tend each vine as if it were part of a home garden. They must untie, lay down, and hill over every cane to prevent winter damage. Their Chardonnay, naturally reduced to about 1.5 t. per acre in 2003, was sold to Huff Estates, where winemaker Frédéric Picard produced one of the county's best white wines. Deep and friable sandy loam soil is peppered with rocky areas, but the limestone base and the 3%-5% southwest facing slope provide a perfect environment for intense mineral-flavoured wines. The couple plans to start their own winery. For now, they're focusing on establishing the vineyard and learning the tricks of the trade.

• **LITTLE CREEK VINEYARDS (Wellington, PEC)** – Ken Burford and Yvonne Millman, both of whom are active in the Ontario Wine Society, purchased a farm in 2000. The 34-acre patch of Hillier clay loam with its rolling terrain is just 3 km away from Lake Ontario, near Closson

Chase winery and The Grange. During 2001 and 2002, they planted 5 acres of Pinot Noir at the ultra-high density of 3,600 vines per acre. They cultivate organically, giving their vines the care a home gardener might give to his roses. Half the vineyard has a northwest aspect while the other half has a southeast exposure. They harvested a grand total of 1,860 kg of fruit in 2003 and 2,670 kg in 2004. The grapes were sold to Domaine Calcaire and Domaine la Reine.

• **London Winery** – This historic Canadian winery was established in 1925 and produced a full range of uninspiring wines, ports, and sherries, as well as communion wine. It was swallowed up by Vincor International Inc. in 1996.

• **LONG DOG VINEYARD AND WINERY INC.** (104 Brewers Road, Milford, ON, K0K 2P0 / Phone: 613-476-2921 or 613-476-4140 / Fax: 613-476-6462 / Email: wine@longdog.ca / Website: www.long dog.ca)

(Est. 2002) James Lahti, an IMAX film producer and editor, his spouse and collaborator, Victoria Rose, and lawyer Steven Rapkin are partners in this 300-acre estate in the southeast corner of Prince Edward County. Over a 5-year period, starting in 1999, they have planted 20 acres of vinifera vines at the medium-high density of 1,650 plants per acre. The property spans several soil types, but the northernmost section, where they've planted, is all Percy fine sandy loam sitting on the ubiquitous fractured limestone bedrock of the county. It is gently sloped southward and the lowest third of the vineyard is tiled for better drainage. There are 6 acres planted with 3 Dijon clones of Pinot Noir, 8 acres with 2 clones of Chardonnay, 4 acres of Pinot Grigio, and 2 acres of Gamay. With Lake Ontario less than 2 km away, there is some moderating effect, but it is felt most significantly during the early fall season. Lake or no lake, winter chills can be devastating so the vines are hilled up to prevent them from freezing. Lahti puts all his reds in French barrels, but for his Chardonnay he prefers Hungarian oak. Current production sits at 1,200 cases, just over a quarter of the volume of 4,000 cases projected for 2006.

Winemakers: James Lahti; Dan Sullivan (consulting) / Vineyard Manager: James Lahti

Chardonnay, Storring Block, Barrel Reserve [PEC, non VQA] **2003** ★ ★ ★ ☆ ↗ Pale straw-gold with a lightly oaked nose. Rich nuances of vanilla and caramelized pear. Clean, soft, light-bodied, but big-flavoured with a stiff spine of zippy acidity. Great start for a young winery. Drink now-2008.

Pinot Noir, Barrel Select [PEC, non VQA] **2002** ★ ★ ★ ☆ ↗ Pale ruby with a lovely bouquet of sweet, ripe, delicate fruit and just the right bitterness to balance. Nuances of strawberry syrup, cherry-pie filling, and ripe red peppers. I find the fragility and delicacy of the flavours combined with the layers of complexity a very exciting omen of future vintages. Drink now-2010.

- **LOWREY VINEYARD (St. David's, NP)** – The first grapes to grow on this 63-acre vineyard on Tanbark Road in St. David's were planted by David Jackson Lowrey in 1869. Five generations later, Howard and Wilma Lowrey still tend the vines, although the old labruscas are long gone. The 20 acres that are cultivated on this gentle north-facing slope of silty clay loam include 4 acres of Cabernet Sauvignon, 1.5 acres of Pinot Gris, 3 acres of Pinot Noir, 2 acres of Sauvignon Blanc, 3 acres of Shiraz, and 6.5 acres of Vidal Blanc. In 1994, when Burgundian winemaker Bernard Repolt agreed to produce "Alliánce" with Inniskillin's Karl Kaiser, 30 barrels of 1993 Pinot Noir were tasted in the winery's cellars. The 5 casks chosen all hailed from this vineyard. Today, the fruit is sold to Creekside Estate Winery. The Lowreys' son, Wes, currently works as winemaker/manager for Blomidon Ridge Estate Wines in Canning, Nova Scotia, a winery owned by the proprietors of Creekside Estate.

- **Loyalist Vineyard** – See County Cider Company

M

- **MAGNOTTA WINERY CORPORATION** (271 Chrislea Road, Vaughan, ON, L4L 8N6 / Phone: 905-738-9463 / Toll-Free: 1-800-461-9463 / Fax: 905-738-5551 / Email: mailbox@magnotta.com / Website: www.magnotta.com)

(Est. 1990) Gabriel Magnotta and Rossana DiZio Magnotta had their first encounters with wine early on. At age 8, Gabe would fill carafes at the family tavern near Naples. When Rossana went through a severe illness as a child, the family doctor recommended daily baths in red wine. The couple started the Festa Juice Company selling winemaking kits and juices to home winemakers and ran the business for 10 years before getting into the commercial side of winemaking. After the provincial government changed the Wine Content Act in 1988 to give Ontario wineries a competitive edge in light of the Free Trade Agreement with the United States, the Magnottas perceived an opportunity. In 1989, they bought the flagging Charal winery in Blenheim for $250,000, moved the equipment to Concord near Toronto, and started bottling "Product of Canada" wines blended from local and foreign grapes, as the new laws permitted. They also discovered that they could sell wines not available at the liquor monopoly, at a significantly lower price than the LCBO would, as the Magnottas would not be required to charge high LCBO markups. They opened up shop, advertised their low, low prices, and by their second year of operation attracted enough sales to become the fifth largest winery in the province. As a result, during the first decade of its existence, the Magnottas were relentlessly persecuted and slandered by the Liquor Control Board, until Gabe Magnotta hired a private detective to capture the defamations on tape and sue the board. After Magnotta won the right for a judicial review in 1996, it took nearly 5 years to mediate an out-of-court settlement. Although all agreements between the parties have remained confidential, at the time it seemed fairly obvious that the LCBO baled from a losing case. Today, the LCBO no longer says nasty things about Magnotta and Magnotta no longer disses the Ontario monopoly. Magnotta wines appear in Ontario liquor stores on a regular basis. In 1995, the winery became a publicly owned corporation. Over the years, it purchased several additional wineries – including sparkling wine producer Montravin Cellars and Northumberland Winery – and relocated the licences to suit its retail needs in more populated centres. The company also has purchased several vineyards in the Niagara-on-the-Lake and Beamsville areas as well as a large tract of land in Chile to supply its needs. Last year the winery produced 370,000 cases of wine. The Magnottas also brew beer and hold a federal licence to distill all sorts of spirits, including whisky, gin, rum, brandy, grappa, and eau-de-vie.

Winemakers: Peter Rotar (1998-present); Marco Zammuner (1999-present); Alejandro DeMiguel; Robert Henn / Stillmasters: Peter Rotar (1998-present); Simon LeChene (1994-1998)

Baco Noir [Ont] **2001** ★ ↻ Deep purple-garnet with a tart, leathery, sweet, hybrid nose. Creamy blackberry flavours and a bitter finish.

Brut Sparkling [Ont] **2002** ★ ↻ Pale straw-gold, fine mousse, crisp palate but has little character and a somewhat bitter finish.

Cabernet Franc Icewine [NP] **2002** ★ ★ ★ ★ ↗ Pale tawny-red with rich, red cherry-berry flavours. Very fruity, luscious, and powerful. Drink now-2012.

Cabernet Franc [NP] **2002** ★ ★ → Ruby-cherry with an earthy nose with hints of rubber, cherry, blackberry, and black-currant jam. Tart applelike acidity with a short astringent finish. **2000** ★ ★ → (Ducks Unlimited Label) Very pale black-cherry colour with an aroma of dried straw in a barn attic. Vegetal with strawberry-cherry flavours and a sharp, bitter finish. Drink up.

Cabernet Franc, Icewine [NP] **2002** ★ ★ ★ ★ → *Best Sweet Red, Cuvée 2005.* Pale tawny-red with rich, red cherry-berry flavours. Very fruity, luscious, and powerful. Drink now-2012.

Cabernet Franc, Limited Edition [NP] **2002** ★ ★ ★ → Although the bouquet includes notes of artificial fruit and hints of Band-Aid, it's actually very pleasant. Lovely big, bold fruit flavours come through despite a dusty, tannic first impression. Drink now-2008.

Cabernet Franc, Sparkling [NP] **1999** ★ ★ ★ → Copper-red with a fresh, sweet strawberry syrup aroma. Sweet, foaming, and jubilant. Drink now-2009.

Cabernet Franc, Sparkling Icewine [NP] **NV** ★ ★ ★ ★ → Cherry hue with a sienna rim. The nose is of cherries soaked in brandy while the taste moves into the realm of cherry jam. Drink now.

Cabernet Franc, Special Reserve [NP] **2001** ☒ Smells of vase rot. Tainted by Asian lady beetle.

Cabernet Sauvignon [nonVQA] **2002** ★ ↻ Browning garnet colour with an extreme black-currant nose at first, typical of Chilean Cabernet. Nose drops off and turns vegetal, grapey, and hybrid within minutes. Not for aging.

Cabernet Sauvignon [NP] **2002** ★ ★ → Garnet colour with a light aroma of generic berries. Balanced, but finish is tough and tannic.

Cabernet Sauvignon, Limited Edition [NP]   2002★★★↗
Gold, Ontario Wine Awards, 2004. Deep garnet with an extreme
black-currant nose that is soon oak-dominated. Tough, tannic, and
powerful. Drink now or hold till 2010.

Cabernet Sauvignon, Toro Nero [nonVQA]   2002★★★→
Dark cherry with fading colour at the rim. Sweet, supple, almost
soft taste with a velvety texture, bright fruit, and good balance.
Ready to drink.

Carmenère, Gran Riserva [nonVQA] 1998★★★→ *Gold, Toronto
Wine & Cheese Show 2004.* Deep cherry hue with a dry red-pepper
bouquet. Dry, dusty, ginseng finish and high alcohol warms the throat.

Chardonnay [NP] 2002★↻ Clean, light, basic, pleasant Chardonnay.

Chardonnay, Limited Edition [NP] 2002★★★→ Bursting with
coconut cream pie aromas, the taste follows with big, fat, caramel
flavours. Drink before 2006.

Chardonnay, Special Reserve, Barrel-Aged [NP] 2002★★★→
Gold, Concours Mondiale, Belgium 2004. Clean, dry, and medium-
bodied. Aroma hints of lemon drops and apple bonbons. Gently
oaked with a soft, fine finish.

Classic Sparkling [NP]   **NV**★↻ Green-gold hue, fine surface
foam, somewhat candied nose of overripe apple, little else.

Enotrium [NP]   Inspired by France and Italy, this wine is made from
the classic Bordeaux grapes, which are first air-dried for 20-30 days
before fermentation in the manner of Amarone. **2001★★★★↗**
(CF25/CS25/M50) Deep garnet with a powerful bouquet of oak,
roasted coffee, herbs, spice, dried black currants, and plum. Very
high alcohol (14.5%), but balanced by dense fruit flavours, velvety
thick texture, and solid tannins. Drink 2007-2014.

Gamay [NP] 2002★★→ Coarse, simple.

Gewürztraminer, Icewine [NP] 1999★★★★→ Cognac colour
and ripe tropical nose of mango, pineapple, and apricot. Spicy palate
with a candied-ginger finish. Drink now-2014.

Gewürztraminer, Special Reserve, Dry [NP]   2002★★→
Clean, crisp, and balanced, with hints of spiced mandarin.

Gewürztraminer, Special Reserve, Medium Dry [NP]
2002★★★→ Pale gold with rose reflections. Bouquet hits on
apple, peach, and 3-citrus marmalade. It's clean, balanced, barely
sweet, and very fresh-tasting. Drink now-2007.

Il Cacciatore [nonVQA] 1998★★★★→ Clean, dry, and intense
with nuances of sour cherry and leather. Mildly astringent but ready
to drink, now-2007.

Marechal Foch, Special Reserve [Ont] 2002★↻ Intense colour
but smell is not for me. Weedy, perfumed, and soapy with hints of
mosquito repellent. Overpowering, tart black fruit with an astringent, thin finish. Relatively well made from a lousy grape.

Meritage, Limited Edition [NP] 2002★★★↗ Garnet hue with
a closed, unyielding nose. A second bottle showed emerging

black-currant notes reminiscent of Chilean Cabernet. Both were supple on the palate, with fullish body and some promise for the future. Drink now-2010.

Merlot, Gran Riserva [nonVQA] **1998**★★★➔ Blackberry, apple, and plum aromas with an astringent, alcoholic finish. Drink now-2007.

Merlot, Limited Edition [NP] **2002**★★★↗ Garnet hue with a nose reminiscent of bicycle tires. Clean and crisp with additional flavours of black currant and black cherry. Tough, tannic finish with good body and balance. Drink now-2008.

Merlot, Special Reserve [NP] **2002**★★★➔ Garnet colour with hints of black currant. Tasty, fruity, and implicitly sweet with a crisp and pleasant if simple finish. Drink now-2006.

Pinot Gris, Special Reserve [NP] **2003**★★★↻ Silvery gold with a shy nose and crisp flavours of pink grapefruit, rosewater, and beeswax. **2002**★↻ Dried-fruit nose with dull, tired flavours.

Pinot Noir, Special Reserve [NP] **2002**★★↗ Garnet with mahogany brown reflections and a somewhat cooked nose. Stemmy flavours with a mean, green streak in the finish. Give it another year to relax.

Riesling, Dry [NP] **2002**★★➔ Zippy, lemon-grapefruit flavours. Clean, light, balanced.

Riesling Icewine [NP] **2002**★★★➔ Marmalade nose, dense and painfully sweet. Drink now-2010. **1998**★★★★☆↗ Amber-gold hue with a lovely, high-toned petrol and minerals bouquet. Bracing acidity and balanced barley sugar sweetness. Drink now-2020.

Riesling, Dry, Special Reserve [NP] **2002**★★★➔ Closed nose at this time, but the palate is warm and inviting. Ripe green fruit sugar, a smidgen of petrol, and a big, fat exciting finish.

Riesling, Medium Dry, Special Reserve [NP] **2002**★★➔ Soft, sweet, and spicy with some fruity and floral nuances. Like a fat Liebfraumilch.

Sauvignon Blanc, Special Reserve [NP] **2003**★★★↻ *Best Sauvignon Blanc, Cuvée 2005.* Silvery gold tint with a strong grassy, grapey aroma and crisp, clean, mildly bitter, off-dry finish.

Sparkling Ice [NP] **2003**★★★★☆➔ Tiny bubbles foam up like a natural fizz. Deep amber-gold with a spicy, high-toned bouquet of dried apricot. Luscious. Drink now-2009. **1996**★★★➔ This first batch was a standard Vidal icewine that had been carbonated in a 50 L beer keg. It was creamy, less sweet than still icewine, and tended to age a smidgen more quickly. Drink up.

Vidal, Harvest Moon [Ont] **2001**★★★➔ Gold with clean, sweetish, apple juice flavours. Drink now-2007.

Vidal Icewine [LENS] **2002**★★★★➔Amber shade with an aroma of apricot jam, bubblegum, and bergamot. Very rich and very sweet with a thick, honeylike texture. Drink now-2015.

Vidal, Icewine [NP] **2002**★★★★➔ *Gold, Challenge International*

Du Vin 2004. Balanced, youthful pear aromas and rich, viscous texture. Drink now-2012.

Vidal, Magnotta Classic Sparkling [Ont] **2002**★★★➔ Foams up and stays frothy for some time. Pleasant and lively nose followed by clean, dry, fullish, fruit flavours and a good finish.

Vidal, Medium Dry [Ont] **2002**★★★➔ Hints of winter melon. Clean and quaffable with good sugar/acid balance and nice lemon and apple flavours.

Vidal, Select Late Harvest [Ont] **2001**★★★★➔ Amber-gold with peach and apricot notes. Balanced, with flavours and bitterness reminiscent of strong orange pekoe tea. Drink now-2011.

White Merlot, Special Reserve [NP] **2002**★↻ Pale pink with a sweetish and relatively full-bodied texture. Candied strawberry flavours with a slightly hot finish.

Other Products:

Vidal Icewine Grappa (a distillate of icewine grape skins) **NV**★★★★☆➔ Frost on the nose, fire in the belly. Gr-r-reat!

• **MALETA VINEYARDS & ESTATE WINERY** (450 Queenston Road, R.R.#4, Niagara-on-the-Lake, ON, L0S 1J0 / Phone: 905-685-8486 / Fax: 905-685-7998 / Email: info@maletawinery.com / Website: www.maletawinery.com)

(Est. 1998) Founders Stan and Marilyn Maleta sold the business in early 2004 to Cadenza Limited Partnership, a company owned by Quebec businessman Daniel Pambianchi, who is also technical editor for *WineMaker* magazine and author of *Techniques in Home Winemaking: A Practical Guide to Making Château-Style Wines*. The Maletas continue to work for and promote the winery. The 16.5-acre estate lies 135 ft. above and about 5 km from Lake Ontario. The soil is Haldiman clay to a depth of 30 ft. over a limestone bedrock. The land is gently sloped, providing a south-facing exposure. Maleta's best wine comes from a 4.5-acre section of Riesling vines planted in 1969. There's an acre of Gamay planted in the same year. In 1996, soon after purchasing the property, Stan Maleta planted 4.5 acres of Cabernet Franc and 1.5 acres each of Cabernet Sauvignon and Merlot for their Meritage red. He added .5 acre of Syrah in 2000 and 1 acre of Chardonnay in 2004. All grapes are planted with a vine density of 1,361 per acre, or 4 ft. apart on 8-ft. rows. Maleta has begun to experiment with Canadian oak, but most wines are aged in American and French oak barrels. Current production is 2,000 cases from estate-grown grapes. Maleta does not buy grapes at this time. By 2010, Pambianchi hopes to be at a full-production level of 5,000 cases.

Winemakers: Daniel Pambianchi (2004-present); Stan Maleta (1998-present) / Vineyard Manager: Stan Maleta

Cabernet-Merlot [NP] **2003** ★ ★ ☆ ➜ (CS60/M40) Garnet with a
creamy herbal, oaky nose. Light, clean, and quaffable. Drink now-
2007.

Chardonnay Reserve [NP] **2001** ★ ★ ★ ★ ➜ Deep yellow-gold
with amazing complexity in the bouquet. Rich and flavourful with
nuances of panna cotta, crème brûlée, toffee, and burnt sugar. Rich,
lingering aftertaste.

Gamay, "View" [NP] **2002** ★ ★ ★ ↻ Ruby-garnet with aromas of
oak and blackberries. Light, fruity, and oaky.

Meritage [NP] **2001** ★ ★ ★ ☆ ➜ (CF30/CS40/M30) Despite a hint
of Asian lady beetle at first nosing, the wine survives and even
rebounds, opening up with lovely blueberry and blackberry aromas.
Well structured with balanced fruit and tannins. Drink now-2010.
1999 ★ ★ ★ ⬈ (CF30/CS50/M20) *Best Meritage, Canadian Wine
Awards, 2003*. Garnet with brick colour around the rim. Zippy fruit
nose with hints of black cherry and cassis. Long, complex aftertaste.
Drink now-2011.

Riesling, Reserve [NP] **2002** ★ ★ ★ ☆ ➜ Brilliant pale-gold hue
with a bouquet of pink grapefruit and orange. Terrific balance, a dry,
flavoury mineral core, and long, lovely aftertaste. A real food wine.
Drink now-2010. **2000** ★ ★ ★ ☆ ➜ Bright gold with a developing
floral, petrol nose. Sweet, ripe applesauce taste. With distinct residual sugar and significantly lower alcohol, this vintage follows a classic
Germanic profile. Drink now-2008.

Rosé, Reserve [NP] **2002** ★ ★ ↻ (CF5/R95) Pale orangey-pink with
an unmistakable tomato-soup nose. Strange, but not at all unpleasant.

Shiraz "View" [NP] **2002** ★ ★ ★ ⬈ Purple-garnet with aromas of
oak and sweetened sour cream with blackberries. Good flavours of
fruit, oak, and nuts with a clean finish. Drink now-2008.

• **MALIVOIRE WINE COMPANY** (4260 King Street East,
Beamsville, ON, L0R 1B0 / Telephone: 905-563-9253 / Toll-Free: 1-866-
644-2244 / Fax: 905-563-9512 / Email: wine@malivoirewineco.com /
Website: www.malivoirewineco.com)

(Est. 1997) What started a decade ago as the casual search for a
weekend getaway home for motion-picture special-effects producer
Martin Malivoire and his investment executive partner, Moira Saganski,
has turned into one of Ontario's most exciting vineyard and winery
projects. With the deeply rooted belief that quality starts in the ground,
the couple refer to themselves as "wine growers" rather than "wine
makers." There are 3 vineyards: the 40-acre Estate Vineyard, which surrounds the winery, 40-acre Moira Vineyard, located a few hundred
metres east of the winery, and the Epp Vineyard, of which 12 acres are
leased and managed by the winery. The Estate Vineyard was purchased
in 1997 and planted the following 2 years with Chardonnay, Chardonnay

Musqué, Gamay, Gewürztraminer, Melon, Pinot Gris, and Pinot Noir. In a 30-ft.-deep ravine cutting through the middle of the site, Malivoire built his 10,000-sq.-ft., gravity-fed winery. The facility comprises a series of Quonset-like huts interconnected to "flow" down the side of the hill and offers separate crush, press, storage, barrel aging, bottling, and warehousing of the wines. The warehouse area empties quickly whenever new wines come into the retail shop. After a disappointing vintage in 1996, most of the Moira Vineyard, which was purchased a year earlier, had to be torn out. It was replanted with Chardonnay, Pinot Gris, and Pinot Noir. Only the Gewürztraminer was kept; however, by 2003, it too was not doing well and was replanted with Pinot Noir. By the end of the following year, Moira Vineyard, qualified for certification as fully organic, although some practices go further, following bio-dynamic principles. Epp Vineyard in nearby Jordan is the source of Malivoire's concentrated Old Vines Foch. These grapes were planted in 1975. While the company does not own this property, it has been under its viticultural control since early 2002. As a result, it qualifies for an "estate" designation. Additional grapes are purchased as required from Wismer Vineyards and Laundry-Mottiar Vineyards. In past years, Riesling grapes also have been purchased from the Honsberger Vineyard as well as from the Misek Vineyard, however those ties have now lapsed. Malivoire uses 100% Ontario grapes and buys nothing from abroad, even during short vintages such as 2003. All grapes are hand-harvested and transferred from tank to tank by gravity flow. This gentle touch reduces the need for filtration, leaving more complex flavour components in the finished wines. In 2001, the year of the dreaded Asian lady beetle, they decided to unceremoniously dump almost the entire production, rather than release tainted wines and damage the company's reputation. Only icewines – picked after the bugs had gone – were produced. And in 2004, Malivoire improved its packaging by switching to modern screw-cap closures. At time of writing, a new 3,000-sq.-ft. barrel cellar was in the plans. The current total annual production of 10,000 cases is projected to peak at 15,000 cases by 2008.

Winemakers: Ann Sperling (1997-present, 2004 Winemaker of the Year); Martin Malivoire (1996-1997) / Vineyard Manager: David Crow

Chardonnay, Estate-Bottled [NP] **2003** ★ ★ ★ ☆ ➔ Gold with a pineapple, mango, and crème anglaise bouquet. Big, pungent, and quite alcoholic. Still very youthful. Drink now-2008. **2002** ★ ★ ★ ☆ ➔ Pale gold with a lively, minty aroma. Packed with exciting, vivacious pear, lemon, and wine-gum flavours. Thick and full-bodied. Drink now-2007. **2000** ★ ★ ★ ☆ ➔ Deep gold with a big, fat, rich, concentrated bouquet and high acidity. Apricot and lemon flavours. Drink now-2006. **1999** ★ ★ ★ ➔ Peaking. Drink up before it tires.

Chardonnay, Moira Vineyard [NP] **2002** ★ ★ ★ ★ ➔ Brilliant pale gold with a lovely nose of fresh cream and the slightest hint of vanilla. Bright, crisp, fresh, lively, and complex with nuances of caramel toffee. Drink now-2009. **2000**★★★★➔ Deep gold with a bouquet of roast coffee, oak, and pine nuts. Great concentration, but oaky tannins overshadow the fruit. Drink now-2009. **1999**★★★★➔ Gold with a profoundly rich nose of oak, herbs, vanilla, and buttered corn. Palate is perfect with supple texture, balance, and length. Drink now-2010.

Chardonnay Musqué, "Spritz" [NP]   **2004**★★★★↻ (C13/ CM87) A significant change in this vintage with the Gewürztraminer replaced by early harvest Chardonnay. Very pale straw-gold and distinctly fizzy when poured. Crisp, fresh, wine-gum and sweet lanolin aroma and charming Moscato d'Asti-like taste. **2003**★★★★↻ (CM89/Gew11) Very pale straw-gold with big bubbles attaching themselves to the inside of the glass. Light, fruity, wine-gum aroma, the result of some Gewürztraminer blended in. Luscious, grapey, foamy, sweet, and ripe.

Gamay, Estate-Bottled [NP]   **2003**★★★↗ Rich cherry-garnet shade with a bold, dense, and perfumed nose of blackberry, cherry, and strawberry. Lovely texture, solid density, and an interesting future, though short-term. Drink now-2007.

Gamay, Single Block [NP]   **2002**★★★➔ Deep black-cherry-garnet with a dense plummy nose and hints of black cherry and raspberry. Vibrant palate, high acidity, and a flavoury finish. Chill lightly to accentuate the fruit. Drink now-2007. **2001** Not produced.

Gewürztraminer, Estate-Bottled [NP]   **2003**★★★↗ Brilliant gold colour with a fabulous concentrated nose of pine sap, wildflowers, apricot jam, mint, bergamot, and Thrills gum. Palate is still young, hot, bitter, and brutal. Drink 2006-2013.

Gewürztraminer, Moira Vineyard [NP]   **2002**★★★★➔ Deep, brilliant gold with rosy reflections. Profoundly rich nose of lychee, lanolin, honey, citrus, spice, and earth. One big mother of a wine with a smidgen of residual sweetness. Drink now-2012.

Gewürztraminer Icewine, Moira Vineyard [NP] **1998**★★★★➔ Cognac-gold with a peppery nose of spiced raisins. Dried-apricot flavours and perfect balance. Drink now-2012. **1997**★★★★➔ *Gold, International Wine & Spirit Competition, London 1999.* Amber-gold with a fruitcake and pear syrup nose. Rich and spirity with a taste more like a fine liqueur made with spiced honey and cognac. Drink now-2010. **1996**★★★★☆➔ Tasted only once and in a restaurant; it made me weak with delight. Drink now-2015.

Melon "Martin's Oyster Wine" [NP]   **2002**★★↻ (Mel90/ Gew10) Very pale silvery-gold. Briny, iodine smell of fresh-shucked oysters spritzed with lemon. Crisp and clean, the perfect foil for a mollusc.

Old Vines Foch [Ont] Aged in American oak and bottled unfiltered. **2003**★★★☆↗ (Gam13/MF87) Opaque garnet-purple with a thick, gamy, herbal nose with nuances of plum and mocha. Tart, juicy, rustic, and oaky. Drink now-2009. **2002 ★ ★ ★ ↗** (Gam13/MF87) Deep purple-garnet with a big, oaky nose with nuances of talcum powder, lipstick, black cherry, herbs, and field flowers. Tastes of warmed plums, cream, nuts, dark chocolate, and herbs. Tremendous depth but high acidity and short, mouth-drying, burnt-toast finish. Drink now-2010. **2000 ★ ★ ★ →** (CF5/MF95) From Epp Vineyard. Garnet with edges beginning to take on a brick colour. Surface bubbles. Berries and cream aroma with a charred woodsy undertone and plummy, blackberry flavours. Mouth-drying tannic finish. Drink now-2008. **1999 ★ ★ ★ ★ ↗** (CF12/MF88) From Epp Vineyard. Garnet with a brick rim. Sweet, sharp, vegetal, hybrid nose to start, develops warm black-cherry and cedar notes with airing. Big, oaky, rustic flavour and terrific balance. Drink now-2010. **1998 ★ ★ ★ ↘** (CF8/MF92) Plastic stopper nearly impossible to remove. Garnet hue with significant orange-brick edges. Maturing nose, hint of wet autumn leaves, earth, mushrooms, a whiff of iodine and ripe, stewed black fruits. Excellent structure and supple texture despite high acidity. Ready to drink now.

Old Vines Foch, Canadian Oak [Ont]   Bottled without filtration. **2002 ★ ★ ★ ★ ↗** (CF13/MF87) Inky purple-garnet. Has a lovely restrained nuttiness and ripe blackberry notes with nuances of oak, smoke, and concentrated black fruit. It has wa-a-ay more elegance than the American-oaked OVF. The domestic oak seems to give support to the fruit, letting it express itself, whereas the American oak seems to dominate the fruit, giving it a warmer caramelized flavour and a hint of stewiness. The taste is lean and concentrated with high acidity, youthful tannins, and a long-lasting finish. Drink now-2012.

Pinot Gris, Estate-Bottled [NP] **2003 ★ ★ ★ →** Straw-gold with pink reflections and a hint of spritz. Bouquet is ripe, bold, and aromatic with nuances of wildflowers, herbs, and spice. Grapefruit flavours with lovely mouthfeel. Drink now-2007.

Pinot Gris, Moira Vineyard [NP] **1999 ★ ★ ★ ★ ↗** Concentrated, peachy, spicy, and exceptionally firm. Drink now-2007.

Pinot Noir, Estate-Bottled [NP] **2003 ★ ★ ★ →** Deep ruby with a spicy, fruity bouquet of Bing cherries. Ripe flavours and substantial body. Lasted for days after opening. Drink now-2012. **2002 ★ ★ ★ →** Another yumster. Light Pinot nose of cherry with cinnamon spice. Pleasant, balanced, short-lived. Drink now-2008.

Pinot Noir, Moira Vineyard [NP] **2000 ★ ★ ★ ★ ↗** Cherry red with tiny bubbles appearing on the surface and rim. Full, deep, classic bouquet of black and red fruits, oak, smoke, toasted nuts, raw meat, and cracked pepper. Drink now-2012. **1999 ★ ★ ★ ★ ↗** Ruby cherry with a red-brick rim. Concentrated bouquet with rich notes of roasted coffee beans, smoked herbs, raw meat, game, and undertones of sandalwood, leather, and spice. Dense, fleshy, and supple with a ripe, sweet finish. Drink now-2013.

Riesling Icewine, Honsberger Farms [NP] **2000**★ ★ ★ ★ ↗ Rich gold with deep amber highlights. Bouquet of warm pastry or butter tarts. Dried peach flavours and great acidity. Has a long future. Drink now-2025. **1999**★ ★ ★ ★ ↗ Cognac-gold with copper reflections. Nose is of dried apricots and warmed walnuts. Has a nuance of "rancio," that wonderful aroma of sun-dried fruits. Stewed and jammy. Drink now-2020.

Riesling Icewine, Misek Vineyard [NP] **2003**★ ★ ★ ★ ↗ Yellow-gold with a fresh aroma of sweet floral blossoms. Tastes of fruit cocktail with plenty of pear and pineapple flavours. Drink now-2020. **2002**★ ★ ★ ★ ↗ Brilliant golden hue with a peachy, luscious bouquet. Clean and lively with a seamless citrus and apricot fusion of flavours. Drink now-2017. **2001**★ ★ ★ ★ ↗ Deep gold with a caramelized fruit nose. Seems advanced and forward. Peach and orange flavours with hints of sun-dried apricot. Drink now-2015.

Rosé, Ladybug [NP] **2003**★ ★ ★ ↻ Pale garnet-pink with a hint of sweetness. Subtle red-fruit flavours. The perfect picnic wine. **2002**★ ↻ Some tasters have told me they loved it. I didn't.

Vidal, Late Harvest [Ont] A blend of 93% second-pressing of Vidal Blanc icewine grapes with 7% late-harvest Pinot Gris. **2002**★ ★ ★ ★ ↗ Thick apple, pear, and peach flavours with bracing acidity. Will shine in 2006, amaze in 2008, wow in 2010, and begin to fade thereafter.

• **Malolactic Fermentation** – A wholly natural or artificially induced process by which a wine's tart malic acidity (which gives a wine an applelike crispness) is converted to lactic acid (which has a softer, creamier taste, typical of cheese, butter, sour cream, or yogourt).

• **MAPLE GROVE ESTATE WINERY** (4063 North Service Road, Beamsville, ON, L0R 1B6 / Office Phone: 905-856-5700 / Winery Phone: 905-562-7415 / Fax: 905-856-8208)

(Est. 1994) Giovanni and Rosanna Follegot came to Canada in 1968 from the Veneto region of Italy, where Giovanni's family had settled for 4 generations after leaving France. In 1992, they purchased a neglected 18-acre vineyard on the Lake Ontario shoreline just west of the picturesque Schuele Vineyard. The relatively flat, mixed-clay and sandy-loam soil is now completely tiled for drainage, and since 1993 has been replanted with Cabernet Franc, Cabernet Sauvignon, Chardonnay, Merlot, Pinot Noir, and Riesling all to a density of 1,210 vines per acre. There's also 1 row of Vidal, from which the Follegots harvest 1 t. of grapes for the production of icewine. All wines are estate-grown and estate-bottled. Production volumes are unknown.

Winemakers: Giovanni Follegot (1994-present); Peter Rotar (1996-1997) / Vineyard Manager: Giovanni Follegot

Wines were not made available for tasting.

• **MARIANNE HILL VINEYARDS ESTATE WINERY** (3953 Hixon Street, Beamsville, ON, L0R 1B7 / Phone: 905-563-5144 / Fax: 905-563-5155 / Email: mariannehill@canada.com)

(Est. 2004) When Gerd and Ingrid Schmitt purchased this 85-acre vineyard in 1980, it was known as the St. Hilarius Vineyard. Located high on the bench of the Niagara Escarpment overlooking Beamsville, it has one of the prettiest vistas across the lake to the Toronto skyline. The soil is Oneida clay loam till with some alluvial deposits over a limestone substrata. Here, so close to the escarpment, the terrain is significantly sloped in places, with grades that vary between 5% and 30%. Most of the property is north-facing; however, there are east- and west-facing exposures too. The Schmitts tend 60 acres of vinifera vines, including 2.5 acres of Cabernet Franc, 2 acres of Cabernet Sauvignon, 12.5 acres of Chardonnay, 4 acres of Gamay, 2 acres of Gewürztraminer, 4 acres of Merlot, and a whopping 33 acres of Riesling clone Weis 21 dating back to 1982. Grapes for icewine production, especially Riesling, are sold to Inniskillin. The Schmitts have a manufacturer's licence, are producing wine to create an inventory, and are in the process of applying for a retail licence. As soon as they open, they will be able to sell what they haven't kept for themselves.

Winemaker: Ingrid Schmitt / Vineyard Manager: Gerd Schmitt

Wines not available for appraisal before press time.

• **MARYNISSEN ESTATES** (1208 Concession #1, R.R.#6, Niagara-on-the-Lake, ON, L0S 1J0 / Phone: 905-468-7270 / Fax: 905-468-5784 / Email: info@marynissen.com / Website: www.marynissen.com)

(Est. 1990) John Marynissen, a professional grape grower and hobby winemaker, immigrated from Holland together with his wife, Nanny, in 1952. The next year he purchased his first parcel of land a mile from the Niagara River and began to plant a vineyard. He later added another parcel, bringing total owned acreage to 70, although only 45 acres are under vine. In the early days, wineries purchased mostly labrusca and some hybrid varieties, but after his Marechal Foch was used by Inniskillin in that winery's first test batch in 1974, Marynissen realized that vinifera vines would play a central role in the future of the wine industry. By 1975, he was shifting emphasis to the European varieties and, by 1978, was awarded for his efforts by being chosen Ontario Grape King.

Although his primary work was as a grape farmer, John made his own wine too, often entering bottles in amateur competitions. When his 1987 Riesling won top prize for Best Estate-Bottled Wine at the American Wine Society in 1989, Marynissen caved in to friends who convinced him it was time to start his own winery. The 2 estate vineyards have no official names but are given lot numbers. Lot 31 is the 27-acre vineyard surrounding the family home and winery. The property is flat, with areas of Jeddo clay loam, Vineland lacustrine sandy loam, and Tavistock loam. On this property, the Marynissens grow Cabernet Sauvignon, Chardonnay, Merlot, and Sauvignon Blanc. Lot 66, a 42-acre parcel with stony gravel, is located along the same side road, just 2 properties north of the home farm. It is planted with Cabernet Franc, Gamay, Gewürztraminer, and a small amount of Petite Sirah. Production at Marynissen is predominantly from estate-grown grapes, although some varietals have been made from purchased grapes. The best known was the 1995 Funk Vineyard Pinot Noir shared by Eddy Gurinskas at Lakeview Cellars and Jim Warren at Stoney Ridge. And the gold medal–winning 1997 Baco Noir produced by John's daughter Sandra came from Muir Vineyard, which is owned by husband Glen Muir's parents. In 2003, Sandra and Glen bought the farm and now make all the wines, although John is still active as company president. Marynissen wines are recognized for their good value, partly because they sell most products through their own retail shop, where they can make a reasonable profit while consumers avoid exorbitant LCBO markups.

Winemakers: Sandra Marynissen (1997-present); John Marynissen (1990-2003) / Vineyard Manager: Glen Muir

Baco Noir [NP] **1997**★★★➔ Gold, All Canadian Wine Championships, 1999. Big and blackstrap with a juicy, fruity blackberry, black-cherry flavour. Drink soon.

Cabernet Franc [NP] **1991**★★★↘ Opaque purple-garnet colour. Pruney, kirschlike nose, lovely supple texture, but drying up to an austere finish. Drink soon.

Cabernet/Merlot [NP] **1991**★★★☆➔ Deep garnet with some browning along the edge. Wide open bouquet of barnyard, cabbage, and sweetened yogourt. Balanced palate with tough tannins, but fruit is holding on. Drink soon.

Cabernet Sauvignon [NP] **1992**↓ Deeply coloured for the vintage. Strong vegetal, green pepper, celery tones. Past its peak. **1990 (Barrel Select)**★★➔ Mulberry-purple colour, minty, black-currant flavours, good balance, and lengthy finish. Ready. **1989**★★↘ A bit strange now; fruit is present, but it's quite vegetal. Drink up.

Cabernet Sauvignon, Lot 31-A [NP] Aged in American oak. **1991**★★★↘ Holding well, with some cassis flavours and hints of cigar box, dill, and other herbs. Drink up.

Cabernet Sauvignon, Lot 31-F [NP] Aged in French oak. 1991 ★ ★ ★ ➔ Some blackberry and black-currant aromas with secondary smells of leather, coffee, chocolate, and toffee. Drink now.

Cabernet Sauvignon, Lot 66 [NP] 1997 ★ ★ ★ ➔ Ruby-garnet with orange hints on the rim. Plummy flavours with a tannic herbal finish. Drink now-2010. 1991 ★ ★ ★ ★ ➔ Dark garnet with significant browning along the rim. Dense aroma of prune and stewed cherry, some herbal notes, and balanced tannins. 500 cases made. Drink now-2008.

Cabernet-Merlot [NP] 1991 ★ ★ ★ ➔ (CF25/CS50/M25) Deeply coloured with an enticing perfumed black-fruit nose. Starting to lose an earlier toughness on the palate. Great balance with concentrated fruit extract. Drink now-2009. 1989 ★ ★ ➘ (CS75/M25) Ruby-cherry colour, gamy leather and sausage nose with some nuttiness. Lean, well-balanced palate. 25 cases made. Drink now.

Gewürztraminer [NP] 2002 ★ ★ ★ ➔ Clean but unexciting flavours of honey and lanolin. 1995 ★ ★ ➘ Soft, subdued ripe peach, pear, and honey aromas.

Merlot [NP] 1998 ★ ★ ★ ★ ➔ Still deep garnet with an opaque centre. Fluffy nose with big fruit flavours, mocha chocolate, and an exotic herbacity. Full-bodied, with a long, thick aftertaste. Drink now-2012. 1997 ★ ★ ★ ➔ Similar flavours to 1998, but with leaner texture, more zippy fruit, less lush velvetiness. Ready to drink, but will keep to 2009. 1991 ★ ★ ★ ★ ➔ Paling ruby colour with a browning rim. Earthy, coffee, black pepper, and cream on the nose, with plenty of boiled-cherry flavours left. A superb, long-lived wine. Drink now.

Merlot, Barrel Select [NP] 2001 ★ ★ ➔ Cooked fruit nose. Dense and concentrated, but not showing well at this time. 1990 ★ ★ ★ ➘ Lovely, ripe plum flavours. Drink soon.

Merlot, Marynissen Vineyard [NP] 1997 ★ ★ ★ ➔ Aroma and flavours of soy, beef bouillon, spice, and a touch of barnyard. Fully mature and beginning to slide. Drink soon.

Pinot Noir, Funk Vineyard [NP] 1995 ★ ★ ★ ➘ Bigger, fuller, richer than any earlier Pinots, almost Californian in style. Unfortunately, fruit now is beginning to dry up. 1992 ★ ★ ➘ Old Pinot flavours reminiscent of over-the-hill Côtes de Nuits.

Pinot Noir, Watson & Voege Vineyards [NP] 1991 ★ ★ ➘ Light and pleasantly barnyardy, but ready to keel over.

Riesling [NP] 1999 ★ ★ ★ ➔ Deep amber gold colour. Has strong, overripe peach and beeswax aromas. 1993 ★ ★ ★ A tank sample was thick and grapey in 1995. Green but concentrated. Not tasted since. 1990 ★ ★ ➘ Fruity and elegant.

Riesling, Barrel Select [NP] 2002 ★ ★ ★ ➔ Softness and implicit sweetness make it very quaffable for now. For short aging only.

Sauvignon Blanc [NP] 1998 ★ ★ ★ ★ ↘ Was crisp, full, zesty, herbal, and big. Now tiring.

Vidal Icewine [NP] 1990 ★ ★ ★ ★ ↘ Lovely, but fully mature with the fruit beginning to dry up. Drink up.

Vidal, Winter Wine [NP] 1994 ★ ★ ★ ↘ This is a second pressing of icewine grapes. Just a bit grassy with an herbal nose, half dry/half sweet palate, clean dry finish. Drink soon.

• **MASTRONARDI ESTATE WINERY** (1193 Concession #3, Kingsville, ON, N9Y 2E5 / Phone: 519-796-0491 / Fax: 519-326-0434 / Email: emastronardi@cogeco.ca)

(Opening: Spring 2006) When Tony and Eadie Mastronardi and Tony's brother Reno bought this 100-acre property in 2002, their primary intention was to tear out all the grapevines and start a greenhouse operation. They were not ready to build, however, and since there was a viable income from the vineyard, they made arrangements to sell the grapes back to the property's previous owners, Colio Winery. With a history of winemaking in Tony and Reno's Italian roots, it didn't take long to spark interest in the wine business. The following year after a devastating winter, Tony learned about the frost protection offered by wind machines and decide to install a half-dozen throughout the vineyard. When the following winter the vineyard produced a bountiful crop despite similar severe conditions, Tony became the Canadian distributor of the American-made machines and last year sold almost 2 dozen to fellow grape growers. The vineyard is situated 2 km north of Lake Erie with an elevation of approximately 10 m above it. The sandy loam soil is fully tiled for drainage and planted with about a dozen varieties at 1,000 vines per acre. Yield is generally 4.5 t. per acre. The oldest planting is an experimental Geisenheim variety that dates back to 1990. In 1996, Colio planted Cabernet Franc, Chardonnay, Gewürztraminer, Pinot Gris, Riesling, Riesling-Traminer, Vidal Blanc, and Zweigelt. The Mastronardis added more Cabernet Franc, plus Cabernet Sauvignon and Merlot in 2004. The Mastronardis have produced approximately 2,000 cases of wine, which should by now be available in a temporary retail store they constructed this past summer. By 2010, they plan to expand production to 400,000 cases annually. For now, most of the fruit is sold to Colio Estate Winery.

Winemaker: Lyse LeBlanc / Vineyard Manager: Jacob Neufeld

Wines not available for appraisal before press time.

• **MAZZA VINEYARD** (Niagara-on-the-Lake, NP) – Welder Angelo Mazza rents this property on the northwest corner of Concession 6 and Highway 55 to Pillitteri Estates. It is flat, fully tiled for drainage, and consists of Chinguacousy clay loam. The entire 10-acre vineyard is planted to Cabernet Franc and Merlot.

• **MCGRADE VINEYARD (Vineland, NP)** – This tiny vineyard owned by Stoney Ridge Estate Winery is situated on the south side of King Street (Regional Road #81), south of Butler's Grant Vineyard. It is only 3.3 acres in surface area, flat, composed of sand and clay, fully underdrained, and planted entirely with Pinot Noir at a plant density of 1,300 vines per acre. Fruit harvested at 3 t. per acre is processed exclusively by Stoney Ridge.

• **MCNAB ACRES (Niagara-on-the-Lake, NP)** – Largest producer of grapes in the Niagara Peninsula, supplying 3,000 t. to Hillebrand Estates for its premium and icewines. Bill Falk manages 14 properties from the Lakeshore to Line 2.

• **MEADOW LANE WINERY** (44892 Talbot Line, R.R.#3, St. Thomas, ON, N5P 3S7 / Phone: 519-633-1933 / Fax: 519-633-1355 / Email: wines@meadowlanewinery.com / Website: www.meadowlane winery.com)

(Est. 1998) Debbie and Walter Myszko farm 45 acres of heavy clay loam 5 km from the shores of Lake Erie. The long, narrow strip is only partially underdrained. Although they are listed primarily as a fruit winery, they also sell wines produced from grapes purchased from Gothic Cottage Vineyard in Norfolk County and from Watson Farms in Niagara-on-the-Lake. The couple grow tree fruits and bush berries and purchase additional fruit from as far away as Parry Sound. They have 5 acres devoted to grapes. In 2000, they put in 2.5 acres of Zweigelt. Two years later, they added .5 acre of the white hybrid variety GM-322-58, also known as Hibernal. In 2003, they planted 1 acre each of Cabernet Franc and Merlot, and .25 acre of Cabernet Sauvignon. Before the end of the decade, they hope to double their current production of 2,100 cases.
Winemaker: Walter Myszko / Vineyard Manager: Walter Myszko

Zweigelt [Ont] 2001 ☒ Nice colour but Asian lady beetle detected.

• **MERTENS VINEYARD (Beamsville, NP)** – Close to the Cave Spring Farm and the Eastman Vineyard, Otto Mertens grows 8 acres of Gewürztraminer, 10 acres of Chardonnay, and some Riesling. He used to sell to Cave Spring, but now deals exclusively with Kittling Ridge.

- **MIKE WEIR ESTATE WINERY** (963 Queenston Road, St. David's, ON, L0R 1J0 / Phone: 905-562-0035 / Toll-Free: 1-877-262-9463 / Fax: 905-562-5493 / Email: retail@weirwines.com / Website: www.weirwines.com)

(Est. 2005) The most recent and heralded announcement in the Ontario industry earlier this year was the founding of a joint venture between Canada's first PGA golfer to win the Masters title, Mike Weir, and Creekside Estate Winery. The concept was loosely patterned after Australia's Greg Norman Estate Wines. A key difference is that all proceeds from the sale of these wines will be directed to Canadian children's charities through the Mike Weir Foundation. Two introductory wines were released in April 2005, and others have appeared since. Until the new winery is completed, production will be carried out at Creekside Estate's existing facility in Jordan. All grapes are harvested from the Beverly lacustrine silty clay of a 50-acre St. David's vineyard planted between 2000 and 2002. There are 40 flat and underdrained acres of Chardonnay, Cabernet Sauvignon, Merlot, Pinot Noir, Shiraz, and Viognier cultivated at a vine density of 1,200 plants per acre. The winery's retail store will open onsite in the spring of 2006, and production is expected to reach 5,000 cases by 2008.

Winemakers: Rob Power; Craig McDonald / Vineyard Manager: Bryson Waind

Wines not available for appraisal before press time.

- **MISEK VINEYARD (Vineland, NP)** — Before escaping communist Czechoslovakia in the late 1960s, Jan Misek worked as a winemaker at the state farm in southern Moravia. After coming to Canada, he settled in as a viticulturalist for Chateau Gai. In 1989, he and his wife, Olga, purchased this 10-acre farm on King Street between Lakeview Cellars and Niagara Bench Vineyard. Misek's first act was to tear out the old labrusca varieties — Concords, Niagaras, and some others. He kept the Vidal Blanc and Chambourcin and added Cabernet Sauvignon, Gewürztraminer, Merlot, and Riesling. A total of 8 acres now are planted on the sloped, east-facing Oneida clay with its many scattered pebbles. The excellent natural drainage of this soil eliminates any need for additional tiling. In an average vintage, Misek will thin about 25% of his fruit at veraison and harvest up to 4 t. per acre. Over the years he has supplied several Bench wineries such as Lakeview Cellars and Malivoire, but, since 2004, his grapes have been sold exclusively to Pillitteri Estates.

- **MOIRA VINEYARD (Beamsville, NP)** — This 40-acre working vineyard was purchased in 1995 by Martin Malivoire and Moira Saganski. After their first harvest in 1996, they tore out all but the Gewürztraminer, replanting with 8.5 acres of Chardonnay at a vine density of 1,000 plants per acre, and 0.4 acres of Pinot Gris plus 2 acres of Pinot Noir (clone 115) at a high vine density of 1,445 plants per acre. The remaining Gewürztraminer was replaced with Pinot Noir (clone 777) in 2004. The vineyard was certified organic late in 2004. All grapes are processed exclusively by The Malivoire Wine Company.

- **MOLEK VINEYARD (Pelham, NP)** — Martin Molek grows Baco Noir, Chardonnay, and Vidal Blanc along with a red Slovenian variety (possibly Plavac Mali) in gravelly, sandy soil, next door to the DeJonge Vineyard. Chardonnay is supplied to Henry of Pelham for its "sur lie" Chardonnay, while other varieties are sold to Andrés.

- **MONTAGUE VINEYARD (Niagara-on-the-Lake, NP)** — Located at the intersection of Carlton Road and Town Line Road directly north of the Niagara District Airport, this 110-acre property is one of Inniskillin's estate vineyards. Chardonnay was planted on the original 50-acre parcel in 1980. In 1993, it was enlarged when a contiguous parcel on the north side was purchased. It isn't particularly fertile, but, with plenty of small stones in the heavy Chinguacousy and Jeddo clay loam soils, the wines produced from this property are full-bodied and packed with character. The vineyard now has 25 acres of Chardonnay, 20 acres of Merlot, 12 acres of Pinot Gris, 25 acres of Pinot Noir, 10 acres of Riesling, 5 acres of Sauvignon Blanc, and 6 acres of Vidal Blanc all spaced at 1,247 vines per acre. Average yield is 3-5 t. per acre, depending on the variety. Originally tended by Rick Hunse, the vineyard has been managed by Gerald Klose since 1993.

- **Montravin Cellars** — This producer of traditional, hand-riddled, sparkling wine succeeded Podamer and, in 1993, was itself swallowed up by Magnotta. Bottles held now would likely be too old.

- **MORGAN VINEYARD (Beamsville, NP)** — Stu and Ginny Morgan are part-owners of Lakeview Cellars Estate Winery. This 11-acre lakeshore property has been their "home farm" since 1994. They cultivate 3 fully tiled acres of grapevines, with 1.5 acres each of Kerner and Sauvignon Blanc spaced at 1,100 vines per acre. The soil here is a fine clay loam. The vineyard is thinned at veraison to yield 4 t. of fruit per acre, all of which is sold exclusively to Lakeview.

- **MORI VINEYARDS AND NURSERIES (Niagara-on-the-Lake, NP)** — A large provider of vine- and rootstock to many Niagara area wineries, it also supplies grapes from the nursery to Hillebrand Estates and Pillitteri.

- **Mounier Brut** — Sparkling wine made by Hillebrand Estates from Chardonnay and Pinot Noir grapes grown in the Niagara Peninsula, using the champagne method. The product was dropped after Andrés bought Hillebrand Estates, but not the Mounier brand name from its German owners. Bottles held today would be too old and oxidized to drink.

- **MOUNTAIN ROAD WINE COMPANY** (4016 Mountain Road, Beamsville, ON, L0R 1B7 / Phone: 905-563-0745 / Fax: 905-563-0650 / Email: info@mountainroadwine.com / Website: www.mountainroadwine.com)

(Est. 1999) Two years after leaving Hungary during the 1956 revolution, Andy and Klara Kocsis purchased the 46-acre mixed-fruit farm that today is the home of this premium winery. Their son, Steve, did his share of chores with the rest of the family until starting his engineering studies at Carleton University and the University of Toronto. After graduating, he started a business that permitted him to retire at age 24. He travelled the world and gained an appreciation for fine food and wine. In 1981, Kocsis bought the family farm to settle down with his wife and young son and live in the country. He took up winemaking as a hobby and planted 13.5 acres of Chardonnay, Gamay Noir, and Vidal Blanc. In 1992, he purchased 2 additional properties nearby and for a while sold all his fruit to neighbouring wineries. Today, wineries still line up to get his grapes, but as he now produces his own wines, there's less to sell. Current volume is 2,000 cases, a quantity with which he is quite satisfied. Peter Kocsis of Crown Bench Estate and Tom Kocsis, who started Thomas and Vaughan Vintners, are Steve's cousins.

Winemakers: John Witkowski (2000-present); Steve Kocsis (1999, table wines); Deborah Paskus (1999, icewine) / Vineyard Manager: Steve Kocsis

Baco Noir [Ont]   From Fly Road Vineyard. **2001 ★ ★ ★ ↗** Opaque garnet with blackberry and brambleberry notes and a nuance of cooked-cherry cough syrup. Taste is tart and underripe. Drink now-2007.

Cabernet [NP]   **2000 ★ ★ ★ →** (CF50/CS50) Garnet-brick colour with a pleasant bouquet of cedar, tobacco, leather, and plum. Nice balance. Drink now-2008.

Cabernet Franc [NP]   From Hillside Drive Vineyard. **2001 ★ ★ ☆ →** Opaque garnet with a shy dusty nose. After several hours, the taint of Asian lady beetle shows up. Big, juicy, luscious flavours, tannic and long-lived, but best to use up while fruit still overshadows the bug. Drink now.

Cabernet Sauvignon, Reserve [NP]   Hillside Drive Vineyard. **2001 ★ ★ ☆ →** This would have been a killer wine if not for the Asian lady beetle. Drink now while the rich, ripe black-fruit flavours eclipse the effects of the bug. **2000** Best of Category, All Canadian Wine Championships, 2004.

Chardonnay, Barrel-Aged [NP] **2000** ★ ★ ★ ➔ A deep yellow shade of gold and strong oaky, toasty, roasted coffee notes. Lingers but only briefly. Drink soon.

Chardonnay, Barrel-Fermented [NP] From Mountain Road Vineyard. **2001** ★ ★ ★ ☆ ↗ Thick gold with an oily look. Bouquet of poached pear, caramel, pralines in cream. Big, buxom, and supple with ripe, concentrated exotic flavours, solid structure, and great length. Doughy aftertaste. Drink now-2008.

Chardonnay, Barrel-Fermented Reserve [NP] Mountain Road Vineyard. **2001** ★ ★ ★ ★ ↗ Brilliant gold with an undemonstrative nose. Powerful, ripe, and implicitly sweet with exotic fruit flavours of pineapple, mango, guava. This is a biggie. Drink now-2011.

Chardonnay, Unoaked [NP] Hillside Drive Vineyard. **2000** ★ ★ ★ ➔ Bleached straw-gold with a clean, light aroma of pears in fresh cream. Taste is fresh and light. Drink now-2006.

Gamay Rosé [NP] Mountain Road Vineyard. **2000** ★ ★ ★ ➔ Onion-skin orange with a vinous nose and clean, balanced, solid, dry finish. Drink now.

Marechal Foch [Ont] Fly Road Vineyard. **2001** ★ ★ ★ ☆ ↗ Opaque garnet with a big plummy aroma. Flavours of plum and black cherry. Not overly tart like many MFs, but well balanced and tannic. Drink now-2009. **2000** *Gold, All Canadian Wine Championships, 2004.*

Mountain Road Red [nonVQA] A blend of 5 grapes (BN/CF/CS/Gam/MF) from 3 vineyards. **NV** ★ ★ ★ ↻ *Best of Category, All Canadian Wine Championships, 2004.* Opaque garnet with a violet edge. Bouquet has fine elements as well as quite rustic notes, i.e., ripe fruits and boiled vegetables. Delightful taste. It would improve with a stretch in a cool cellar but, without a vintage date on the label, it's not worth the risk of leaving it too long. Drink now.

Riesling [NP] Hillside Drive Vineyard. **2002** ★ ★ ★ ➔ Pale green-gold with an herbaceous nose of grapefruit, field flowers, and plastic. Ripe and racy lemon-lime notes, grapefruity flavours, good concentration, and tough, tight structure. Drink now-2009.

Vidal, Icewine [NP] Grapes are from the Mountain Road Vineyard. **1999** ★ ★ ★ ★ ☆ ➔ *Gold, Ottawa Wine & Food Show, 2004.* Deep amber hue. Rattles the teeth with its intense sweetness. Concentrated, jammy, apricot marmalade and honeyed pear flavours. Drink now-2010.

Vidal, Special Select Late Harvest [Ont] Grapes are from the Mountain Road Vineyard. **2003** ★ ★ ★ ★ ↗ Bright gold hue with an aroma of pear essence. Lovely soft texture, alluring rich taste, and perfect balance. More satisfying than any icewine. Drink now-2010.

• **MUIR VINEYARD (Niagara-on-the-Lake, NP)** – This property is flat and composed of relatively heavy clay. Owners Earle and Sheila Muir are situated a couple of concessions over from the Marynissens. Their son, Glen, is married to Sandra Marynissen. The grapes for Sandra's gold medal–winning 1997 Baco Noir were sourced here. The Muirs are primarily tender-fruit growers and the grapes have never been a huge source of income. There's talk of tearing them out in the future.

- **MURRAY VINEYARD (Niagara-on-the-Lake, NP)** – Now owned by Kathleen Murray and her son, Shawn, the 12-acre property on Lakeshore Road at McNab Corners has been in the family since 1950. The 1984 Pinot Noir grown here was used in Inniskillin's first commercial production of this variety.

- **MYERS FARMS (Beamsville, NP)** – The Myers family has farmed this 67-acre property on Greenlane since 1890. It is fairly flat with Jeddo clay loam over a bedrock of clay shale, and is both tiled for drainage and irrigated against drought. Bill Myers cultivates 2 acres of very old Cabernet Franc (planted in 1983), 1 acre of Gewürztraminer (2002), and 21 acres of Riesling, some of which dates back to 1983. Unfortunately, 12 acres of Cabernet Sauvignon, Chardonnay, Sauvignon Blanc, and Zweigelt were pulled out after suffering severe winter damage in 2003. They were replanted with the much hardier Riesling vines. Vines are spaced at 950 plants per acres and thinned to yield 5 t. of fruit per acre. Although grapes were sold to several wineries in the past, Myers Farms now sells its fruit exclusively to Cave Spring Cellars.

N

- **NADJA'S VINEYARD (Jordan, NP)** – A 2.5-acre section of Riesling (Weis clone) planted in 2001, high up on the upper bench of the Niagara Peninsula above Jordan, where there is a highly variable mixture of stratified silt and silt on clay loam over a gravel subsurface. It is a slightly sloped, south-facing part of the Flat Rock Cellars Estate Vineyard, which was isolated after they noticed that, due to its height and exposure to higher winds, this section experienced an overall climate about 2 degrees cooler than the surrounding vineyards. The result is a lower natural yield, giving the fruit higher natural acidity and greater concentration. In 2003, the vineyard generated 800 kg per acre, about one-third what the remaining acreage would produce in a normal harvest.

- **NEUDORF VINEYARD (Jordan, NP)** – Owners of the new Le Clos Jordanne Winery have negotiated a long-term lease with the Neudorf family to cultivate an 8.3-acre portion of this farm. Situated near the intersection of 11th Street and King Street (Regional Road 81), the silty clay soil over glacial till was planted entirely with Pinot Noir in 2002 at a vine spacing of 2,160 plants per acre. Drainage is installed between every row, and cover crops are grown alternate years between every second row to improve the soil structure and to increase competition for water. Over-the-row tractors are used to lessen soil compaction. Yields are exceptionally low for now, but will increase to a maximum of 2 t. per acre at maturity. All treatments are organic, and the plan is to certify the vineyard as such, then to introduce bio-dynamic farming practices within a few years.

- **NEUFELD VINEYARD (Niagara-on-the-Lake, NP)** – Owner John Neufeld served for several years as head of the Association of Grape Growers of Ontario. His 118-acre farm is situated 300 m from the lake at 911 Lakeshore Road on the south side, between the Falk and Froese farms. It's a reasonably flat piece of land, with mostly clay loam and a lot of deep rocks, some sandy pockets, and some pebbles. There's a rocky ridge running through the property, so only 85 acres are planted. Neufeld grows 7 acres each of Cabernet Franc and Seyval Blanc, 20 acres each of Cabernet Sauvignon and Chardonnay, 9 acres of Gamay (planted in 1975), 7 acres of Gewürztraminer (from 1975), 6 acres each of Geisenheim 318 and Merlot, 11 acres of Vidal Blanc, and 5 acres of Zweigelt. All grapes were sold to Vincor until Neufeld started his own winery, Palatine Estate.

• **NIAGARA BENCH FARMS (Beamsville, Vineland, NP)** – Two properties owned by Judith and Marcel van Doorslaer and managed in partnership with Vailmont Vineyards. The Beamsville block is on Cave Springs Road north of Cave Spring and west of Plekan Vineyard. It is essentially flat with a very slight north-facing slope and is composed of Oneida clay loam over a limestone base. There are 6 acres planted at this time, with additional planting scheduled for 2006. Currently, the Pinot Gris and 2 clones of Riesling, harvested at 4 t. per acre, are sold exclusively to Cave Spring Cellars. The Vineland block is off Regional Road 81 (King Street) and is bordered by Willow Heights to the north, Kacaba to the east, Lastiwka Vineyard to the south, and Jan Misek to the west. There are 2 separate fields, both composed of Oneida clay loam with a total of 5.5 acres under vine. One has Pinot Noir and some Gamay planted in a north-south direction; the other has Merlot and the remaining Gamay Noir, with rows running east to west. Vines in both fields are spaced at 1,345 plants per acre. After thinning at veraison, an average yield of 3 t. per acre is sold to Angels Gate Winery.

• **Niagara Cellars Inc.** – Holding company owned by Susan O'Dell and Murray Watson. Holdings include EastDell Estates, EastDell Estate Vineyards, and, since 2004, Thomas & Vaughan.

• **NIAGARA COLLEGE TEACHING WINERY** (135 Taylor Road, R.R.#4, Niagara-on-the-Lake, ON, L0S 1J0 / Phone: 905-641-2252 / Fax: 905-988-4309 / Email: sgill@nctwinery.com / Website: www.nctwinery.ca)

(Est. 2002) Teaching winery for vitivinicultural technicians, assistant winemakers, and winery assistants. Each class cares for the school's teaching vineyards and makes wine under the supervision of industry-experienced instructors. The school's 2001 Chardonnay took top prize in the Canadian Wine Awards, beating every other winery in the country, while the 2002 Pinot Noir was the highest scoring wine at the Ontario Wine Awards. The 6-acre Jack Forrer Vineyard is used as a teaching and research vineyard in the Winery and Viticulture Technician program.
Instructor: Jim Warren (1997 Winemaker of the Year) / Winemakers: Second-year students / Vineyard Managers: First-year students

Cabernet Franc, Barrel-Aged [NP] **2002** ★ ★ ★ ↗ Deep garnet with violet reflections and a dense, reserved, plummy, Bordeaux-like nose. Lasting flavours, but hollow mid-palate and hard, dusty, herbal finish. Needs mucho relaxo. Drink 2007-2012.

Cabernet Sauvignon, Barrel-Aged [NP]   **2002** ★ ★ ★ ↗ Inky purple-garnet hue with notes of apple skin, plums, and toasted nuts. Lean on the palate, with mouth-drying tannins and a zippy, tough finish. Drink 2007-2014.

Chardonnay, Barrel Fermented [NP]   **2003** ★ ★ ★ ☆ → Pale gold with a hazelnutty-oak overtone. Great structure with all elements in proportion: ripe fruit, balancing acidity, and supportive oak. Did I mention, it tastes good too. Drink now-2008. **2002** ★ ★ ★ → Green-gold hue with a big nose of oak, toasted bread, vanilla, caramel, and a peachy, floral undertone. Almost as good as . . . **2001** ★ ★ ★ ★ → Best White Wine, Canadian Wine Awards 2003. Has power, delicacy, and great length.

Chardonnay, Reserve [NP]   **2003** ★ ★ ★ ★ → Rich straw-gold with a very big, oaky, caramel nose. Outstanding depth and flavours of cream, lemon, pear, peach, and mango. Complex and luscious. Drink now-2008.

Chardonnay, Warren Classic [NP]   **2003** ★ ★ ★ ☆ → Pale gold with a sweet oaky nose. Taste is dominated by residual sugar. A variation on Stoney Ridge Charlotte's Chardonnay. Drink now-2008.

College Red [Ont]   (Zweigelt, Cabernet Franc, and Chardonnay) **2002** ★ ★ ★ ↺ Some gamaylike berry notes; fullish, sweet, and ripe with flavours of cherry and skin of red apple. Good acidity.

College Rosé [Ont]   (BN/Gam) **2003** ★ ★ ↺ Pink with dry, crisp, citrusy aroma. Clean pink grapefruit flavour, pithy finish.

College White [Ont]   (VB) **2003** ★ ★ ★ ↺ Silvery-gold with a sweet, candied apricot nose. Off-dry but balanced.

Meritage, Barrel-Aged [NP]   **2003** ★ ★ ★ ☆ ↗ Garnet with a perfumed nose of black currant and raspberry. Sweetish with high-toned fruit flavours. Tannic yet soft. Drink now-2011. **2002** ★ ★ ★ ↗ Deep garnet with a rich nose of dark fruits. Great depth and complexity, dark berries, earth, nuts, and spice. Drink 2006-2012.

Merlot [NP]   **2002** ★ ★ ★ ↗ Purple-black with a concentrated but utterly closed nose. Dense ripe black-fruit flavours need time to develop. Drink 2006-2010.

Pinot Noir, Barrel-Aged [NP]   **2002** ★ ★ ★ ★ ↗ Gold & Wine of the Year, Ontario Wine Awards 2004. Pale ruby-garnet with a deep, elegant, typically Burgundian nose. Ripe, soft, red-fruit flavours with nuances of sandalwood and truffle. Great balance, good weight, lovely texture, and profound, classic finish. This class deserves an "A."

Riesling [NP]   **2003** ★ ★ ★ ★ → Gold, Ontario Wine Awards 2004. Crisp, green, grassy nose with ripe, sweet Granny Smith apple flavours and a soft, supple, fullish palate. Could do with a smidgen more acidity. Drink now-2009.

Rosé [NP]   **2003** ★ ★ ↺ Clean, light, pleasant.

Sauvignon Blanc [NP]   **2003** ★ ★ ★ → Silvery-gold with an intense, grassy, asparagus nose. Clean, crisp flavour of veggies sautéed in lemon butter. Some residual sugar but well balanced. Drink now.

Vidal Icewine [NP] **2002** *Gold, Toronto Wine & Cheese Show 2004.*
Vidal Late Harvest [Ont] **2003** ★ ★ ★ ☆ ↗ Gold with a baked
pear aroma, flavours of fruit tea, and cleansing, citrusy finish. Drink
now-2008.

• **NIAGARA PENINSULA** [NP] – This is the largest designated viticultural area in the country and includes all the land bounded by Lake
Ontario to the north, the Niagara River to the east, the Welland River
to the south, and Highways 56 and 20 to the west. It takes in all the
non-urban land between Niagara-on-the-Lake and Grimsby. The region
has more than 70 wineries with 18,500 acres (7,500 hectares) of vineyards and accounts for almost 90% of Ontario-grown wines. Wedged
between 2 of the 5 Great Lakes, the region benefits significantly from
the moderating effects of Lakes Erie and Ontario, as well as from the
protective influence of the Niagara Escarpment. Globally, the region is
situated on a par with the Provence region of France, Italy's central
Tuscany, and the Rioja region of Spain. In the last year there has been
an industry push to subdivide the Niagara Peninsula into almost a
dozen subregions, based on minor differences in soil, aspect, climate,
and lake effect.

• **NOKARA ESTATE (St. David's, NP)** – Supplied Chardonnay and
Riesling to Château des Charmes until 2002. Now sells its fruit to Vincor.

• **NORMAN HARDIE WINERY** (1152 Greer Road, Wellington,
ON, K0K 3L0 / Phone: 613-778-4508 / Email: njh@rogers.com /
Website: under construction)

(Est. 2004) Partners Oliver Lennox King and Norman Hardie are the
owners of 2 properties totalling 86 acres. The larger 51-acre site, where
the grapes are planted and the winery stands, lies just across the road
from Carmela Estate Winery, where Hardie also is the winemaker. After
leaving the Four Seasons Hotel as restaurant manager for Truffles,
Hardie learned his winemaking skills by working 12 vintages over a 6-
year span in 4 countries and 2 hemispheres. The properties have gently
sloped north- and south-facing aspects and are entirely Hillier clay loam
over fractured limestone. There's no need to install drainage as the fractured substrata naturally release excess rainfall; nor is there need for
irrigation with the water-retentive clay in the soil. To date, the partners
have been using organic practices but are undecided as to whether to
apply for certification. They planted 6 acres of Pinot Noir in 2003 and
added 1 acre of Chardonnay and 2 acres of Pinot Gris in 2004, all at the
high density of 2,200 vines per acre. By severe cluster-thinning each
year once the vineyard is established, they plan to limit yields to 1 kg
per plant or about 2 t. per acre. This year, they anticipate their first crop

to achieve no more than 0.5 t. per acre. In 2004, they produced 750 cases of wine using Chardonnay, Pinot Noir, and Riesling grapes purchased from Wismer Vineyards and from Creekside Estates' St. David's Vineyard. Their short-term objective is to increase production to 2,500 cases by 2007.

Winemaker: Norman Hardie / Vineyard Manager: Norman Hardie

Wines not available for appraisal before press time.

- **Oak** – Just as a chef may use a handful of herbs or spices to help generate the myriad flavours that make an ordinary dish a masterpiece, so, too, a winemaker will employ a few flavouring agents to improve his wine. I don't mean chemical soups from a jar or artificial essences from a vacuum pouch, I'm talking about natural flavouring from genuine wood and, in almost all cases, that means white oak. Wine needs to rest after the vinification process. It can taste rough, sharp, or simply unknit for a few months or for as much as several years after it undergoes the transformation resulting from alcoholic fermentation. It may yet benefit by undergoing a secondary "malolactic" fermentation before it is ready to drink. Storing wine in an impermeable glass or stainless-steel tank allows it to lose some of its rough edges, without dramatically changing its fruit flavours. A wooden vat or cask, however, permits additional modifications to occur that, invariably, alter the flavour of the wine. Winemakers generally use casks of oak grown in France, Hungary, or the United States. Ideally, the wood is hand-split and air-dried for a minimum of 24 months. French oak (*Quercus alba*) is grown in the central forests of Allier, Nevers, and Tronçais, and in the northern Vosges forest near the region of Alsace. It tends to have a tighter grain and smaller pores than American oak. American barrels are produced from the same species of white oak tree, usually grown in the Carolinian forests of the lower Great Lakes area and the floodplains of the Mississippi River, including Alabama, Arkansas, the Carolinas, Indiana, Kentucky, Missouri, Ohio, Tennessee, and Virginia. According to the French cooperage firm of Seguin-Moreau, American oak has components that give it 2-5 times the aromatic potential of European oak. In 1999, 2 Canadians started a company dedicated to manufacturing wine barrels from rare Carolinian oak trees grown within a tiny area of southern Ontario. Dr. Jim Hedges, a cardiac surgical assistant at Hamilton General Hospital, and Dr. Michael Risk, a retired geology professor at McMaster University, established Canadian Oak Cooperage Inc. after successfully experimenting with small barrels they had made from the wood. They were thinning out some overmature trees on Hedges's sister's woodlot in order to supply more light to the younger saplings when they recognized the Carolinian species. Before long the amateur winemakers began to wonder if they could use it to make themselves a few wine barrels. Hedges, a woodworker by hobby, tried to construct a small wine cask but quickly discovered coopering is a skill best left to professionals. As there are no qualified wine-barrel makers in Canada, Hedges and Risk loaded up 4 hockey equipment bags with hand-cut staves and carried them to Gibb Cooperage in Hot Springs, Arkansas. Four days later they returned with 3 miniature 10-gal. casks with which to experiment. Preliminary attempts at aging Sauvignon Blanc, Chardonnay, and Cabernet Sauvignon for varying lengths of time in the new barriques were rewarded with surprise and satisfaction. The Canadian oak barrels imparted a flavour similar to that of French oak. By 2001, not yet ready to commercialize their idea, they convinced Derek Barnett, winemaker at high-end Lailey Vineyards, to produce side-by-side bottlings of his estate-grown Chardonnay aged in 30-gal. barrels of Canadian and American oak. Barnett concluded that the Canadian oak had real potential. He agreed that the flavours seemed a bit stronger than French oak, but said he needed more time to learn the nuances of the wood. Nevertheless, the single barrel of Lailey 2001 Canadian Oak Aged Chardonnay was so well received by local wine media and collectors, Barnett put a 1-bottle limit on purchases. With the 2002 vintage, Barnett bought 6 full-sized (225 L) casks from 100-year-old heartwood that had been air-dried for 24 months and coopered by A & K Cooperage of Missouri. Several other Ontario wineries produced trial batches as did Dave Cofran, retired general manager of California winery Silver Oak Cellars. Cofran produced 3 Merlots, 1 each in full-sized barrels of Canadian, French, and American oak harvested in Missouri. Cofran described his results as follows: "Our own Missouri oak had the strongest vanilla flavours, the French was more like cigar box, and the Canadian wood was midway between the two." He explained that the character of the Canadian oak was neither better nor worse than that of the others and that it was unique enough to merit further testing. Ann Sperling, winemaker at Malivoire Wine Company, also experimented with Canadian oak. She agrees that it is distinct from French or American oak and says that the flavours are closer to oak from the Vosges forest of France, which is a cooler growing region, much like our own Niagara Peninsula. She, too, concluded that the full range of its characteristics would take time to discover. In 2003, Canadian Oak Cooperage produced 120 classic 59-gal. barrels for sale at $850, as well as a few 15-gal. kegs at $375 for the home winemaking market. "As soon as the market accepts us, we could gear up to make several hundred," Hedges said. "I'd hate to sell this stuff as flooring," Wineries currently working with Canadian oak include: Featherstone Estate, Lailey Vineyards, Daniel Lenko Estate, Malivoire Wine Company, Marynissen Estates, and Thirty Bench Winery.

- **Oak Ridge Wines** – Brand owned by Andrés Wines. Generic nonVQA varietals produced from imported wine, juice, or grapes.

Tasting notes listed under Peller Estates.

- **OCALA ORCHARDS FARM WINERY LTD.** (971 High Point Road, R.R.#2, Port Perry, ON, L9L 1B3 / Phone: 905-985-9924 / Toll-Free: 1-866-985-9924 / Fax: 905-985-7994 / Email: ocala@sympatico. ca / Website: www.ocalawinery.com)

(Est. 1995) Irwin Smith and his wife, Alissa, make a variety of products from the grapes and fruits they grow on their property near Lake Scugog. The farm was purchased in 1915 by Irwin's grandfather George, who tended a 4-acre orchard and ran the rest as a dairy farm. George's son, Lloyd, expanded the size and selection of fruits in the orchard and developed a pure-bred Holstein herd to supply the demand for high-quality milking stock. It was 1992 when Irwin, a hobby winemaker from the mid-1980s, decided to experiment with a small vineyard of his own. The vines needed to be tucked down to the ground and ploughed over to survive, but they did survive and, soon after, Irwin applied for a wine manufacturing licence. Today, the Smiths grow 20 acres of vinifera and hybrid grapes producing as much as 5,000 cases of wine in a good year. They also make fruit wines, sell non-alcoholic grape juice to a distributor in Jamaica, apple juice to home cider-makers, and grow cash crops like fall wheat, seed barley, and hay for feed. The vineyard is very gently sloped, south-facing, and composed of equal portions of clay loam and sandy loam. Spaced at a density of only 550 vines per acre, the varieties are Auxerrois, Baco Noir, Cabernet Sauvignon, Chardonnay, Marechal Foch, Pinot Gris, Riesling Seyval Blanc, Syrah, and Vidal Blanc. Smith also recently planted some hybrid stock purchased from Wisconsin, including Frontenac and Sabrevois. These will be used in the production of house wines and inexpensive banquet wines. A tiny amount of Cabernet Franc is purchased from Reuther Farms in the Niagara Peninsula.

Winemaker: Irwin Smith / Vineyard Manager: Irwin Smith

Baco Noir [Ont] 2002 ★ ★ ☆ → Dull garnet with an aroma of blackberries and blueberries macerated in sweetened sour cream. Soft palate with decent fruit. Drink now-2007.

Riesling [Ont] 2002 ★ ★ ★ → Silvery-gold with light lime and poached pear aromas. Off-dry taste with an apricot-peachiness in the finish. Drink now-2008.

- **ONTARIO** [Ont] – The appellation officially includes all vinifera, hybrid, vintage-dated, and non-vintage wines produced from grapes grown in the province. Wines produced from hybrid varieties must carry the Ontario appellation unless they have been made into icewine. Viniferas blended with hybrids must carry the appellation. Grapes grown outside the 3 designated viticultural areas (Lake Erie North Shore, Niagara Peninsula, and Pelee Island) qualify for the Ontario appellation.

P

• **PALATINE HILLS ESTATE WINERY** (911 Lakeshore Road, R.R.#3, Niagara-on-the-Lake, ON, L0S 1J0 / Phone: 905-646-9617 / Fax: 905-646-5832 / Email: palatinewines@sympatico.ca / Website: www.palatinehillsestatewinery.com)

(Est. 1998) John and Barbara Neufeld have been growing grapes since 1972, the year that John graduated from university and purchased his parents' fruit farm. He enlarged his holding later, when he purchased 115 acres of the adjacent Tobe Vineyard. (A 40-acre parcel was later sectioned off for his brother, who eventually sold it to Walter Burkhardt.) For many of Neufeld's grape-growing years, harvests were sent off to Brights for use in the production of sweet ports and sherries, but he was one of the early farmers to foresee the rapid changes coming to the wine industry. He responded by switching production to vinifera grapes as early as 1975. As demand for better grapes grew, he was able to supply premium fruit. Upon establishing Palatine Winery, he entered his first commercial wine, 1998 Vidal Icewine, in the 2003 Ontario Wine Awards and won the grand prize of Wine of the Year. The first vintage for table wines was 2001, and the retail shop opened in 2003. Neufeld now farms 118 of his 120 acres. The vineyard is flat, underdrained, and irrigated, with a rich complexity of soils, including areas of Chinguacousy clay loam, reddish Vineland fine sandy loam, and Peel lacustrine silty clay over clay loam. There are 5 acres of Baco Noir, 25 acres of Chardonnay, 27 acres of Cabernet Sauvignon, 4 acres of Geisenheim, 15 acres each of Gewürztraminer and Merlot, 7 acres of Riesling, 5 acres of Sauvignon Blanc, 5 acres of Seyval Blanc, and 10 acres of Vidal Blanc, all spaced at a vine density of 1,200 plants per acre. Production was 6,000 cases last year. Neufeld hopes to have that up to 10,000 cases with the 2005 harvest. Grapes are still supplied to Vincor International and are exported into New York and Pennsylvania. Neufeld was chairman of the Grape Growers of Ontario in the mid-1980s.

Winemaker: David Hojnoski / Vineyard Manager: John Neufeld

Cabernet Franc [NP] **2002 ★ ★ ★ →** Rich garnet hue with light brick edges. Perfumed and intensely fruity with nuances of stewed orange. Supple texture and lingering gamy flavours. Drink now-2008.

Cabernet Sauvignon, Neufeld Vineyard, Proprietor's Reserve
[NP] 2002★★★★↗ Garnet with a obliging nose, offering nuances of cream, herbs, black fruits, oak, smoke, and a hint of tar. Still somewhat closed but has finesse. Complexity will come in time. Drink 2007-2014.

Chardonnay [NP] 2002★★★→ Straw-gold hue with mild, vanilla-coconut aroma. Light and clean. Drink now-2006.

Chardonnay, Neufeld Vineyard, Proprietor's Reserve [NP] 2003★★★→ Pale gold with tiny bubbles forming inside the glass. Aroma of lemon-butter, perhaps a hint of hollandaise. Clean, light, pear-flavoured with big body and balanced acidity. Drink now-2007.

Gewürztraminer [NP] 2003★★★☆→ Pale straw-gold with hints of grapefruit, lychee, and lanolin. Drier than the previous vintage but still has a kiss of peachy sweetness. Drink now-2007. 2002★★→ Made in a demi-sec style. Good aromatic nose, medium body, and a grapefruit pith finish. Drink now-2007.

Gewürztraminer Icewine [NP] 2002★★★★→ Amber gold with tiny bubbles forming on the wall of the glass. Secretive nose, doesn't reveal much except the slightest hint of lanolin. Teeth-shatteringly sweet. Not cloying but needs higher acid to balance. Drink now-2008.

Meritage [NP] 2002★★★★↗ Ruby garnet with a soft, inviting, red fruit, milk chocolate, and table cream bouquet. Supple and velvety, with flavours of cedar, Virginia tobacco, cherry, and plum. Elegant. Drink now-2012.

Merlot, Neufeld Vineyard, Proprietor's Reserve [NP] 2002★★★↗ Garnet with a charred cherry, smoked blueberry nose. Good, thick, ripe fruit with soft tannins and a short, velvety finish. Drink now-2010.

Sauvignon Blanc [NP] 2002★★★→ Pale straw-gold with bubbles forming inside the glass. Grassy with asparagus and celery notes. Clean, crisp, thick, and supple, with a nice herbal bitterness in the finish. Drink now.

Vidal Icewine [NP] 2002★★★★→ Amber colour with concentrated honey nose. Mild bitterness in the finish. Drink now-2008. 2000★★★★→ Amber gold with a nose of honey, dried pear, corn syrup, and herbs. Concentrated, ultra rich, yet balanced. Drink now-2010. 1998★★★★→ *Wine of the Year, Ontario Wine Awards 2003.* A surprise and a delight. Nice balance. Drink now.

Vidal, Select Late Harvest [Ont] 2001★★★★↗ Gold with aromas of honeyed pear, orange, lemon, and mango. Rich and luscious without being overly sweet. Great balance. Drink now-2008.

• **PARAGON VINEYARD (Jordan, NP)** – Proprietor Lou Pavan's fine Chardonnay finds its way into Thirteenth Street Winery's sparkling wine. The vineyard is located directly across the road from the Thirteenth

Street Winery on a patch of Oneida clay loam till. Lou is a first cousin of Angelo Pavan, winemaker and partner in Cave Spring Cellars.

- **Paul Bosc Estate Vineyard** – *See* Château des Charmes

- **PELEE ISLAND** [PI] – The appellation officially includes all the land within the geographical limits of Pelee Island, bounded by the waters of Lake Erie. Situated 3 km south of Point Pelee, the island is 13.5 km long and 5.5 km wide, with a total surface area of approximately 15,000 acres (6,250 ha) Elevation ranges from 6-18 ft. (2-5 m) above the water level. Water around the island plays a significant temperature-moderating role as coolness in the spring delays budding but simultaneously protects the 650 acres (260 ha) of grapevines from late-spring frosts. It also helps to prolong the growing season, giving the grapes a longer period in which to mature slowly and thoroughly. The island is planted mainly to vinifera varieties although some hybrids such as Scheurebe, Seyval Blanc, and Vidal Blanc are appearing. Soil is primarily dark Toledo clay with some patches of shallow light loam, all of it resting on a hard limestone bedrock. At 41°N latitude, this is the southernmost "inhabited" area in Canada. Only the tiny uninhabited Bass Island is farther south by approximately 1 km. Although there is one commercial licence issued on Pelee Island, the Pelee Island Winery is actually located on the mainland in the Lake Erie North Shore viticultural area, at Kingsville.

- **PELEE ISLAND WINERY** (455 Seacliff Drive, Kingsville, ON, N9Y 2K5 / Phone: 519-733-6551 / Toll-Free: 1-800-597-3533 / Fax: 519-733-6553 / Email: pelee@peleeisland.com / Website: www.pelee island.com / Pelee Island Wine Pavilion: 20 East West Road, Pelee Island, ON, N0R 1M0 / Phone: 519-724-2469 / Fax: 519-724-2507)

(Est. 1979) Wine production in Canada has deep roots on Pelee Island. The first commercial winery was established here as Vin Villa Vineyards in 1868 by some American entrepreneurs. Today, there's little evidence of what was once the biggest winery in Canada, beyond a few wild vines and a decaying stone ruin. In its place, though, a new powerhouse winery has emerged. Pelee Island Winery started with a dream and fewer than 10 acres of grapes planted by Walter Strehn in 1979. However, the building of a winery required more money than Strehn had, so in 1983 Wolf von Teichmann and a pair of German partners invested enough to construct a winery on the mainland at Kingsville. In the same year Walter Schmoranz joined the company as general manager. The soil on the island is essentially Toledo clay, from 3-20 ft. in depth, sitting on a very tough limestone base, which permits excellent drainage. Varieties grown include Baco Noir, Cabernet Franc, Cabernet

Sauvignon, Chardonnay, Gewürztraminer, Merlot, Pinot Gris, Pinot Noir, Riesling, Sauvignon Blanc, Scheurebe, Seyval Blanc, Shiraz, and Vidal Blanc. With additional land purchases over the years, the winery now has holdings of 1,200 acres on the island, of which 550 are in full production. They plant an additional 30-50 acres of vines each spring, so vine age ranges from 1 to almost 25 years. Pelee Island holds 2 winery and retail licences. The primary production facility is on the mainland at Kingsville. The island facility is more of a tourist-oriented wine pavilion with entertainment, picnicking, touring, and retail space. In 2004, the Pelee Island Winery celebrated its 25th year in business by breaking previous production records, with a volume exceeding 300,000 cases.

Winemakers: Martin Janz (1997-present); Walter Schmoranz (1983-present); Walter Strehn (1979-1983) / Vineyard Manager: Bruno Friesen

Baco Noir [Ont] **2003** ★ ★ ★ → Healthy purple colour with a juicy fresh blackberry taste. Drink now-2007.

Blanc de Blanc, Seyval/Vidal [Ont] **2003** ★ ☆ ↻ Pale straw-gold with a lemony nose and green apple flavours. Crisp, clean, simple.

Battle of Lake Erie [NP] **NV** ★ → Ordinary but clean and balanced bubbly.

Cabernet [Ont] **2002** ★ ★ ★ ↗ Healthy fruit and soft tannins. May improve but too good now to wait. Drink now-2008.

Cabernet Franc [Ont] **2002** ★ ★ ★ → Soft, light, straightforward. Fresh berries on the boil. Drink now.

Cabernet-Merlot, Vinedressers [Ont] **2002** ★ ★ ★ ☆ ↗ Oaky and earthy at present, but rewards are hiding for the patient. Beneath the massive structure is a workhorse of a wine that will, one day, deliver the goods. Drink 2007-2012.

Chardonnay, Barrique [PI] **2003** ★ ★ ★ ☆ → Rich gold colour with an oaky vanilla aroma, good body and balance, solid caramelized apple and pear flavours with a clean finish. Drink now.

Chardonnay, Non-Oaked [NP] **2003** ★ → Crisp and clean, but basically nondescript with relatively high residual sugar.

Chardonnay, Premium Select [Ont] **2003** ★ → Dull, nondescript. Some caramel and praline flavours. **2002** ★ ★ ★ → Full and soft with an open, appealing buttered-toast aroma and light pear flavour. Drink now.

Eco-Trail Red [Ont] A blend of Cabernet, Zweigelt, and Gamay Noir. **2002** ★ ★ ★ ↻ Ruby-garnet with a winy nose and soft, balanced, straightforward taste.

Eco-Trail White [Ont] A blend of Scheurebe, Riesling Italico, and Pinot Blanc. **2002** ★ ★ ↻ Pale straw with a Muscat-like nose. Crisp, fresh, fruity, simple.

Gamay Noir-Zweigelt [Ont] **2003** ★ ★ ★ → Ruby-garnet hue with a subdued, green, leafy nose and light cherry-berry flavour. Drink now-2007.

Gewürztraminer [nonVQA] **2003**★★↻ Pale gold with a peach, mango, and grapefruit aroma. Sweetish with apple acidity.

Meritage, Vinedressers [PI] **2000**★★★☆↗ A dark and brooding wine. Very slow to open up and will be slow to develop. Hints of prune, tobacco leaf with high alcohol and high tannins. Drink now-2010.

Merlot [Ont] **2002**★★★☆↗ Juicy, fruity, clean, fresh, packed with flavours of pure brambleberry with subtle hints of blueberry. Delicious. Drink now-2008.

Merlot-Cabernet [nonVQA] **2003**★★★→ Garnet with orange around the rim. Oaky nose and palate with some minty berry flavours. Drink now-2008.

Pinot Blanc [Ont] **2003**★★↻ Straw-gold with a nondescript nose and vague, vinous flavour.

Pinot Gris [nonVQA] **2003**★★☆↻ Straw-gold with a blush of pale pink. Nondescript nose, pleasant ripe-apple flavour, and dull, flabby finish.

Pinot Gris, Vendenge Tardive [PI] **2002**★★★→ *Gold, Ontario Wine Awards 2004.* Rich gold hue with amber-pink reflections. Soft taste has hints of spice, herbs, and orange pith. Could do with a touch more acidity. Drink now.

Pinot Noir [Ont] **2003**★★☆→ Ruby-garnet with a mildly acetic smell. Very tart and juicy with medium body. Drink now-2008. **1998**★★★→ Ruby colour. Mature, light aroma leans to canned Bing cherries. Still packed with tannins. Drink now-2007.

Pinot Noir Reserve, Vinedressers [PI] **2002**★★★↗ Rich, ruby-garnet. Healthy bouquet with floral moments. Taste is fleshy and plump with a sharp finish. Drink 2006-2012. **2001**☒ Another unfortunate victim of Asian lady beetle taint. Tasted equally bad on 5 occasions.

Red Icewine [nonVQA] **1992**★★★☆→ Luscious with amazing red-fruit influences. Never sold but on rare occasions can be sampled at the winery.

Riesling [Ont] **2002**★★↻ Pale straw with a mildly floral aroma. Hints of spice, herbs, and lemon, but otherwise little flavour.

Rosé [Ont] From Cabernet and Zweigelt grapes. **2002**★☆↻ Ruby-crimson with a candied strawberry aroma. Just a hint of residual sugar lifts the fruitiness.

Sauvignon Blanc, Vinedressers [nonVQA] **2003**★★☆↻ Pale straw-gold with tiny bubbles forming inside the glass. Light with a hint of grassiness and a taste of white peach, with a bitter peach-pit finish.

Scheurebe, Late Harvest [Ont] **2002**★★★→ Golden with a lovely greengage plum aroma. Sweet and fruity with a mild herbal bitterness. Light and refreshing. Drink now-2007.

Shiraz-Cabernet [nonVQA] **2003**★★★→ Garnet with a sweet oak and red-fruit aroma and sweet berry flavours. Tough oaky tannins though. Drink 2006-2009.

Vidal, Icewine [PI]   **2003** ★ ★ ★ ★ ⬀ Bright gold with a light, fresh pear nose. Soft and sweet with applelike acidity. Drink now-2009. **2002** ★ ★ ★ ★ ⬀ Lemon-glazed tarte tatin. Balanced and beautiful. Drink now-2010. **1995** ★ ★ ★ ★ → Orange, mandarin, and apricot perfume. Exotic, tropical flavours, incredibly sweet with a soft finish. Drink soon.

Vidal, Late Harvest [Ont]   **1996** ★ ☆ ⬋ Candied lemon-apple fruitiness and balanced acidity. Drink soon.

Vidal, Monarch [Ont]   **2003** ★ ★ ★ ☆ ↻ Straw-gold with an orange-nuanced aroma and clean, crisp flavours.

• **PELLER ESTATES WINERY** (290 John Street East, R.R.#1, Niagara-on-the-Lake, ON, L0S 1J0 / Phone: 905-468-4678 / Toll-Free: 1-888-673-5537 / Fax: 905-468-1920 / Email: info@peller.com / Website: www.peller.com)

(Est. 2001) Although a generic Peller Estates brand had been around for a full decade, manufactured and bottled at Andrés Winona plant, a state-of-the-art Peller Estates winery was opened only in June 2001. Here, the focus is on the classic Bordeaux varieties: Cabernet Franc, Cabernet Sauvignon, and Merlot. The winery is situated on a plot of land within walking distance from the Old Town of Niagara-on-the-Lake. The 25-acre John Street Vineyard was chosen to exploit the moderating effect of nearby Lake Ontario, which prolongs the season by up to several weeks. The soil is Vineland lacustrine fine sandy loam with some Maplewood silty clay in the southwest corner of the vineyard. The property was not tiled for drainage, in order to force vine roots to stretch deep into the ground in search of moisture. Varieties planted include Cabernet Franc, Cabernet Sauvignon, Chardonnay, and Merlot for the production of dry wines as well as Riesling and Vidal for late harvest and icewines. Peller owns 145 acres of estate vineyards, including the 50-acre Carleton Vineyard and 70-acre Clark Farm, and supplements its needs by purchasing additional fruit from more than 20 Niagara area growers. Annual production is 25,000 cases. Peller Estate produces fruit-forward wines with a lightness and crispness, as compared with the wines of sister winery Hillebrand Estates, whose wines are somewhat more reductive with earthy flavours. Peller regularly holds back a small percentage of its best wines to stock a Vintage Library. These back vintages are available for purchase at the winery.

Winemakers: Rob Summers (1997-present); Jamie MacFarlane (1997-2003) / Vineyard Manager: David Mines

Andrew Peller Signature Series

Cabernet Franc [NP] **2001** ★ ★ ★ ☆ ↑ *Best of Category, All Canadian Wine Championships 2004.* Brilliant garnet hue with dense black-fruit nose. Scented with black currant and raspberry notes. Tight, tannic, and needing a couple of years to open up. Drink 2007-2014. **2000 ★ ★ ★ ↗** Very pale garnet with some browning around the rim. Advanced taste with nuances of caramel and boiled veggies. Fruit beginning to dry up. Drink now-2008. **1999 ★ ★ ★ ★ ↑** *Gold, All Canadian Wine Championships 2003.* Still quite closed. Fruit is dense but currently overpowered by tannins. Chewy, thick, and complex. Drink 2006-2013.

Cabernet Franc Icewine [NP]   **2002 ★ ★ ★ ★ ↗** Rich red, portlike nose; very fruity, very berry. Intense, juicy, strawberry, red currant, cherry-pie filling flavours, with a hint of walnut-skin tannins in the end palate. Drink now-2012.

Cabernet Sauvignon [NP]   **2001 ★ ★ ★ ☆ ↑** Dark garnet with a ripe, sweet, plummy aroma. Soft texture with a cocoa, condensed milk, and crushed berry flavour. Needs time. Drink 2009-2016. **2000 ★ ★ ★ ↑** Light garnet centre with brick around the edge. Somewhat disjointed at present with a hard, tart taste. Mildly stewed flavours. Drink 2007-2012. **1999 ★ ★ ★ ☆ ↑** Garnet hue with rich plummy notes. Packed with flavours of smoke, nuts, herbs, and veggies. Clean and lingering taste. Drink 2007-2015.

Chardonnay, Sur Lie [NP]   **2002 ★ ★ ★ →** *Best of Category, All Canadian Wine Championships 2004.* Golden hue with sweet, ripe, buttery, vanilla, crème anglaise flavours. Soft, fresh, and lasting. Drink now-2007. **2001 ★ ★ ★ →** Pale gold with ripe, vanilla, caramel flavours, a hint of spice, and distinct oaky bitterness in the finish. Fully mature. Drink now-2006.

Merlot [NP]   **2001 ★ ★ ★ ☆ ↗** Purple with blue reflections. Soft and lovely with lush, ripe flavours of blueberries and plum pie. Drink 2006-2014. **2000 ★ ★ ★ ↗** Pale garnet with a spicy nose of orange peel and apple skin. Lean texture with tough, unyielding tannins. Drink now-2010. **1999 ★ ★ ★ ★ ↑** *Best Merlot, Cuvée 2004.* Garnet with a plump, sweet, ripe, complex nose. Hints of spice and plums. Velvety texture and long-lasting aftertaste. Drink 2006-2012.

Riesling Icewine [NP]   **2002 ★ ★ ★ ★ ↑** Big on sugar, short on flavour at this point in its development. Solid texture with hints of pear, baked apple, and petrol already emerging. Expect it to relax and show real finesse within a year or two, but ideally drink 2008-2020. **2000 ★ ★ ★ ★ ☆ ↗** *Gold, All Canadian Wine Championships 2002.* Rich and luscious. Drink now-2015

Vidal Icewine [NP]   **2002 ★ ★ ★ ★ ☆ ↗** *Citadelles du Vin, VinExpo 2004; Gold, Concours Mondiale, Belgium 2004; Gold, Cuvée 2004.* Sweet, soft, and balanced with nuances of honey and poached Bosc pear. Outstanding. Drink now-2010.

Founder's Series

Cristalle, Sparkling [NP]   **NV ★ ★ ★ →** *Gold, Ontario Wine Awards 2004. Gold, All Canadian Wine Championships 2001.* A dollop of icewine was added as the final dosage. Clean, slightly candied taste. Minor variation from batch to batch.

Vidal, Icewine [NP] **2000** ★ ★ ★ ☆ → *Gold, Monde Selection, Brussels 2002.* Amber-yellow. Peach and pear flavours. Palate cleansing acidity. Drink now-2010.

French Cross Series

Blush [nonVQA]   **NV** ★ ↻ Off-dry, international-blend rosé. Sweetish, candied, strawberry bonbons.

Chardonnay [nonVQA]   **NV** ★ ☆ ↻ Dry, crisp, international-blend white.

Cabernet-Merlot [nonVQA]   **NV** ★ ☆ ↻ Dry, international-blend red. Light berry flavour. Better with red meat than on its own.

Red [nonVQA] **NV** ★ ↻ Dry, red, international blend. Clean, simple, uncomplicated.

Sauvignon Blanc [nonVQA] **NV** ★ ★ ↻ Crisp, dry, white, international blend with zippy lemon-grass flavours.

White [nonVQA] **NV** ★ ↻ Dry, white, international blend. Pleasant.

Heritage Series

Baco Noir [Ont] **2003** ★ ★ → Deep garnet red. Aroma of spiced blackberries macerated in sour cream. Soft, almost mushy flavours with a refreshingly tart finish. Drink now. **2002** ★ ★ ☆ → Exceptionally deep garnet with a concentrated blackberry aroma. Very tart taste of blackberries and underripe cranberries.

Chardonnay [NP] **2002** ★ ★ ★ → Gold with a full, fat bouquet of lemon, apple, and pear with notes of vanilla and heavy cream. Excellent value.

Cabernet Franc [NP] **2002** ★ ★ ★ → Pale cherry-garnet with strong varietal character. A tough but luscious mouthful. Veggies, herbs, red-fruit flavours are all in balance. Drink now-2007.

Cabernet Sauvignon [NP] **2003** ★ ★ → [nonVQA] Garnet with a somewhat sharp nose. Tannic finnish. Drink now.

Gamay Noir [NP] **2003** ★ ★ → [nonVQA] Deep ruby. Fresh, simple, and fine with burgers or pizza. **2002** ★ ★ ☆ → Ruby-cherry colour with a soft pleasant aroma of strawberry jam. A simple but "happy" wine. Drink up.

Gewürztraminer [NP] **2002** ★ ★ ★ → Gold with a mildly aromatic smell that appeals less than the palate. Perfectly balanced and tasty.

Merlot [NP] **2003** ★ ★ → Pale ruby-garnet with a varietally pure though dreadfully simple aroma. Youthful, juicy taste, but a touch vegetal with a hint of bitterness in the finish. Drink now through the end of 2006.

Muscat [NP] **2002** ★ ★ ★ → Silvery-gold colour with a terrific bouquet of wildflowers, wine gums, lychee, lime, linalool, and bergamot. Ideal paired with steamed asparagus with hollandaise.

Pinot Grigio [nonVQA] **2003**★★☆→ Lovely flavours of pink grapefruit and strawberries. Clean, crisp, and fresh.

Pinot Gris [NP] **2002**★★★→ Lovely, grapey, honeyed citrus flavours with some spice notes. Medium-bodied, fresh, and balanced. Drink up.

Riesling, Dry [NP] **2002**★★☆→ A soft wine, without the usual Riesling "snap." Clean and pleasant nevertheless – a cheery patio wine.

Sauvignon Blanc [NP] **2002**★★→ Straightforward, with minimal varietal intensity, a smidgen of residual sugar, and fairly ordinary flavours.

White (Vidal) [Ont] **2002**★★→ Aromatic with good body, smooth texture, and a clean finish. Apple and peach kernel flavours.

<u>Oakridge Wines</u>

Cabernet Sauvignon [nonVQA] **NV**★☆↻ Garnet with a reserved nose. Perfectly competent but uninteresting.

Cabernet-Shiraz [nonVQA] **NV**★★↻ Garnet-purple hue with an understated nose of blackberry and white pepper. Simple but pleasant.

Chardonnay [nonVQA] **NV**★★↻ Pale gold with a sweet, buttery caramel nose. Simple, straightforward, and appealing.

Gamay Noir [nonVQA] **NV**★★↻ Ruby-cherry with clean, light, and pleasant flavours of strawberry.

Merlot [nonVQA] **NV**★☆↻ Ruby-garnet. Clean, soft, fresh, and quaffable.

Pinot Noir [nonVQA] **NV**★↻ Pale cherry-tawny with a tired mushroomy nose.

Sauvignon Blanc [nonVQA] **NV**★↻ Light, crisp, fresh, and mildly grassy.

Zinfandel-Cabernet [nonVQA] **NV**★★☆↻ Cherry-garnet hue. Fine blackberry and cranberry flavours with great acidity.

White Zinfandel-Gamay [nonVQA] **NV**★★↻ Pale pink hue. Sweetish strawberry syrup flavour with good balance.

<u>Private Reserve Series</u>

Cabernet Franc, Barrel-Aged [NP] **2001**☒ Spoiled by Asian lady beetle. **2000**★★☆→ Ruby-garnet with a darkening rim. Beginning to show its age with nuances of leather, spice, and wood. Drink up.

Cabernet Sauvignon, Barrel-Aged [NP] **2001**☒ Spoiled by Asian lady beetle.

Chardonnay, Barrel-Aged [NP] **2001**★★☆→ Clean, simple, soft, approachable, nondescript but highly quaffable. **2000**★★★→ Brilliant gold colour with a toasty, nutty aroma. Big, tart, oaky, and well balanced.

Gamay Noir [NP] **2002**★★★➜ Deep black-cherry colour with a refreshing cherry aroma. Mildly tannic but very quaffable. **2001**☒ Tainted with the odour of Asian lady beetle.

Merlot, Barrel-Aged [NP] **2001**☒ Spoiled by Asian lady beetle.

Riesling, Dry [NP] **2002**★★★➜ *Gold, All Canadian Wine Championships 2003.* Lean, tight structure. Straightforward. For drinking now.

Sauvignon Blanc [NP] **2002**★★☆➜ Aroma suggests warmed apples. Soft palate with fullish body. Not especially vivacious, but chill well and pair with starters. **2001**☒ Has the odour of Asian lady beetle.

Vineyard Series

Gewürztraminer [NP] **2001**★★↻ Pale straw with floral bouquet over a fruity backdrop. Clean, simple, straightforward. Drink up.

- **PENINSULA RIDGE ESTATES WINERY** (5600 King Street West, Beamsville, ON, L0R 1B0 / Phone: 905-563-0900 / Fax: 905-563-0995 / Email: info@peninsularidge.com / Website: www.peninsula ridge.com)

(Est. 2000) Norman Beal, a native of nearby Fonthill, slaved as a high-octane petroleum trader in the global oil industry for years before deciding to trade it all in for a dream. Connecticut-based at the time, the broker considered key U.S. wine regions – California, Washington, and Oregon – before settling on the Niagara Peninsula on the advice of his sister Theresa, who had just completed her viticultural studies at Brock. Two years and $5 million later, he had the best 11,000-sq.-ft. winery money could buy, 80 acres of prime land on the Niagara bench, levelled, contoured, and planted with 38 acres of vinifera vines, a fully restored Victorian house converted into a fine-dining restaurant, a coach house for corporate events, a new career, a major lifestyle change, and time to spend with his growing family. Beal Vineyards includes all the land surrounding the winery, along with another property near Cave Spring Cellars. Both properties have sandy loam soils and are given over primarily to Bordeaux varieties, with 5.5 acres of Cabernet Franc, 12 acres of Cabernet Sauvignon, and another 12 acres of Merlot. There are also 7 acres of Chardonnay and 2 of Syrah, all of which supply up to 65% of the winery's grape requirements. The soil is already relatively friable; nevertheless, undrainage is provided throughout. Vines are spaced at a density of 1,345 per acre, or 4 ft. apart in 8-ft. rows (or, 1 m apart on 3 m rows). And all varieties have been grafted onto vigour-reducing rootstocks to shorten the growing season and produce riper fruit earlier in the season. One of Beal's greatest achievements has been to seduce French winemaker Jean-Pierre Colas, former head winemaker at Domaine Laroche in Chablis, to move to Canada and join in the adventure of producing Bordeaux-style red wines and Burgundy-style whites. In 1998, Colas won the highly coveted Wine Spectator "Best White Wine of the Year" Award for his 1996 Chablis Grand Cru, Le Clos. In 2004, Peninsula Ridge's annual production was 17,000 cases, barely half of what Beal intends to produce by the end of the decade.

Winemakers: Jean Pierre Colas (2000-present); Brian Schmidt (1999, consulting) / Vineyard Manager: Peter Graham

Arcanum [NP] **2002**★★★★↗ Deep garnet with a tough, closed nose. Packed with black fruit and berry flavours, but its true colours are still submerged beneath the oaky tannins. Drink 2007-2015.

Cabernet [NP] **2002**★★★☆→ Garnet with a leafy aroma of McIntosh apple and its skin. Tart and fresh with some plummy nuances beginning to appear. Finishes with soft tannins. Drink now-2010.

Cabernet Franc [NP] **2002**★★★↗ Clean, tart, and juicy, with flavours of ripe blackberry and green herbs. Needs time to reveal itself. Drink 2006-2010.

Cabernet Franc, Icewine [NP] **2001**★→ Funky nose of pimento, sundried tomato, and pizza sauce. Strange and untypical. Could this be Asian lady beetle?

Cabernet Franc, Reserve [NP] **2001**☒ Sadly, affected by Asian lady beetle. **2000** *Gold Award, Cuvée 2002.*

Cabernet Sauvignon, Reserve [NP] **2001**☒ It takes a half-hour of aeration, but the Asian lady beetle appears.

Chardonnay [nonVQA] **2003**★★★↻ A blend of Niagara and Loire Valley grapes. Pale gold with a restrained nose of pastry dough and fresh cream. Soft and fullish texture and a definite French slant to the flavours.

Chardonnay, Inox [NP] **2003**★★★★↗ Pale straw-gold with, once again, a bouquet reminiscent of Chablis, with a sweet face-powder overtone and a hint of lime beneath. Clean, ripe, implicitly sweet with terrific balance and structure. Drink now-2008. **2002**★★★→ Silvery gold with a wonderful Chablis-like odour. Clean, firm mineral notes with a somewhat earthy finish. Seductive. **2001**☒ Asian lady beetle taint subtly present.

Chardonnay, Reserve [NP] **2002**★★★★↗ *Prestige Award, Citadelles du Vin, Bordeaux 2004.* Thick bouquet balances apple and pear fruit note with hazelnutty oak. Well structured and muscular with a litheness and elegance. Drink now-2009.

Equinox [NP] **2002**★★★→ (C50/SB20/V20) Brilliant pale gold with a lemon, oak, smoke, toast, and nut bouquet. Thick, lush palate seems mildly over-oaked. A gentle monster. Drink now-2008. **2001**☒ Asian lady beetle taint present.

Merlot [NP] **2002**★★★↗ Deep purple with clean, lovely black-fruit nose. Has plenty of submerged black cherry and blackberry fruit beneath a tough and tannic exterior. Hope the fruit survives the wait. Drink 2008-2014.

Merlot, Reserve [NP] **2001** ☒ Ruined by Asian lady beetle.

Merlot-Cabernet Reserve [NP] **2000** (CS49/M51) Not tasted.

Ratafia [NP] Unfermented juice of Chardonnay grapes fortified with Kittling Ridge plum brandy in the style of Pineau des Charentes. **2002**★★↻ Brilliant golden hue. Disjointed spiry nose of bread yeast, chlorinated water, cardamom, and rosewater. Sweet, thick palate, but the plum brandy overpowers any fruit and leaves a hot, alcoholic finish. Next batch may benefit from more time in barrel to meld.

Rosé [NP] **2003**★★★→ Solid salmon-pink colour with a some-what innocuous nose. Off-dry palate has hints of strawberry and tart cherry. Drink now.

Sauvignon Blanc [NP] **2003**★★★★→ *Gold, Ontario Wine Awards 2004.* Lovely, intense, herbaceous nose of green beans and day-old hay with an undertone of ripe, citrus-spritzed passion fruit. Crisp, firm, tight, and ever-so refreshing. Drink now-2007.

Syrah [NP] **2002**★★★★↗ *Gold, Ontario Wine Awards 2004.* Deeply coloured and profoundly flavourful. Inky garnet-purple, nose and palate hint at black fruits, spice, and citrus. Great acidity makes for a lean but lingering aftertaste. Drink now-2012.

• **PILLITTERI ESTATES WINERY** (1696 Niagara Stone Road [Highway 55], R.R.#2, Niagara-on-the-Lake, ON, L0S 1J0 / Phone: 905-468-3147 / Fax: 905-468-0389 / Email: winery@pillitteri.com / Website: www.pillitteri.com)

(Est. 1993) After immigrating to Canada from his native Sicily in 1948, Gary Pillitteri became a dedicated fruit farmer and grape grower. In 1981, he was chosen Ontario's Grape King. The public appearances that followed gave him a taste for politics, and in 1993 he won a seat in Parliament and handed the management of his newly built winery and vineyards over to his children. He was re-elected 3 times thereafter and retired from federal politics in 2004. The winery, renovated and expanded in 2003, is located 4 km from the lake on the main highway into Niagara-on-the-Lake and includes a greenhouse, garden market, bakery, and a substantial retail operation. Total fermentation capacity is 400,000 L while storage capacity is almost 600,000 L. A recently built underground barrel cellar holds more than 300 casks, of which 70% are American oak and the remainder, French. Annual crush includes 450 t. for the production of table wines (big reds and luscious whites) and 500 t. of icewine. Half of all Pillitteri wines are exported.

Winemakers: Sue Ann Staff (1997-present, 2002 Winemaker of the Year); Joe Will (1993 to 1997) / Vineyard Manager: Jamie Slingerland

Baco Noir [Ont] **1999** All was lost when vandals drained 2 outdoor storage tanks, spilling 30,000 L of unfinished wine. **1997**★★↘

From 25-year-old vines grown on one of the Niagara Estates vineyards belonging to Jack Hernder, blended with a small portion from Westphalen Vineyard. Fullish nose with hints of fresh-baked cinnamon bread. Tart, juicy black-fruit flavours suited to big game – moose, bear, boar, or even well-charred, all-dressed cheeseburgers. Drink up.

Cabernet Franc [NP]   **1999** ★ ★ ★ → Terrific nose, developing sweet, ripe, and fruity aromatics. Plush, velvety texture with loads of flavour. Drink now-2009. **1994** ★ ★ ↘ Lean with tart, plummy flavours. Drink up.

Cabernet Franc, Family Reserve [NP]   **2002** ★ ★ ★ ★ ↗ Deep purple with a pink edge. Smoky, herbal, black-tea bouquet with concentrated black-fruit flavours and lean texture. Developing well. Drink now-2011.

Cabernet Franc Icewine [NP]   **2003** ★ ★ ★ ★ → Copper colour with pinpoint-sized bubbles forming on the inside of the glass. Aromas of burnt sugar on crème caramel. Light but complex flavours of raspberry, prune, and fig. Drink now-2010. **2002** ★ ★ ★ ★ → Sweet strawberry-cherry notes with a nice balance of mouth-cleansing acidity. Drink now-2012.

Cabernet-Merlot [NP]   **2002** ★ ★ ★ ☆ ↗ Garnet with a pink rim. Deep, concentrated black currant and brambleberry fruit with a leafy undertone. Taut palate, ready to explode with ripe flavour. Mildly bitter finish. Drink now-2010.

Cabernet Sauvignon [NP]   **2002** ★ ★ ★ ☆ ↗ Dark garnet with a violet rim. Leafy, floral aromas with a narrow spectrum of ripe berry flavours. Tough and tannic but expect solid and steady development over the next few years. Drink now-2012. **1994** ★ ↘ Unripe herbal nose with hints of celery and cucumber. Has balance but lacks body. Drink up.

Cabernet Sauvignon Icewine [NP]   **2003** ★ ★ ★ ★ → Onion-skin shade with a fabulous caramel-apple nose. Faint flavour of strawberry and red-cherry syrup. Drink now-2010. **2002** ★ ★ ★ ★ ↗ Bright red hue with an intense aroma of red apple, cherry, and black raspberry. Concentrated fruit sugar and perfectly balanced acidity. Thick and luscious. Drink now-2017.

Chambourcin, Special Select Late Harvest [Ont]   **2000** ★ ★ ★ ☆ →. Deep ruby-garnet with a jammy bouquet of strawberry, raspberry, and blackberry. Sweet and viscous with intense berry flavour like fresh-pressed juice; nevertheless, the variety's hybridity comes through. Drink now-2010.

Chardonnay, Barrel-Aged [NP]   **2002** ★ ★ ★ ★ ↗ Straw-gold with aromas of nutty oak, vanilla, roasted coffee beans, and popcorn. Burst with ripe fruit flavours. Fresh and vibrant with great balance of components. Drink now-2008. **1999** The volume of this vintage was reduced to nearly nothing when vandals drained 2 outdoor storage tanks, spilling 30,000 L of unfinished wine.

Chardonnay, Barrel-Fermented [NP] 1994★★➘ Fuller, softer, and richer than oak-aged version. Higher alcohol too. Drink soon.

Chardonnay, Icewine [NP] 2000★★★☆→ Deep gold with rich toffee and brown-butter aromas. Sweet marmalade flavour and unctuous mouthfeel. Drink now.

Gewürztraminer [NP] 2000★★★→ Has 30% Riesling blended in, giving it a sharper fruit focus on the nose and palate. Clean, crisp, and superb, but not for aging. Drink now.

Gewürztraminer Icewine [NP] 2002★★★★→ Pungent with herbal spicy notes. Concentrated and complex. Drink now-2010. 2000★★★★→ Brilliant amber-gold. Has spicy bouquet with pungent, herbal nuances of caramelized onions and bacon fat. Syrupy and a touch sharp in the back palate. Drink now-2007.

Gewürztraminer-Riesling [NP] 2003★★★☆→ Pale straw-gold with a hint of spritz. Lemony nose with nuances of ripe peach, lychee, and wildflower honey. Flavour combines McIntosh apple flesh and Bartlett pear skin. Drink now.

Merlot [NP] 1997★★★➚ A small portion of grapes from the Puglisi Vineyard was blended with estate-grown grapes. Full fruit aroma, tons of tannin. No hurry to drink. 1994★★➘ Thick, creamy texture; sweet berry flavours, clean finish of mid-length. Drink now.

Merlot, Reserve [NP] 2002★★★★➚ Garnet with a pink rim. Smoky, creamy, chocolaty with green, floral notes. Lush texture and concentrated ripe fruit flavours. Lingers in the aftertaste. Drink now-2010. 1999★★★➚ Garnet with pale cherry edges. Well-developed nose of fruit compote, spices like cardamom, allspice, and clove. Complex fruitcake flavour. Beginning to dry up. Drink now-2007.

Riesling [NP] 1999★★→ Lovely full-blown petrol nose, but with an undesirable undertone of yeastiness; ripe and multilayered flavours. Drink now. 1997★★★→ Brilliant gold with hints of petrol aroma, lemon zest, and wet stones. Firm mineral structure and baked apple flavours. Drink now. 1995★➘ No longer zesty. Lemony notes and lively taste of youth are gone. Drink now-2006. 1994★★★☆→ From 12-year-old vines. Deep gold with amber reflections. Advanced maturity has brought aromas of orange peel, lemon, petrol, and beeswax. Lovely caramelized apple flavours. Nice, clean finish. Drink up.

Riesling Icewine [NP] 2002★★★★↑ Intense aroma of poached pear and marmalade. Terrific acidity balanced the high sugar. Drink 2008-2020. 1995★★★★★➚ *Civart Trophy, International Wine Challenge, France 1996.* Rich and generous aroma of orange, apricot, vanilla, and toffee. Superbly balanced. Drink now-2015.

Riesling, Select Late Harvest [NP] 2003★★★★➚ Pale straw-gold with a honeyed aroma, racy acidity, and delicate, high-toned flavours. Drink now-2015.

Riesling, Sparkling Icewine [NP] **2000** ★ ★ ★ ★ ➔ Foams up a lot, then quickly subsides. Medium-sized bubbles adhere to the glass while tiny ones rise occasionally. Rich old-gold colour with a bouquet of vanilla apple custard. A terrific nectar but it's advancing quickly and has developed a mucoid texture. Drink up.

Sauvignon Blanc [NP] **1997** ★ ★ ↘ A soft, fruity style, lacking the intense green chlorophyll-like grassiness that often predominates in cool climates.

Trivalente [NP] **1999** ★ ★ ★ ★ ↗ Garnet with very ripe raspberry, cassis note and coffee, dark chocolate, gunpowder, and mineral nuances. Oh, yum! Still youthful but already sexy and seductive. Lush fruit, charming personality. Drink now-2014.

Vidal Icewine [NP] **2003** ★ ★ ★ ★ ☆ ↗ Gold hue with a fragrance that reminds me of expensive, fruit-scented soap. Concentrated pear and bubblegum nuances. Tastes of boiled-down applesauce with orange peel and clove spicing. Has great acidity. Drink now-2012. **2002** ★ ★ ★ ★ ★ ↗ *Grand Gold, VinItaly 2004; Great Gold, Concours Mondiale, Belgium 2004.* Brilliant gold with honeyed pear flavours and a painfully sweet finish. Drink now-2012. **1996** ★ ★ ★ ➔ Huge but candied, cloying, and out of balance. Massive concentration with pungent flavours of tarte tatin. Drink up. **1994** ★ ★ ➔ Rich and thick but somewhat clumsy. Drink up.

Vidal, Late Harvest (Semi-Sweet) [Ont] **1994** ★ ➔ Perfumed nose, then too dry and herbal on the palate.

Vidal, Semi-Dry [Ont] **2003** ★ ★ ★ ↻ Silvery-gold with a crisp, bright, grapefruity aroma with hints of fresh-cut grass. Mouth-watering grapefruity taste.

Vidal, Select Late Harvest [Ont] **2003** ★ ★ ★ ★ ➔ Powerful pop. Pale yellow-gold with very fine beads of tiny bubbles rising slowly. Exotic pear and pineapple bouquet. Vibrant and joyous flavours. Will hold till 2010, but it's perfect for immediate self-pleasuring.

Vidal, Sparkling Icewine [NP] **2003** ★ ★ ★ ★ ★ ➔ Bright gold with rich flavours of pear syrup. Drink now-2009.

• **PLEKAN VINEYARD (Beamsville, NP)** – Mike and Mimi Plekan's small property is located on Cave Spring Road above Beamsville on one of the higher Benchland peaks of the Niagara Escarpment. They have a couple of acres each of Cabernet Franc and Chardonnay both planted in 1993 and about 4 acres of Riesling planted in 1984 at a density of 960 vines per acre. The Plekans do not use chemical fertilizers and they shun chemical weed control, preferring horse manure and companion planting instead. They work the land very little except to turn the soil over between the rows early in the season. Though the property is not undertiled for drainage (except an area at the bottom near a gully), they are able to enter their field soon after it rains "because of all the dew worms." They tend to pick 2-4 weeks later than their neighbours and typically get sugars of higher Brix values. Grapes are sold to Stoney Ridge Estate Winery.

- **POLANA VINEYARD (Beamsville, NP)** – Jan and Krystyna Tarasewicz treat their Mountainview Road vineyard the way one might tend a garden. There are just over 21 acres of vines cultivated on this under-drained 40-acre patch of Chinguacousy clay loam. Cabernet Franc, Cabernet Sauvignon, Chardonnay, Gewürztraminer, Petit Verdot, Riesling, Syrah, Viognier, and some Merlot was planted in 2001. Sub-sequently, the couple added more Merlot as well as small parcels of Pinot Noir and Sauvignon Blanc, all planted at a density of 1,200 vines per acre. Grapes are thinned about 30% at veraison to yield no more than 2 t. per acre. Fruit is sold to the Angels Gate Winery close by.

- **POOLE FARM (Beamsville, NP)** – Jim Poole's 30 north-facing acres along Thirty Road are managed in partnership with Vailmont Vineyards. The soil is Oneida clay loam over a limestone base with partial under-drainage. There are 21.5 acres of Cabernet Franc, Cabernet Sauvignon, Chardonnay, De Chaunac, Gamay Noir, Merlot, and Vidal, averaging 957 plants per acre. Fruit was sold to EastDell in 2004 and to Kittling Ridge in 2005.

- **PRINCE EDWARD COUNTY [PEC]** – Although it is not yet officially designated a viticultural area of Ontario, this isthmus jutting out into Lake Ontario 200 km east of Toronto is a de facto wine-growing zone. The potential is huge as the land mass is enormous and popula-tion is still sparse. PEC enjoys a growing season that's much like that of the Niagara Peninsula in length and average summer temperatures but winters are much harsher and, most importantly, the soil is completely different. Currently, there are approximately 630 acres devoted to grape culture with about two-thirds of them now in production. The area around Hillier in the southwestern end of the island has the highest concentration of clay and limestone as well as the largest number of new vineyard plantings. The areas surrounding the hamlet of Waupoos and around South Bay, in the extreme southeastern corner, are also emerging as wine-producing districts. As "The County" becomes chic and trendy, new wineries sited around Adolphustown would like to catch some of the falling gold dust by being included in an official designation of Prince Edward County borders, but these are mainland wineries in another county altogether.

- **Prydatkewycz Vineyard** – See Rosomel Vineyard

- **PUDDICOMBE ESTATE WINERY** (1468 Highway #8, Winona, ON, L8E 5K9 / Phone: 905-643-1015 / Fax: 905-643-0938 / Email: info@puddicombefarms.com / Website: www.puddicombefarm.com)

(Est. 2001) Originally established in 1797, Puddicombe Farms is owned by seventh-generation farmer Murray Puddicombe, who until 1998 was a partner in Stoney Ridge Estate Winery. The farm grows apples cherries, peaches, pears, raspberries, strawberries, and a variety of vegetables as well as labrusca, hybrid, and vinifera grapes for sale to home winemakers and to other commercial wineries. Grapes grown include Auxerrois, Baco Noir, Cabernet Franc, Cabernet Sauvignon, Chardonnay, Colombard, De Chaunac, Gamay, Gewürztraminer, Marechal Foch, Merlot, New York Muscat, Niagara, Pinot Noir, Riesling, Sauvignon Blanc, Seyval Blanc, Vidal Blanc, Viognier, and 23-512. The operation also encompasses numerous other interests with a fully licensed café, banquet facilities, a petting farm, choo-choo train, kiddie days and birthday parties, a general store with jams, jellies, pies, gift baskets, seasonal novelties, candles, and kitchen items. Total juice production is 220,000 L, but most of it is sold off to Stoney Ridge Estate Winery and to Vincor. Puddicombe keeps about 15% for his own winemaking needs. Tender fruits are also processed to make fruit wines.

Winemaker: Lindsay Puddicombe / Vineyard Manager: Murray Puddicombe

Chardonnay, Barrel-Fermented [NP] **2000** ★ ★ ➔ Gold colour with amber highlights. Buttery nose with a canned-pear nuance. Drink up.

Meritage [NP] **2000** ★ ★ ☆ ➔ Garnet with a firebrick rim. Aroma of prune compote, black tea, and hints of saddle leather. Balanced but light with a short finish. Drink now–2008.

Vidal Icewine [NP] **1998** ★ ★ ★ ➔ Amber-gold with a very sweet aroma of peach and pineapple. Slight chemical impression. Drink now.

- **PUGLISI VINEYARD (Niagara-on-the-Lake, NP)** — Pillitteri's vineyard manager, Jamie Slingerland, manages this 50-acre site on Line 2 between Concessions 3 and 4 for property owner Lou Puglisi. Forty-five acres are planted with Cabernet Franc, Cabernet Sauvignon, Chardonnay, Gewürztraminer, Pinot Gris, Riesling, and Vidal Blanc. The flat vineyard has a graduated mixture of soils with a higher concentration of fine sand at the front and more clay loam at the back. It is fully tiled to provide drainage and has an irrigation system in place, but the winery is irrigated only in the worst drought conditions. Grapes are sold exclusively to Pillitteri Estates.

- **PUMA VINEYARD (Niagara-on-the-Lake, NP)** — Another Pillitteri exclusivity is this 20-acre site located on the south side of Line 1 between Concessions 3 and 4. The flat, underdrained vineyard has several silty alluvial deposits, sandy knolls, and clay loam patches. There are 16 acres under vine, including Cabernet Franc, Chardonnay, Merlot, Pinot Gris, and Riesling.

- **QUAI DU VIN ESTATE WINERY** (45811 Fruitridge Line, R.R.#5, St. Thomas, ON, N5P 3S9 / Phone: 519-775-2216 / Fax: 519-775-0168 / Email: info@quaiduvin.com / Website: www.quaiduvin.com)

(Est. 1990) Roberto and Lisa Quai originally started with the intention to make wines solely from his own vineyards, but business has been so good the winery now supplements its own harvest with grapes brought in from local growers, as well as from the Niagara Peninsula. Estate wines are without a VQA designation since the 50-acre property is situated near the town of Sparta in Elgin County, outside the provincially regulated designated viticultural areas of either Niagara Peninsula or Lake Erie North Shore. Quai has 20 acres of vines, including 1 acre of 10-year-old Aurore, 1 acre of 20-year-old Chardonnay, 4 acres of ancient Concord, 3 acres of recently planted Merlot, 2 acres of 15-year-old Riesling, 4 acres of 28-year-old Seyve-Villard 23-512, and 5 acres of young Vidal Blanc, all spaced at 800 vines per acre. Quai du Vin is about 6 km from Lake Erie at the highest point in Elgin County. At this altitude, there's a fair amount of breeze, so the vineyard is slightly cooler and later budding/ripening but completely protected from humidity-induced vine diseases. The soil is primarily clay loam over a terminal moraine, with a considerable amount of gravel just beneath the surface. Production in 2004 was 7,500 cases, all of which is sold at the winery.

Winemakers: Jamie Quai (2005-present); Roberto Quai (1990-2005) / Vineyard Manager: Roberto Quai

Chambourcin [nonVQA] **2001** ★ ☆ → Pale cherry-garnet with smoky aromas. Tart, smoky with sour cherry flavours. Drink with cheese or charcuterie.

Elvira [nonVQA] **2001** ★ ★ → Yellow-gold hue with a grapey, labrusca nose and light hints of smoked meat. Clean, balanced with pleasant grape marmalade flavours. Chill well.

- **QUARRY RIDGE VINEYARD (Beamsville, NP)** – Stuart and Robert Reimer now farm this property, which has been in the family since 1944. It is located on Quarry Road opposite DeSousa Winery.

- **QUARRY ROAD VINEYARD (Beamsville, NP)** – A 26-acre property purchased by Gabe Magnotta and Josef Zimmermann in 1993. The latter was subsequently bought out. There are 5 acres of Cabernet Franc, 2 acres of Pinot Noir, and 5 acres of Riesling.

R

- **RED TAIL VINEYARD (Consecon, PEC)** – This 11-acre site on Partridge Hollow Road is owned and operated by Pauline Joicey and Gilbert Provost. Since purchasing the land in 2002 they have planted 0.3 acre of Pinot Gris and 0.7 acre of 2 Dijon clones of Pinot Noir at an average spacing of 3,630 vines per acre. By the end of 2006, they plan to have an additional 8,500 vines in the ground for a total of 2.5 acres. The soil is Hillier clay loam over limestone, and the couple farm it using organic practices modelled on some pocket-sized Burgundy vineyards.

- **REIF ESTATE WINERY** (15608 Niagara Parkway, R.R.#1, Niagara-on-the-Lake, ON, L0S 1J0 / Phone: 905-468-7738 / Fax: 905-468-5878 / Email: wine@reifwinery.com / Website: www.reifwinery.com)

(Est. 1982) Ewald Reif emigrated to Canada in 1977 from Neustadt, Germany, where the family had been winemaking for 12 generations. He bought a 135-acre property near the banks of the Niagara River on the west side of the Niagara Parkway at Line 2. He immediately began to plant vinifera grapes. Five years and many test batches later, he concluded very good wine could be made in Niagara and proceeded to establish a formal winery. Meanwhile, back at the old homestead, nephew Klaus, who had visited his uncle in Canada in 1978, decided he, too, loved this country and wanted to come here to make wine. He studied marketing and business management, then entered the world-renown Geisenheim Institute to learn oenology and viticulture. Upon completing his degree in 1987, Klaus and his young bride, Sabina, moved to Niagara-on-the-Lake to help his uncle Ewald manage the vineyards and winery. The relatively flat and entirely underdrained property currently comprises 127 acres of Jeddo clay loam till. (Uncle Ewald severed a few acres off the original farm for his retirement home.) The winery's entire production was 100% estate-grown and bottled until 2002, after which Reif began to purchase grapes from neighbouring farms. Currently, about 20% of production is from purchased grapes. Reif was honoured with the top award for Canada's Best Winery at VinItaly in 1999 and at the International Wine & Spirit Competition in London in 2002.

Winemakers: Roberto DiDomenico (1990-present); Klaus W. Reif (1987-present) / Vineyard Manager: Klaus Reif

Black Oak [Ont] 2002★★↻ A blend of Baco Noir, Cabernet, and Shiraz, it has plenty of fruit and surprising depth and elegance.

Cabernet Franc, Estate-Bottled [NP] 1995★★★→ Garnet with a pale brick rim. Inviting aromas of roasted coffee and plum tarts. Mature soft palate. Drink now.

Cabernet Franc Icewine [NP] 2002★★★★↗ Salmon-flesh hue with amber reflections. Has a nice aroma of candied strawberry and flavour of strawberry jam. Touch of bitterness in the finish says it needs time to develop. Drink 2007-2012.

Cabernet-Merlot [nonVQA] 2002★★☆→ Garnet with lovely aromas of plum butter and nuts, but there's a less than pleasant hint of bitterness in the finish. Drink now.

Cabernet-Merlot, Estate-Bottled [NP] 2002★★★↗ Garnet with a tight, tough herbal nose with hints of blackberry and raspberry. Starts sweet with black-cherry flavours and finishes pleasantly with apple-skin bitterness and balanced acidity. Drink now-2008. **2000★★★→** *Best General List Red, Cuvée 2003.* Garnet with blackberry and blueberry flavours. Supple and round palate. Drink now-2008.

Cabernet Sauvignon, First Growth [NP] 2003 Not made. **2001★★★★↗** *Best Cabernet Sauvignon, Cuvée 2004.* Deep garnet to the rim with a nose dominated by new oak. Cassis and black-cherry aromas are present, though completely overshadowed by wood at this time. Flavours range from wild strawberry extract to cough syrup and bitters. Balanced and clean with a rigid structure – more bones than flesh – and a tough, tannic finish. Drink 2008-2015.

Canadian Champagne [nonVQA] NV★★→ A blend of Chardonnay and Riesling. Light, fruity, tart, and even charming. Has enough residual sugar to qualify for a "sec" (off-dry) rating.

Chardonnay, All Natural [NP] Same grapes as for Chardonnay Reserve but fermented on its own natural yeasts. 1994★★★↘ Soft, complex, and long on the palate. Only 60 cases produced. Past its prime.

Chardonnay, Premium Select [nonVQA] 2002★★★↻ Pale gold with aromas of oak and burnt butter. Clean, straightforward, pleasant.

Chardonnay, Reserve, Estate-Bottled [NP] Grapes are taken from the oldest block and barrel fermented in new oak. Recent vintages have spent more time in cask than those from the 1990s. **2001★★★→** Billowing with lemon-butter, oak, and toast flavours. A fat wine. Drink now-2007. **1999★★★→** Bright yellow-gold hue. Bouquet developing nicely with ripe, fat, buttery flavours of caramel, nuts, oak, vanilla, pineapple, and coconut. Yum. Drink now-2006. **1996 ★ ★ ↘** A difficult vintage. Drink up. **1994 ★ ★ ★ ↘** Now amber gold; implicitly sweet nose; soft and richly layered with luscious caramel-coated pear flavours. Still drinking well but not for long. 220 cases made.

Gewürztraminer [NP] **2002 ★ ★ ★ →** Grapes are from the Estate and the Wiens Vineyard. Light, with hints of spice, apricot, wine gums, and canned pears in syrup. Bright taste, quick finish. Drink now.

Meritage, Estate-Bottled [NP] (CF10/CS40/M50) **2001 ★ ★ →** Tiny bubbles surface upon opening, hinting that this wine may still be "working" – not a healthy sign. Bouquet severely subdued by oak, although taste suggests red and black fruits. **2000 ★ ★ ★ →** *Best Red Wine, Cuvée 2003.* Deep garnet with aromas of black currant, cedar, black pepper, and plum. Rich aftertaste with soft tannins. Drink now-2010.

Merlot, Estate-Bottled [NP] **2001 ★ ★ ★ ↗** Garnet with a pale ruby rim. Subdued nose of red fruit, cigar box, forest floor. Lively, spicy palate full of developing flavours. Drink now-2009.

Merlot, First Growth [NP] **2003** Not made. **2001 ★ ★ ★ ↗** Garnet colour. Oak-dominated nose is tight, closed, with a hint of egginess. Plummy fruit, lean structure, and tons of tannin for a bitter apple-skin finish. High alcohol and high acidity suggests a long, slow development. Drink 2006-2012.

Pinot Grigio, Estate-Bottled [NP] **2002 ★ ★ ↻** Unexpectedly grapey with tropical nuances of mandarin, papaya, and lychee. Solid mouthfeel.

Pinot Noir [NP] **1995 ★ ★ ★ ↘** Still has good nose and relatively vibrant fruit, but it's a bit over-oaked. Drink now.

Pinot Noir, First Growth [NP] **2003** Not made. **2001 ★ ★ ★ ↗** Ruby-garnet with a brick colour seeping into the edge. Forward earthy nose with hints of cherry pie, cranberry sauce, boiled cabbage, and mushrooms. Dusty tannins and bitter finish in this over-oaked wine. Wait till 2006-2009.

Riesling, Estate-Bottled [NP] **2002 ★ ★ →** Gold with a caramel and petrol nose. Has a green, underripe taste and an oxidative finish. Seems to be advancing rapidly. **2001 ☒** Has the taint odour of Asian lady beetle.

Riesling Icewine [NP] **2002 ★ ★ ★ ★ ↗** Thick, viscous, and extraordinary. Packed with nuance – lemon, apple, pineapple, and grapefruit. Great concentration and high acidity promising a long life. Drink 2007-2020.

Riesling, Icewine [NP] **2002 ★ ★ ★ ★ ★ ↗** Brilliant golden hue. Rich candied pear and wildflower honey aromas. Squeaky-clean texture with its high acidity. Despite its intensity, there's a playful lightness about it. Drink now-2018. **1997 ★ ★ ★ ★** *Gold, Ontario Wine Awards 1999.* Great acidity, flavour of pear concentrate. Drink now-2012. **1995** *Gold, All Canadian Wine Championships.*

Shiraz, Estate-Bottled [NP] **2002** ★★★➔ Deep indigo-purple with a light nose of blackberries in sweetened sour cream. Tannic but soft. Good now-2007.

Tesoro [NP] **1995** ★★★★➔ (CF10/CS50/M40) Garnet hue with a mature Bordeaux-style nose of plum, fading rose, and cigar box. Balanced, ripe, supple, and fully mature. Drink now-2010.

Vidal, Select Late Harvest [NP] **2001** *Best Dessert Wine, All Canadian Wine Championships 2003.* **2000** *Gold, All Canadian Wine Championships 2003; Gold, Toronto Wine & Cheese Show 2004.*

Vidal, Icewine [NP] **2002** *Gold, Toronto Wine & Cheese Show 2004.* **2001** ★★★★↗ Amber-gold hue with nuances of dried fruit, ripe orange, pastry dough, and nuts. Very sweet with high, balanced acidity. Can drink now but, really, wait a couple of years. **2000** *Best Icewine, International Wine & Spirit Competition, London 2002; Best Sweet Wine, Cuvée 2002; Gold, Toronto Wine & Cheese Show 2002.* **1999** *Gold, Vinexpo 2001; Gold, Concours Mondial, Belgium 2001; Gold, Toronto Wine & Cheese Show 2001.* **1998** *Gold, International Wine & Spirit Competition, London 2002.* **1996** *Grand Gold, Vinltaly 1998; Gold, World Wine Championships 1998.* **1993** *Grand Gold, Vinltaly 1995.* **1987** ★★★↘

Vintner's Cuvée Red [nonVQA] **NV** ★★↻ A blend of Cabernet Sauvignon and Gamay, it has plenty of fruit and surprising depth and elegance.

White Sands [nonVQA] **NV** ★★↻ A fruity wine produced from Riesling and Vidal. Pale gold hue, light beeswax aroma, with pleasant flavours of lemon drops and white peach.

Zinfandel [NP] Canada's only VQA producer of this variety, planted in 1996. **2001** ★★★➔ Bright purple-garnet with a bouquet temporarily dominated by new oak. Aromas of raspberry, red currant, and spice emerge with airing. Good body, balance, and depth indicating plenty of potential for future vintages. There's the slightest hint of Asian lady beetle but not enough to spoil the wine. Drink now through 2006.

• **REIMER VINEYARD (Niagara-on-the-Lake, NP)** – On a 62-acre vineyard purchased in the late 1970s by George Reimer. His son Art grows Pinot Noir and other vinifera and hybrid varieties for next-door neighbour Donna Lailey.

• **REPKO VINEYARD (Kingsville, LENS)** – Brothers Paul and Robert Repko farm almost 1,000 acres of land, with corn and other crops. In the late 1980s, they planted 29 acres of Cabernet Sauvignon, Cabernet Franc, Zweigelt, and Lemberger, which was sold to the neighbouring LeBlanc Estate Winery. Since LeBlanc closed in 2002, the grapes have gone to Pelee Island Winery.

- **REUTHER FARMS (Virgil, NP)** – Alex Reuther grows Cabernet Franc, some of which is sold to Ocala Orchards Farm Winery in Port Perry.

- **RIDGEPOINT WINES** (3900 Cherry Avenue, Vineland, ON, L0R 2C0 / Phone: 905-562-8853 / Fax: 905-562-8854 / Email: info@ridge pointwines.com / Website: www.ridgepointwines.com)

(Est. 2003) Mauro and Anna Scarsellone are likely the only brother-sister team currently running an Ontario winery. They bought the 20-acre property above the escarpment in 1995 and began planting the following year. As grape growers, they sold their fruit to established wineries like Cilento Wine, Willow Heights Estates Winery, and Kacaba Vineyards. Now that they have both winery and retail licences, they retain more of their fruit each year. They have 18 acres of Cabernet Sauvignon, Merlot, Nebbiolo, Pinot Noir, Riesling, Sangiovese, and Vidal Blanc, spaced at an average density of 1,100 vines per acre. Ridgepoint thins severely at veraison to maintain a crop weight of 2 t. per acre; however, that was unnecessary in 2003 after spring frosts significantly reduced their yield. The winery was able to produce 1,000 cases that year and hopes to grow to 4,000 cases by the end of 2006. Ridgepoint also makes fruit wines.

Winemakers: Arthur Harder (2003-present); David Johnson (2001-2002) / Vineyard Manager: Claus Wolf, Custom Farm Services

Merlot [NP] **2002** ★ ★ ★ → Solid garnet with an oaky, creamy, juicy, brambleberry aroma. Sweet oaky flavour with lean fruit and high alcohol. There's a genuine cheeriness to the taste. Drink now-2007.

Nebbiolo [NP] **2003** Not produced. Frost wiped out the crop. **2002** ★ ★ ★ → Pale cherry-red colour and open, approachable floral aroma. Taste of ripe, spicy red cherries with an undertone of sourdough rye. Juicy, clean, dry, tart, and tannic with a soft, expansive finish. Drink now-2008.

Riesling [NP] **2003** ★ ★ ★ → Pale straw-gold with a light, white-peach aroma. Clean, with firm structure and a kiss of sweetness. Drink now-2006.

Riesling, Medium Dry [NP] **2003** ★ ★ ★ → Pale straw-gold with an apple, lemon, and white-peach nose. A bit hollow in the mid-palate, but otherwise has solid structure. Drink now-2006.

Vidal [Ont] **2003** ★ ★ ☆ ↻ Silvery-gold with an aroma of Golden Delicious and Spy apples. Hint of residual sugar and balanced acidity. Nice quaffer.

- **RIVERBEND VINEYARD (Niagara-on-the-Lake, NP)** – This 45-acre property adjacent to and immediately north of Riverview Cellars is owned by Frank and Sue Pohorly. The vineyard is situated on a substantial knoll, giving it both north- and south-facing slopes, and, as it is so close to the Niagara River, it gets slightly warmer winter conditions and cooler summer temperatures. The concentration of Vineland fine sandy loam is highest at the eastern edge of the property, with increasing clay loam as one moves westward. Thirty acres are under vine with Cabernet Franc, Cabernet Sauvignon, Chancellor, Chardonnay, Chenin Blanc, Merlot, Pinot Noir, and Vidal. The fruit is sold to Frank's brother, Joseph Pohorly, who owns Joseph's Estate Winery, and to Vincor International.

• **RIVERVIEW CELLARS ESTATE WINERY** (15376 Niagara Parkway, Niagara-on-the-Lake, ON, L0S 1J0 / Phone: 905-262-0636 / Fax: 905-262-0462 / Email: winery@riverviewcellars.com / Website: www.riverviewcellars.com)

(Est. 2000) Sam Pillitteri owns 25 acres of land, in a long, narrow patch that runs from the Niagara Parkway to Concession 1. It is sandwiched between van de Laar to the north and Tregunno Farms on the south, and Marynissen on the other side of the road to the west. Roughly 17 acres are planted in 2.5-acre blocks with Cabernet Franc, Cabernet Sauvignon, Chardonnay, Gewürztraminer, Merlot, Riesling, and Vidal Blanc. Although the soil is sandier on the Niagara River side of the property and gets heavier as one moves farther way, the entire property is tiled for drainage. Production last year was about 5,000 cases, all of which is sold through the retail shop or via the Internet. Once the vineyard is mature, volumes should reach close to 10,000 cases.

Winemakers: Fred DiProfio (2004-present); Sam Pillitteri (2000-2003) / Vineyard Manager: Sam Pillitteri

Wines not available for appraisal before press time.

• **ROBERT THOMAS ESTATE VINEYARD** (Cherry Valley, PEC) – This 58-acre farm is one of only a few vineyards in the county owned and operated by locally born individuals. Debra Marshall, whose United Empire Loyalist ancestors came to the region in the 1780s, inherited the farm from her parents, Robert and Ruth Hook. Soon afterward, she and her husband, Thomas, began to plant a vineyard. In 2003, the couple's daughter, Sarah, and her husband, Jason Babutac, became partners in the operation. Currently, they grow almost 6 acres of Pinot Gris, a little over 1 acre of Pinot Noir, and 3 acres of Zweigelt, all spaced at 1,210 vines per acre. They also have 0.3 acres of Landot Noir and other experimental varieties. The vineyard is composed primarily of Ameliasburg clay loam with fractured limestone deposits throughout and more of them in the area closest to County Road 18. It is neither tiled for drainage nor irrigated. All care is given to keep the farm in tone with its heritage and its history. For now, grapes are sold to a number of local wineries. In the future, the 3 generations of the family plan on opening a small farmgate winery.

- **ROCKWAY GLEN GOLF COURSE ESTATE WINERY** (3290 9th Street Louth, St. Catharines, ON, L2R 6P7 / Phone: 905-641-1030 / Toll-Free: 1-877-762-5929 / Fax: 905-641-2031 / Email: rockway@ niagara.com / Website: www.rockwayglen.com)

(Est. 2000) With a links-style 18-hole championship golf course designed by Robert F. Moore, plus separate putting and chipping greens, a pro shop, glassed-in restaurant, a banquet hall to accommodate up to 200 people, an estate winery, a retail shop both for wine and wine accessories, as well as a small wine museum with genuine French antiquities from the 18th and 19th centuries, owners Bruce and Catherine Strongman manage to cover a lot of ground. Two hundred acres, to be specific. There are 40 acres under vine, including parcels of Baco Noir, Cabernet Franc, Gewürztraminer, and Merlot. The winery itself is housed in the 10,000-sq.-ft. clubhouse. Current production is 2,500 cases last year and plans are in place to expand to 10,000 cases by the end of 2006.

Winemakers: Jeff Innes (2004-present); Peter Warkentin (2000-2004); Klaus Reif (2000-2002, consulting) / Vineyard Manager: Andre Pelletier

Wines not available for appraisal before press time.

- **RONALD MOYER LTD. (Grimsby, NP)** – Arthur Moyer and his wife, Marlene, farm just a few acres of grapes on this 300-acre escarpment property owned by his father, Ronald Moyer. In addition to apples, cherries, and pears, the couple chose a small section with heavier clay soil to cultivate Cabernet Franc, Chardonnay, Pinot Noir, and Villard Noir for Colio Estate Wines. Moyer Sr. sold a second property in Colchester to Colio a decade ago.

- **ROSOMEL VINEYARD (Beamsville, NP)** – Roman Prydatkewycz is one of Canada's leading pioneers of premium grape growing. In the early 1970s, when most grape growers preferred to take the easy road of low-maintenance, high-yield labrusca and hybrid vines, Prydatkewycz spent an enormous amount of his own money to recontour his property, install a drainage system, and plant some of the province's first Chardonnays and Merlots. He followed up by developing special techniques of canopy management to increase the grapes' ripeness. His Chardonnay (planted in 1976) was used to launch Hillebrand's ultra-premium Trius Chardonnay, and most recently surfaced in Thirty

Bench's single vineyard series. His concentrated Cabernet Sauvignon (planted in 1981) and Merlot (1978) appeared in Vineland Estates' outstanding Meritage wines, and his delightful Riesling (1977) is featured by Legends Estates. The 26-acre property – severed from the original Stouck Vineyard – has 20 acres under vine, including Gewürztraminer (from 1981), Malbec (2000), Pinot Noir (1980), Sauvignon Blanc (1982), and Vidal Blanc (1979), all at a vine density of 900 plants per acre. It is composed of Oneida loam over a bed of limestone. With the Niagara Escarpment as its southern border, it slopes 12 degrees toward the Stouck Vineyard on its northern edge and adjacent to the Eastman Vineyard on its western side. Fruit is thinned 10%-20% at veraison to yield an average of 3.5-4.5 t. per acre in an average vintage. Late in 2004, Harald Thiel of Hidden Bench purchased the farm. Prydatkewycz will continue to oversee its care, and all grapes from the 2005 and future vintages will appear in Hidden Bench wines.

- **ROWAN VINEYARD (Niagara-on-the-Lake, NP)** – Excellent quality Chardonnay is grown in this parcel, at Line 5 and Concession 1, for Lailey Vineyards. Great care is taken with vineyard, which is slowly converting to a Scott Henry trellising system.

- **ROYAL DEMARIA WINES** (4551 Cherry Avenue, Beamsville, ON, L0R 1B0 / Phone: 905-562-6767 / Toll-Free: 1-888-793-8883 / Fax: 905-562-6775 / Email: icewine@royaldemaria.com / Website: www.royaldemaria.com)

(Est. 1994) Toronto barber Joseph DeMaria still clips hair a day or two a week, but he prefers to clip grape bunches in the dead of winter. "Canada's Icewine Specialists" is what he and his company call themselves. In fact, he has trademarked the phrase. DeMaria started his internationally recognized company following a series of mishaps. First, he offered to help some friends with their vineyard and acquired the necessary winemaking and export licences to do so, but before he could make any wine, the friends backed out. Next, he bought his own vineyard and began to sell grapes to local wineries. The following year, after buying wine presses to squeeze the juice, his buyers fell through. What could he do? DeMaria decided to produce his own wine. Despite his lack of experience, the wine was good and Joseph DeMaria discovered his calling. Today, he makes only one type of wine – icewine – but does it from numerous varieties. Current production averages 3,000-4,000 cases from a dozen varieties. His goal is to make as many as 20 different icewines by 2006 and to build his export business to 75% of production. The 25-acre property DeMaria purchased in 1996 is called RDW Vineyards and has 22 acres under vine. The site is north-facing with a 20% grade. The soil is a mix of Jeddo clay loam and Vineland fine sandy loam. It is irrigated between every row and cultivated with organic farming practices, although it is not a certified organic vineyard. His Vidal Blanc dates back to 1974, while the Riesling vines were planted in 1978. The remaining 11 varieties, including Cabernet Franc, Chardonnay, Chenin Blanc, Gamay, Gewürztraminer, Merlot, Muscat Ottonel, Pinot Blanc, Pinot Gris, Pinot Noir, and Sauvignon Blanc, were planted between 1996 and 1998 at vine densities averaging 1,000 to 1,300 plants per acre, depending on the variety. DeMaria holds 3 international records for most gold medals for dessert wines won in a single wine competition, and is recognized for producing the world's most expensive icewines. His wines were requested by Her Majesty Queen Elizabeth II during her Jubilee visit and appear regularly on the dining tables of other notables.

Winemaker: Joseph DeMaria / Vineyard Manager: Joseph DeMaria

The owners of Royal DeMaria Wines did not wish to provide samples for tasting. The following notes were scribbled under varying circumstances – at wine-judging events or over display tables at trade functions – not the ideal conditions of a clinical tasting room.

Cabernet Franc Icewine [NP] 2002★★★★↗ Very pale tawny-orange with a rich, clean aroma. Taste is rich, sweet, and balanced but somewhat vague in fruit flavours. Drink now-2009.

Cabernet Sauvignon Icewine [NP] 2002★★★★↗ Coral colour with candy-floss bouquet of red cherries in sweet syrup. Long-lasting aftertaste but a bit clumsy in the finish. Drink now-2010.

Gewürztraminer Icewine [NP] 2002★★★★☆↗ Bright gold with light amber reflections. Herbal, spicy, honeyed nose with very concentrated spicy, sweet flavours. A touch sharp in the finish. Drink now-2012.

Meritage Icewine [NP] 2002★★★★☆↗ Lovely, soft, sweet, clean, and complex flavours. Lush strawberry jam. Drink now-2011.

Merlot Icewine [NP] 2002 ★★★★★↗ *Gold, Citadelles du Vin, VinExpo 2004.* Incredibly complex and perfumed nose reminiscent of wild manuka honey. Intense blend of fruit and herb flavours. Drink now-2010.

Vidal Icewine [NP] 2002★★★★↗ The bouquet hints of DEET to start, with herbal, vegetative, and buttermilk notes. Later, it develops a lovely marmalade fragrance. Soft and sweet. Drink now-2009.

- **Saignée** – A French word that means "to bleed." Essentially, a red grape variety is crushed and tanked. After just a few hours or up to a day, some of the juice, which has by now taken on a pink colour from the red skins, is bled off to another tank. The original tank is left with a greater proportion of skin to juice, so that over the remaining period – during which the skins and juice are kept together – a more-concentrated red colour and flavour is extracted. The pink juice that is poured off is fermented into a rosé wine, while the original wine becomes redder and more concentrated than it would have been if all the juice had been left alone.

- **Salmon River Cellars** – Brand name owned by Birchwood Estate Winery. Wines are VQA blends, except in 2003 when content rules were waived after a severe winter caused a short crop.

*Tasting notes listed under **Birchwood Estate Winery Ltd.***

- **SANDBANKS ESTATE WINERY** (17598 Loyalist Parkway, Wellington, ON, K0K 3L0 / Phone: 613-399-1839 / Fax: 613-399-1456 / Email: catlan@allstream.net)

(Est. 2004) Driving west past By Chadsey's Cairns Winery & Vineyard, it's easy to miss Sandbanks on the north side of the road. Quebecer Catherine Langlois is reluctant to go for the big bold signs until the winery is a bit more established and the vines more mature. Her past experience in the food business has demonstrated that it's best not to make a splashy entrance until all systems are running smoothly. She cultivates 6 acres of vines on a south-facing slope just 300 m from Lake Ontario. Langlois grows Baco Noir, Cabernet Franc, Pinot Noir, Riesling, and Vidal Blanc, and will add more acreage as demand grows. The soil is Ameliasburg clay loam soil nearest to the lake, with some Brighton sandy loam farther back, and all of it sitting on a solid limestone base. Black Prince Winery buys her Baco Noir, Marechal Foch, and Vidal Blanc. Her total production in 2004 was just 100 cases. She expects to build that to about 800 cases by the end of the decade.

Winemaker: Catherine Langlois / Vineyard Manager: Catherine Langlois

Cabernet Franc [Ont] **2003** ★ ★ ★ ➜ Garnet with a soft aroma, akin to light toast with wild blackberry jam. Light taste has strong black-fruit influences with a mildly herbal backdrop of green pepper. Drink now-2008.

• **SANDSTONE VINEYARD (Niagara-on-the-Lake, NP)** – Grape growers Erwin and Esther Willms sold their crops to Château des Charmes for almost 20 years before getting into the winemaking business themselves. They own the vineyard outright, but in 1999 they partnered with St. Catharines lawyer Ken Douglas to create Sandstone Vineyards Inc., a separate holding company that is half-owner of the Thirteenth Street Winery. The 18-acre vineyard is bounded by 4 others: Pillitteri on the north, Puglisi to its south, H.H. Wall Farm to the east, and Dizio Vineyard (a table-grape farm) on the west. Fifteen acres of well-cared-for vines include 2 acres of Cabernet Franc (planted in 1993), 2 acres of Cabernet Sauvignon (also 1993), 5.5 acres of Chardonnay (1983 and 1995), 3 acres of Gamay (1983, 1987), and 2.5 acres of Riesling (1983). All grapes are planted at a density of 1,100 vines per acre. The flat surface soil consists primarily of loam and clay-loam, but plenty of stones and gravel are scattered throughout. The vineyard is fully tiled for drainage and yields about 3.5 t. per acre in an average vintage. Grapes not used in Thirteenth Street's Sandstone Vineyard label have been sold to Malivoire and Warren Ridge in the past, recently to Stratus and Strewn, as well as to a Pennsylvania-based operation called Presquille.

• **SANSON ESTATE WINERY** (9238 Walker Road, R.R.#1, McGregor, ON, N0R 1J0 / Phone: 519-726-9609 / Email: bacosbest@sansonestatewinery.com / Website: sansonestatewinery.com)

(Est. 2000) Situated in the Canard Valley in Anderdon Township, Sanson Estate is the first stop on the wine route when travelling from the city of Windsor. It borders on the Texas Road Cemetery, which locals consider to be the most haunted graveyard in southern Ontario. The cemetery is a constant reminder to Dennis Sanson of how he got to where he is today. In 1990, he was nearly killed in a head-on collision when a teenage driver blindly passed a plough in a snowstorm. His recovery was long, slow, and painful, but his determination to return to a normal life drove him to work hard at rebuilding his strength. It also brought him the financial opportunity to bring to fruition a dream he had cherished during his long convalescence. In 1997, Sanson purchased the 100-acre farm that lies equidistant to Lake St. Clair, Lake Erie, and the Detroit River. The fairly flat site is composed entirely of Brookston clay. Sanson has planted 7 acres of grapes, which provided

30% of his production requirements. He supplements his needs by purchasing fruit from a local grower, Smith & Wilson Farms. Current production is 3,500 cases, which is projected to grow to 10,000 cases by 2012.

Winemaker: Dennis Sanson / Vineyard Manager: Dennis Sanson

Baco Noir, Reserve [Ont] **2003** *Gold, All Canadian Wine Championships 2004.* **2002**★★★☆**↗** Deep, inky, opaque garnet-black pigment stains the glass. Big, bold, juicy, fruity with flavours of black cherry and blackberry. Balanced despite the 15% (!) alcohol. A powerhouse of flavour with a heady finish. Drink 2006-2010.

Bird Dog Red [Ont] **2002**★★★**↗** Garnet colour with a soft, restrained yet elegant bouquet. Ripe, red fruit flavours with palate-cleansing apply acidity. Drink 2006-2011.

Cabernet Franc [LENS] **2002**★★★☆**↗** Cherry-garnet hue with an oaky, smoky aroma of Virginia tobacco. Great depth, ripe, concentrated yet lean fruit, with a good, lingering finish. Drink now-2009.

Shiraz [LENS] **2002**★★★**↗** Garnet-purple with an herbal nose hinting of dusty tannins. Palate has lovely flavours of cassis, blackberry, and raspberry, though the dusty herbal thing put me off a bit. Drink now-2008.

• **Sawmill Creek** – National brand owned by Vincor International Inc. Generic nonVQA varietals produced with imported wine, juice, or grapes.

Tasting notes listed under **Vincor International Inc.**

• **ST. URBAN VINEYARD (Vineland, NP)** – The rolling hills of this vineyard surround the Vineland Estates Winery, providing one of the more scenic vistas in the region. The 50-acre property was first planted in 1979 with 3 acres of Chardonnay, 35 acres of Riesling, 5 acres of Seyval Blanc, and 5 acres of Vidal Blanc. An additional 2 acres of Pinot Noir were planted in 1990 and 1 acre of Viognier was added in 1993. All plantings have been spaced at an average density of 1,120 vines per acre. There's a gentle, 4-degree north-facing slope and the soil is predominantly Oneida clay loam till with some Chinguacousy, and a few patches with alluvial deposits.

• **SCHUELE VINEYARD (Beamsville, NP)** – Martin Schuele and his father, Reinhold, baby this picture-book vineyard situated next door to George II Farms on the flat Chinguacousy clay loam and silt that lies along the lakeshore between Beamsville and Vineland. Their 120-acre farm is planted 960 vines per acre with 7 acres of Auxerrois (planted in

1990 and 1991), 3.5 acres of Cabernet Franc (1989), 14.5 acres of Chardonnay (1983 and 1990 plantings), 2 acres of the German red crossing Dornfelder (1993), 6.5 acres of Geisenheim 318 (1987), 5.5 acres of Merlot (1992), 7 acres of Pinot Gris (1994), 5.5 acres of Pinot Noir (from 1988), 15 acres of Riesling (planted in 1983 and again in 1994), 7 acres of Sauvignon Blanc (2002), 9 acres of Vidal Blanc (1983 and 1984), and 8 acres of Zweigelt (1992 through 1998). Grapes are sold exclusively to Inniskillin, and special single-vineyard designations have regularly been given to their Chardonnay and Merlot. Wines from this vineyard are medium-bodied, with delicate tropical aromas that reflect the lighter soil and lakefront terroir.

• **SCHWENKER VINEYARD (St Catharines, NP)** – Gordon Schwenker was chosen Grape King in 1960. He sold exceptional quality Auxerrois and Cabernet Franc grapes to Stoney Ridge Estate Winery and all other vinifera varieties to Andrés. In 1997, after severing an acre off the 58-acre property to build a retirement home, he divided the rest into 2 lots and sold them to Doug Whitty and Josef Zimmermann. Whitty lives on his section and continues to grow grapes as well as strawberries and other tenderfruits that he sells through a roadside stand. Zimmermann, one of the pioneers of the wine industry, transformed the acreage into King's Court Estate Winery and sells his grape production to several Quebec wineries, a few Ontario producers, and into the export market.

• **SCOTCH BLOCK COUNTRY WINERY** (9365 10th Sideroad, R.R.#5, Milton, ON, L9T 2X9 / Phone: 905-878-5807 / Fax: 905-878-4997 / Email: farm@andrewsscenicacres.com / Website: www.scotch block.com)

(Est. 2002) Bert and Laurie Andrews and their 3 children established this 97-acre, all-purpose farm in 1980 among rolling hills in the regional municipality of Halton. They offer a market garden specializing in all sorts of fruits, vegetables, grains, pumpkins, as well as a pick-your-own operation with weekly activities for kids and city slickers alike. Nestled in the Scotch Block – named after the Scottish pioneers who first settled the area in the 1820s – this rich, fertile, rolling farm community lies just below the Niagara Escarpment about 10 miles north of the town of Milton. In 2000, they dedicated a 6-acre section off Highway 25 to vines, calling it the Toccalino Vineyard. They had tried viniferas, but the heavy clay soil, severe winters, hungry birds, and hard-to-control powdery mildew convinced them to focus on hybrids. Today, they grow approximately .5 acres each of Baco Noir, Cayuga White, De Chaunac, L'Acadie Blanc, Leon Millot, Marechal Foch, Seyval Blanc, and Vidal Blanc. In fact, most of the Andrewses' production is fruit wine; however, their Halton Red and White are from their estate-grown grapes, while the remaining vinifera blends are made from grapes purchased in the Niagara Peninsula.

Winemaker: Fred Bulbeck / Vineyard Manager: Bert Andrews

Wines not made available for tasting prior to publication.

- **SEEGER VINEYARD (Niagara-on-the-Lake, NP)** – Originally owned by Inniskillin, this vineyard was sold to Albrecht Seeger to help finance the winery's expansion in 1980. The property is 135 acres of Chinguacousy and Jeddo clay loam with significantly more sand and stone outcroppings than Klaus Reif's vineyard to the immediately north or Inniskillin's Brae Burn Estate on the south side of the road. A total of 110 acres are planted at an average density of 1,600 vines per acre. Auxerrois, Cabernet Franc, Chardonnay, Gamay, Gewürztraminer, Pinot Noir, Riesling, Vidal Blanc, and Zweigelt are cultivated with tender, loving care. Seeger's Chardonnay vines are more than 25 years old. Average yields are 3-4 t. per acre, and produce fuller-bodied whites with mature, complex, and distinguished flavours. Seeger was chosen Ontario Grape King in 1998.

- **SERVOS VINEYARD (Niagara-on-the-Lake, NP)** – Located at the southwest corner of Irvine Road and Church Road just south of the Stonechurch Vineyards winery, David and Shirley Servos continue to care for the 50-acre farm that's been in the family for more than 100 years. In the early years it was used to herd cattle and sheep and grow grain. David's father, Peter, planted his first Concords in 1941 and the fruit from those ancient vines continues to be sold to Welch's juice company to this day. In 1963, the existing hybrids were planted, including De Chaunac, Marechal Foch, Seyve-Villard 23-512, and Vidal Blanc. Around 1974, David began planting viniferas, starting with Riesling. Other viniferas cultivated include Cabernet Sauvignon, Chardonnay, Gamay, Gewürztraminer, Sauvignon Blanc, and the Viognier that Inniskillin regularly bottles with the single-vineyard indication. The terrain is very flat and smooth, and composed of Tavistock silty clay loam with plenty of fieldstones scattered through the site. There is a small 10-acre section in the back corner where sand is more evident. Fruit is contracted to Vincor and Inniskillin, except for the labruscas, which are turned into juice. David was chosen Ontario Grape King in 1980.

- **SHOEMAKER VINEYARD (Jordan, NP)** – When Dan Shoemaker purchased this tract of land in 1979 is was called Fry Farm. It had been planted in 1972 and the first grapes were to be sold to a brand-new winery called Inniskillin. Today, Shoemaker supplies Marechal Foch and Vidal Blanc to Kittling Ridge, and Seyval Blanc to Silver Peak Wine

Cellars. A property formerly owned by Dan's father, also once called Shoemaker Vineyard, used to supply the Chardonnay that appeared on Hillebrand's Trius labels during the late 1980s and early 1990s. That property was sold to Cave Spring Cellars in the late 1990s, and now forms part of the enlarged Cave Spring Vineyard.

- **SHORT HILLS VINEYARD (St. Catharines, NP)** – When the Masterson family sold their 88-acre farm, the Speck brothers of Henry of Pelham bought one-half while the other half was sold to Fred Hernder. Short Hills is the Speck-owned section that lies between 8th Avenue and Pelham Road and between 3rd and 5th Streets Louth. The soil is a reddish sand with some clay patches.

- **SILVER ACRES FARM (St. Catharines, NP)** – Situated at 4th Avenue and 3rd Street Louth, this 99-acre plot is one of many owned by Fred Hernder, the largest grape farmer in Canada. Ninety flat acres of clay loam soil are planted, including 8 acres of Chardonnay, 6 of Chardonnay Musqué, 8 of Chenin Blanc, 12 of Gewürztraminer, 4 of Marechal Foch, 12 of Merlot, 30 of Riesling, and 10 Vidal Blanc at a plant density of 1,400 vines per acre. All the fruit is harvested by machine and processed at Hernder Estates.

- **SILVER PEAK WINE CELLARS** (36 Cawthra Avenue, Toronto, ON, M6M 5G3 / Phone: 416-767-7600 / Fax: 416-763-7236 / Email: info@silverpeakwines.com)

(Est. 1998) After making wine for the family from childhood at his father's side, then winning numerous awards for the wines he was producing commercially for others, Angelo Rigitano finally applied for his own wine manufacturer's licence. Since he has no vineyards, though, he cannot open a retail store or sell directly to the public. Silver Peak wines are available in numerous restaurants throughout the Greater Toronto Area. Last year, Rigitano produced 500 cases using grapes purchased from well-known Niagara growers, including Walter Burkhardt, Steve Kocsis, Dan Shoemaker, and Roger Vail. He has 11 oak barrels, mostly French, some American, as well as 3 Hungarian casks in which he prefers to age his Chardonnays. He hopes to build the business to 1,500 cases by 2007, and continues to look for just the right piece of land to take things to the next level.
    Winemaker: Angelo Rigitano

Baco Noir [Ont]   **2003** ★ ★ ★ ☆ ➚ An exceptional Baco! Opaque purple-garnet with a ripe, concentrated nose of black fruits and berries, a hint of cream and oaky smoke. Lovely, sweet, rich, juicy taste with a terrific lingering finish. Drink now-2011.

Chardonnay [NP] 1999 ★ ★ ★ ☆ → Brilliant straw-gold with a clean, lean, Chablis-like bouquet. Good body, with firm mineral notes and a gentle richness from light oaking. Drink now-2007.

Gamay Noir, Steve Kocsis Mountain Road Vineyard [Ont] 2003 ★ ★ ★ ☆ → Ruby-garnet with a classic Gamay nose of raspberry, bitter cherry, and ripe strawberry. Pure fruit flavours, good depth and balance. Drink now-2006.

Muskat Ottonel, Walter Burkhardt Vineyard [NP] 2003 ★ ★ ★ ☆ → Rich yellow-gold with a wild, floral, perfumed, lanolin bouquet. Soft, unctuous, and yummy. With ripe apple flavours and rich mouthfeel. Drink now-2007.

Riesling [NP] 2003 ★ ★ ★ → Silvery-gold with the slightest blush of orange-pink. Subdued grapefruity nose with orange and apple flavours. Balanced and pleasant. Drink now-2008.

Seyval Blanc, Shoemaker Vineyard [Ont] 2004 ★ ★ ↻ This tank sample had a lemony nose and taste, but finished somewhat yeasty. Filtration before bottling should correct that. 2003 ★ ★ ☆ ↻ Pale straw-gold with a touch of oak and an exotic aroma of lemon wine gums. Fullish, soft, vinous, and interesting.

• SKUBEL VINEYARD (Virgil, NP) – Ted Skubel has long supplied grapes to Vincor. His Cabernet Sauvignon and Merlot are included in the winery's cross-country Unity brand.

• **SMITH & WILSON ESTATE WINES** (R.R.#1, Blenheim, ON, N0P 1A0 / Phone: 519-676-5867 / Fax: 519-676-7371 / Email: smith. wilson@southkent.net)

(Est. 2004) High up on a 60-ft. bank overlooking the edge of Lake Erie, George and Mary Jane Smith have cultivated tender fruits since 1984. In 1990, they planted their first grapes, 6 acres of Vidal Blanc. Since then, they have periodically added more acreage so that today 50 of their 100 acres are dedicated to viticulture. In addition to the Vidal, they have small blocks of Baco Noir, Cabernet Franc, Cabernet Sauvignon, Chambourcin, Chardonnay, Gamay, Gewürztraminer, Merlot, Petit Verdot, Pinot Gris, Riesling, Sauvignon Blanc, Syrah, Viognier, and Zweigelt, all spaced at 1,200 vines per acre. The lakeshore soil is clay, with a moderate south-facing slope. Portions of the harvest are sold to Pelee Island Winery, Sanson Estate, and Viewpointe. Their first estate wines were produced in 2004, with none yet available for sale, but by 2008 the Smiths plan to be making 3,000 cases annually.

Winemaker: Mary Jane Smith / Vineyard Manager: George Smith

Wines not available for appraisal before press time.

- **Sola-Nero** – Brand owned by Vincor International Inc. Generic nonVQA varietals produced from imported wine, juice, or grapes.

Tasting notes listed under Vincor International Inc.

- **SOUTHBROOK WINERY** (1061 Major Mackenzie Drive, Richmond Hill, ON, L4C 4X9 / Phone: 905-832-2548 / Fax: 905-832-9811 / Email: office@southbrook.com / Website: www.south brook.com)

(Est. 1991) In 1984, Bill and Marilyn Redelmeier set up a roadside picnic table in front of their farm just north of the city of Toronto, to sell fresh corn to cottage-country commuters. Business was good, so they turned it into a small market garden store a few years later. They also ran a large pick-your-own jack-o-lantern business every autumn. (They sell 300,000 lb. of pumpkins every year.) By the end of the 1980s, they decided to try their hand at making and selling a few boxes of wine as well. Little did they know, it would eventually become the main focus of their business. The winery operation was started by "the 3 bald guys" – Redelmeier and his friends Derek Barnett, who ran the market garden store, and Toronto wine merchant Ian Hanna – fine winelovers who liked to hang out together. (There also were early consultations with Australian winemaker Brian Croser.) The threesome bought some grapes from Donna Lailey Vineyards, converted an empty, century-old dairy barn into a makeshift winery and barrel room, and started fermenting. In no time at all, the wines began to garner awards. Suddenly, it was time to get serious. Southbrook does not own any vineyards. Grapes are purchased at a premium price from several top growers in the Niagara Peninsula, including Lailey, Watson, and, until the end of 2001, Reif vineyards. For their fruit wines, berries are purchased from a wide variety of Ontario growers. The house style has always been high acidity and new oak. But after Southbrook's first winemaker, Derek Barnett, left to join Lailey Vineyards in 2000, there was a noticeable change in the wines, especially in the Chardonnays. They still have tons of oak and acid, but the greater emphasis on blending grapes from different vineyards has given the wines a fuller, fatter taste and, some would argue, more complexity. I like both styles, for different reasons and with different foods. Combined annual production is 12,000 cases. About 10% is exported, primarily to the United Kingdom, but also to France, Germany, Hong Kong, Taiwan, and the United States.

Winemakers: Colin Campbell (2001-present); Derek Barnett (1991-2000, 2000 Winemaker of the Year)

Cabernet Franc [NP] **1995** ★ ★ ★ ↘ *Gold & Trophy, Ontario Wine Awards, 1996.* Red-brown hue with a mature bouquet of dried apple chips, fading rose, and forest floor. Holding, but beginning to fade. Drink up.

Cabernet Franc, Lailey Vineyard [NP] 1998★★★★↗ Drink now-2018. 1995★★★★➔ Gold, All Canadian Wine Championships, 1997. Big, balanced, and beautiful. Drink now-2007.

Cabernet Franc, Watson Vineyard [NP] 2002★★★★↗ Deep garnet with a clean bouquet, rich with new oak, fruit jam, dill, and coffee-mocha aromas. Very elegant with well-integrated flesh and bones. Complex, supple, and fine but a smidgen over-oaked. Drink now-2012. 2001★★★↗ Early bottles had lovely, creamy berry flavours with balanced acidity. More recently, the wine tasted better than it smelled. Perfumy soaplike nuances gave way to a balanced, supple, ripe, and sweet palate. In a gawky phase. Drink 2006-2012.

Cabernet-Merlot [NP] 2001★➔ Garnet hue with vegetal notes and a hint of Asian lady beetle. A touch odd, sweet, sour, bitter, weedy, and vegetal. May improve, but I doubt it.

Cabernet-Merlot, Triomphe [NP] From Lailey and Watson grapes. 2001★★★★↗ Garnet with strong flavours and rich texture. Hint of Asian lady beetle but ripeness and oak masks it for the most part. Drink now-2012. 2000★★➔ Garnet with a hint of mercaptan, giving it an unpleasant nuance of garlic in the finish. Tough, vegetal flavours and a mild burnt-rubber stink. Out of character – could this be a dumb phase? 1999★★★↗ Lovely. Balanced and full-flavoured. Still seems very young. Drink 2007-2014.

Cabernet Sauvignon, Lailey Vineyard [NP] 2001★★★★↗ Big, tough, and tannic with rich, full black and red berry flavours. Drink 2006-2012. 1998★★★★↗ Profoundly deep garnet colour with hints of red brick creeping into the solid rim. Big bouquet with a slight eggy reek to start. That blows off quickly, revealing a full, classic California-style Bordeaux – restrained exuberance, dense plummy fruit, solid but gentle tannins and tremendous balance. It's that last feature that makes me confident this superb red will last a couple of decades. Drink now-2015. 1995★★★★➔ Gold, Toronto Wine & Cheese Show 1997; Red Wine Trophy, Ontario Wine Awards 1997.

Cabernet Sauvignon, Triomphe [NP] 2002★★★↗ Garnet colour with an undeveloped nose. Hints of mocha and red fruit. The taste has an element that at times seems like fresh tartness and at times like sourness. Good fruit, herb, and earth flavours, with that little bit of an edge. Drink now-2015.

Chardonnay, Lailey Vineyard [NP] 2000★★★★➔ Pale yellow-gold with a crisp, fine, delicate bouquet of vanilla ice cream with pralines. Implicitly sweet, with a lovely creamy caramel taste and clean finish. Drink now-2010.

Chardonnay, Triomphe [NP] A blend of grapes from Lailey, Watson, and Reif vineyards. 2002★★★↗ Bright yellow-gold hue with an expressive nose that starts with smoked sausage and quickly turns lemony, floral, fruity, and exotic. Fresh, fruity flavours with a lingering, slightly tropical finish. Drink now-2009. **2001★★★➔** Deep yellow-gold colour, a thick, oaky, toasty bouquet with rich nuances of warmed butter. Big, concentrated, lush flavours perhaps a touch overblown. Drink now-2008. **2000★★★➚** Restrained nose at first, opens to oaky, toasty, vanilla, baked-pear flavours. Burgundian in style with bright, youthful acidity and an oaky, latex finish. Drink now-2008. **1999★★★➔** Soft nose with hints of brown butter and caramel, slightly oxidative. Drink now-2007. **1998★★★★➔** *Gold, Ontario Wine Awards, 2004.* Big and buxom with toasted coconut and toffee flavours. Drink now.

Chardonnay, Triomphus [NP] A selection of the top 2 or 3 barrels in each vintage, bottled unfiltered. **2002★★★★➚** *(barrel sample)* Deep yellow-gold, still murky from the cask. Bright, crisp, fresh, lemony nose. Tart and sharp at first with huge depth of flavours lurking beneath. Drink 2006-2012. **2001** Not produced. **2000★★★★➔** Yellow-gold with fading brilliance. Thick, oaky smoky, buttered toast with nuances of fresh-brewed coffee. Mouth-watering acidity, lemon marmalade flavours, and a slightly nutty finish. Drink now-2008. **1999★★★★➔** Yellow-gold with a full-blown oak nose and a strong whiff of brown butter. Packed with concentrated flavours of spice, nuts, dehydrated pears, a veritable monster wine. Drink now-2008. **1998★★★★★➚** Comparatively pale yellow-gold for its age. Soft, creamy, with terrific complexity. Shows its age in well-developed oxidative flavours, yet retains enough acidity to permit further growth. Balanced, full-bodied, and difficult to put down, even for a moment. Drink now-2010.

Gewürztraminer Icewine [NP]   Regrettably, no longer made. **1995★★★★➔** Orange apricot and creamy canned-corn bouquet. Delicate flavours with a clean spiced finish. Yumsters! Drink up.

Marechal Foch [Ont]   **2001★★➔** Green vegetables and fruit salad. Not to my taste.

Merlot, Lailey Vineyard [NP]   **1999★★★➔** Lovely, balanced, soft fruit nose and palate, but flavours stop short. Drink now-2008.

Pinot Gris [NP]   **2001★★★➔** Pale, soft gold with strong aromas of mandarin and quince. Nose grows to include ripe grapes, water-melon cocktail, maraschino cherries. Medium-full body and rich mouthfeel with sweetish flavours of white plum, apples, and wine gums. Drink now-2007.

Pinot Noir [NP]   **2000★★★➔** Cherry-garnet with a browning rim. Earthy, herbal, pencil-lead nose; tart with hints of sour cherry and cranberry. Drink now-2008.

Pinot Noir, Triomphe [NP]   Grapes are from the Lailey Vineyard. **2001★★★➚** Pale ruby with a tart cherry aroma. Quite closed the first time I tasted it in January 2003. It's softer now with cherry, strawberry, and plum flavours, but retains its tough, tannic afterbite. Drink now-2009.

Sauvignon Blanc [NP] **1996** ★ ★ ↘ Nose of nearly ripe honeydew melon and touched by oak. Dry, light, and barely kicking. **1995**↓ *Gold, All Canadian Wine Championships, 1997.* **1994**↓ Ripe nose of creamed asparagus, celery, sweet apple, and skin of Bartlett pear.

Sauvignon Blanc, Triomphe [NP]   From the Watson Vineyard. **2003** ★ ★ → Clean, green nose but falls flat on the palate. **2002** ★ ★ ★ → Straightforward green apple notes with terrific acidity. **2001** ★ ★ ↘ Oxidative, buttery nose with a slightly tart taste and some bitterness in the finish. Seems tired. **1998** ★ ★ ★ → *Gold, Ontario Wine Awards, 1999.* Big, full, and fat for a wine that's normally crisp and light. Fully mature and about to descend.

Trillium, Lailey Vineyard [NP]   **1995** ★ ★ ★ → A Bordeaux-style blend. (CF25/CS50/M25) Soon after this wine was released, Redelmeier received a lawyer's letter telling him to stop using the name; someone else had already registered it. He renamed the series "Triomphe." Concentrated, flavourful, with nuances of cedar, leather, autumn leaves, and charred plums. Well balanced and fully mature. Drink now.

Vidal, Icewine [NP] **2001** ★ ★ ★ ★ → Really delicious, rich, soft, and balanced. Drink now–2013.

Vidal, Icewine, Triomphus, Canadian Oak [NP] **2003** ★ ★ ★ ★ → Pale amber-golf with a fresh peach and apple cider opening followed by nuances of wildflower honey and candied pineapple. Peachy and oh so sweet. Drink now–2015.

White [nonVQA] **NV** ★ ★ ↻ A blend of Vidal from at least 2 vintages and a tiny percentage of Chardonnay. Gold with a fairly nondescript nose and a sweet-tart taste. Lively acidity with good balance.

Fruit Wines

Blackberry [QC] **NV** ★ ★ ★ ↻ Clean and balanced but the least intense or exciting of this group of fruit wines. My least favourite of this bunch.

Blueberry [QC] **NV** ★ ★ ★ ★ ↻ Intensely rich and sweet. Varietally pure as blueberry pie filling.

Cassis [QC] **NV** ★ ★ ★ ★ ↻ *Platinum, World Wine Championships, 1997; Gold, International Wine & Spirits, 1997; Best Red Wine Trophy, New Zealand International Fruit Wine Competition, 1997.* An intensely flavoured, tough, tannic, fortified wine produced from black currants gathered in the Kingston area. Unidimensional but deliciously black curranty. Fabulous in champagne, on ice, on ice cream, with chocolate, or in clear tea or black coffee.

Framboise [QC] **NV** ★ ★ ★ ★ ★ ↻ *Gold, Toronto Wine & Cheese Show 2004; Gold, World Wine Championships; Gold, International Wine & Spirits; Best Red Wine Trophy, New Zealand International Fruit Wine Competition 1995.* Liquid raspberry. Early versions (pre-1992) were more bitter until then winemaker Derek Barnett developed more thorough methods for seed removal prior to fermentation.

Framboise d'Or [QC] **NV**★★★★★↻ Produced from golden raspberries that cost, on average, $26,000 per t. Nuances of orange pekoe tea, white plum. Outstanding.

• **SPRUCEWOOD SHORES ESTATE WINERY** (7258 Heritage Road, County Road 50, Harrow, ON, N0R 1G0 / Phone: 519-738-9253 / Fax: 519-738-9253 / Email: gord@sprucewoodshores.com)

(Est. 2004) There are 6 pairs of hands in this budding hands-on operation. The Mitchell family, Gordon and Hannah, and their 4 children, Stephen, Marlaina, Tanya, and Jake, all take responsibility (and credit) for the successes achieved to date. There are 35 acres under vine on the 52-acre farm, including 4.7 acres of Cabernet Franc, 5.2 acres of Cabernet Sauvignon, 8.9 acres of Chardonnay, 1.7 acres of Gamay Noir, 2.1 acres of Merlot, 2.6 acres of Pinot Gris, 3.5 acres of Pinot Noir, 5.4 acres of Riesling, and 1 acre of Riesling-Traminer and Vidal Blanc. All blocks were put into the ground between 1991 to 1993. The Perth clay loam soil of the vineyard has a moderate south-facing slope and runs right down to the lake. It is tiled for drainage and irrigated with an overhead boom system when required. With some of the highest heat units anywhere in Canada, summertime day/night differentials in temperature, and the prolonged fall harvest period of the Lake Erie shoreline, the Mitchells believe they can consistently develop high levels of ripeness and excellent flavour elements in their red varieties. Gordon Mitchell is particularly optimistic about the future of Cabernet Franc from here. Average yield is 3.5 t. to the acre, and until 2 years ago, everything was sold to Colio Estate or Pelee Island wineries. The Mitchells produced 460 cases in 2004 and plan to grow to 12,000 cases annually by 2009.

Winemaker: Tanya Mitchell / Vineyard Manager: Gordon and Steve Mitchell

Wines were not ready for appraisal before press time.

• **STAFF HOME FARM** (Jordon, NP) – The original homestead of the Staff family still stands on this 200-year-old, 80-acre spread. H. Lavelle Staff (the 1967 Ontario Grape King) lives here, though the property is cared for by son Howard (1996 Grape King) and daughter-in-law Wendy. Situated on a 5-degree, north-facing slope on the brink of the Niagara Escarpment on Staff Avenue between Pelham Road and Highway 8, this property has a huge pond and two airstrips that are used mainly during spring frosts. The soil is predominantly clay loam with a solid limestone bedrock. Fifty acres are planted to grapes, including 25 acres of Niagara, 20 acres of Concord, and 5 acres of Baco Noir put into the ground in 1997. All grapes are sold to National Grape

(Welch's) in the United States except for the Baco Noir, which is destined for the fermentation tanks at Pillitteri Estates, where granddaughter Sue Ann Staff is the head winemaker.

- **STEFANIK VINEYARD (Beamsville, NP)** – For more than a decade, Willow Heights Estates Winery has been the exclusive buyer of grapes from this 10-acre site near Kew Vineyard on King Street (Regional Road 81) at Bartlett Avenue. Owner Dave Stefanik rents the property to Roger Vail's company, Vailmont Vineyards. The north-facing terrain is significantly sloped and composed of Oneida clay loam. Vail cultivates Cabernet Franc, Cabernet Sauvignon, Chardonnay, Gewürztraminer, Merlot, Riesling, and Vidal Blanc at an average density of 957 plants per acre. Average yield is 4 t. per acre.

- **STEVE KOCSIS FLY ROAD VINEYARD (Beamsville, NP)** – Kocsis bought this existing 12.7-acre vineyard on the northeast corner of Fly Road at Mountain Road in 1992. It has a gentle south-facing slope and a combination of Chinguacousy and Oneida clay loam tills. The vineyard is completely underdrained. Concord and Fredonia grapes were put into the ground in 1949. Here, above the Niagara Escarpment, vinifera varieties have reduced prospect of surviving the winter so, in 1996, Kocsis added 4 acres of the hybrid varieties, Baco Noir, Marechal Foch and Vidal Blanc. He harvests about 4 t. per acre for his Mountain Road Wine Company. Occasionally Lakeview Cellars buys some of the fruit.

- **STEVE KOCSIS HILLSIDE DRIVE VINEYARD (Beamsville, NP)** – This 11-acre vineyard purchased in 1992 is on the outskirts of Beamsville, bordered by Hillside Drive to the south, Aberdeen Vineyard to the east, Marianne Hill Estate Winery to the south, and Csets Vineyard to the west. There are 7 acres of Cabernet Franc, Cabernet Sauvignon, Chardonnay, and Riesling planted at 1,210 vines per acre in the Chinguacousy clay loam till. Kocsis practises minimal use of insecticides and herbicides, although the parcel is by no means cultivated organically. He thins the grapes ruthlessly at veraison to limit yields to between 1.5 t. and 3 t. per acre. All fruit is directed to his Mountain Road Wine Company. Kocsis hopes to use this site to construct a new winery in the future, but that depends on the Niagara Escarpment Commission, which has jurisdiction over the location.

- **STEVE KOCSIS MOUNTAIN ROAD VINEYARD (Beamsville, NP)** – Winelovers first took notice of this 45-acre property in the early 1990s after the release of the first Temkin-Paskus Chardonnay, which was produced from several rows of grapes leased from Steve Kocsis. The resulting wine was so good that other wineries jumped onto the bandwagon, putting the Kocsis Vineyard name on their bottles too. Kocsis bought the family farm from his parents in 1981 and, 2 years later, planted 13.5 acres of Chardonnay, Gamay Noir, and Vidal Blanc at a density of 960 vines per acre. The soil is Chinguacousy clay loam till, although there is more sand here than in surrounding vineyards and several pockets of gravelly subsoil, which improve drainage and allow for earlier warming of the ground in spring. The site is underdrained, irrigated with a drip system, and cultivated with minimal herbicide and insecticide use. Grapes are severely thinned at veraison and most of the fruit is used by Mountain Road Wine Company. Kocsis also sells grapes to Andrés, Angels Gate, Closson Chase in Prince Edward County, Lakeview Cellars, Stoney Ridge, the new Tawse Family Winery, and Thirty Bench. The property is situated east of EastDell Estate within Beamsville city limits and is therefore zoned for development. Kocsis successfully fought city hall to save the site from developers. It is one of the very rare properties on the Niagara Bench that has southeast-facing sections.

• STONECHURCH VINEYARDS (1242 Irvine Road, R.R.#5, Niagara-on-the-Lake, ON, L0S 1J0 / Phone: 905-935-3535 / Toll-Free: 1-866-935-3500 / Fax: 905-646-8892 / Email: winery@stonechurch. com / Website: www.stonechurch.com)

(Est. 1990) Rick Hunse has been a grape grower since 1972, long before the idea of starting his own winery came up. For many years, he managed vineyards for Inniskillin and others. The 200-acre farm less than 1 km from the lake is composed of very fine, reddish-hued Grimsby sandy loam and Tavistock loam over lacustrine silt. It is planted with Baco Noir, Cabernet Sauvignon, Chardonnay, Gewürztraminer, Morio Muscat, Pinot Noir, Seyval Blanc, and Vidal Blanc. Hunse also grows peaches, although some acreage is to be torn out to make room for more grapes. Current production averages 30,000 cases.

Winemakers: Terence J. van Rooyen (2004-present); Jens Gemmrich (2000-2004); Tatjana Cuk (1994-1999); David Hulley (1989-1993) / Vineyard Manager: Rick Hunse

The winemaker at Stonechurch would not provide vineyard information or samples for tasting. The following notes were scribbled under varying circumstances – at wine judging events, display tables, trade functions – not the ideal conditions of a clinical tasting room.

Cabernet Franc [NP] 1997⊠ Unpleasant mercaptan nose and chemically taste.

Cabernet Sauvignon [NP] 1998☐↘ Eggy and unappealing. 1990★★★☆➔ Pale mahogany with a fully mature nose of dried cherries, raspberry jam, and a hint of sundried tomato. Light-bodied but well balanced. Ready to fade. Drink up

Pinot Noir [NP] 1999☐↘ Ruby-firebrick colour with an odd fried-onion smell. Taste lacks ripeness or sweetness and ends with a bit of an edge.

Riesling [NP] 1998☒ Dirty nose. I did not wish to taste this.

Riesling, Icewine [NP] 1990★★★★☆→ Amber-gold colour with a penetrating nose of honey, broiled pineapple, and essence of pear. Racy acidity is perfectly balanced with the rich, syrupy fruit. Drink now–2015.

Vidal, Icewine [NP] 1990★★★★→ Deep amber hue with an opulent bouquet of dried apricots, peaches, orange zest, and honeycomb honey. Drink now.

Vidal, Late Harvest [NP] 1999☐↘ Smells of old apples.

• **Stone Road Wines** – Brand name owned by Andrés subsidiary Hillebrand Estate Wines. Wines are nonVQA blends produced from domestic and imported juices.

Tasting notes listed under **Hillebrand Estate Wines.**

• **STONEY RIDGE ESTATE WINERY** (3201 King Street, Vineland, ON, L0R 2C0 / Phone: 905-562-1324 / Fax: 905-562-7777 / Email: store@stoneyridge.com / Website: www.stoneyridge.com)

(Est. 1985) This tiny boutique winery was founded by Jim Warren, a former high-school teacher and amateur winemaker. The wines he produced were good, but production was severely restricted by the size of his small facility. Consequently, growth proceeded at a snail's pace. In 1989, Warren partnered with fruit and grape grower Murray Puddicombe and built new facilities at Puddicombe's farm. The winery grew rapidly, further expansions were carried out, and the wines garnered many awards. Differences between the partners led to a split in 1997 and a new group of investors joined Warren and relocated to larger facilities at the current location on Regional Road 81. With new money and a strong marketing team, the winery flourished for a while, but conflicting views among the partners over direction led to Warren's announcing his retirement in 1999. Warren smoothly transitioned winemaking responsibilities to Liubomir Popovici, a recent Romanian immigrant with a strong winemaking background. Early in 2002, some of the partners liquidated their shares and a new management team emerged under Barry Katzman. The winery returned its focus to producing premium Niagara wine and renewed its relationship with Jim Warren, who was invited to return as founding winemaker and produce a signature label. During the course of cleanup and inventory assessment, a large cache of older wines was uncovered and, following extensive tastings, the winery established The Wine Library, a unique collection of back vintages and limited-edition wines. Many of these rare bottles are still available for purchase at the winery. Last year Katzman left to join another winery and Mark Bonham took over as president of Stoney Ridge. The winery sources its fruit from the vineyards it owns or manages, including Cuesta, Kew, McGrade and Troup, and Zimmerman, as well as from several local grape growers including Wismer Vineyards. Recent production was 30,000 cases, but with slow, steady growth the target is 50,000 cases before the end of the decade.

Winemakers: Liubomir Popovici (1999-present); Jim Warren (1986-2000, 1997 Winemaker of the Year) / Vineyard Manager: Mladen Stegnjaic

Baco Noir, Barrel Select [Ont] **2003** ★ ★ ★ ➔ Deep garnet with a hot, cooked nose reminiscent of blackberry jam and stewed plums. Full-bodied with solid texture, but the tartness is a bit much for me. Not bad for a hybrid. Drink now-2009.

Cabernet, Reserve [NP] **1995** ★ ★ ★ ★ ↘ Grapes were from Lenko Vineyard. Big, hot, and forward. Drink now.

Cabernet Franc [NP] **1991** ★ ★ ★ ★ ↘ Bright garnet with mahogany core and brick-red edges. Cooked fruit, green herbs, and mint bouquet with a spicy taste, gracefully passing into its twilight years. Drink now.

Cabernet Franc, Bench [NP] **2002** ★ ★ ★ ➔ Black-cherry colour with aromas of candied fruit and perfume. Dry, dusty, herbal, tannic flavours and a short finish. Drink now-2007.

Cabernet Franc, Fox Vineyard Reserve [NP] **2002** ★ ★ ★ ↗ Aged in new American oak barrels. Richly layered with overtones of vanilla, chocolate, coffee, and smoke. There's a distinct fruity cassis note waiting to emerge, hidden by strong dusty tannins. Hide until after 2006. **2000** ★ ★ ★ ➔ Mildly vegetal undertones with big, forward black fruits and some malolactic cheesiness in the finish. Drink now.

Cabernet Franc, Wismer Vineyard Reserve [NP] **2002** ★ ★ ★ ★ ↑ Best Red Wine, Cuvée 2004; Gold, Toronto Wine & Cheese Show, 2004. Deep garnet with viscosity so thick it hold bubbles on the surface for a long time. Bouquet packed with smoky, oaky, coffee notes and ripe, vanilla-scented black fruits. Soft, lush, silky, and packed with big, alcoholic, pungent black-cherry and raspberry fruit flavours that last and last. Peak drinking: 2010-2018. **1997** ★ ★ ★ ★ ↗ Fat and lovely, beginning to open up gracefully. Drink now-2012.

Cabernet Franc, "Old Vines" [NP] **1997** ★ ★ ★ ★ ↗ A blend of Kew and Wismer grapes. Big, juicy, and tannic, beginning to show personality but still needs a half-dozen years to open fully. Black-cherry flavours, lead-pencil notes, and a hint of wild game – like a southern Rhône wine.

Cabernet-Merlot, Bench [NP] **2002**★★➔ Somewhat green with a tart, veggie nose. Taste is underripe too.

Cabernet-Merlot, Eastman Vineyard [NP] **1995**★★★★➔ Maturing slowly but oh-so-graciously. Still tough and tannic with evolving plum and cherry flavours. Complex, balanced, rich, and long-lived. Some bottles still available for purchase at the winery. Drink now-2015.

Chardonnay [NP] **1996**★★➔ Good value. Clean, straightforward, with ripe apple and vanilla tones.

Chardonnay, Bench [NP] **2000**★★★↻ Big buxom wine with a crisp palate and hot finish. Drink up.

Chardonnay, "Charlotte's," Founder's Signature Collection [NP] From Dim, Kew, and Koscis vineyards. **2003**★★★★↻ *Gold, Ontario Wine Awards, 2004; Best White Wine, Cuvée 2004.* Packed with fresh and tropical orange, mango, and peach flavours with hints of nutmeg and clove. Rich and lush with a kiss of residual sugar. Best consumed within 3 years of vintage.

Chardonnay, Kew Vineyard Reserve [NP] **2002**★★★↗ A seductive wine from old vines planted in the mid-1970s. Rich golden hue with solid structure and a lively spritz on the palate. Sweet, ripe, honeyed, creamy vanilla nose. Full of flavour with nuances of wine gums, honey, crème brûlée. Drink now to 2007.

Chardonnay, Lenko Vineyard [NP] **1994**★★★★➔ Fully mature now with lively flavours of toasted coconut, brown butter, and coffee notes. Clean, balanced palate. Drink now-2009.

Chardonnay, "Old Vines" (Cuesta Label) [NP] Grapes from Lenko Vineyard. **1997**★★★★➔ *Gold, Ontario Wine Awards, 1999.* Amazing depth and balance. Concentrated flavours of vanilla, pear, pineapple, oak, smoke, coconuts, caramel, and lemon.

Chardonnay, Reserve [NP] **2003**★★★➔ Pale gold with green reflections and soft, creamy peachy aroma. Subtle vinous flavours but taste is dominated by residual sugar. Drink now-2006 **1994**★★★☆↘ Grapes from Eastman Vineyard. Reductive and advanced but still good with hazelnut, toast, and browned butter flavours. Drink up. **1990**★★★★➔ Flavours of yogourt and sweetened sour cream. Still good, but this is one of those "acquired" tastes. Drink now.

Country Selection [Ont] **NV**↻ Predominantly Marechal Foch. Very pleasant, but a touch tart. Dried cherry fruit with an oaky, gamy nose.

Gewürztraminer, Butler's Grant Vineyard [NP] **1997**★★★★↘ Extreme concentration and perfect balance. Flavours of spice, apricot, and mango. Drink now-2009. **1995**★★☆↘ Deep gold colour; slightly perfumed spicy nose; sweet flavour and oily texture with enough acidity for short-term cellaring. **1994**★☆↘ Light spice with tropical peachy-lychee fruit.

Gewürztraminer Icewine [NP] **1997** ★ ★ ★ ★ ★ ➔ Intensely perfumed, almost to the point of hotel soap. Fabulous concentration. Drink now-2010.

Meritage, Founder's Signature Collection [NP] **2002** ★ ★ ★ ★ ↗ Opaque purple black with a strong, toasty, nutty black-cherry and plum flavour. Very complex with hints of black olive, tobacco, chocolate, and cream. Big, rich, supple, and mouth-filling. Drink 2007-2012.

Merlot Reserve [NP] **1994** ★ ★ ★ ☆ ➔ Aging exceptionally well. Restrained but blueberry, blackberry, and plum flavours are clean, fresh, and healthy. Drink now-2010.

Merlot Reserve, Butler's Grant Vineyard [NP] **1997** ★ ★ ★ ★ ☆ ↗ Even better than the 1995. Garnet with a dark brick rim. Developing nose with some jammy notes of black currant, plum butter, orange zest, sage, spices, and black tea. Brilliant. Still hiding a few cards. Drink now-2015. **1995** ★ ★ ★ ★ ➔ *Gold, VinExpo 1997.* Pale ruby-garnet with significant brick reflections. Smoked plums, pencil shavings, and black-cherry ice cream. Plenty of fruit on the palate and plenty of oak. Drink now-2010.

Merlot Reserve, Kew Vineyard [NP] **2002** ★ ★ ★ ★ ↗ *Gold, Ontario Wine Awards, 2004; Best Limited Edition Red Wine, Cuvée 2004.* Solid black-cherry hue with soft, fruity, blueberry, cherry, and plum flavours. Velvety texture, full-bodied taste, with a clean, well-balanced, lingering finish. Drink 2006-2014.

Pinot Noir, Bench [NP] **2002** ★ ★ ★ ➔ Pale garnet hue with a candied black-cherry aroma. Has a taste reminiscent of creamy, chocolate-coated, caramel candies. Drink now to 2008. **1999** ★ ★ ★ ➔ Light, balanced, and lovely. Classic aroma of flowers, cherry, and forest earth. Drink now. **1997** *Gold, Ontario Wine Awards, 1999.*

Pinot Noir, Butler's Grant Vineyard [NP] **1997** ★ ★ ★ ➔ Ruby with an orange rim. Vanilla oaky nose with hints of chocolate sauce and cherry compote. Fully mature and luscious. Drink now.

Pinot Noir, Funk Vineyard [NP] **1995** ★ ★ ★ ➔ Ruby-garnet with hints of brick along the edge. Fullish soft nose of black-cherry Jello. A mouthful with a supple texture and lovely ripeness. Fully mature; drink now.

Riesling, Bench [NP] **2003** ★ ★ ★ ➔ Pale gold with an orange, apricot, petroleum-jelly bouquet. Confected fruit flavours, a mineral undertone, and some depth and complexity. Drink now-2010.

Riesling, Puddicombe Vineyard Reserve [NP] **1995** ★ ★ ★ ★ ➔ One of Jim Warren's favourite "children." Pale colour, big developed nose of lime, honey, and kerosene, balanced, soft, and lingering. Some life left but beginning to show signs of age. Drink now to 2007.

Riesling Reserve [NP] **1999** ★ ★ ★ ★ ➔ Clean, nicely balanced fruit and alcohol, aroma of lemon-lime and petrol with lively acid finish. Drink now-2011. **1994** ★ ★ ★ ★ ➔ Fully mature. Showing tremendous flavours of butterscotch, buckwheat honey, and broiled citron. Drink now-2007.

Riesling-Traminer, Select Late Harvest [NP] **1997** *Gold, Ontario Wine Awards, 1999.*

Sauvignon Blanc [NP] **2003**□ Tasted twice. Both bottles corked.

Vidal Icewine [NP] **1999** *Gold, Ontario Wine Awards, 2004; Gold, Toronto Wine & Cheese Show, 2004.*

Vidal, Late Harvest [Ont] **1999** ★ ★ ★ ☆ ➜ Golden hue with a lovely nose of pears boiled in syrup. Medium-sweet and medium-bodied with superb balance and a clean, vibrant finish. Drink now-2010.

* **STOUCK ESTATE FARM (Beamsville, NP)** – This property has been family owned since 1899. Today, it is run by Brian and Shirley Stouck and, increasingly, by their son, Daniel. The first cultivated grapes appeared on the farm in 1928 and, although they have all been torn out and replanted since, there remains 13 acres of Concord and Niagara dating back to 1945. These are sold to Motts, the juice company. In 1957, the late Henry Stouck, who planted those vines, was chosen Ontario Grape King, the province's second person to be so titled. Two years later, Henry's son, Brian, was chosen as the province's first Grape Prince in 1959, a 4-H club honour no longer in practice. The original property was subdivided in the early 1970s with a parcel at the south end just below the escarpment sold to Roman Prydatkewycz and one on the west sold to Roman's brother-in-law Simon Trochanowski. (Prydatkewycz, who called his section Rosomel Vineyard, resold the property to Harald Thiel's Hidden Bench Estate Winery last year. Trochanowski continues to farm his piece.) The Stouck property is 25 acres in size with 23 of them dedicated to vines. It has an undulating terrain with east and west exposures and a soil of Oneida clay loam over a limestone base. In addition to the 13 acres of labrusca vines planted at 550 vines per acre, there are 4 acres of Cabernet Sauvignon and 3 acres each of Gewürztraminer and Merlot, spaced at 950 vines per acre. All the vinifera fruit is thinned to 3.5 t. per acre before being turned over to Lakeview Cellars Estate Winery.

* **STRATUS VINEYARDS** (2059 Niagara Stone Road [Highway 55], Niagara-on-the-Lake, ON, L0S 1J0 / Phone: 905-468-1806 / Fax: 905-468-0847 / Email: info@stratuswines.com / Website: www.stratus wines.com)

(Est. 2004) Starting on the ground floor and reaching for the clouds is nothing new to David Feldberg. He's the president and CEO of Teknion Corporation, the largest contract furniture-manufacturing company in Canada. Although Feldberg has kept a low profile since purchasing the

62-acre property next door to Jackson-Triggs on Niagara, his ambitions have reached into the "stratus-sphere." The vineyard sits primarily on moderately well-drained Oneida clay loam till, essentially flat with a negligible north-facing slope. Combining existing vines with new plantings, there now are 50 acres of grapes, including Cabernet Franc, Cabernet Sauvignon, Chardonnay, Gamay Noir, Gewürztraminer, Malbec, Merlot, Petit Verdot, Sauvignon Blanc, Semillon, Syrah, and Viognier, all spaced at the medium density of 1,150 vines per acre. All vine stock was brought in from highly rated French nurseries. Vineyard fans have been installed to extend the growing season and to optimize grape maturity. Low cropping is practised throughout the vineyard – the vines are meticulously tended, employing cluster thinning, leaf-plucking, and green harvesting practices to ensure yields are kept to a maximum of 1-2.5 t., per acre depending on variety and vintage. The vineyard is hand-hoed to preclude chemical weed spraying, and grapes are hand-picked into small boxes to avoid bruising them before they are hand-sorted at the winery. Only perfect grapes enter the fermenters. Every aspect of viticulture is focused on the production of super-premium wines with a high level of terroir expression. The obsession continues beyond the vineyard into the winery. Large French oak fermenters are computerized for temperature control. Sophisticated elevator tanks are installed to allow complete gravity handling of wines without need for harsh, mechanical pumps. The building itself has been certified for its ecological and environmental design. The structure is super-insulated with a galvanized roof to reflect heat while a ground loop geothermal system uses the earth's natural energy to heat and cool the building through a series of 25 wells dug 270 ft. into the ground. In its first year of production, the winery bottled 5,000 cases. By 2009, Stratus expects to produce 10,000 cases annually.

Winemaker: J-L Groux (1998 Winemaker of the Year) / Vineyard Manager: Bert Ediger

Cabernet Franc [NP] **2002** ★ ★ ★ ★ ↑ Not a very dark shade of garnet but densely pigmented. Elegant, youthful, concentrated, balanced, ripe, complex, and classic. Hints of raspberry, black cherry, black currant, iodine, and a nuance of charred wood. Ripe and sweet palate with firm body and soft tannins. Lean but muscular. Drink 2007-2015.

Chardonnay, Barrel-Fermented [NP] **2002** ★ ★ ★ ★ ↗ Brilliant, viscous gold colour with a rich, vanilla, caramel, butter taste and a delicate oak undertone. Tastes like liquid wine gums with this implicitly sweet texture, full body, and layers of flavour from yellow pear through licorice. Very high alcohol, but there is finesse in the finish. Drink now-2009.

Chardonnay, Reserve [NP] **2002** ★ ★ ★ ★ ☆ ↗ Pale straw-gold, it pours like oil. Very French nose is still restrained by its youth. Massive body, supple, oily texture, stunning complexity, and richness.

High alcohol, yet this wine has terrific equilibrium and harmony. Drink now-2012.

Merlot [NP] **2002** ★ ★ ★ ★ ☆ ↑ Solid garnet hue with a tightly restricted, juicy, brambleberry nose. Palate is finely structured, vibrates with focused fruit flavours, and teases the tastebuds with the promise of a complex and wonderful future. Drink 2008-2018.

Red [NP] **2002** ★ ★ ★ ★ ↑ Solid garnet with violet reflections in the rim. Full, round nose of red and black fruits. Plummy palate is intense, ripe, tannic, and harmonious. Drink 2007-2016.

Riesling Icewine [NP] **2003** ★ ★ ★ ★ ★ ↗ Brilliant straw-gold with a bouquet of fresh pear nectar and poire william eau-de-vie. I know this may sound geeky, but I also sense an aroma of distant hillside wildflowers when there is a nip of frost in the air. Perfect luscious texture characterized by thick, syrupy viscosity and a delicate, palate-cleansing acidity. Supple, lingering, and superb. Drink now-2025.

White [NP] **2002** ★ ★ ★ ★ ☆ → Brilliant pale gold with clean, floral aromas and a crisp, fruity taste. Thick and supple but without the fruit development of the older vintage. Has tremendous promise for those with patience. Drink now-2010. **2000** ★ ★ ★ ★ → Rich, viscous gold hue with a powerful nose of insanely ripe fruit. Peach and apricot wine gums come to mind and the multidimensional flavours suggest multiple varieties, late-harvested, and cropped very low. Simply brilliant. Drink now-2009.

• **STREHN FARMS (Pelee Island)** – One of the original partners in the Pelee Island Winery, Walter Strehn still holds about 100 acres of vineyards on the island. He sells most of his grapes from the Pelee Island property to Colio Wines.

• **STREWN WINERY** (1339 Lakeshore Road, Niagara-on-the-Lake, ON, L0S 1J0 / Phone: 905-468-1229 / Toll-Free: 1-888-478-7396 / Fax: 905-468-8305 / Email: info@strewnwinery.com / Website: www. strewnwinery.com)

(Est. 1997) Husband and wife Joe Will and Jane Langdon bought the abandoned Niagara Canning Company in 1996 and slowly began to convert the sprawling 50-year-old brick cannery into a wine and food lover's paradise. Together with business partner Newman Smith, they cultivate 2 vineyards planted exclusively with vinifera grapes (and one hybrid, Vidal Blanc, for late harvest and icewine). Strewn Lakeshore Vineyard is a small property adjacent to the winery. It is 10.5 acres in size, with 5 acres planted at a density of 930 vines per acre. Most of the vineyard is flat with Vittoria reddish-hued sand over lacustrine silt loam. The western third of the property has a significant west-facing slope down to the eastern edge of Four Mile Creek and is composed of clay alluvium with variable floodplain deposits of clay and loam. There are 2.5 acres of Gewürztraminer, 1 acre of Pinot Blanc, and 1.5 acres of Sauvignon Blanc, all dating back to 1997. These 3 cold-sensitive varieties were chosen for this site because of the proximity of the lake and its moderating effects in winter and also because they ripen early in a "cool summer location." The other Strewn Vineyard on Line 1 is a 21-acre parcel with almost 16 acres under vine. This is a flat and gently undulating site with mostly sandy soil including a few patches of clay and some of sandy loam. It is irrigated and underdrained. Here, the plant density is 910 vines per acre with 1.25 acres of Cabernet Franc, 4.25 acres of Cabernet Sauvignon, 2.3 acres of Merlot, 1.5 acres of Pinot Blanc, 2.2 acres of Riesling, and 2.5 acres Vidal Blanc. Most of these vines were put into the ground between 1995 and 1999. Will practises shoot thinning, leaf removal, and top trimming to manage vigour, irrigates only when the vines are severely parched, crop thins to limit tonnage, and harvests as late as possible to maximize ripeness. Additional grapes are purchased from up to 10 neighbouring vineyards. Besides the winery, the couple runs Canada's first winery cooking school and have leased space to a restaurant. The Wine Country Cooking School, managed by Langdon, explores the relationship between wine and food. Local food experts conduct hands-on and demonstration classes using local produce and, of course, the very local wines. The restaurant, called Terroir La Cachette, is an all-window dining room with an outdoor patio and features Provençal-style bistro menus using regional and seasonal ingredients to highlight the quality and style of Strewn wines.

Winemaker: Joe Will / Vineyard Manager: Joe Will

Strewn wines are distinguished as follows:
Strewn Two Vines: Affordable introductory-level wines.
Strewn: Premium wines in a variety of styles.
Strewn Terroir: Super-premium wines made only in great years and only of the best grapes of the particular vintage. Prior to 1999, these were labelled "Strewn Vineyard," and before 1996 as "Reserve."

Strewn Two Vines Label
Riesling-Gewürztraminer [NP] **2003** ★ ★ ★ ☆ → Very pale gold with some peach-pink reflections. Inviting bouquet of orange, peach, lemon, honey, and confectioner's sugar. Balanced palate with a nice mix of sweetness and bitterness. Perfect for Raclette cheese. Drink now-2009.
Cabernet Merlot [NP] **2002** ★ ★ ★ → Garnet with red fruit and black-berry aromas. Light, fresh, and quaffable. Drink now-2007.

Strewn Label
Cabernet Franc [NP] **2002** ★ ★ ★ ↗ Garnet with an aroma that starts off leafy, turns creamy, then hints at charred plums. Soft

creamy texture with focused flavours of raspberry and bramble-berry. Green leafy aftertaste. Drink now-2010.

Cabernet Sauvignon [NP] **2002** ★ ★ ★ ↗ Garnet with a tobacco-leaf aroma. Clean, pure, red-fruit flavours. Drink now-2012.

Riesling [NP] **2003** ★ ★ ★ → Pale straw shade with bouquet of grapefruit, lime, and ginger ale. Tart, fresh taste. Drink now-2008.

Riesling, Botrytis-Affected [NP] **2001** ★ ★ ★ ★ ↗ *Gold, Toronto Wine & Cheese Show 2003.* Pale amber gold. Striking nose of honey, crème brûlée, and white-chocolate truffles. Rich, lush, and complex with unctuous flavours of orange zest and burnt brown sugar. Drink now-2013.

Riesling, Late Harvest [NP] **2001** ★ ★ ★ ↗ Bright gold with an off-putting pickle and sauerkraut nose. Tastes fine with a soft medium sweetness. Drink now-2007.

Riesling, Semi-Dry [NP] **2003** ★ ★ ★ → *Best General List White, Cuvée 2005.* Silvery gold with green reflections. Aromas of white peach and lemon and a soft, fresh, balanced taste. Drink now-2007.

Sauvignon Blanc [NP] **2003** ★ ★ ☆ ↻ Pale gold with a clean grassy aroma with hints of raw asparagus. Lemony palate with a hint of pithy bitterness in the aftertaste.

Strewn Terroir Label

Cabernet Franc [NP] **2001** ★ ★ ★ ↗ Starts out funky, with sour milk and hydrogen disulfide notes, but soon opens to dense, toasty, oaky, chocolate, and spice flavours. I'd prefer to see more fruit flavour but that could still emerge with aging. Drink 2006-2009. **1999** *Gold, All Canadian Wine Championships 2001.*

Cabernet Sauvignon [NP] **2002** ★ ★ ★ ☆ ↗ Garnet with a wild black-cherry fragrance and zippy black-currant flavours. Expect this to develop quite slowly. Drink now-2014.

Chardonnay, French Oak [NP] **2002** ★ ★ ★ ★ ↗ Straw-gold with an elegant caramel, vanilla, smoke, and oak bouquet. Delicate flavours in a full-bodied wine. Gulpable and classy. Drink now-2008.

Chardonnay, Strewn Vineyard [NP] **2001** ★ ★ ★ ☆ ↗ Gold hue with a lovely caramel, vanilla, and light cream nose. Full-bodied with a dusty texture of unfiltered black coffee and nut skins. Drink now-2007. **1998** *Gold, All Canadian Wine Championships 2000.*

Gewürztraminer [NP] **2000** *Gold, All Canadian Wine Championships 2003; Gold, Ontario Wine Awards 2003.*

Merlot, Strewn Vineyard [NP] **2001** ★ ★ ★ ☆ ↗ *Gold & Best of Category, All Canadian Wine Championships 2004.* Deep garnet with green pepper notes. Big, fruity, and tannic with a taste of barely ripe plum. Drink 2007-2013.

Riesling [NP] **2002** ★ ★ ★ → Petrol notes are beginning to emerge but cosmetic flavours dominate at this time. **2000** *Gold, Concours Mondial, Belgium 2003.*

Riesling Reserve [NP]   **1995**★★↘ Lemon-lime with good balance, though flavours are a bit light. Drink soon.

Strewn Three [NP]   The winery's flagship red, produced only in the best years. **2002**★★★★↗ (CF10/CS30/M60) Garnet with a dense but undeveloped nose. Sweet, lush black-cherry fruit flavours and mouth-drying pencil-lead tannins. Should grow up to be a very fine and elegant wine, but for now it needs its beauty sleep. Drink 2008-2015. **2001**★★☆→ (CF10/CS45/M45) Dark garnet with a subdued leafy nose with a barely noticeable undertone of Asian lady beetle. Big black cherry-fruit with dusty tannins but the ALB spoils the finish. Drink now-2011. **1999**★★★☆↗ (CF45/CS35/M20) Light garnet with a milk chocolate and brambleberry bouquet. Silky, smooth palate with light plum flavours. Drink now-2014. **1998**★★★★↗ (CF25/CS35/M40) Deep garnet with a concentrated black-fruit nose. Beginning to soften up but far from ready. Juvenile fruit juice flavours for now. Drink 2008-2020.

Riesling Icewine [NP]   **2002**★★★★↗ Gold, Concours Mondiale, Belgium 2004. Like a concentrated pear compote. Light, sweet, and ridiculously luscious. Drink now-2015. **2000** Gold, Challenge International du Vin, France 2002; Gold, Toronto Wine & Cheese Show 2002. **1999** Gold, Toronto Wine & Cheese Show 2001.

Vidal, Icewine [NP]   **2002**★★★★→ Citadelles du Vin, VinExpo 2004. Harvested later than most. Pale gold colour with a taste that's sweet almost to the point of pain; not cloying, just super-concentrated with flavours of pineapple and triple sec. Drink now-2010. **2000** Gold, All Canadian Wine Championships 2002. **1999** Gold, Toronto Wine & Cheese Show 2004. **1997** Grand Gold, VinItaly 1999. **1996**★★★★→ Jury Prize for Highest Scoring Canadian Wine, Séléctions Mondiales, Montreal 1998. A huge icewine now fully mature.

• **SUGARBUSH VINEYARDS LTD.** (1286 Wilson Road, R.R.#1, Hillier, ON, K0K 2J0 / Phone: Not yet installed / Email: robert@sugar bushvineyards.ca / Website: www.sugarbushvineyards.ca)

(Est. 2002) There's no wine to sell yet, but Robert and Sally Peck have plans to build a winery and produce up to 6,500 cases within 10 years. So far, they've planted 8.5 of their 47 acres on Wilson Road not far from The Grange of Prince Edward and Huff Estates wineries. They grow Cabernet Franc, Chardonnay, Gamay, Gewürztraminer, Pinot Noir, and Riesling, all of it planted in 2002/2003 at a density of 1,200 vines per acre. The terrain is relatively flat with clay limestone soil.

    Winemaker: Robert Peck / Vineyard Manager: Robert Peck

Wines not yet available.

- **Sur Lie** – The wine was kept for a period of time in barrel or tank "on its lees." This is a production technique wherein spent yeast cells are left in the barrel along with the wine while it ages, helping to preserve the wine's youthful, fruity flavours and giving it a light, slightly spritzy zing. Some winemakers will stir the lees on a regular basis to develop more richness to the wine's fruitiness.

- **Sussreserve** – German expression for the small portion of sweet unfermented grape juice reserved for adding back to a fully fermented wine. The process gives sweetness to the wine while maintaining its natural balance and proportion.

- **SWALLOW VINEYARDS (Vineland, NP)** – Immediately south of Misek Vineyard.

- **TAWSE FAMILY WINERY INC.** (3955 Cherry Avenue, R.R.#1, Vineland, ON, L0R 2C0 / Phone: 905-562-9500 / Fax: 905-562-9600 / Email: info@tawsewinery.ca / Website: www.tawsewinery.ca)

(Est. 2001) Bay Street financier and Burgundy wine lover Moray Tawse bought the Vinc Vineyard immediately south of Lakeview Cellars. The property backs on to the escarpment with exposures to the north, east, and west and a gentle overall slope toward the lake. The soil here is entirely Chinguacousy clay loam till with irregular stones scattered throughout the soil. Seven acres of Chardonnay dating back to 1979 and 1.3 acres of Riesling from 1976 have been preserved, but other varieties were uprooted and replaced in 1998 with 2 acres of Cabernet Franc and 6 acres of Merlot. Tawse added an additional 2 acres of Pinot Noir in 2002. Supplemental fruit was purchased from the Eastman, Hughes, and Laundry-Mottiar Vineyards to produce a total of 2,500 cases in 2003. The winery's objective is to make 5,000 cases annually by 2007.

Winemaker: Deborah Paskus / Vineyard Manager: Deborah Paskus

Cabernet Franc [NP] **2002**★★★☆↗ Deep garnet with a violet-pink rim. Nose offers dense black-fruit aromas and a hint of anti-septic powder. Thick, lush texture, sweet flavours of black cherry and table cream, and a tannic, slightly bitter finish. Drink 2006-2010.

Riesling, Semi-Dry, Carly's Block [NP] **2002**★★★☆↗ Beginning to show exciting hints of lime and petrol in the bouquet. Austere at first but opens to lemon-lime flavours and grapefruit finish. Racy acidity and mineral structure bode well for the future development of this wine. Drink now-2012.

- **Temkin-Paskus** – They call themselves cultivators of fine wine, but they're much more than that. In the late 1980s, Toronto writer and wine lover Stephen Temkin founded and wrote *The Wine Companion*, a newsletter of wine-tasting notes à la Robert M. Parker Jr.'s *The Wine Advocate*. After its run of about 3 years, Temkin worked as a wine buyer for Scaramouche, a top-ranked Toronto eatery. On one of his many visits to wine country, he met Deborah Paskus, a grape grower and vineyard manager at French Oak Vineyards, now called Thirty Bench Vineyards. During that first encounter, Temkin postulated that great wine could never be made in Niagara unless certain conditions and traditions were followed. Over time, they talked, they debated, they argued. Then, they agreed to co-produce a special cuvée of Chardonnay following his model. Paskus would do the winemaking, while Temkin would coach her in the traditional Burgundian techniques of the great producers. These included: strict vineyard management and ruthless crop thinning at verai-son to produce low yields of less than 3 t. per acre, full physiologic and phenolic maturation on the vine, hand-harvesting, careful sorting to discard unhealthy or underripe bunches, whole-cluster pressing, slow fer-mentation in barrel, undisturbed lees contact, and gentle gravity bottling without filtration. The results were stunning. The wine sold out quickly in the restaurant under the exclusive Scaramouche label. Prior to the com-pletion of their third vintage, Temkin parted company with the restaurant and the pair decided to sell their wine privately, labelled "Cuvée Temkin-Paskus." To do this they would have to produce it under the licence of an existing winery. Their first 2 crushes (1991 and 1992) were at Reif Estate; in 1993, they switched to Cave Spring Cellars, then in 1994 to Thirty Bench. There, they produced 2 barrels of wine, one of which was left to ferment completely on its own, using natural ambient yeast. The experi-ment worked and the 1994 vintage was an exceptional Chardonnay. In an August 1995 letter to friends and customers, Temkin wrote, "It smells so good, we're having trouble keeping our noses out of the bung hole." In 1997, they moved to the Malivoire winery, then Thirteenth Street, and currently the wine is being produced at Tawse Family Winery. The primary achievement of the Temkin-Paskus co-production was to create Canada's first cult wine and, thus, to force the industry to face the reality that better wines could be made in Ontario. Although many of the established wineries do their best to ignore the "dynamic duo," several new players have joined the industry in recent years with a similar passion for finding the purest expression of Ontario soils.

Chardonnay, Cuvée Temkin-Paskus [NP]   **2001** Not produced due to Asian lady beetle. **2000** Not produced. Deborah had a busy year and was not able to baby the wine in her usual manner. **1999** ★ ★ ★ ★ ☆ → Deep gold. **1998** ★ ★ ★ ★ ★ → A small per-centage of Eastman Vineyard grapes were blended in. Absolutely sweet with ripeness. Rich, potent, packed with complexity and showing a wide range of flavours including lemon peel, tangerine, guava, apricot, buckwheat honey, mango chutney, nutmeg, clove, and even goose fat. Profoundly deep and complex with wave after wave of flavour. Clarified butter, butterscotch, almond tuiles, toasted hazelnuts. Thick texture perfectly balanced with mouth-cleansing acidity. Drink now-2010. **1995** ★ ★ ★ ★ → Two barrels produced. **1994** ★ ★ ★ ★ → Yield approached 2.5 t. per acre. Two barrels produced. One was inoculated with yeast; the other left to ferment on its own natural yeasts. The final blend was comprised of 40% inoculated wine and 60% naturally fermented wine. It is softer, deeper, more forward, and more giving than previous vintages. It has higher alcohol (14%) and slightly lower acidity. Richly layered and tremendously complex, when I tasted it, in March and again in December 1996, it was still undeveloped and somewhat subdued by oak. By December 1997, it had opened considerably, with a perfectly balanced lemony acidity, a sweet, pie-crust toastiness, coconut, white chocolate, and a buttery toffee taste reminiscent of Polish "cow" candies. About 525 bottles produced. Drink now. **1993 ★ ★ ★ ★ →** Yield was 1.5 t. per acre, more by nature than by choice. Fermented in a refinished Vosges oak barrel, left on the lees for 15 months, and bottled in January 1995. Caramel, burnt butter, pastry with custard, and baked apple flavours. Extremely rich, alcoholic (13.8%), very complex with good high acidity and great structure. Reminiscent of a very fine white Burgundy from a top producer. Only 296 bottles produced. Drink up. **1992** Not produced. The pair were unhappy with the results, so they sold the entire production. **1991 ★ ★ ★ ↘** Grapes were from Kew Vineyard. Rich, deep hue; viscous with thick, hanging legs; nose full of ripe fruit with undertones of hazelnut, clarified butter, and fresh-baked pastry dough; mouth-filling, alcoholic (13.2%), and heavily layered with rich fruit flavours. Outstanding. By December 1997, bottle #96 had developed notes of oxidation as well as some lactic/sour cream flavours. Acidity and high alcohol continue to preserve it. There were 240 bottles (all gone now) produced under the Scaramouche Restaurant label and another 282 with the Temkin-Paskus label, though I doubt there's more than a half-dozen bottles still in existence today. Drink soon or hold for its historic value and/or its collector appeal.

- **Terroir** – A descriptive term of French origin that takes into account all the factors that can affect the quality of the fruit of the vine: climate, weather, surface soil, bedrock, latitude, elevation, aspect and slope, orientation of the vine rows and neighbouring geological properties. Also, a brand name used by Strewn Winery.

- **THIESSEN VINEYARD (Niagara-on-the-Lake, NP)** – This property on the East West Line grows Cabernet Sauvignon, Chardonnay, Pinot Noir, and Vidal Blanc. Grapes were sold to Pillitteri but now are sold to various other wineries.

- **THIRTEENTH STREET WINERY** (3983 Thirteenth Street, Jordan Station, ON, L0R 1S0 / Phone: 905-562-9463 / Fax: 905-562-8766 / Email: craftwines@13thstreetwines.com / Website: www.13th streetwines.com)

(Est. 2000) Equal partners in the winery are Gunther H. Funk Vineyard Inc. – which in turn is owned by Gunther Funk and Herb Jacobson – and Sandstone Vineyard Wine Inc. – owned by St. Catharines lawyer Ken Douglas and grower Erwin Willms. Wines are made from grapes sourced from 25 acres of owned vineyards as well as from grapes purchased from neighbours such as Paragon Vineyard, located directly across the road from the winery and from other growers, including David Dyck and Don Eastman. Current volume is about 2,700 cases in an average vintage; however, the group plans to cap production at 4,000 cases.

Winemakers: Herb Jacobson (1998-present, Funk Label); Ken Douglas (1998-present, Sandstone Label) / Vineyard Managers: Gunther Funk (G.H. Funk Vineyard); Erv Willms (Sandstone Vineyard)

Cabernet-Merlot, G.H. Funk Vineyards [NP] **2002**★★★↗
Deep garnet with a clean, thick, ripe, jammy nose of fruits and berries. Big, juicy flavours, lean structure, and a slightly dusty, tannic finish. Drink 2006-2012.

Chardonnay Reserve, Sandstone Vineyard [NP] **2002**★★★★↗
Deep gold with an oaky, vanilla, lemon, caramel, and smoked herbal bouquet. So ripe it has rich, implicit sweetness. Powerful, opulent, and extremely concentrated. Drink 2006-2010.

Gamay, Estate-Bottled, Sandstone Vineyard [NP]
2002★★★☆↗ Brilliant ruby colour with a jammy black raspberry and tobacco nose. Superb depth – the fruit sings a high-pitched melody to my palate – and has terrific, balanced acidity. Awesome for a simple Gamay. Drink now-2007.

Gamay Reserve, Sandstone Vineyard [NP] **2001**★★★★→
Ethereal floral notes with flavours of raspberry and blackberry. Drink now-2009. **2000**★★★☆→ Lovely texture with vibrant cassis notes. Drink now-2007. **1999**★★★★→ Deep raspberry flavours that remind me more of an adolescent Bordeaux than a Gamay. Drink now-2007. **1998**★★★☆→ Holding up, like an old northern Rhône wine with intense black cherry, tobacco, chocolate, leather, and game flavours. Supple texture. Drink now.

Erv's Burger Blend [NP] **2002**★★★↻ Packed with bold blackfruit flavours. Big boned and somewhat rustic, but perfect for the intended target.

Meritage, Sandstone Vineyard [NP] **2000**★★→ A horrible year for Bordeaux varieties. Harsh, weedy, with green pepper flavours. Drink now or give away.

Merlot [NP] **2002**★★★↗ Garnet with a high-toned berry nose of cassis, raspberry, and cranberry and an undertone of licorice. Smooth, supple, and very delicious. Drink now-2010.

Merlot, Funk Vineyard [NP] **2001**★★★★↗ Deep garnet with a brilliant, pure fruit nose. Soft, supple, and full-bodied. Drink 2007-2012. **1998**★★★★↗ A field blend of approximately CS20/M80.

Opaque garnet with brooding black-fruit flavours. Tough structure but great balance. Drink now-2012.

Pinot Gris, Late Harvest [NP] **2002**★★★↻ Full, rich, balanced, simple, and quaffable.

Pinot Noir, Funk Vineyard [NP] **2002**★★★★↑ Rich ruby with a ripe cherry and warm, damp-earth bouquet. Hints of cherry, plum, and spice. This is a truly lush mouthful. Hold for more complexity. Drink 2006-2010. **2001**★★★★☆→ Quite closed when I last tasted it; however, it was solid, with dense fruit and sturdy tannins. Should be coming around nicely now. **2000**★★★→ Nice cherry-berry flavours, but it's a touch alcoholic. Drink now. **1999**★★★↘ Fabulous but showing considerable maturity now. **1998**★★★★→ Very Burgundian with a silky, sweet mid-palate. Drink now.

Premier Cuvée, G.H. Funk Vineyards [NP] A Chardonnay/Pinot Noir blend. **2002**★★★★↗ Brilliant, silvery-gold hue with a rich, creamy mousse and everlasting beads of pinprick-sized bubbles. Extremely fine nose of toast, lemon, and well-aged Columbian weed. Fresh limey taste with some complexity. Aging will bring more depth to the glass. Drink now-2008. **1999**★★★★→ Outstanding mousse of minuscule, fast-rising bubbles. Flavours of lemon, grapefruit, roasted almonds, and yeasty bread dough. Great length and elegance. Will hold at least till 2009.

Riesling, Funk [NP] **2003**★★★☆↗ Silvery with a hint of lime and nuances of lemon drops coated in confectioner's sugar. Lovely taste with more sweetness than a Kabinett but less than a Spätlese. Drink 2006-2013. **2002**★★★★↗ Colourful fragrance. Lime, orange, and lemon aromas seem to play off each other. Terrific zing. Drink now-2014.

Riesling, Sparkling Wine, Paragon Estate Vineyards [NP] **NV**★★★↻ Brilliant silvery hue with a delicate, biscuity, tobacco, floral bouquet. Clean, candied, apple-y flavour. Best drunk young and fresh.

Rosé, Sparkling Wine, Funk [NP] **2002**★★★☆↻ Pretty pink colour with an exceptionally foamy mousse that takes forever to subside. Fine, light strawberry and red-currant aroma. Clean with a red-apple flavour. Best drunk fresh.

Syrah [NP] **2001**☒ Asian lady beetle taint present. **1997**★★☆→ Solid structure with good balance but not a lot of character when I tasted it in 2002.

• **THIRTY BENCH WINES** (4281 Mountainview Road South, Beamsville, ON, L0R 1B0 / Phone: 905-563-1698 / Fax: 905-563-3921 / Email: wine@thirtybench.com / Website: www.thirtybench.com)

(Est. 1994) Incorporated in 1980 as the collective venture of a casual group of home winemakers to secure their own source of grapes. They first purchased a fruit farm near Thirty Mile Creek along the edge of the Beamsville Bench, called it Heritage Vineyards, and planted 25 acres of Riesling. In 1983, the name was changed to French Oak Vineyards. The small quantity of grapes that made up their first harvest was sold to members of the collective but, as quantities grew, outside buyers were courted. In 1985, Andrés bought 5 t. of the Riesling grapes and, the following year, French Oak Vineyards began to supply Cave Spring Cellars. Interest in premium Ontario wines was increasing annually at a staggering rate during these preVQA years and the need for quality grapes kept surging. By 1991, the consortium added 5 acres of red varieties, with Cabernet Franc, Cabernet Sauvignon, Merlot, Pinot Meunier, and Pinot Noir. In 1993, a small winery was built and the name changed again, to Thirty Bench Vineyard and Winery. The numbers and names of members in the consortium has changed over the years, but the key players are 3 original winemaker partners. Each has his own specialty, each his own particular domain. Dr. Tom Muckle makes the unoaked Chardonnays, the unoaked reds, and the Rieslings – oaked, unoaked, limited yield, dry, semi-dry, whatever. Professor Yorgos Papageorgiou creates the BIG reds and the BIG whites – Meritage, the Reserve red blends, as well as barrel-fermented and barrel-aged Chardonnays. Franz Zeritsch produces the late harvest and icewines, the sherry-style wine and Mountainview Blush. Two vineyards owned by the winery include the 34-acre Thirty Bench Vineyard – the original fruit farm located on the east side of Mountainview Road – and a newer, larger parcel adjacent to it on its north side, which runs all the way down to Highway 8. Together, the two parcels completely surround the winery buildings. The older vineyard is a 35-acre parcel with a north/northeast facing slope of Oneida clay loam on the first bench of the Niagara Escarpment. Almost all of it is planted with Riesling at 1,150 vines per acre. There are 3 acres of Geisenheim clone #3 (a Rheingau clone) planted in 1980 and another 20 acres of the more aromatic Weis clone #21 (a Mosel clone). The field to the right of the winery, on the south side of the buildings, is the first experimental block of reds, including Cabernet Franc (.33 acre), Cabernet Sauvignon (2.5 acres), Merlot (.5 acre), Pinot Meunier (.5 acre), and Pinot Noir (.33 acre), with 3 rows of 24 additional experimental varieties. The "new" vineyard, as they continue to refer to it, lies on the north side of the older one, with Lenko Vineyard just east of it. It is a 42-acre property with 35 acres planted in 1999, predominantly with red varieties to supply the demand for their concentrated reserve reds, but also has the winery's first Chardonnay planting, which some day will be used to make a reserve wine. Vineyard manager Marek Maniecki sees to it that Thirty Bench grapes are some of the last to be harvested in the region. Over the years, grapes also have been purchased from neighbouring vineyards, including Atalick, Caralou, Steve Kocsis, Prydatkewycz, Reif Estates, and Van Bers. Labels of premium wines often indicate the name of the source vineyard. Winemaking philosophy here is to make many small artisanal lots from classic varieties with heavily restricted yields picked much later than normal harvest times. Consequently, navigating one's way through the vast array of labels can be confusing. Reds are left to macerate on the skins for 3 or more weeks after fermentation in the belief that the astringent tannins that leach into the juice during fermentation will drop out in the fourth week or so. Most of the reds, as a result, are softer and more approachable in their youth, while still having serious aging potential. Prices are high, but the quality of the finished product is, in many cases, stunning. Current production is 9,000 cases annually.

Winemakers: Jessica Ash (assistant); Thomas Muckle; Yorgos Y. Papageorgiou; Franz Zeritsch / Vineyard Manager: Marek Maniecki

Baco Noir [NP] **2003** ★ ★ → Intensely fruity smell but at the same time it has a dirty twang to it. Flavour leans to blackberry with a tart, dried-fruit note and somewhat coarse finish. Drink now-2008.

Cabernet [NP] Grapes were thinned to 2 t. per acre 1 month before harvest, macerated on the skins for 3 full weeks, and 1 year in Allier casks, then bottled unfiltered. **1994** ★ ★ ★ → *Best Canadian Red, Toronto Wine & Cheese.* (CF18/CS80/M2) Sweet and herbal with concentrated berry and asparagus nuances. 78 cases made. Fully mature. Drink now-2010. (*In 1995, this wine was renamed Reserve Blend and, in 2000, became part of the Benchmark series.*)

Cabernet Franc, "American Oak" [NP] **2002** ★ ★ ★ ★ → Rich, full, oaky nose with a pralines-and-cream sweetness and black-cherry pie flavours. Drink now-2012.

Cabernet Franc, Atalick Vineyard [NP] **2002** ★ ★ ★ ★ ↗ Cherry-garnet colour with a light, strawberry-cherry flavour. Bright fruity taste and clean finish. Drink now-2012.

Cabernet Franc, "Canadian Oak" [NP] **2002** ★ ★ ★ ★ ↑ Deep, rich, elegant bouquet of black cherry, raspberry, oak, and hazelnut skins, like baked pastry. Plummy with greater finesse than the American oak version. Drink 2006-2014.

Cabernet Franc, "No Oak" [NP] **2002** ★ ★ ★ ↻ Pale garnet with a jammy, fresh nose of black cherry and raspberry. Drink now.

Cabernet Franc, Reserve [NP] **1999** *Gold, International Wine & Spirit Competition, London.* Drink now-2010. **1998** ★ ★ ★ ★ ↗ Just beginning to enter its peak years. Opaque garnet with a brick-coloured rim. Closed unyielding bouquet to start, over the hours it generates layer after layer of interesting spices and flavours. With 15.2% alc./vol., there's no hurry. Drink now-2020. **1996** ★ ★ ★ ↘ Pale strawberry red with some browning around the edge. Taste still has healthy fruit flavour but smell was funky at opening. Ten (!) days later the same bottle was much improved, displaying pruney, dried-fruit flavours. Drink now-2010. **1995** ★ ★ ★ ★ → Harvested at 2 t. per acre from the Thirty Bench estate vineyard. Deep, dark, and densely purple, concentrated black currant, and plum aromas, oak, sweet vanilla, toasted bread, roasted nuts, spice, and a huge tannic structure. 30 cases made. Drink now-2010.

Cabernet Franc, Tradition [NP]   Grapes are from the van Bers Vineyard. **2000**★ ★ ★ ➔ Ruby-garnet with a freshly cooked aroma of black currant and creamed corn. Good body with satiny texture and a clean, jammy finish. Drink now.

Chardonnay, Bench, Barrel Select [NP]   **2002**☒   Oxidative, chemical nose with a yeasty flavour. Two bottles tasted.

Chardonnay, Bench, Single Barrel Select [NP]   **2002**★ ★ ★ ☆ ➔ Yellow-gold with a subdued fruit nose and overtones of vanilla and oak. Big, potent, and mouth-filling. Only 250 numbered bottles produced. Drink now-2007.

Chardonnay, Estate [NP]   **2002**★ ★ ★ ↻ Good. Clean, light, fresh, ready.

Chardonnay Reserve, Reif Vineyard [NP]   From a 3-acre leased section of Klaus Reif's estate vineyard. Grapes are reduced to about 2 t. per acre. **2000**★ ★ ➔ Full-blown buttery nose, heavily oaked, lactic, and somewhat alcoholic at 14.2% alc./vol. Gawky now, may still improve. Drink now-2007. **1999**★ ★ ★ ★ ➔ Bright gold with a fresh churned-butter aroma. 14.9% alc./vol. Full, rich palate, with tropical flavours of broiled grapefruit, vanilla cream, and honey. Drink now. Match with lobster or crab. **1998**★ ★ ★ ★ ↘ Rich gold colour with a thick bouquet of brown butter and toasted rye. Much improved from the "monster" status of its youth. Supple and strong but still a touch hot at 14.3% alc./vol. Drink now-2008. **1995**★ ★ ★ ↘ *Two Golds, Toronto Wine & Cheese, 1997; Gold, Hamilton Wine & Food Expo, 1997.* Good concentration with flavours of lemon and thickened cream. Now passing its prime.

Gewürztraminer, Late Harvest [NP]   **2002**★ ★ ★ ⬈ Still somewhat undeveloped with weak aromatics. Balanced with flavours of apple skin and orange pith. Drink now-2010.

Gewürztraminer-Pinot Gris, Late Harvest [NP]   **2002** ★ ★ ★ ⬈ In this 50/50 blend, the PG adds flesh to the bones of the Gewürz. Herbal, oily, spiced, and citrusy. Drink now-2011.

Kokkineli [nonVQA]   **NV**★ ★ ↻ Special-edition Greek-style red released in time for the Athens Olympics. Four varieties blended and flavoured with genuine Aleppo pine-tree resin. Sure tastes resinated . . . not bad, though.

Merlot, Estate-Bottled [NP]   **2002**★ ★ ★ ➔ (Unfiltered) Lovely, brooding wine with aromas of strawberry jam and scorched plums. Velvety texture with a hot, jammy finish. Drink now-2008. **1995**★ ★ ★ ★ ➔ *Gold, London International Wine & Spirit Competition, 1996.* Explosive nose of blackberry, black tea, and dark chocolate. Only 100 bottles produced. Drink now-2015.

Mountainview Blush [Ont]   **2002**★ ↻ (CF5/VB95) Onion-skin hue with oxidative notes. Flavours are of strawberry jam and old apples.

Mountainview White [Ont] **2000**★★↻ (R50/VB50) Gold with a slightly oxidative, candied grapefruit flavour. Sweetish and quaffable.

Pinot Gris-Gewürztraminer, Late Harvest [NP] **2002**★★★★↗ (Gew5/PG95) An unctuous, opulent, and amazing wine. A pleasure to hold, to swirl, to smell and, especially, to swallow. Drink now-2010.

Pinot Meunier-Riesling [NP] **1996**★★↘ (PM60/R40). Weird nose but tasty overall. Red currant and lime flavours. Imagine red Gewürztraminer. Fading.

Pinot Meunier-Rosé [NP] **1995**↓ A small portion of Cabernet Franc was added to boost colour and body. Very pale cherry red. Delicate nose of gently spiced, oxidized strawberries, sweet ripe flavour. Now dead.

Pinot Noir, Caralou Vineyard [NP] **1995**★★↘ Light and forward. Drink up. **1993**★★★↘ Deep and rich. Drink up.

Pinot Noir, Estate-Bottled [NP] **2002**★★★★↗ Powerful, totally juvenile, and packed with perfectly balanced cherry-berry fruit. Nuances of sandalwood, incense, earth, spices, and herbs grow with aeration. Long-lived and sensuously delicious. Drink now-2015. **2000** Gold, Canadian Wine Awards, 2003.

Reserve Blend [NP] **1998**★★★★↗ (CF28/CS58/M14) Opaque garnet to the rim. Plummy, powerful, rich, complex, and lasting. 15.1% alc./vol. Drink now-2018. **1997**★★★★→ (CF50/CS25/M25) Gold, London International Wine & Spirit Competition, 2000. Nature had its way with thinning these grapes. Deep ruby-garnet, watery around the rim. Bouquet of charred oak and baked fruit, plum pie. Full-bodied, plush mouthfeel. Maturing nicely. Drink now-2014. **1995**★★★★→ (CF25/CS50/M25) Two Golds, Toronto Wine & Cheese Show, 1998. Harvested at 2 t. per acre from the Thirty Bench estate vineyard. Gripping yet delicate. Huge, still-closed bouquet of flowers, berries, cedar, spices, and mocha. Only 30 cases made. Drink now-2020. (For earlier vintages, see Cabernet above; for later vintages, see Benchmark Label below.)

Retsina [nonVQA] **NV**★★★↻ Greek-style white released in time for the Athens Olympics. Chardonnay and Riesling blended and flavoured with genuine Aleppo pine-tree resin. Overpoweringly resinated flavour, but I would argue this is better than the imported stuff.

Riesling, Botrytis-Affected, Late Harvest [NP] **1994**★★★★→ From hand-picked grapes 85% affected by botrytis. Rich nose of boiled pear, peach, orange, fig, butter, and honey with elegant mushroom undertones. Like a classic German or Austrian Trockenbeerenauslese. Drink now-2020.

Riesling, Botrytis-Affected, Select Early Harvest [NP] **1995**★★★★→ From hand-picked grape bunches 35% affected by botrytis. Huge nose, wonderful complexity, deep flavours of apple, peach, and apricot with a walnut-skin aftertaste. Drink now-2015.

Riesling, Dry, Estate-Bottled [NP] **1999** ★ ★ ★ → Rich, implicitly sweet, and full-bodied but has an oxidative note. Drink soon. **1995** ★ ★ ★ → An almost oily texture results from high alcohol (14.1% alc./vol.), giving this wine a ponderous Alsace-like intensity. A honeyed, floral perfume is followed by pure, ripe fruit flavours. Drink now-2007. **1994** ★ ★ ↘ Light, nondescript nose. Clean, dry, and citrusy. Just 400 cases made. Drink up.

Riesling, Dry, Reserve [NP] Produced from the Geisenheim clones. **1995** ★ ★ ↘ Deep flavours of tart orange candy. Drink now. **1994** ★ ★ ↘ Picked at 21-degree Brix with a touch of botrytis, giving it a nose that's both exciting and offensive. At first it seems oxidized and musty, but sweet lemon-custard flavours come through. Tom Muckle says it just needs time. Just 130 cases produced.

Riesling, Early Harvest [NP] **2003** ★ ★ ★ ★ → Only 5% alc./vol. Yummy with a fresh, light, juicy, clean, sweet, and appetizing taste of crisp white fruits. Has a hint of spritz. Drink while young and fresh.

Riesling, Icewine [NP] **2000** ★ ★ ★ ★ → Amber-gold with a bouquet of dried mango, candied papaya, and caramelized sugar. Sweet and slightly nutty. Drink now-2020. **1999** ★ ★ ★ ★ → Pale amber-gold with a smell of new plastic and aromas of candied pineapple, applesauce, and canned fruit cocktail. Very sweet and tart with hints of broiled lemon and walnut skin. Drink now-2020. **1998** ★ ★ ★ ★ ☆ → Amber hue with hints of dried orange peel and honey. Thick and very sweet with flavours of honey, spice, and orange-butter sauce, as for Crepes Suzette. Drink now-2020. **1996** ★ ★ ★ ★ → *Gold, Hamilton Food & Wine Expo, 1998.* Intense spiced apple, pear, and lychee flavours. Drink now-2010. **1995** ★ ★ ★ ★ →. Drink now-2015. **1994** ★ ★ ★ ★ → Lemon, asparagus, new plastic, honey, mango, papaya, creme, caramelized sugar. Great acidity, adds a razor-thin edge to this very sweet wine, giving it a long and cleansing aftertaste. Drink now-2012. **1992** ★ ★ ★ ★ → Less acid zing than the 1994 but somewhat more exotic flavours and thicker texture in the middle palate. Drink now.

Riesling, Limited Yield, Barrel-Fermented, Dry [NP] **1999** ★ ★ → Over-oaked. Fruit is completely overshadowed. Drink now. **1998** ★ ★ ★ → The first experimental batch. Fruit is boxed in by a nutty, woody taste. Drink now or hope it survives to 2008.

Riesling, Limited Yield, Canadian Oak [NP] **2003** ★ ★ ★ ☆ → Walks a tightrope with delicate balance of dry, spicy oak and sweet, mandarin-orange flavours.

Riesling, Limited Yield, Semi-Dry [NP] **2003** ★ ★ ★ ★ → Sweet Auslese-style with delicious peach and lemon-custard flavours. Balanced and luscious. Drink now-2013.

Riesling, Semi-Dry [NP] From the Weis clone. **1999** ★ ★ ★ ↘ Rich gold with a well-developed petrol nose. Honey, apple, and cooked egg whites in a crisp, clean, fine product. Drink now-2007.

1994★★→ *Gold, Toronto Wine & Cheese, 1996.* A small percentage of icewine was added in place of sussreserve. Crisp, clean, deeply perfumed, with intense tangerine hints. Beautifully balanced with pure fruit sweetness and racy acidity. 130 cases made. Drink now.

Riesling, Semi-Sweet [NP] Geisenheim clone. **1999★★★↘** Wow! Sweet as a German Auslese with rich, liquerlike flavours of pear, apple, honey. Lively, with time to go. Drink now-2011. **1995★★★↘** A blend of the Riesling Dry with 8% fresh juice and 4% icewine blended back. Well balanced, fruity, fresh, and delicious. Drink soon.

Riesling, Select Dry, Thirty Bench Vineyard [NP] **1996★★★↘** Has creamy, cheesy notes with a taste of tart russet apple and a washed-out mid-palate. Drink soon.

Riesling, Select Semi-Dry, Thirty Bench Vineyard [NP] **1998★★★↗** Fresh and grapefruity with thick syrupy texture and solid structure. Drink now-2008.

Riesling, Thirty Bench Vineyard [NP] **2000★★★→** Aromatic with nuances of spice, herbs, earth, and sweat. At its peak. Drink now.

Riesling, Very Early Harvest [NP] **2004★★★↻** *(Tank sample)* Bursts into fizz as soon as the cork is pulled. Silvery-gold shade with some sedimented tartrate crystals falling into the glass. Aroma similar to Moscato d'Asti, but there's an unfiltered, yeasty flavour that should disappear once the wine is fined, filtered, and bottled.

Solara [NP] **NV★★★↻** Vidal and Sauvignon Blanc blended, fortified, and aged from 4-7 years as sherry would be in the south of Spain. Strong, nutty, medium-dry, and terrific. Try over ice with lemon and soda or sip lightly chilled to warm up an autumn appetite.

Trillium Red [NP] **1999★★↻** Five classic vinifera varieties (both red and white) are blended into this light, floral, fruity, and clean Lambrusco-like sipper. A perfect little patio wine. Drink now.

Vidal-Riesling [NP] A "fun" wine with the fuller texture and peachy fruit flavours of Vidal combined with the lemony acidity and spiciness of Riesling. Later renamed Mountainview White. **1996★★↘** (60/40) Once crisp, clean, now tired. **1995★↘** (70/30) Peachy flavours, short finish. Tired.

Benchmark Label

Blend [NP] **2002★★★☆↑** (CF35/CS15/M50) Deep garnet with black-cherry and plum flavours. Lush texture and excellent balance. Drink 2007-2016. **2002★★★☆↑** (CF50/CS25/M25) Another version of the basic blend. Garnet with a closed, plummy nose with nuances of chocolate pudding. Tart, plummy fruit flavour. Drink 2006-2014. **2001★★★★↗** (CF50/CS25/M25) Deep garnet with a sweet fruit surface smell and green, leafy undertones. Seems a touch sharp and out of kilter at first, but within the hour it opens up lean, balanced fruit. Drink now-2013. **2000★★★★☆↗** (CF40/CS12/M48) Garnet and more open than younger wines. Bouquet of black currant, black cherry, raspberry, and plum. Charming. Drink now-2016.

Cabernet Franc, Reserve [NP]　**2002★★★☆↗** Garnet with a slightly pruney and raisiny nose that suggests cough syrup. Concentrated fruit and mouth-drying tannins. Somewhat unidimensional. Drink now-2012.

Cabernet Sauvignon, Reserve [NP]　**2002★★★↑** Garnet with distinctly hotter fruit. Perhaps more charred than stewed. Very, very tasty with stiff fruit flavours that still need relaxing. Drink 2007-2016.

Chardonnay, Prydatkewycz Vineyard [NP]　**2002★★★→** Rich gold hue with a light, scented pear and honey bouquet. Brilliant balance of oak and fruit. Drink now-2010. **2001★★★→** Gold with an aromatic nose of spiced nuts, orange, toffee, vanilla cheesecake, and fruit salad. Full-bodied. Drink now-2008.

Chardonnay, Steve Koscis Vineyard [NP]　**2000★★★→** *Gold, Canadian Wine Awards, 2003.* Big, buxom, complex, and alcoholic. Smells of well-buttered corn on the cob. Highly extracted, sweet, thick, and syrupy texture. Drink now-2010. **1998★★★★→** Golden hue with nose of warm croissant. Youth is gone but middle age looks good. Drink now-2008. **1995★★★★↘** Amazingly deep flavour concentration. Pear syrup, mandarin essence, light toast, well buttered. Drink soon. **1994★★☆↘** Barrel-fermented and barrel-aged. Fullish, good concentration of flavours though light structure. "Burgundian" with long, clean fruit finish. Only 48 cases made.

Chardonnay, Thirty Bench Vineyard [NP]　**2002★★★→** Amber-gold with a peachy aroma. Big, full, fat, and almost sticky-sweet in ripeness. Drink now-2008.

Pinot Noir [NP]　**2002★★★↑** Very dark ruby with concentrated pigment to the rim. Herbal, slightly vegetal nose with a dense, sweet, and ripe flavour and a tough, tannic finish. Needs time to relax. Drink 2008-2014.

Reserve Blend [NP]　**2002★★★★☆↑** (CF25/CS25/M50) A firecracker of a wine. Spot on. Inviting nose, plush palate, massive fruit, powerful tannins, long, tasty, harmonious, well-balanced finish. Drink 2007-2018. **2001★★★☆↑** (CF50/CS25/M25) A warm, maturing nose with a jammy side to it. Excellent body and balance, still has more to reveal. Drink 2006-2013. **2000★★★→** (CF40/CS12/M48) Ripe though not as deep and rich as the 2001. Also has a mildly disturbing dirty note right from the start. Maturing early but graciously. Drink now-2010. **1999★★★↗** *Gold, Toronto Wine & Cheese Show, 2002.* (CF27/CS27/M46) Drink now-2015. (*For earlier vintages, see Reserve Blend in the regular section.*)

- **THIRTY THREE VINES VINEYARD & WINERY** (9261 Loyalist Parkway [Highway 33], Conway, ON, K0K 2T0 / Phone: 613-373-1133 / Email: 33vines@sympatico.ca / Website: www.pec.on.ca/33vines/index.html)

(Est. 2004) Paul and Marylin Minaker are still at the good intentions stage. In 2003, they purchased a 13-acre farm with a house, a 100-year-old barn, and a red caboose in the County of Lennox and Addington overlooking Adolphus Reach Inlet. Since taking over the property, they have planted 5 acres of vines at 1,250 vines to the acre. There are 1.5 acres each of Chardonnay and Pinot Noir and 1 acre each of Cabernet Franc and Riesling. The vines are on a moderately steep, south-facing slope of clay loam over limestone about .5 km from the water. The Minakers will harvest their first crop in 2006. In the meantime, they plan to convert the barn into a production facility.

Winemaker: TBA / Vineyard Manager: Paul Minaker

Wines not yet produced.

- **THOMAS & VAUGHAN** (4245 King Street, Beamsville, ON, L0R 1B1 / Phone: 905-563-7737 / Fax: 905-563-4414 / Email: retail@thomasandvaughan.com / Website: www.thomasandvaughan.com)

(Est. 1998) Namesakes Thomas Kocsis and Barbara Vaughan started with 500 cases in their first year of production and built it up tenfold in 5 years. In June 2004, they sold the business – lock, stock, and French oak barrels – to Niagara Cellars Inc., a holding company that also owns EastDell Estates. The new ownership plans to turn the winery into a showcase of premium wines. The 40-acre estate lies across the road from Malivoire Wine Company. Thirty acres of south-facing, red clay loam soils are under vine. Plantings include Baco Noir, Cabernet Franc, 2 sections of Cabernet Sauvignon (4.5 acres planted in 2003 and a .5-acre block planted in 1998.) Chardonnay, De Chaunac, Merlot, Pinot Gris, Syrah, and 20-year-old Vidal Blanc. Vine density throughout is about 1,000 plants per acre. Annual production reached 5,000 cases in 2003, all of it produced exclusively from estate-grown grapes.

Winemakers: Scott McGregor (2004-present); Jason James (2004-present); Tom Kocsis (1999-2004); Megan Schofield (1998); Deborah Paskus (1997-1998, consulting) / Vineyard Manager: KCMS Consulting

Baco Noir [NP] **1999 ★ ➘** Inky-garnet colour. Awkward, floral nose of peony, geranium. Skunky, hybrid taste. Sharp acidity and astringent finish.

Cabernet [NP] **1997 ★ ★ ➘** Zippy, fresh, juicy fruity flavours of a few years ago have gone. A mushy blueberry/strawberry jamminess has set in. Drink now.

Cabernet Franc [NP] **2002**★★★☆↗ *Gold, All Canadian Wine Championships 2003; Gold, Toronto Wine & Cheese Show 2003.* Garnet with a rich black-fruit bouquet and charming minty notes. Big and full with some tough tannins in the background but plenty of complex fruit flavours that linger well into the aftertaste. Drink now-2012. **2000**★★★↗ Garnet with a bright, fruity, pine-resin bouquet. Supple texture, fruit flavours developing nicely. Drink now-2009.

Cabernet Franc, Reserve [NP] **2000**★★★★↑ *Gold, All Canadian Wine Championships 2004.* Deep garnet that is solid to the rim. Shy, closed nose at first, slowly opens to black tea, cedar, and cassis. Dry, dusty palate indicates much aging may be required. Drink 2007-2015.

Cabernet Sauvignon [NP] **1998**★★★☆→ *Gold, All Canadian Wine Championships 2001.* Intense, dark garnet hue with a superb bouquet of cassis, plum, tobacco, cedar, and spice. Ripe and nicely balanced. Drink now-2012.

Chardonnay, Vintners' Select [NP] **1997**★★★↘ Amber-gold with a rich aroma of peanut brittle. Medium-bodied, dry, and balanced. Drink up.

Chardonnay, Estate Reserve [NP] **2001**★★★→ Rich gold with tiny bubbles forming onto the inside surface of the glass. Full, oaky, buttered rum, caramel, and vanilla bouquet, big, bold flavours, and a powerful, balanced finish. Drink now-2007.

Marechal Foch [NP] **2002**★★★→ Deep garnet with a bright violet rim. Smoky, rustic black-cherry nose and taste with lean texture and a sweaty, herbal undertone. Drink now-2008. **2001**★★★→Opaque, inky-garnet colour with a thick, rustic plum and sour-cherry nose. Big, bold, full, and fat with balanced tannins. Drink now-2007. **1998**★★↘ Inky garnet with a mahogany rim. Characteristic gamy hybrid nose of wet earth, cooked black plums, ripe blackberry, and sweaty leather. Sweet vegetal bitterness in the finish. Drink up.

Meritage [NP] **2002**★★★☆↑ Deep garnet with a mahogany rim. Oaky herbal nose with locked-in flavours of plum and roasted coffee. Drink 2008-2016. **2001**☒ Overwhelming Asian lady beetle. **2000**★★★☆↗ *Gold, International Wine Challenge 2003; Gold, Ontario Wine Awards 2003; Best Red Wine, Toronto Wine & Cheese Show 2003.* (CF20/CS40/M40) Garnet hue with a rich coffee aroma. Has the signature plumminess. Drink now-2010. **1998**★★★☆→ Deep garnet. Rich, full nose of plums, vanilla, white chocolate, and cassis. Fleshy and full with lovely balance. Drink now-2015.

Meritage, Estate Reserve [NP] **2000**★★★★↗ *Gold, Ontario Wine Awards 2004.* Deep garnet colour with a thick black-fruit bouquet backed by green pepper notes. Still tough and tannic but plenty of fruit to balance. Drink now-2013.

Merlot [NP] **2001** ☒ Tainted with Asian lady beetle.

Pinot Grigio [NP] **2003** ★ ★ ☆ → Pale gold with miniature bubbles forming on the inside surface of the glass. Nondescript winy nose, simple flavours, solid texture, and refreshing acidity. Perfect with light hors d'oeuvres as it offers refreshment, without competing with delicate flavours. Drink now-2006.

Vidal [Ont] **1998** ★ ↘ Once light and spritzy, now tired.

Vidal, Icewine [NP] **2002** ★ ★ ★ ★ → *Best Dessert Wine, All Canadian Wine Championships 2004.* **1997** ★ ★ ★ ★ → Brilliant gold hue. Aromas of custard, baked apple, and spiced pear. Thick with the flavour of apple-butter. Not overly sweet. Drink now-2011.

Vidal, Old Vines [Ont] **2002** ★ ★ → Quaffable but unexciting. Off-dry.

Vidal, Semi-Sweet [Ont] **1999** ★ ★ ★ → *Gold, Burlington Wine Show 2001.* Bright, limpid, pale straw-gold. Healthy citrus nose with apple and spice notes. Balanced, medium-bodied, very pleasant. Drink now.

• **TINTERN VINEYARD (Vineland, NP)** – A 12-acre, west-facing vineyard owned by Vineland Quarries Ltd. and leased to Vailmont Vineyards. There are 3.5 acres of Cabernet Franc, 2.5 acres of Cabernet Sauvignon, and 4 acres of Chardonnay planted at a density of 1,281 vines per acre in the underdrained Oneida clay loam. Vines are bloom-thinned early in the season and fruit-thinned at veraison to provide an average yield of 4 t. per acre. Grapes are sold to Kittling Ridge Wines.

• **TOBE VINEYARD (Niagara-on-the-Lake, NP)** – This property near the lakeshore is managed by Kevin and Peter Buis. The fruit is sold to Hillebrand.

• **TOCCALINO VINEYARD (Milton, Ont.)** – One of the few successful vineyards cultivated outside of the standard DVAs. All grapes are grown on a 6-acre section of Andrews Acres, off Highway 25. Bert Andrews tried growing viniferas, but the heavy clay soil, severe winters, hungry birds, and hard-to-control powdery mildew convinced him to focus on hybrids. He has approximately .5 acre each of Baco Noir, Cayuga White, De Chaunac, L'Acadie Blanc, Leon Millot, Marechal Foch, Seyval Blanc, and Vidal Blanc. Most of the grapes are used to produce Halton Red and Halton White, the mainstay grape wines at Scotch Block Winery.

• **TREGUNNO FRUIT FARMS INC. (Niagara-on-the-Lake, NP)** – Philip and Lorna Tregunno and their three sons, Philip Jr., Ryan, and Jourdan, own 600 acres of land in 13 individual parcels along the Niagara Parkway between Line 4 and Line 6. The majority of their land is dedicated to cultivating tender fruits, including peaches, plums, and cherries. There are 85 acres of vinifera grapes planted at 1,200 vines per acre. They have 7 acres of Auxerrois, 8 acres of Cabernet Franc, 18 acres of Cabernet Sauvignon, 12 acres of Gamay Noir, 11 acres of Merlot, 8 acres of Riesling, 7 acres of Sauvignon Blanc, and 14 acres of Syrah. Soils range from the round river rock of the ancient riverbed along the Niagara Parkway to the Jeddo clay loams ubiquitous around Concession 1. This area historically gets the highest heat units in the peninsula. All fruit is contracted to Cave Spring Cellars and Andrés Wines.

- **Trius** – The premium brand of Hillebrand. VQA varietals are produced from estate grapes blended with purchased juice. The brand was introduced in 1989 with a wine labelled simply "Red." It was blended from the 3 classic Bordeaux grapes: Cabernet Franc, Cabernet Sauvignon, and Merlot. The series included a high-end Riesling, 3 Chardonnays, each from a different vineyard, and a sparkling wine produced using the traditional champagne method. In 2000, the winery introduced Grand Red, combining the 20 best barrels of each variety, and with the 2002 vintage, they added 3 single varietal reds.

Tasting notes listed under **Hillebrand Estates.**

- **Twenty Valley** – Brand name used by Cave Spring Cellars for wines produced from late-harvested Vidal Blanc and icewines. Most are sold to the local restaurant trade or in the export market. Some have found their way into Ontario's Vintages stores.

Tasting notes listed under **Cave Spring Cellars.**

- **TWOBRIDGES VINEYARDS (Milford, PEC)** – Peter and Renee Wheeler own 300 acres of prime land off Crowes Road near the village of Milford west of South Bay. They run a 50-acre woodlot and lease 200 acres to a local farmer. Since 2001, they have planted 7 acres of Baco Noir, Gamay Noir, Gewürztraminer, Pinot Noir, and St. Laurent at a density of 1,000 vines per acre. They intend to continue planting an additional 2 acres of grapes each year until they have 50 acres. Except for some ditching between the rows, there is no drainage system installed in their deep limestone soil and the gently sloped south-facing vineyards are not irrigated. By 2006, the Wheelers hope to farm completely organically. For now, the grapes are sold to Carmela Estates, but eventually they'll build their own winery. Their neighbours include Huff Estates Winery to the east, Black River Winery to the south, and Marshall Estates Winery to the west of their property.

- **VAILMONT VINEYARDS (Beamsville, Campden, Vineland, NP)** – Not so much a vineyard but a vineyard management company that looks after a group of leased, "custom care," or partnership sites under the direction of Roger Vail, the 1993 Ontario Grape King. These include CherryVail Vineyard, Niagara Bench Farms, Poole Farm, Stefanik Vineyard, Tintern Road Vineyard, and Vieni Estates. (See individual vineyard listings for details.)

- **VAN BERS VINEYARD (Jordan, NP)** – See Emerald Shore Vineyard

- **VAN DE LAAR FARMS (Niagara-on-the-Lake, NP)** – Second-generation grape growers Peter and Cathy Van de Laar have been supplying premium grapes for many years to Vincor for Inniskillin wines, for the Jackson-Triggs Grand Reserve series, and most recently for Vincor's transcontinental Unity label. The flat, 65-acre farm is situated next to the Niagara Parkway, sandwiched between the Inniskillin winery to the north and Riverview Cellars to the south. Here the soil is deep Chinguacousy clay loam, underdrained every 9 ft. and irrigated. Sixty acres are cultivated with Auxerrois (planted in 1983), Cabernet Franc (1988 and 1994), Cabernet Sauvignon (1989), Chardonnay (1980 and 1995), Gamay (1984), Merlot (1990), Riesling (1985 and 2002), Seyval Blanc (1998), Shiraz (2002), and Vidal Blanc (1980 and 1990), all spaced at 1,200 vines per acre. Fruit is thinned at veraison and leaf removal is practised to obtain optimal ripeness and quality. Viniferas are cropped at 3 t. to the acre, while hybrids average approximately 8 t. In 1985, Peter was chosen Ontario's Grape King.

- **Veraison** – This is the moment at which grapes begin to ripen. Having been hard and green for most of the summer, the fruit starts to change skin colour to yellow-green or red-black. The grapes enlarge, soften, and accumulate large amounts of fructose and glucose. This process normally occurs in August, once the grapes reach a Brix level of about 7 degrees. By thinning or cutting away some of the fruit at this time, the remaining grapes will ripen more quickly and achieve higher levels of concentration. Some growers refer to this process as green harvest.

- **Verjus** – From Old French, translated as green juice. Grapes cut away at the beginning of veraison are crushed and turned into a very sour juice that is used in medicine production or in cuisine in place of lemon or vinegar.

- **VIENI ESTATES INC. (Campden, NP)** – A large, north-facing, variably sloped property above the Niagara Escarpment on Fly Road near the village of Campden. Almost 126 of the 170 acres are planted with labrusca, hybrid, and vinifera varieties in the mixed Chinguacousy and Oneida clay loam till soils. Labrusca grapes are sold to Motts for juice, while other fruit is shared by Magnotta Winery and Stonechurch Vineyards.

- **VIEWPOINTE ESTATE WINERY** (151 County Road 50 East, Harrow, ON, N0R 1G0 / Phone: 519-738-4718, 519-738-2421 / Fax: 519-738-2211 / Email: jfancsy@viewpointewinery.com / Website: www.viewpointewinery.com)

(Est. 2001) Perhaps it's trite word play to call this a Fancsy winery, but once you've seen it, you may forgive me. Brothers John and Steve Fancsy and Steve's wife, Jean, have brought their shared vision to life with years of careful planning, inexhaustible energy, and barrels of money. Starting with the family farm, they saw an opportunity to develop a winery that would attract attention to Essex County as the economically and recreationally exciting region it was almost a century ago. There are 3 vineyards with 44 acres under vine. The oldest is Walnut Grove Vineyard, the 28-acre family farm that sits on the Lake Erie shoreline. Seventeen acres planted in 2000 and 2001 at a vine density of 1,360 plants per acre provide Auxerrois, Cabernet Franc, Cabernet Sauvignon, Chardonnay, Gewürztraminer, Merlot, Pinot Noir, Riesling, Sauvignon Blanc, Semillon, and Syrah. This parcel is south-facing, gently sloped toward the lake, and composed of lightly undulating Berrien sand. Surrounding the winery is the Viewpointe Vineyard, a 26-acre south-facing lakefront property with clay and Harrow sandy loam soil. There are 10 acres planted in 1999 with Cabernet Franc, Cabernet Sauvignon, and Merlot at 1,160 vines per acre. Opposite the winery on the north side of County Road 50, there is another 17-acre section the Fancsys call Viewpointe North Vineyard. It has similar soil with sand, clay, and loam features and a 1% south-facing slope. This is a catch-all vineyard with .5-2.5-acre parcels of Auxerrois, Cabernet Franc, Cabernet Sauvignon, Chardonnay, Gewürztraminer, Merlot, Pinot Gris, Pinot Noir, Sauvignon Blanc, Syrah, Tempranillo, and Viognier. All vineyards are fully tiled for drainage. Vines are leaf-thinned to provide extra sunshine to the grapes and shoot- and cluster-thinned to reduce crop size. Yields average 3.5-4 t. per acre. With its own grapes and those purchased from other vineyards, Viewpointe produced 4,000 cases in 2004 and plans to grow that to 15,000 cases by 2007, when all its existing vine-yards achieve optimum yields.

Winemakers: Jocelyn Clark (2004-present); John Fancsy (2002-present); Sal D'Angelo (2001-2004, consulting, 2005+) / Vineyard Manager: Dave Hildebrand

Cabernet Franc [LENS] **2002**★★★★↑ (*Barrel sample*) From Viewpointe and Walnut Grove vineyards. Garnet with an oaky and undeveloped nose. Shows solid structure, lovely fruit, and delicate balance. Drink 2007-2011. **2001**★★★☆↑ Grapes from View-pointe Vineyard and D'Angelo Farm. Garnet colour with an iodine, oak, and mint bouquet with a bitter herbal note. Good depth and length but needs time to show its charm. Drink 2006-2009.

Cabernet-Merlot [LENS] Grapes exclusively from Viewpointe Vineyard. **2002**★★★↑ (CF34/CS39/M24/PV3) This *barrel sample* had a nice perfuminess in the nose and was bigger, deeper, and richer than the previous vintage. It would have scored higher but for a bitter note in the finish. Time may correct that. Drink 2007-2014. **2001**★★★↑ (CF40/CS35/M25) Loads of depth and complexity in this well-balanced, supple, and flavourful blend. Drink 2006-2012.

Chardonnay [LENS] Grapes are exclusively from Walnut Grove Vineyard. **2002**★★→ Silvery-gold with a mild apple and honey-dew melon aroma. Sweetish taste with distinct residual sugar. Light flavour with relatively high alcohol. Drink soon.

Pinot Noir [LENS] Grapes from Walnut Grove Vineyard and Euro Farm. **2002**★★★↑ (*Barrel sample*) Lively ruby hue with a clean, healthy nose. Strawberry-cherry fruit is just beginning to emerge. Drink 2006-2010.

Sauvignon Blanc [LENS] Grapes are exclusively from Walnut Grove Vineyard. **2002**★→ Pale, silvery-gold with some apple aromas. The alcohol is a bit high for a wine of this light concentration and there's a hint of filter-pad flavour in the finish.

• VINC VINEYARD (Beamsville, NP) – Once owned by George Vinc and planted in 1976 with Chardonnay, Riesling, Welsh Riesling, and Vidal Blanc. Vinc Vineyard appeared on early bottles of Lakeview Cellars wines, although grapes were also supplied to Inniskillin. Moray Tawse purchased the vineyard in 1999 and built the Tawse Family Winery.

• **VINCOR INTERNATIONAL INC.** (*Administrative Head Office:* 441 Courtney Park Drive East, Mississauga, ON, L5T 2V3 / Phone: 905-564-6900 / Toll-Free: 1-800-265-9463 / Fax: 905-564-6909 / Website: www.vincorinternational.com / *Niagara Cellars Winery:* 4887 Dorchester Road, Niagara Falls, ON / Phone: 905-357-2400)

(Est. 1993) Canada's largest wine company and the world's eighth largest producer, marketer, distributor, and retailer of wine and wine-related products. When John Labatt Breweries Ltd. decided to rational-ize its diversified interests and concentrate on making beer, a group of executive employees headed by Don Triggs, Rick Thorpe (currently British Columbia's minister responsible for regulating the alcohol indus-try), and former winemaker Allan Jackson purchased Ridout Wines, the wine division with Château Gai and Casabello its main brands. The name was changed to Cartier Wines. From its earliest days Cartier has been on an endless buying spree. First, it bought Canada's oldest winery, Barnes Wines. In 1992, Cartier acquired Inniskillin Wines and, the following year, merged with T.G. Bright & Co. and changed its oper-ating name to Vincor International Inc. In subsequent years, Vincor has taken over established competitors Jordan & Ste. Michelle Wines and London Wines, then moved on to the oldest estate winery in B.C.'s Okanagan Valley, Sumac Ridge and its sister property, Hawthorne Mountain. It also purchased Okanagan Vineyards and renamed it Inniskillin Okanagan. Once Vincor solidified its position in Canada, with operations in British Columbia, New Brunswick, Ontario, and Quebec, it set it sights on the global assets, targeting name wineries in New World wine regions. Foreign interests now include the massive R.H. Phillips of California, Hogue Cellars in Washington state, Amberley Wines and Goundrey Wines in Australia, Kim Crawford Wines in New Zealand, and Kumala Wines in South Africa. If Vincor has not pur-chased a winery in Chile by the time you read this, it soon will. The company produces every wine product imaginable and quite compe-tently. It has developed several successful new brands, including Jackson-Triggs, Ancient Coast, Sawmill Creek, and Sola-Nero, and reju-venated tired old brands, such as L'Ambiance, Entre-Lacs, President Champagne, and Spumante Bambino. Vincor also participates in 3 major joint ventures: Le Clos Jordanne in the Niagara Peninsula in asso-ciation with Burgundy's most successful wine merchants, the Boisset family; Osoyoos-Larose in the Okanagan Valley with Groupe Taillan of Bordeaux; and Nk'Mip winery in British Columbia in co-operation with the Osoyoos Indian Band. The company produces cider under the Grower's banner, numerous coolers and RTDs under several labels, and has a series of shops to serve the home winemaking market. Grapes for the wines produced in Ontario are sourced from more than 90 growers in the Niagara region.

Winemakers: Mira Ananicz; Rob Scapin; Tom Seaver; Susan Szwec

Ancient Coast Label

Baco Noir [Ont] **2002** ★★☆↻ Creamy plum and cherry flavours are simple and pleasant. NonVQA 3 L bag-in-the-box version tastes a bit more forward; however, after opening, it keeps much better than an unfinished 750 ml bottle. Chill lightly to improve and drink within a year of release.

Cabernet Franc [NP] **2002**★☆➜ Green and stemmy with the flavour of underripe cherries. Hard, dusty, tannic finish. May soften in a year, but don't count on it. **2000**★☆➜ A semi-elegant food wine. Very pale with a slight veggie odour and a dry, dusty finish. Needs a good cut of red meat to bring out what little fruit there is.

Cabernet Sauvignon [NP] **2002**★☆➜ Relatively good fruit flavours at first sniff, but high alcohol overpowers other components and puts the wine out of balance. Cheddar cheese and crackers will fix that, though.

Chardonnay [NP] **2002**★★➜ Like well-buttered toast with grapefruit marmalade. Straightforward, full-bodied, and pleasant.

Gamay [NP] **2002**★★↻ A lovely poseur, it tastes more serious than it is. Clean, dry, verging on complex, with a slight Burgundian "stink." **2001**☒ A victim of Asian lady beetle.

Gamay Nouveau [NP] **2004**★☆↻ Fresh, clean, dry, simple, light. Could do with more colour and flavour.

Merlot [NP] **2002**★★➜ Soft, clean, light, balanced, and ready. Drink now-2006.

Riesling [NP] **2002**★★★☆➜ Yowza! Lovely, unexpected petrol nose. Lemon-lime, honey, wildflowers, with great structure and decent length. Drink now-2006.

Vidal [Ont] **2003**★★☆↻ Clean, mouth-filling, ripe, and pleasant. New, nonVQA 3 L bag-in-the-box version keeps fresh for months in the fridge. **2002**★★↻ Sprightly and refreshing with off-dry flavours of apple flan, gooseberry, and white grape juice. Good body and balance to go with many light foods.

Brights Label

Baco Noir, Late Harvest, T. Ghetti Estate [preVQA] One of the highlights of the old T.G. Brights portfolio. There may still be a few bottles in private cellars, which is why I have included these tasting notes. **1989**★★★➘ Deep, mahogany garnet with a concentrated bouquet of apple, red cherry, and rhubarb with a gritty, apple-skin finish. Alive but sliding fast. **1988**★★★☆➜ Tasted only once several years ago at a time when I was not taking notes. I remember it to be quite rich and full-bodied, with delicious, concentrated fruit and real zip. Not unlike Henry of Pelham's 1991 Baco Noir. **1987**★☆➘ Fruit is now drying up, exhibiting tart cherry and prune flavours.

Entre-Lacs, Red [nonVQA] **NV**☆↻ Almost interesting. Has some red fruit flavours and good body.

Entre-Lacs, White [nonVQA] **NV**★↻ A touch too much sulphur but otherwise a good choice for large gatherings.

House Wine, Dry White [nonVQA] **NV**★↻ Generic and quaffable.

House Wine, Red [nonVQA] **NV**★★↻ A light and simple red for pizza and poker. If served from a decanter, many drinkers might take it for a Eurowine.

House Wine, White [nonVQA] **NV★↻** Has a superficial aroma of confectioner's sugar that makes the wine moderately interesting. Perfect for noisy banquet halls.

Maria Christina, Red [nonVQA] **NV☆↻** The smell is quite appealing with a creamy, oak/berry aroma, but there's too much residual sugar added as a reminder that this is the stuff of morning-after headaches.

Maria Christina, White [nonVQA] **NV★☆↻** Nose of bubblegum, flowers, and candied fruit. This basic white is better than most of the cheap German Liebfraumilchs offered in Ontario.

Pale Dry Select Sherry [nonVQA] **NV★↻** Pale amber-brown colour with a mildly foxy *Vitis labrusca* nose. An amontillado-style sherry with perceptible but minimal sweetness. Nutty finish.

Private Stock Port [nonVQA] **NV★★★↻** Rich carmine colour with a spirity, plum-jam aroma. Well balanced with a rich, soft, very pleasant finish. Serve in a decanter and fool your friends.

President, Cuvée 2004 "Canadian Champagne" [nonVQA] **NV★☆→** Rich froth to start, beads of fine bubbles later. Sweetish taste hints of candied pear.

President, Dry Sparkling [nonVQA] **NV★★★→** Surprisingly good with a spiced honey nose suggesting Riesling and light flavours of apple and Bartlett pear.

President, Rosé Sparkling [nonVQA] **NV★★→** Pretty colour, hints of red fruit on the nose, and a good dollop of residual sugar softens the bite.

Rosato Bambino [nonVQA] **NV★★→** Lovely apple, strawberry, and rhubarb flavours and a balanced, sweet, fruity finish. Only 7% alc./vol.

Spumante Bambino [nonVQA] **NV★★→** Sweet with an apple-sauce nose and a very pleasant Asti-like finish. Has only 7% alc./vol.

Cartier Label

Capistro [nonVQA] **NV★☆↻** Very light in colour, nose, body, and flavour. Floral aroma and fruity taste but a touch watery. May make a pleasant patio spritzer without adding soda. Just toss in chopped fruit and a twist of lemon, orange, or lime.

Imperial Canadian Sherry [nonVQA] **NV★★☆↻** Pale amber colour with a fine nose of walnut skins, dried fruit, orange peel, spice, and lemon tea. Medium-sweet palate with a hint of raw alcohol in the finish. Very tasty and relatively complex. Not just for rubbies.

L'Ambiance, Red [nonVQA] **NV★↻** Competently made but quite ordinary. Pair with frozen pizza.

L'Ambiance, White [nonVQA] **NV☆↻** Palatable, but why waste a drinking opportunity on this?

London Wines
Canadian Chablis [nonVQA] **NV**☐↻ The name alone is a crime.

Sawmill Creek "Barrel Select" Label
Autumn Blush [nonVQA] **NV**★☆↻ Clean and lively with aromas of candied orange peel, pink grapefruit, and pink lemonade. Sweetish but well balanced.

Cabernet Sauvignon [nonVQA] **NV**★★↻ Lean and muscular, all you need in a Cab and nothing more.

Chardonnay [nonVQA] **NV**★☆↻ Oak-flavoured with a hint of fruit.

Dry Red [nonVQA] **NV**★★↻ A decent, inconspicuous red. Clean, dry, nicely balanced with decent red-fruit flavours.

Dry White [nonVQA] **NV**★★↻ Lemony with nutty nuances. Dry, clean, balanced, straightforward, and pleasant.

Merlot [nonVQA] **NV**★★☆↻ A bricks-and-mortar red. All business. Clean, balanced, solid, and unexciting.

Riesling [nonVQA] **NV**★★ ↻ Aroma and taste of lightly honeyed grapefruit. Off-dry, but balanced with a clean finish.

Sauvignon Blanc-Chardonnay [nonVQA] **NV**★ ↻ Boiled asparagus nose, dry, medium-bodied, with a mildly bitter finish.

Shiraz-Cabernet [nonVQA] **NV**★★☆↻ A show-off. There's some pizzazz, but you know it's shallow beneath the surface. Clean and balanced with blackberry fruit flavours.

Vidal Icewine, Bin 88 [NP] **2001**★★★☆➜ Bright gold colour with a nose reminiscent of pear syrup. Rich, voluptuous taste with a crisp finish. Yum.

Sola-Nero Label
Nero, Red [nonVQA] **NV**★★↻ Dry, with a hint of red-fruit character. Flawless but without any personality.

Olera, Port [nonVQA] **NV**★★↻ Deep carmine colour with a rich, plummy milk-chocolate nose. A touch hot (spirity) on the palate and a smidgen too sweet.

Sola, White [nonVQA] **NV**★★↻ Off-dry with an aroma of tropical fruits and a taste of candied grapefruit. A decent generic.

Vena, Blush [nonVQA] **NV**★★↻ Quite sweet with an aroma that's somewhere between strawberry Popsicle and cherry Jello. Very picnicky.

Unity Label
Cabernet Sauvignon-Merlot [nonVQA] A innovative concept, combining 50% Ontario wine with 50% from British Columbia. **2002**★★★★↑ (CF8/CS47/M45) Ontario component came from George II Farms, Skubel, and van de Laar vineyards. Deep garnet with aromas of mint, black fruit, tar, and hints of cassis struggling to emerge. Palate has balance and finesse. Drink 2007-2015.

2001 ☒ Unfortunately, in this, the first vintage, the Ontario component seems to have been tainted by Asian lady beetle, leaving unpleasant nuances in the final blend.

Chardonnay [nonVQA]   As with the red, the wine is blended from half Ontario wine with half British Columbia wine. **2002** ★ ★ ★ ★ → The Ontario grapes were harvested at George II Farms and van de Laar Vineyard. Golden hue with a lush nose of fruit cocktail, vanilla, and coconut shavings. Vibrant taste of citrus-spritzed pear, vanilla, butterscotch, and toasted brioche. Drink now-2008. **2001** ☒ Asian lady beetle taint appears to have marred the Ontario component, affecting the entire blend.

Inniskillin, Jackson-Triggs, & Le Clos Jordanne wines:

Listed separately under their individual names.

- **VINELAND ESTATES WINERY** (3620 Moyer Road, R.R.#1, Vineland, ON, L0R 2C0 / Phone: 905-562-7088 / Toll-Free: 1-888-846-3526 / Fax: 905-562-3071 / Email: wine@vineland.com / Website: www.vineland.com)

(Est. 1983) The vineyard and winery were originally established by German winemaker and nursery owner Hermann Weis, producer of some of the world's finest Rieslings at the family-owned Weingut St. Urbanhof in the Mosel Valley. Weis sold the operation in 1993 to John Howard, who transformed the Mennonite homestead that dates back to 1845 to the beautiful destination it is today. In 1998, Toronto businessman Alfredo "Fred" De Gasperis became a shareholder in the winery. When Howard retired in 2004, he sold the balance of his shares to the De Gasperis family. The winery is now run by Allan Schmidt, the winery's original winemaker and by his brother, Brian Schmidt, the winery's current winemaker and vineyard manager. The estate vineyard, called St. Urban Vineyard, backs onto the Niagara Escarpment just south of the village of Vineland. It is a hilly and undulating 75-acre property with Oneida clay loam soils modified by lacustrine processes and loamy textures over clay loam till and was originally planted in 1979 with 50 acres of Riesling, clone Weis 21B. Additional land purchases over the years have brought total holdings to 250 acres, with about 160 under vine. Today, the winery grows Cabernet Franc, Cabernet Sauvignon, Chardonnay, Merlot, Pinot Blanc, Pinot Gris, Pinot Meunier, and, of course, Riesling, all at an average vine density of 1,200 plants per acre. Vineland's focus from the beginning has been on the Riesling grape, and up to 50% of the winery's production is of that variety. Total production in 2003 was 42,000 cases, which should grow to 50,000 by the end of next year. The winery offers a retail wine boutique stocked with current and older vintages, a Four Diamond gourmet restaurant with lovely views of the vineyards and of Lake Ontario, a renovated carriage house originally built in 1856 for small banquets and functions, and a bed-and-breakfast cottage at vineyard's edge for overnight guests.

Winemakers: Brian Schmidt (1991 to present); Allan Schmidt (1983 to 1993) / Vineyard Manager: Brian Schmidt

Cabernet Franc [NP] **2002★★★☆↗** *Gold, Ontario Wine Awards, 2004.* Dense and elegant, fruity, herbal nose, soft tannins, and a ripe, candied finish. Drink now-2010.

Cabernet-Merlot, Reserve [NP] **2002★★★★☆↑** Deep garnet with a purple-pink rim. Ripe, closed, dense nose with hints of blackberry, black currant, and raspberry peeking through. Superb balance, tremendous fruit concentration, and a taste of minerals in the background suggest a long, slow, refined future. Already beginning to show signs of complexity. Drink 2008-2016.

Cabernet Reserve [NP] **1997★★★★→** (CF60-*Wismer Vyd*/ CS40-*Rosomel Vyd*) Still black as ink with terrific concentration of berry, plum, herb, and spice flavours. 525 cases produced. Drink now-2012.

Cabernet Sauvignon [NP] **2002★★★★↑** Ripe cassis nose. Still young and closed up with an acid bite, but there are hints of its greatness. Gawky to start, but it opens up beautifully after a couple of hours. Drink 2008-2015.

Chardonnay Reserve [NP] **1992★★★★↘** Big, rich, oaky style with plenty of fruit. Well structured for average aging of 4-6 years; however, the high acidity of this vintage has preserved it much longer. Drink up, though, it's fading.

Gewürztraminer [NP] **2002★★★☆→** Silvery-gold with an undeveloped nose, likely held back by the whiff of sulphur. Soft, off-dry taste of ripe apples spritzed with lime. Drink now-2009. **1998★★★★☆→** Deep gold hue. Despite hints of maderization and dried fruit, this wine will continue to develop for some time. Ripe and excellent with spicy and exotic fruits. This almost-dry style works especially well with Asian foods. Drink now-2008.

Gewürztraminer, Frontier Vineyard Reserve [NP] **1998 ★★★★★→** Pale amber gold. Aging beautifully with years to go. Aromas of rosehips, orange blossom, lychee, and tarragon. Ripe, seductive, and finely balanced with layers of complexity. Drink now-2018.

Meritage, Rosomel Vineyard Reserve [NP] **1999★★★☆→** Deep garnet with a complex bouquet of cream, herb, coffee, chocolate, caramel, and plenty of fruit. Well structured and still fresh. Drink now-2009. **1998★★★★↗** Deep garnet and solid to the rim. Bouquet is expansive and growing with aroma of warm plums. Luxurious flavours are profoundly deep and lasting. Some hints of oxidation appear. Drink now-2012. **1997★★★☆→** Deeply coloured with a lovely nose of cream chocolate, raspberry, and plum. Tremendous complexity and terrific length. 140 cases made. Drink now-2012.

Merlot [NP] **1995** ★ ★ ★ ★ ☆ ➔ A blockbuster, tasted only once (June 1999) at the winery. It was deep garnet to the rim with a dense, plummy black-fruit nose and lush, full, velvety palate with an unending finish. At the time, I estimated 10-15 years of peak drinking. Drink now-2012.

Pinot Noir, Reserve [NP] **2002** ★ ★ ★ ↗ Cherry colour with a bouquet of light fruit, herbs, and fresh-turned earth. Lean and light with a hard, closed-up finish. **1998** ★ ★ ★ ★ ↗ Cherry with mahogany reflections. Big, bold, and seductive nose of sandalwood, spice, autumn leaves, earth, truffles, and rich, plummy fruit. Ready for action. Drink now-2010.

Riesling, Cuve Close Sparkling [NP] **2000** ★ ★ ★ ☆ ➔ Rich straw-gold colour with long beads of very fine bubbles. Fresh, vibrant grapefruity aroma with a clean and refreshing taste. Drink now-2007.

Riesling, Dry [NP] **2003** ★ ★ ★ ☆ ↑ Pale straw-gold with citrus and minerals on the nose but little development to date. Green, firm, and sliced down the middle with racy acidity. Needs food now, or a period of aging. Drink 2007-2013. **1999** ★ ★ ★ ☆ ➔ Very pale straw colour with a hint of sulphur on the nose. It blows off quickly, revealing intriguing oil and mineral notes. Bright, crisp, lemon-grapefruit flavours and a refreshing, balanced finish. Drink now-2010. **1997** ★ ★ ☆ ➔ Pale straw with a creamy, lactic grapefruity nose. Simple. Drink up. **1996** ★ ★ ★ ↘ Straw gold with a caramelized nose of baked apples and aged cheese. Tart finish. Drink up. **1995** ★ ★ ★ ☆ ➔ Pale gold with a powerful bouquet of minerals and pine. Full, ripe honeyed-lemon flavour. Gripping finish. Drink now-2010. **1994** ★ ★ ★ ☆ ↘ Rich gold hue with a beeswax, petrol, and wet earth nose. Elegant structure, crisp flavours, and complex finish. Drink now-2006. **1993** ★ ★ ★ ➔ Pale gold with sweet fruit nose, brutal acidity, and a wonderfully refreshing finish that lasts. Drink now-2008. **1992** ★ ★ ☆ ↘ Bright straw colour with a severe nose. Caramel and coffee-bean flavours. Well past its peak. **1991** ★ ★ ★ ☆ ➔ Old gold with an oxidative nose of beeswax and petrol. Full, rich, fat texture and fine grapefruity flavours. Lingering finish. Drink now.

Riesling, Icewine [NP] **1998** ★ ★ ★ ★ ★ ➔ *Grand Gold, Riesling du Monde 2001*. Rich, old-gold colour with a deep, high-toned lemon, custard, and applejack nose. Exquisitely balanced, rich, sweet, raisiny, fresh, and juicy, and only now beginning to show some of its potential. Drink now-2020.

Riesling, Reserve [NP] **2003** ★ ★ ★ ☆ ↗ Green-gold colour and lovely fresh green citrus nose. Firm, tight, and balanced. Should develop nicely. Drink now-2015. **1998** ★ ★ ☆ ➔ Straw coloured with a clean, tart, fruity, petro-chemical nose and light, thin body.

Drink up. **1997**★★★☆➔ *Gold, Ontario Wine Awards 1999.* Pale straw with a still youthful lime and grapefruit bouquet. Some muddled, earthy nuances, but fruit stands up. Drink now-2009. **1994**★★★☆➔ Gold with a youthful nose of lemon and white pepper. Ripe grapefruity flavours and a long, dense finish. Drink soon. **1993**★★★➔ Gold with a candied-lemon nose. Zippy flavour and good level of minerality. Drink now. **1992**★★↘ Nice colour but has astringent, grapefruity flavours. In decline. **1990**★★★★➔ Old-gold shade with a nose of lime and minerals. Wonderful complexity with fullish, creamy flavours and an elegant finish. Terrific length but drink now.

Riesling, Semi-Dry [NP] **2003**★★★☆↗ Pale straw-gold with a grapefruity aroma. Residual sugar softens the rasp of the high acidity. Already good but will improve. Drink now-2011. **2000**★★★☆↗ Bright gold with tiny bubbles forming inside the glass. Subdued lemon-apple nose. Fresh, crisp, spritzy taste with great balance and a good-looking future. Drink now-2012. **1997**★★★☆➔ *Gold, Ontario Wine Awards 1999.* Floral nose with more tropical notes than the usual grapefruitiness of many Bench Rieslings. **1991**↓ Medium-bodied, citrusy, apricot tones, easy-drinking. **1990**★★↘ Slightly fuller-bodied, developing mature petrol nuances, well balanced with a clean finish.

Vidal Icewine [NP] Up to 15% Riesling icewine is added to boost acidity and complexity. **2003**★★★★☆➔ Bright gold with amber highlights and aromas of fresh peach and apricot. Intensely sweet and rich with mouth-watering acidity. Very long in the aftertaste. Drink now-2011. **2002**★★★★☆➔ Brilliant gold with a concentrated pear purée nose. Soft with a delicate, expressive palate and a long, clean, lingering finish. Drink now-2012. **1996**★★★★➔ Wonderful balance of sweetness and acidity. Baked pear, spice, and a hint of nuttiness. Drink now-2006. **1994**★★★★➔ Excellent structure, rich texture, balanced acidity, and long aftertaste. Drink soon. **1992**★★★★➔ Exotic fruit flavours include peach, pineapple, mango, papaya, etc. Rich, excellent sugar-acid balance. Drink now.

Vidal, Select Late Harvest [NP] **1996**★★★☆➔ Nice clean flavours of baked apple combined with fresh apple. Fully mature. Drink now.

• **VINOTECA INC. PREMIUM WINERY** (527 Jevlan Drive, Woodbridge, ON, L4L 8W1 / Phone: 905-856-5700 / Toll-Free: 1-866-313-5700 / Fax: 905-856-8208 / Website: www.toronto.com/vinoteca)

(Est. 1989) Giovanni and Rosanna Follegot came to Canada in 1968 from the Veneto region of Italy, where Giovanni's family had settled for 4 generations after leaving France. They built up their financial reserves by engaging in many businesses, including the importation of Ferrari cars and the selling of grape juice to home winemakers. Initially established as the Greater Toronto Area Winery, it was renamed Vinoteca after the Follegots purchased a vineyard in the Vineland area. They supplement their domestic harvests with imported grapes from a vineyard they own in Italy.

Winemakers: Giovanni Follegot (1989-present); Peter Rotar (1996-1997) / Vineyard Manager: Giovanni Follegot

Cabernet Franc [NP] 1995 ★ ★ ★ ☆ → *Gold, Ontario Wine Awards 1997.* Ripe and oaky. Fully mature.

Cabernet Sauvignon [NP] 1999 *Gold, Ontario Wine Awards 1997.* 1991 ★ ★ ★ ↘ Big, juicy, strapping, full-bodied, high-acid wine with excellent fruit. Drink up.

Pinot Noir [NP] 1991 ★ ★ ★ ↘ Delicate Pinot nose with a hint of residual sugar in the finish. On the slide.

Riesling [NP] 1991 ★ ★ → Hints of pickle on the nose when young. Short but lively. Drink soon.

- **VOEGE VINEYARD (Niagara-on-the-Lake, NP)** – This farm was recently sold by Kip and Sue Voege, who grew high-quality Cabernet Sauvignon, Chardonnay, Chelois, Gamay, and Merlot from this 15-acre property on the Niagara Parkway near Line 3. Grapes were sold to a number of wineries through Donna Lailey's D&D Farms.

- **W FARMS (Niagara-on-the-Lake, NP)** – One of the larger farms on the Niagara plains, this 136-acre vineyard on Line 2 is owned by Ernie Wiens and farmed by his son, James. The property is flat, composed of sandy-loam soil, and fully underdrained and irrigated. There are 14 acres of Baco Noir, 18 acres of Cabernet Sauvignon, 15 acres of Chardonnay, 13.5 acres of Gamay, 15 acres of Merlot, 4.5 acres of Pinot Noir, 12 acres of Riesling, 4 acres of Shiraz, and a whopping 40 acres of Vidal Blanc. Grapes are thinned to reduce yields to a maximum of 3.5 t. per acre and all fruit is contracted to Andrés Wines.

- **WAGNER VINEYARD (Niagara-on-the-Lake, NP)** – Jerry Wagner grew 10 acres of Cabernet Sauvignon, Cabernet Franc, Chardonnay, Geisenheim, and Marechal Foch, often selling his grapes through Donna Lailey. Wagner sold the vineyard in 2003.

- **WALNUT GROVE (Harrow, NP)** – This 28-acre family farm owned by Steve and Jean Fancsy, who are partners with Steve's brother, John, in Viewpointe Estate Winery, sits on the Lake Erie shoreline. This terrain is south-facing, gently sloped toward the lake, and composed of lightly undulating Berrien sand. Seventeen acres planted in 2000 and 2001 at a vine density of 1,360 plants per acre provide Auxerrois, Cabernet Franc, Cabernet Sauvignon, Chardonnay, Gewürztraminer, Merlot, Pinot Noir, Riesling, Sauvignon Blanc, Semillon, and Syrah.

- **WATSON VINEYARDS (Niagara-on-the-Lake, NP)** – John Watson and his son, Kevin, farm this property just across the road from Reif. They have Cabernet Franc, Chambourcin, Chardonnay, Gewürztraminer, Pinot Noir, and Syrah, which is sold to Marynissen, Southbrook Farm, By Chadsey's Cairns, and others.

- **WAUPOOS ESTATES WINERY** (3016 County Road #8, Waupoos, ON, K0K 2T0 / Phone: 613-476-8338 / Fax: 613-476-1355 / Email: info@waupooswinery.com / Website: www.waupooswinery.com)

(Est. 2001) The modern pioneers of Prince Edward County wine are Ed Neuser and Rita Kaimins. Neuser, a German-born machinist who came to Canada in 1956, purchased the 100-acre farm and century-old house in 1983. The lakeshore property is on Prince Edward Bay, a few kilometres east of Picton. To date, the sloped south-facing marl soils have been planted with almost 20 acres of Auxerrois, Baco Noir, Chardonnay, De Chaunac, Geisenheim, Gewürztraminer, Pinot Gris, Pinot Noir, Riesling, St. Laurent, Seyval Blanc, and Vidal Blanc. Because temperatures can dip to -36°C, Neuser ploughs over the vinestocks with up to 18 in. of soil from between the rows. The oldest surviving vines are the Vidal, first planted in 1993. Total production currently hovers around 8,000 cases, sold exclusively through the winery retail shop, the on-site dining room, and a few local restaurants. Most wines are from estate-grown grapes, but varieties not grown locally, such as Cabernet and Merlot, are purchased from Niagara-area vineyards. Neuser also produces 600 L of maple syrup every spring.

Winemaker: Jason MacDonald

Chardonnay Reserve [Ont] **2002**★★➔ Oaky with light but exotic aromas of coconut and pineapple. Not enough fruit to support the heavy oak. Drink now-2008.

Chardonnay Select, Unoaked [Ont] **2002**★★☆➔ Clean and fruity with an apple and lemon aroma and taste. Drink now.

Pearl Noir [nonVQA] **2002**☒ Black with orange-brown edges. Nose is stewed, pruney, and volatile. Taste is unpleasantly vegetal and cooked.

St. Laurent [nonVQA] **2002**☆➔ Tasted twice. One bottle was ruby-cherry with a rustic nose of sweet hay and saddle leather. The second smelled so sick, sour, and vinegary that I refused to taste it.

• **WEIS VINEYARD (Jordan, NP)** — Situated off 19th Street on the upper bench of the Niagara Escarpment, this 65-acre property was purchased by Thomas Pennachetti and Anne Weis-Pennachetti in 1998. The site has a moderate northeast-facing slope and soil composed of stony Chinguacousy clay loam till rich in limestone and shale. Almost 60 acres now are planted at 2,200 vines per acre. There are 8.5 acres of Chardonnay, 4.5 acres of Pinot Noir, 2 acres of Sauvignon Blanc, and 31 acres of Riesling, clone Weis 21, which was developed by Anne's father, Hermann, at the family vine-breeding nursery at Weingut St. Urbanhof in the Mosel Valley, Germany. An additional 13.5 acres of the Riesling were planted during 2003 and 2004. The Pinot Noir is crop-thinned at veraison from 20%-30%, depending on the vintage, and average yield is 3-3.5 t. per acre. All fruit is sold to Cave Spring Cellars.

- **WESTPHALEN VINEYARD (Niagara-on-the-Lake, NP)** – Mark Neufeld sells to several Niagara Peninsula wineries, as well as to Black Prince Winery in Prince Edward County.

- **WEST GLEN FARM (St. Catharines, NP)** – This huge property, which borders on the Rockway Conservation Area and Rapids, provides the base location for the Hernder Estate winery. It's almost 3 km long, 2 km wide at one end, and 1 km wide at the other, running all the way from the escarpment to Highway 8. Of the 254 acres of continuously rolling hills of Chinguacousy clay, almost 140 are given over to vines. Niagara and Concord are grown on 90 acres. There are 10 acres planted with Chardonnay and Vidal, and another 20 acres of Riesling and Baco Noir. Vinifera vines are underdrained between every row.

- **WICKED POINT VINEYARD (Picton, PEC)** – Owned by Don Kerr since 2001, this south-facing vineyard with sandy clay loam over fractured limestone has almost 9 acres planted at an average spacing of 1,089 vines per acre. Baco Noir, Chardonnay, Gewürztraminer, Melon de Bourgogne, and St. Laurent were planted between 2002 and 2004. Fruit should come off the oldest vines for the first time this year. A winery is planned for the future.

- **WIENS VINEYARDS (Niagara-on-the-Lake, NP)** – Abe and Ernie Wiens are the second largest grape supplier to Hillebrand Estates. In an average vintage, they can provide 2,000 t. They have several vineyard plots located in and around Niagara-on-the-Lake and run a large, efficient pressing facility for icewine. They grow Cabernet Franc, Cabernet Sauvignon, Chardonnay, Gamay, Merlot, Pinot Gris, and Riesling.

- **WILEY VINEYARDS (Niagara-on-the-Lake, NP)** – Dave Wiley is one of the biggest growers in Niagara. Cabernet Sauvignon, Merlot, and Pinot Noir are supplied to Henry of Pelham.

- **WILLOW HEIGHTS ESTATE WINERY** (3751 King Street [Regional Road #81], Vineland, ON, L0R 2C0 / Phone: 905-562-4945 / Fax: 905-562-5761 / Email: info@willowheightswinery.com / Website: www.willowheightswinery.com)

(Est. 1994) Ron Speranzini worked for 29 years as a quality assurance manager at Stelco. His hobby was winemaking, and from 1984 to 1991 the prize for best amateur wine went to him or to 1 of his 3 closest winemaking buddies, Eddy Gurinskas, John Marynissen, and Jim Warren. Donald Ziraldo and Leonard Pennachetti encouraged him to "go pro," saying the Ontario industry needed more good Italians to set it straight. In 1992, Speranzini applied to the Liquor Licence Board on a lark and 2 years later was granted a wine manufacturer's licence. At first, grapes were purchased from Dieter Guttler, and Willow Heights leased a small vineyard on Cherry Avenue next to South Service Road. His first wine, 2 barrels of Chardonnay vinted from severely thinned Beamsville Bench grapes, brought him immediate attention when he took the top prize at Cuvée 1995. It was the industry equivalent of winning an Oscar. From day one, Speranzini has lived by the theory that the only way to get quality is to reduce yield in the vineyard. In 1998, Speranzini was forced to relocate after the Cherry Avenue property was sold. He and his wife, Avis, and daughter, Nicole, moved Willow Heights to a 12-acre property on the north side of Regional Road 81 (King St.), just west of Vineland. Here at the current site, the land is smooth and very gently sloping with a soil that consists of Trafalgar reddish-hued silty clay loam over a bed of Queenston shale. The vineyard is currently under redevelopment for new vinifera plantings. In 2003, Willow Heights purchased a second vineyard in the Grimsby area. It was named Il Vigneto, which translated from Italian means The Vineyard. It is a flat piece of land, 180 acres and almost entirely clay limestone soil. Prior to 1980, it was planted with 6.5 acres of Chardonnay, 7.8 acres of Riesling, 12.5 acres of Vidal Blanc, and an additional 20 acres of miscellaneous red and white hybrid varieties. Last year, Speranzini put into the ground an additional 5 acres of vinifera vines, including small plots of Pinot Gris, Pinot Noir, and Syrah. The winery also buys about as much fruit as it grows, especially from the Hughes and Stefanik Vineyards. Total production is 20,000 cases with up to 5% sold in the export market.

Winemaker: Ron Speranzini / Vineyard Manager: Ron Speranzini

Cabernet Sauvignon [NP] **2002** ★ ★ ★ ☆ ↑ Tough and tannic but lovely full ripe fruit. Flavours of cassis, red apple, plum, and black-cherry Jello are exciting signals of a wine that should delight the palate for years to come. Drink 2006-2012.

Chardonnay, Sur Lie [NP] **2002** ★ ★ ★ ↻ Clean, straightforward, varietally pure Chardonnay. All you'd want but nothing more.

Chardonnay Reserve [NP] **1999** *Gold, Ontario Wine Awards, 2002.* **1998** *Gold, Ontario Wine Awards, 2001.* **1992** ★ ★ ★ ★ ↘ *Best White Wine, Cuvée 1995.* Big, balanced, and flavoury with lemony acidity, nutty oak, and sweet fruit. A stunning accomplishment for a winery in its first year of production.

Chardonnay Reserve, Lenko Vineyard [NP] **1995** ★ ★ ★ ☆ ↘ In its youth, it had clean, lemony acidity and some enticing white peach and creamy pear flavours. More recently, I have found some bottles tasting over-oaked, the fruit demolished by barrel aging, while others show great complexity with balanced vanilla, caramel, baked pear, toast, and nut flavours.

Chardonnay Reserve, Stefanik Vineyard [NP] **2002** ★ ★ ★ ☆ ↗ *Gold, All Canadian Wine Championships 2004.* Rich straw-gold colour with a thick, buttery, toasted oak, vanilla cream nose with subdued hints of pear and lemon. Brawny palate has stick-to-the-roof-of-your-mouth nutty flavours. Excessive alcohol dulls the distinctive-ness of the fruit. Drink now-2008. **2001 ★ ★ ★ ★ ⌐** Full-flavoured oaky fruit, powerful and elegant. Tremendous balance of compo-nents with flavours of pear, tropical fruit, honey, and spiced butter. Drink now-2007.

Gamay [NP] **2003 ★ ★ ★ ☆ ↻** Absolutely wild with vibrant black-raspberry aromas. Full fruit flavour, though lean (not thin) in texture. A wonderful food wine.

Gewürztraminer [NP] **2002 ★ ★ ★ ⌐** Pale straw-gold with a sweetish aroma. Slow-starting, the bouquet opens to orange and lime flavours with spice and buckwheat honey. Balanced palate, with solid structure, full body, and a distinct orange-mandarin undertone. Drink now-2012

Merlot [NP] **2002 ★ ★ ★ →** Deep garnet. Exotic, balsamic nose with hint of dill. Chutneylike pickled fruit with green herb nuances. Drink now-2009.

Merlot Reserve [NP] **1995 ★ ★ ★ →** Tough and dense but fruit stands up to tannins. Combines plum and mulberry flavours. Drink now-2008.

Pinot Noir Reserve [NP] **1994 ★ ★ ☆ ↘** Simple, straightforward, balanced, and pleasant. Now fading.

Tresette [NP] **1999 ★ ★ ★ →** Garnet with some brick-red reflec-tions along the rim. Soft nose, Bordeaux-like bouquet but with a meaty nuance combining earth, leather, game, and plum butter. Well balanced with an edgy acidity. Drink now-2007.

Tresette Reserve, Hughes Vineyard [NP] **2002 ★ ★ ★ ☆ →** (CF24/CS44/M32) Bright ruby-garnet with some raspberry nuances but a strong, leafy overtone. Light, lean palate with good juvenile acidity and some black-currant flavours sneaking in at the end. Drink now-2010.

Vidal Icewine [NP] **2002 ★ ★ ★ ★ →** Brilliant gold with an intense, spiced pineapple nose and thick peach and citrus marmalade flavours. Drink now-2010. **1998 ★ ★ ★ ★ ☆ →** *Gold, Ontario Wine Awards 2000; Best of Show Trophy, International Wine Challenge, London 2000.* Rich, rich, rich. Intense bouquet of white peach jam with nuances of clove and cardamom. Drink now-2010.

• **WILLOW LAKE VENTURES (Niagara-on-the-Lake, NP)** – This 70-acre property owned by James & Monica Froese is on Lakeshore Road sandwiched between Glenlake Vineyard and Palatine Estate Winery. They bought the vineyard in 1996 already planted with 3 acres each of Gamay and Vidal Blanc, plus some smaller sections of Cabernet Sauvignon, Pinot Gris, and Pinot Noir, all spaced at 1,281 plants per acre. Over the years, they have added 3 acres of Cabernet Franc, several acres of Cabernet Sauvignon, 3 of Chardonnay, 3.5 acres of Merlot, as well as some more Pinot Gris and Pinot Noir, bringing total vine coverage to 50 acres. The sandy loam soil is both tiled between the rows for drainage and irrigated against drought. Grapes are regularly thinned at veraison and fruit is sold exclusively to Vincor.

- **WILLOW SPRINGS WINERY** (5572 Bethesda Road, R.R.#2, Stouffville, ON, L4A 7X3 / Phone: 905-642-9463 / Fax: 905-642-2251 / Email: julie@willowspringswinery.ca / Website: www.willowsprings winery.ca)

(Est. 2001) Gino Testa immigrated from Italy to build a new life for his family, and to do so he worked hard in the construction industry. In 1955, he purchased a 158-acre farm on Highway 404 at the Stouffville Side Road. The south-facing property with clay loam soil was used to grow a bit of hay, some soybeans, and other cash crops. Being Italian, Gino also tended a small Concord vineyard from which he made wine for the family every year. In 1996, son Mario and his wife, Julie, bought a 15-acre section of the farm from his parents, installed tile drainage, and began to plant a vineyard, starting with 2 acres of Geisenheim 318. Adding small parcels irregularly over the past 9 years, the couple now cultivates 11 acres of vines, including Baco Noir, Chardonnay, Frontenac, Marechal Foch, Pinot Gris, Sabrevois, and Seyval Blanc at an average density of 1,100 vines per acre. Willow Springs buys additional grapes from well-known Niagara growers, including Steve Kocsis Vineyards, Watson Farms, and Wismer Vineyards. In past years, a larger percentage of the production was fruit wine; however, the Testas have torn out their apple orchard and now focus exclusively on grape wines. Theirs is the only commercial winery cultivating grapes in York Region at this time. Production in 2004 was 3,000 cases. The goal is to grow to 5,000 cases by 2010.

Winemaker: Mike Traynor / Vineyard Manager: Mario Testa

Cabernet [NP] **2002**★★➜ Garnet with a light aroma of black and red fruits. Light and lean with more complexity than the single varietals. Drink now-2006. **2001** [Ont]★★☆➜ Garnet with a sweet aroma of new oak and vanilla, caramel and coconut. Oak-dominated taste requires quick drinking before the fruit fades. Drink now.

Cabernet Franc [Ont] **2002**★★➜ Garnet with a blackberry fruit bouquet. Juicy with high acids and tough with hard tannins but balanced. Drink now-2007.

Cabernet Sauvignon [Ont] **2002**★★➜ Garnet with smells of berries, cream, and plastic. Slightly underripe taste with a light bitterness. Nevertheless, there is plenty of berry flavour. Drink now-2006.

Chardonnay [Ont] **2002**★★☆ Rich gold with a nose of Kraft caramels and a soft, mild taste of caramel apple and poached pear. Drink now-2006.

Riesling [Ont] **2002** ★ ☆ ↻ Straw gold with a shy, lemony aroma and a clean, vinous taste.

Testa Meritage [NP] **2002** ★ ★ ★ → Garnet with a stewed-fruit nose. Some plummy flavours and a lot of oak. A gentler hand with the wood is required. Only 600 bottles produced.

- **WISMER VINEYARDS (Jordan/Vineland, NP)** – The collective name given to a grouping of 7 contiguous properties situated approximately at the intersection of Victoria Avenue at 5th Avenue. Total area is about 260 acres covering a large section of Benchland immediately south of Vineland and just west of Jordan near Ball's Falls. All 7 blocks share similar though slightly differing soils, combining Chinguacousy, Jeddo, and Oneida clay loam till with one patch of sandy loam. There are several owners; however, all the properties are managed by Phil Clarke and his company, Glen Elgin Vineyard Management. The best-known parcel is the Foxcroft Block, which over the years has been referred to as Fox Vineyard, Fox Den, Fox Run, and so on, all incorrectly. It isn't expressly better than the other blocks, simply better known. It is unusual as well for its very gently sloping west-, south-, and east-facing exposures. There are 41 acres of Cabernet Franc, Chardonnay, Chardonnay Musqué, Gamay, and Riesling, all planted in 1998 and 1999 at 1,210 vines per acre. Average harvest is 3 t. per acre and fruit is sold to Angels Gate, Flatrock, Hernder, Lakeview, Malivoire, Peninsula Ridge, Stoney Ridge, and Vineland Estates in the Niagara Peninsula, and to Carmela Estate, Hardie Wines, and Huff Estates in Prince Edward County. The Glen Elgin Block is a 29-acre property with 9 acres under vine, including Cabernet Franc, Gewürztraminer, Pinot Noir, and Zweigeltrebe, planted variously from 1994 to 2000. It has gentle north- and south-facing slopes. Harvested at 4 t. per acre, the fruit is sold to Angels Gate, Fielding, Hernder, Lailey, Niagara College Teaching Winery, and Vineland Estates. The 67-acre Homestead Block sits adjacent to Butler's Grant Vineyard on its north side. It is a flat vineyard with 23 acres of Cabernet Franc, Merlot, Pinot Noir, Sauvignon Blanc, and Vidal Blanc. Grapes harvested at 3 t. per acre are sold to Lailey Vineyards, Lakeview Cellars Estates, Malivoire Wine Company, and Vineland Estates in Niagara and to The Grange of Prince Edward Estate Winery in Prince Edward County. Lakeview Blocks I and II combined are 23 acres with 14 under vine. The gentle north-facing slope was planted from 1997 through 1999 with Cabernet Sauvignon, Gewürztraminer, Riesling, and Sauvignon Blanc. Fruit is sold to Fielding Estates, Legends, Malivoire, Niagara College Teaching Winery, Peninsula Ridge, Rockway Glen, and Stoney Ridge Estate Winery. Of the 7 blocks, the 9-acre Parke Block is the only one not tiled for drainage. This flat vineyard has parcels of Pinot Noir and Syrah harvested at 2 t. per acre and sold to Kacaba and Niagara College Teaching Winery plus Hardie Wines in Prince Edward County. The largest of all the properties is Wingfield Block, though only 9 acres are under vine. Wingfield and Glen Elgin are the 2 blocks that still remain Wismer family holdings. Cabernet Franc, Cabernet Sauvignon, and Chardonnay are grown on this flat site. Fruit is sold to Colio Estate in the Lake Erie North Shore region and to Fielding, Stoney Ridge, and Vineland Estates. Fruit from any of these blocks is generally identified as Wismer Vineyards on wine labels.

- **ZABEK VINEYARDS (Niagara-on-the-Lake, NP)** – Rick and Jim Zabek grow 150 acres of Vidal Blanc, Seyval Blanc, Cabernet Franc, and some Geisenheim varieties. Soil is clay with gravelly pockets. There's a cooler environment in this lakeshore vineyard that results in more aromatic fruit with a higher degree of acidity. Some of Hillebrand's best barrel-aged Vidal icewines were made from grapes hand-picked here. In recent years, the grapes have been sold to Vincor.

- **ZIMMERMAN AND TROUP VINEYARDS (Beamsville, NP)** – Two contiguous properties east of Cave Springs Farm owned by Cuesta Vineyard Corp. and managed by Stoney Ridge Estate Winery. There are 11 acres of Cabernet Franc and 13 acres of Cabernet Sauvignon. All the fruit is processed at Stoney Ridge Estate Winery.

Ontario VQA Vintage Chart, 2004-1988

About the Ontario VQA Vintage Chart

Winemakers from every commercial grape winery in Ontario were asked to rate their own wines according to 2 criteria: (1) "How well did specific grape varieties perform in each of the years listed?" and (2) "How ready and drinkable are the wines made from those varieties today?"

Ratings on this vintage chart reflect information gathered solely from these wine producers; that is, the "vinsiders." And thanks to the wide range of large and small wineries that returned the survey, it was possible to come up with truly representative averages for each grape variety.

Vintages have been given a numerical rating from 1 to 100. (I'd say anything with a score over 80 is a safe buy.) The arrows indicate the current drinkability of each variety during the next year or two.

As with every vintage chart, I encourage you to view this one as a starting point rather than as the final word. After all, these are only averages. There are always winemakers capable of overcoming the challenges of a lousy harvest and making decent wine, and there are also bumblers who turn the best grapes into dreck.

One thing I can absolutely guarantee: If you use this vintage chart regularly, you will increase your chances of drinking a decent wine to 98.7%, 19 times out of 20.

LEGEND

Vintage Quality

0 = worst
100 = best

Current Drinkability

↑ = still needs more age
↗ = can be drunk now but will improve
→ = at its peak
↘ = should be drunk soon
↓ = probably over the hill

Ontario VQA Vintage Chart, 2004-1988

Quick Chart	2004	2003	2002	2001	2000	1999	1998
Ontario Reds	78↑	72↑	88↗	83→	76→	87→	90→
Ontario Whites	82↗	78↗	84→	78→	76↘	77↘	81↘

Red Varieties	2004	2003	2002	2001	2000	1999	1998
Baco Noir	86↑	78↗	87↗	75→	76→	81↘	86→
Cabernet Franc	73↑	69↑	91↗	84↗	74→	90→	94↗
Cabernet Sauvignon	67↑	68↑	89↗	79↗	69↘	85→	96↗
Gamay	77↗	69↗	87→	86↗	75→	86→	89→
Marechal Foch	80↑	77↗	83↗	87→	81→	88→	86↘
Merlot	74↑	68↑	90↗	87↗	67→	91↗	92↗
Pinot Noir	92↑	83↗	93↗	89↗	83→	86→	87→
Syrah/Shiraz	75↑	65↗	88↗	80→	—	—	—
Zweigelt	81↗	68↗	85→	83→	79→	78↘	78↘

White Varieties	2004	2003	2002	2001	2000	1999	1998
Chardonnay	80↑	77↗	83↗	73→	78→	79↘	81↘
Gewürztraminer	71↑	73↗	83→	80→	70→	73↘	82↘
Pinot Gris	81↗	63→	79→	76↘	74↓	78↓	75↓
Riesling (Dry)	82↑	77↗	80↗	73→	79→	75→	75↘
Riesling (Late Harvest)	90↑	87↗	88↗	73→	78→	83→	87→
Sauvignon Blanc	80↗	80→	80→	82↘	74↓	73↓	86↓
Viognier	89↗	86→	93→	80↘	80↓	77↓	80↓

Icewines	2004	2003	2002	2001	2000	1999	1998
Cabernet Franc	86↑	75↗	90↗	69→	71→	—	—
Gewürztraminer	92↑	88↗	85↗	72↗	70↗	80↗	81→
Riesling	93↑	90↑	82↗	81↗	83↗	84↗	91↗
Vidal Blanc	88↗	85↗	89↗	83→	86→	79→	89→

Lake Erie North Shore and Pelee Island

	2004	2003	2002	2001	2000
Baco Noir	84↑	78↗	83↗	79→	78→
Cabernet Franc	78↑	68↗	91↗	90↗	76→
Cabernet Sauvignon	69↑	70↗	87↗	88↗	73→
Chardonnay	80↗	75→	80→	76→	78→
Merlot	76↑	70↗	90↗	88→	72→
Pinot Noir	80↑	71↗	94↗	89→	80→
Riesling	79↑	75↗	82↗	76→	78→

1997	1996	1995	1994	1993	1992	1991	1990	1989	1988
77↘	65↓	86↘	75↓	80↘	64↓	88↘	73↓	77↓	63↓
81↘	71↓	81↘	76↓	75↓	69↓	77↓	77↓	77↓	76↓

1997	1996	1995	1994	1993	1992	1991	1990	1989	1988
80↘	73↓	82↘	73↓	79↓	73↓	87↓	78↓	82↓	75↓
79↘	58↓	87→	71↓	72↓	53↓	89↘	71↓	81↓	59↓
79↘	51↓	90→	70↓	71↓	53↓	90→	66↓	79↓	59↓
73↓	62↓	83↓	73↓	71↓	62↓	84↓	79↓	70↓	69↓
81↓	70↓	75↓	75↓	92↘	68↓	82↘	69↓	67↓	50↓
81↘	58↓	93→	75↓	83↓	61↓	94↘	75↓	80↓	64↓
75↘	74↓	87↘	79↓	81↓	67↓	86↘	73↓	78↓	65↓
—	—	—	—	—	—	—	—	—	—
72↓	70↓	58↓	85↓	90↓	72↓	90↓	—	—	—

1997	1996	1995	1994	1993	1992	1991	1990	1989	1988
82↘	69↓	84↓	81↓	81↓	69↓	79↓	81↓	73↓	75↓
80↓	74↘	78↓	74↓	76↓	74↓	71↓	76↓	75↓	80↓
75↓	69↓	78↓	63↓	57↓	75↓	80↓	—	—	—
87→	79↘	81↘	77↘	67↓	75↓	74↓	66↓	81↓	83↓
75↘	72↓	86→	84→	93→	50↓	80↘	83↘	77↓	65↓
82↓	61↓	64↓	—	—	—	—	—	—	—
—	—	—	—	—	—	—	—	—	—

1997	1996	1995	1994	1993	1992	1991	1990	1989	1988
—	—	—	—	—	—	—	—	—	—
71→	89→	—	—	—	—	—	—	—	—
87→	84→	90↗	85→	90→	68↘	81→	83→	90→	73→
67→	76→	73→	79→	78→	73↘	78→	73↘	88→	75↘

Prince Edward County

	2004	2003	2002	2001	2000
Cabernet Franc	68↑	67↗	—	—	—
Cabernet Sauvignon	65↑	63↗	—	—	—
Chardonnay	78↑	81↗	71→	—	—
nay	78↗	70→	85→	—	—
ot	67↑	67↗	—	—	—
Noir	90↑	84↗	87→	—	—
	79↑	74↗	78→	—	—

Acknowledgements

Writing about wine may be a pleasure, but it's hardly a lucrative career. Many of the thousands of bottles opened in the writing of this book were drawn from my personal collection, particularly the older vintages; but it would not have been possible to complete this project without the co-operation of the many Ontario winery owners and managers who sent sample bottles for tasting. Thank you for your generous contributions.

At a meeting in the spring of 2004, the senior editorial team at McClelland & Stewart asked many challenging questions about the concept for this book, but there was one person in the room who needed no convincing. Alex Schultz believed in the project from the beginning, and it was my good fortune that, ultimately, he became my editor. His inspiring words have provided constant support. Thanks also to Heather Sangster for her fine editing skills.

Many personal friends were supportive, but none more than Michael Sullivan and Esther Benaim. Their interest in the project as it evolved, and their continuing moral support, proved invaluable.

And then there's the real insider, my partner and confidante, Talin Vartanian, who has been with me since long before I declared, "I have this idea for a book." Her eagle eye has passed over the manuscript numerous times. T has shared in the anxieties and joys of bringing this project to completion, and for that I am forever grateful.

Index of Industry People